CW00750044

GROUND TRUTHS

To Laureen

Ground Truths

*British Army Operations in the
Irish War of Independence*

Edited with an introduction and commentary by

W. H. KAUTT

IRISH ACADEMIC PRESS

First published in 2014 by Irish Academic Press
8 Chapel Lane
Sallins
Co. Kildare, Ireland

© 2014 W. H. Kautt

British Library Cataloguing in Publication Data
An entry can be found on request

ISBN: 978 0 7165 3219 4 (cloth)
ISBN: 978 0 7165 3220 0 (paper)
ISBN: 978 0 7165 3218 7 (ebook)

Library of Congress Cataloging-in-Publication Data
An entry can be found on request

Printed in Ireland by
SPRINT-print Ltd.

All rights reserved. Without limiting the rights under copyright reserved alone, no part of this publication may be reproduced, stored in or introduced into a retrieval system, or transmitted, in any form or by any means (electronic, mechanical, photocopying, recording or otherwise) without the prior written permission of both the copyright owner and the above publisher of this book.

Contents

List of Maps viii

Abbreviations ix

Acknowledgements xiii

Foreword xiv

Prologue xvi

Editor's Introduction, Original Foreword and Introduction 1

'The Record of the Rebellion in Ireland, 1919–1921 and the
Part Played by the Army in Dealing with it.'

Chapter I   The Situation in Ireland at the end of
             1919 to April 1920   20

Chapter II   Policy and Leadership Changes, May to
             August 1920   56

Chapter III A New 'Campaign', September 1920   87

Chapter IV   Introduction of Martial Law   104

Chapter V   Elections for Northern and Southern Parliaments,
             December 1920   124

Chapter VI   Opening of Northern Parliament, May 1921   151

Chapter VII Cessation of Active Operations   164

Chapter VIII The Agreement of 11 July 1921 and the 'Treaty'   179

Original Appendices
    Appendix I – The Military Situation in Ireland at the
        end of September, 1921.   197

*Appendix II – Some Examples of Gallant Actions for
which Rewards have been Granted.*   202

Appendix III – Orders   207
    Special Order Of The Day, Wednesday 14 April, 1920.   207
    Special General Routine Order, Tuesday 17 August, 1920.   207
    Special Order Of The Day, Thursday 2 December, 1920.   208
    Special Order Of The Day, Friday 25 February, 1921.   209
    Special Order Of The Day, Monday 2 May, 1921.   210
    Special Order Of The Day, Monday 15 August, 1921.   210
    Special Order Of The Day, 17 January, 1922.   211

*Appendix IV – Note on the views expressed by Military Authorities
in Ireland in December, 1920, with regard to the Partial or
Universal Declaration of Martial Law in Ireland.*   213

Additional Appendices—Documents to which the original text refers   217

*Appendix A—The Present Military Situation in Ireland and
the Proposed Military Policy during the Coming Winter,
26 July, 1920.*   217

*Appendix B—Text of The Defence of the Realm Act and
Regulations 9AA and 14B.*   222

*Appendix C—Draft of a Bill to Make Provision for the
Restoration and Maintenance of Order in Ireland, A.D. 1920.*   225

*Appendix D—Report of the Situation in Ireland by
the General Officer Commanding-in-Chief for
Week Ending 13 November, 1920.*   227

*Appendix E—General Officer Commanding-in-Chief,
the Forces, Ireland to The Secretary, the War Office,
Memorandum No. 2/26908(A), 1 September 1920.*   228

*Appendix F—The Irish Situation; Memorandum by
the Secretary of State for War, 3 November 1920.*   229

*Appendix G—Jeudwine to The Chief Secretary for Ireland,
5 December 1920.*   231

*Appendix H—Meeting held at 10 Downing Street, on
Wednesday 29 December, 1920.*   232

*Appendix I—Situation in the 5th Division Area,
14 February, 1921.*   236

*Appendix J—Report by the General Officer
Commanding-in-Chief on the Situation in Ireland for
Week Ending 14 May, 1921.*　　　　　　　　　　　238

*Appendix K—Report by the General Officer
Commanding-in-Chief on the Situation in Ireland for
Week Ending 23 April, 1921.*　　　　　　　　　　241

*Appendix L—Memorandum 'A' by the
Commander-In-Chief, The Forces in Ireland,
23 May, 1921*　　　　　　　　　　　　　　　　243

*Appendix M—Memorandum 'B' by the
Commander-In-Chief, The Forces in Ireland,
23 May, 1921*　　　　　　　　　　　　　　　　244

*Appendix N—Speech of King George V Opening the
Northern Ireland Parliament, 22 June, 1921*　　　246

Appendix O—Appendix V, CAB 24/126/283—4 CP 3134　　247

Bibliography　　　　　　　　　　　　　　　　　249

Index　　　　　　　　　　　　　　　　　　　263

List of Maps

1. 5th Division Area   xix
2. 6th Division Area   xix
3. Dublin District Areas   xx
4. Divisional Areas   xx

Abbreviations

ADM—Admiralty papers
Adm—Admiral
ADRIC—Auxiliary Division Royal Irish Constabulary
ASU—Active Service Unit
BA—Bachelor of Arts
Bart—Baronet
Bde—Brigade
BEF—British Expeditionary Force
Bn—Battalion
Brig-Gen—Brigadier-General
Bvt—Brevet
Cdt—Cadet
CAB—Cabinet Papers
CAI—Cork Archives Institute
Capt—Captain
CD—Contemporary Documents
CIGS—Chief, Imperial General Staff
CMA—Competent Military Authority
CMG—Companion of St Michael and St George
Cmdt—Commandant
COIN—Counter-insurgency
CO—Colonial Office
Co—County
Col—Colonel
Cpl—Corporal
DC—Divisional Commissioner
DCIGS—Deputy Chief, Imperial General Staff
DDMO&I—Deputy Director Military Operations and Intelligence

DI—District Inspector
Div—Division
DMP—Dublin Metropolitan Police
DOCEX—Document exploitation
DORA—Defence of the Realm Act
DOW—Died of Wounds
DRR—Defence Of the Realm Regulations
DSO—Distinguished Service Order
ER—East Riding
FGCM—Field General Court-Martial
FM—Field Manual; Field Marshal
GCB—Grand Cross of the Bath
GCVO—Grand Cross of the Victorian Order
GCMG—Grand Cross of St Michael and St George
Gen—General
GHQ—General Headquarters
GOC—General officer commanding
GOsC—General officers commanding
GOCinC—General officer commanding-in-chief
GSO—General Staff Officer
HMSO—His Majesty's Stationary Office
I-G—Inspector-General
IGS—Imperial General Staff
IRA—Irish Republican Army
IRB—Irish Republican Brotherhood
IWM—Imperial War Museum
KBE—Knight Commander of the British Empire
KC—King's Counsel
KCMG—Knight Commander of St Michael and St George
KIA—Killed in Action
KSOB—King's Own Scottish Borderers
KCB—Knight Commander of the Bath
KP— Knight of St Patrick
L/Cpl—Lance Corporal
Lieut—Lieutenant
Lieut-Col—Lieutenant-Colonel
LLD—Doctor of Laws
Lt—Lieutenant

Abbreviations

Lt-Col—Lieutenant-Colonel
Lt-Gen—Lieutenant-General
MA—Military Archives, Dublin
MI4—Directorate of Military Intelligence, Section 4—Maps
Maj—Major
Maj-Gen—Major-General
MO3—Administration and Special Duties Section
NAUK—National Archives of the UK
ND—No Date
NLI—National Library of Ireland
NR—North Riding
O/C or OC—officer commanding
OBE—Officer of the British Empire
OM—Order of Merit
PRO—Public Record Office
Prov—Provisional
Pte—Private
QMG—Quartermaster General
ROIR—Restoration of Order in Ireland
RAF—Royal Air Force
RAOC—Royal Army Ordnance Corps
RASC—Royal Army Service Corps
RE—Royal Engineers
RGA—Royal Garrison Artillery
Rgt/Regt—Regiment
RHA—Royal Horse Artillery
RIC—Royal Irish Constabulary
RMLI—Royal Marines Light Infantry
RM—Royal Marines
RN—Royal Navy
ROIA—Restoration of Order in Ireland Act
S/Constable—Special Constable (in Ulster)
SF—Sinn Féin
Sgt/Sjt—Sergeant / Serjeant
SIC—Situation in Ireland Committee
SR—South Riding
T/Constable or T/Const.—Temporary Constable (Black and Tans)
Tpr—Trooper

UVF—Ulster Volunteer Force
WS—Witness Statement
WO—War Office
WR—West Riding

Acknowledgements

On such a project as this, there are many people to thank. Amongst the many people are those who have gotten me to this point in my academic career. I owe a great debt of thanks to Geoffrey Parker, Joe Guilmartin and Allen Millet for their help in my formation as a historian. Of course, I greatly value Keith Jeffery and his continued kind mentorship and guidance through the years.

I must also thank those who have read the various drafts of this in various forms: Ken Ferguson was instrumental in suggesting publishing this. My thanks is also due to my former students, Jesse Abreu, Adam Bancroft, Nathan Biddle, Erik Booker, Victor Bowman, Jason Burke, Robert Crowley, Kevin Donley, Adam Ennis, Michael Fletcher, Bryan France, Charles Gallion, Joshua Hegar, Mark Herold, William Hollander, Jerry Landrum, Barry Level, Matthew Linehan, Christopher Lynch, Sean McCafferty, Robert McCracken, Paul Moreshead, Mark O'Brien, Lance O'Bryan, Daniel Parrott, Gareth Prendergast, John Price, Peter Rayls, Sean Reilly, Terry Soule, Timothy Taylor, Michael Teaster, Brendan Toolan, Kevin Wainwright and Bryan Woodcock for having read the text.

Thanks to Dr Wm. Barry Sheehan for his guidance and suggestions, and to the National Archives of the United Kingdom for permission to publish this volume (WO 141/93) and their staff who have been so helpful over the years in my research.

Finally, my thanks goes to my family; my lovely wife Laureen and my children, Stephen, Chloe and Taylor, who have suffered through both the research and writing as well as endless discussions of the project. I could not have accomplished any of this without their love and support.

There are many others whom I cannot name specifically, but my thanks to you all as well. The editing team were outstanding and any mistakes contained herein are mine.

Foreword

The 'Record of the Rebellion in Ireland, 1919–1921', the British army's in-house account of its operations in the Irish War of Independence, was a particularly elusive document for those of us who in the 1970s began researching that period. Despite the introduction of the 'Thirty-Year Rule' in 1966 (replacing a 'Fifty-Year Rule') many relevant official documents were subject to an extended closure, sometimes for as much as a hundred years. Among these was the 'Record of the Rebellion'. But historians are (or should be) not easily put off, and enjoy nothing so much as the thrill of the (paper-) chase. Thus, pioneers in the field, above all Charles Townshend, found versions of the official record preserved in private collections in such places as the Imperial War Museum. Often we have reason to be very grateful that participants in modern historical events have illicitly retained secret and confidential papers, which might otherwise never have seen the light of day (or, at least, not for a very long time). Indeed, for the purposes of posterity we perhaps ought to encourage (though that might qualify as 'aiding and abetting') people to continue to keep sensitive official documents that they strictly should not have. The final release of the 'Record of the Rebellion' to the United Kingdom National Archives in 2001, nevertheless, means that the entire British official version of events is publicly accessible at Kew, and this scholarly edition prepared by William Kautt means that the text will be much more widely available than ever before. The Record is full of fascinating detail, and explanations advanced by soldiers who had lost the campaign in Ireland. It would have been of tremendous assistance after 1969 when British troops once more were deployed in Ireland against a violent republican challenge, but there is no evidence that in the late 1960s anyone thought to revisit the experience of the early 1920s to ascertain if there might be any 'lessons learned' of use in the new situation. Only now, when we hope we have seen the last of British troops in action in Ireland, is their account available to us all. But it provides a fascinating narrative of events, and

Foreword

a snap-shot of contemporary attitudes, which make a real contribution to our understanding of the violent and tragic events of 1919 to 1921. This edition, meticulously prepared by William Kautt, should be read by anyone keen to know what 'actually happened' during the Irish War of Independence.

Keith Jeffery
Queen's University Belfast

Prologue

This project was born of a desire to provide a resource useful to students of Irish military history of the early twentieth century. Others have edited the other volumes of *The Record of the Rebellion*, but none have undertaken a project such as this: a critical examination of the text with all the supporting documentation. I have tried to find a happy medium between letting the British army staff officers give their testimony across time, while providing sufficient examination, documentation, correction and resources to be useful to the reader. The text contains the original spellings, misspellings, typos and other errors. I have used extensive notes to provide information, sources and critique.

Since at the time of writing most of the survivors of these events were still alive, many on the British side went unnamed in the text. In most instances where the authors mention a person, I have given his name, and, where possible, given basic biographical detail relative to his importance. I have done the same with military and police units on both sides. In addition to these basics, I have provided dates and locations where the text does not, or where it gets them wrong.

In terms of critique, there are many places where the authors made mistakes or held a differing view to that of the republicans. Without trying to debate the topics too much, I have sketched the opposing views. At some points, I have criticized the authors for logical fallacies, incoherent logic and other biases, with care given to respect their heartfelt angst.

Finally, I have, in many places in the text, provided bibliographic endnotes giving relevant primary and secondary sources. In the case of the former, whenever a primary document is referenced in the text, but not quoted or otherwise provided, I have placed the document in the Additional Appendices with a footnote indicating its provision. In the instance of the former, in many instances I have added footnotes providing bibliographic sources. In this manner, I hope to make this valuable document useful to all without encumbering with unnecessary additions.

Prologue

The Operations volume is divided into eight chapters, running primarily chronologically through the war itself, with each detailing a different period or series of topics of the conflict. It began with a foreword from the general staff of the War Office and an introduction. The first chapter establishes the status quo by covering the relevant information to the end of 1919. Chapter two tells of the conflict in 1920, beginning with May, the month the leadership changes in the government and military in Ireland were completed, following through to August of that year. In the third chapter, the authors examined the effects of policies, new organizations and the general situation at the end of September 1920.

Chapter four continues on from three, but details internment, martial law, official reprisals and other new measures. In the fifth chapter, some of the more propagandistic and other opinion-affecting aspects come through, as well as perceived results of earlier decisions. Chapter six covers May to June 1921, looking at the military and political situation, various rebel attacks and the British responses to them.

In chapter seven, the study examines the events of the rest of June through July, the Truce, their expectations that the Truce would fall apart and the state of affairs in the autumn of 1921. Chapter eight details the Truce. It looks at the terms, violations, and the military's 'impotence' under the terms and notes about belligerent status of the IRA.

There are also four original appendices. The first concerns the military situation in September 1921. The second surveys some of the decorations for gallantry awarded,[1] providing some details on the events. Three provides various special orders issued, primarily by the Irish Command. Finally, four provides comments made in December 1920 about the use of martial law in Ireland.

The original pagination has not been maintained. Finally, the index, not original to the text, is divided into names, places and topics. The intent is to make this resource more valuable than it already is.

W. H. Kautt, August 2013

NOTES

1. The use of the word 'gallantry' had been ruled inappropriate by the government since they determined that the forces in Ireland were not on 'active service' because they did not want to admit to making war on His Majesty's subjects. See DCIGS (Maj-Gen C. H. Harington) to Secretary of State for War (Churchill), 10 August 1920; Military Secretary (Philip W. Chetwood) to Secretary of State for War (Churchill), 30 October 1920, National Archives of the UK, hereafter NAUK WO 141/42; and DCIGS to Adjutant General, 30 June 1920, WO 32/4309.

MAPS

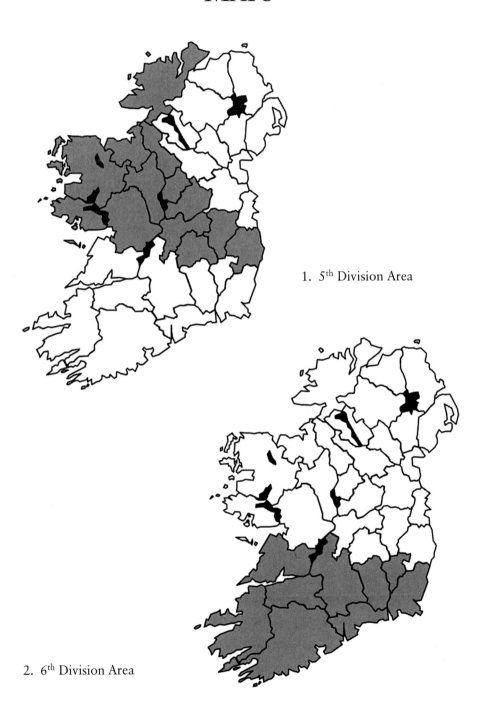

1. 5th Division Area

2. 6th Division Area

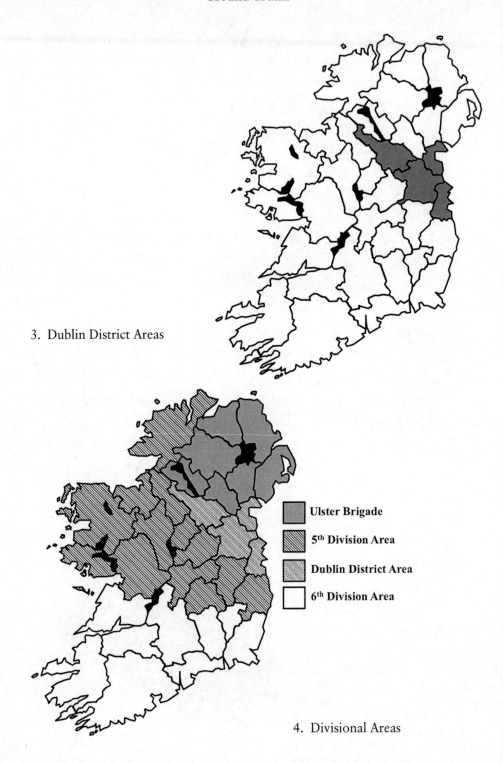

3. Dublin District Areas

Ulster Brigade

5th Division Area

Dublin District Area

6th Division Area

4. Divisional Areas

Editor's Introduction

When soldiers speak of 'ground truth', they are referring to the peculiar reality that the actual situation on the battlefield defies adequate translation into written form through the various types of reports available. The closer one is to the fight, the more 'real' it is; conversely, the further one is from it, the more abstract it becomes. At the 'hotter' end of the spectrum of the myriad of reasons for this is the phenomenon of 'tunnel vision'.

After speaking with hundreds of combat veterans over the course of the past two decades of his professional life, the present author has found what countless others have; in combat, soldiers are by necessity very narrowly focused. Under direct fire, they will experience what is sometimes called 'tunnel vision', in which their span of view is limited in being focused on remaining alive. This is part of the 'fight or flight' response, and is quite normal, but it also means that they will be unable to explain what happened just a few yards away, because their minds blocked it out as unnecessary for survival. Thus, it is quite difficult to establish what happened based on the testimony of these eyewitnesses.

At the other end of this spectrum are the higher headquarters with their requisite staff officers. For the commanders of these echelons and their staffs, the situation is quite different, but no less perplexing. When subordinate units encounter the enemy, they will receive reports of those actions. Depending on proximity and communications, they may receive earlier, less complete reports, and maybe even appeals for help. The staff officers will gain an understanding of the war through this information, as well as information received through intelligence reporting and analysis. Their views will be sympathetic to their combatant comrades, but must necessarily be different. This is one of the reasons why staff officers are sent out to line units during the fighting: they go to assess the situation and report back to their headquarters the 'ground truth' of the situation.

For that very reason, the assessment of the situation, the ground truth, the best line officers are experienced line officers. But herein is the problem: how relevant one's experience is to the situation at hand. Experience as a company or battalion officer commanding in a large-scale war may not help in assessing a guerrilla war. One may misread the signs and signals. If one fought in World War I, will one understand military relations with a civilian populace in a guerrilla war at home? How will one interpret symbolic actions when one is schooled in a different kind of war and when one is from a different society? All of these issues and more will influence how one views the conflict, both while in the midst of it and in later interpretation when it is over.

In Ireland, the staff officers also had reports in the press – hostile, neutral and friendly. Further, there were the coroners' inquests, which tried to establish the legal facts. Even after these ceased to function, the military courts of inquiry acted in the same manner. The staff officers formed their opinions based on these sources in addition to the others. This necessarily influenced their views of the conduct of the war.

The four-volume *The Record of the Rebellion in Ireland in 1920–21, and the part played by the Army in dealing with it* is an invaluable source for students of the Irish revolutionary era because it provides a unique view into British military thought on the conflict, as well as their ideas on the best means of prosecuting this type of war in general at the time. This is not to suggest that the views and information presented in it are accurate to historical fact. Much of the information presented in these volumes is subjective, and not all relevant information was available to the authors. In some instances, it appears almost as if they lied deliberately. Nonetheless, this volume represents their view of what they witnessed and did, albeit tempered by their culture and experience, as well as the political sensitivity of not wanting to insult the government too directly.

The study, then, is a snapshot in time. It is singular in that it was written at a time of great upheaval in the British army. During the years leading up to its writing, the army had reduced from its wartime strength of 3.9 million in 1919 to just 250,000 by 1921.[1] This vastly reduced force, ill-equipped and ill-trained, was deployed in twenty-seven commands around the world, and included active combat operations in both Mesopotamia and the Northwest Frontier. At the same time, they were undertaking more traditional 'imperial policing' missions in India, Khartoum and Palestine, while performing occupation duties in the Baltic, Black Sea, China and, of course, Germany. Of the 250,000 men of the army, some 163,736 (65.49 per cent) were deployed to dangerous regions of the world. Thus, the army was overcommitted and, as a result, stretched thin. At the end of the War for Independence in 1921, the Irish Command mustered about one-fifth of the British army; only the India Command[2] was larger. By 1922, the time of writing, the army's situation had begun to stabilize, or perhaps they had simply adapted to instability.[3]

While the *Record of the Rebellion* may have been written at other times, it was fresh on the minds of its authors and represents one of the few outlets available to them to express their angst.[4] Since there was no existing counter-insurgency doctrine on which to rely at the time, there was no theoretical basis to place their experiences into context, personally or professionally. Interestingly, much the same also held true for the former rebels. In this respect, this study is somewhat similar to the later 'fighting story' series by the former rebels.[5] Obviously, these were stories by individuals rather than by an institution, and they were never meant to establish a methodical and systematic study of their actions. Another aspect for the authors was that the Civil War had broken out while they were writing, the political situation and the military situation in Ireland, or at least their outcomes, were unclear, even their former Chief of the Imperial General Staff (CIGS) was murdered in London by two IRA men, and so the authors did not necessarily know what would happen.[6]

What they 'knew' was that they had been put into a seemingly impossible situation, and given a seemingly impossible mission, with inadequate resources and almost no guidance. The guidance they received was frequently in the negative and often *ex post facto*. Their frustrations with this come through in their commentary. Thus, they may have had more than one truth.

Background to the Irish Revolution, 1916–23

As the reader of such a volume as this is likely already quite familiar with the circumstances that led to its creation, only a brief examination of the Irish revolutionary era is necessary.[7] Frequently, the beginning of the Irish Revolution is usually listed as the 1916 Rising[8], but it would be too much to say that the revolutionary period actually did not begin until the Easter Rising, for many events happened before, but for the purposes here, it is simply enough to acknowledge this.

So although the Easter Rising was not the beginning of the revolutionary era, it was the commencement of the first large-scale revolutionary violence in Ireland in more than two generations. It was from this tragic and heroic event that the new form of Irish rebellion was born, the *petite guerre*, the small war or guerrilla war. The few surviving leaders and some new ones came to recognize that they would likely never be militarily strong enough to *drive* the existing government or its forces from Ireland in any conventional sense, while at the same time they also began to realize that they did not necessarily have to do so.[9]

The rebels entered, or more precisely, started, the war in 1919 without a clear strategy beyond not wanting to be trapped in static defence as in 1916. Over the course of the year, they developed their tactics through trial and error, while conducting raids for arms, attacking barracks and orchestrating ambushes. In this instance, much of the doctrine and strategy followed, or derived from, tactics. As the year progressed, the rebel units learnt what worked. By the end of 1919, the Irish Volunteer GHQ began to examine history for examples to help formulate their strategy and doctrine.

While no evidence has come to light that the Irish Volunteers' leaders ever read him, they decided to fight their new war against what Clausewitz described as the 'centre of gravity'[10], or the place upon which all else depends in the enemy's mind. It is clear that the war was fought against the British politicians as well as the British electorate, through propaganda in newspapers in addition to the more immediate targets of governance and the military in Ireland. This was, then, a strategy using the three parts of Clausewitz's 'paradoxical trinity' of the people, government and military, which, when manipulated, produced different effects.[11] Thus, the Irish Volunteers used military action against the elements of British rule in Ireland. In so doing, they actually targeted the will of the people and the patience of the politicians. Although the struggle between the IRA, the British army and the RIC was frighteningly violent, the true battleground lay in the realm of information: a war of perception.

Although the theory of what is now called 'information operations'[12] is relatively new as a codified concept, the various components of it, especially propaganda, have existed for centuries. In a war largely over perception, what people *believed* happened was frequently more important than the kinetic truth. This means, for example, that there will likely always be debate about the effects of the 28 November 1920 Kilmichael Ambush on C Company, Auxiliary Division, RIC (ADRIC). Physically, one could question how effective C Company was after losing nineteen men, nearly one-fifth of their strength, and two vehicles in one attack. More importantly, what were the ambush's propaganda and psychological effects? It certainly boosted republican morale; it created shock, horror and outrage in the British forces and fostered feelings of anger, despair and impotence amongst British politicians. Although the military and police certainly wanted to strike back at Barry's flying column, they were faced with the stark reality that they could not, if for no other reason than because they could not find it.[13]

Although it took little time for the politicians to decide that they were not willing to give the police or the army in Ireland a free hand, it took considerably longer for them to conclude that they were going to have to negotiate with those whom they had stated publicly they never would. It is by no means clear that the police and the army would have succeeded if they had *carte blanche*, but clearly the army, at least, felt that they would have. They just needed more time, authority, manpower and the support of their government to win, or so they thought. Mistakenly, some in the army thought that they could solve a political problem with military force. Given what has occurred in the past decade in the Middle East, they perhaps may be excused, considering there are many today who believe the same, despite almost a century of experience to the contrary. Interestingly, they mentioned this only in the last chapter of their official history. Yet, despite Sir Hamar Greenwood's statements to the contrary, the Cabinet *were* willing to sit down with the 'ruffians' and 'cornerboys' they had continually derided the rebels for being. It took time for them to get past this prejudice, if they ever did.

Although few expected the Truce to last, it did, and both sides had to make concessions, eventually coming to the compromise of the treaty. There are some interesting points regarding this that shed light on the army's apparent attitude throughout the *Record of the Rebellion*. The first of these, as noted by the eminent Charles Townshend, was that by reporting the truce to the newly created League of Nations, the Cabinet granted the IRA what is legally known as 'combatant' status as a 'legitimate' army. Further, the negotiations were conducted between legal 'equals'. This is not to say that the Cabinet saw the republicans as their equals, but that their formal actions constituted *de jure* legal recognition of such status. This, then, legitimized many IRA actions over the previous five years.[14]

The second point emanates from the first; the careful reader will note that the authors of *Volume I* do not seem to have liked referring to the Truce as a 'truce', frequently using it only in quotation marks when they could. In *Volume I*, the word appears just twenty-seven times in sixty-five pages, but twelve of these are as part of a formal subtitle. Of the remaining fifteen occurrences in the main text, just three are without quotation marks.

In the 5th Divisional history, the primary author, Col. Maxwell-Scott, used the word only three times in its 131 pages, and then, only in quotation marks. The first time he used it was to explain that the 'words "truce" and "armistice" had no application in the situation where one side had no belligerent rights'. Indeed, the chapter in which it lay, Chapter IV, 'January, 1921 to the date of "The Suspension of Activities," 11 July, 1921' would not use the word either.[15] There is, however, more to this than just one man's opinion about the word. The last time it was used was as a direct quotation from Maj-Gen Sir H. S. Jeudwine, proscribing its use in a letter to his brigade commanders about the truce agreement, which is worth quoting in full:

> The word 'truce' has been applied to this Agreement and the situation which follows from it. This word is generally understood as applicable to an armistice between recognized belligerents. It is preferable, therefore, that it should not be used by us in this instance, but that the statement of terms should be referred to as the 'Agreement' and its effects as a 'suspension of activities.'[16]

However much the use of the word 'truce' offended Jeudwine, it is clear that he was not the only one. Thus, this was Jeudwine's means of protesting, in a permanent way, against the Truce itself.

The 6th Division's history was also sparing in its use of the word, occurring only twenty-three times in the volume. Of these, only fourteen were in the main text, which ran to some ninety-three pages. The Dublin District's history used the word seventeen times in its fifty-nine pages.[17] Clearly, the officers were upset by this word because of its *de jure* recognition. Perhaps their reaction seems strange given that it was only a word, but soldiers guard their status jealously, and do not admit people easily into the ranks of equals. This was their means of making a statement against their enemies and against their civilian leaders. The wound caused by what they saw as the betrayal by their own government had still not closed when the time came to write this history. It was under this backdrop that, shortly after the ratification of the treaty, the army began to write its history of the conflict.

The Writing of 'The Record of the Rebellion'

The Record of the Rebellion was written by members of the general staffs of the 5th and 6th Infantry Divisions, the Dublin District and General Headquarters (GHQ) of the Irish Command. The first three general staffs wrote the component parts of *Volume IV*, the Divisional histories, while the GHQ general staff wrote the other three volumes. Compiled in the spring and autumn of 1922, the four-volume history was meant to be a record of the conflict according to what the army did during the course of the conflict.

Several of the four volumes of the *Record of the Rebellion* have recently been published in whole or in part. First to appear was *Volume II*, 'Intelligence', edited and combined by the late Peter Hart with the RIC intelligence final report. Next came Parts III and I of *Volume IV*, the Dublin District and 5th Infantry Divisions' histories, respectively, edited by Dr W. Barry Sheehan. The Military History Society of Ireland released Part VI, 6th Infantry Division history recently, and Dr Kenneth Ferguson is publishing Volume III: Law.

As both Hart and Sheehan have noted in their edited volumes of the *Record of the Rebellion*, the aggravation and puzzlement of British army authors came through in this study. Indeed, Hart referred to it as a 'vast accumulation of frustration, error and confusion...', while Sheehan noted that 'No single view of the IRA emerges...', which was one of the many reflections of that great angst.[18] The army authors knew that they had learnt a great deal about fighting insurgency during this conflict; this knowledge would have come in handy in their operations in Palestine and other locations, as well as, perhaps, former colonies after the Second World War. Not the least of this knowledge was how to use an all-arms approach, including the first doctrine for the use of motorized vehicles, as well as armoured cars, against insurgent threats.

If one assumes, as stated in the original introduction to *Volume I*, that the army authors were writing this to pass along 'lessons learnt', one will be disappointed. For although that was the stated purpose, and while accepting the criticality of a narrative historical element, there were few actual lessons mentioned as such in this overview of the other volumes. The caveat to this was that many of the lessons were interspersed throughout the study, being drawn from and written into the historical narrative. In some cases they are obvious, in others they are implied. The actual phrase 'lessons learnt' occurs only four times, and only in Parts I (5th Infantry Division) and II of *Volume IV* (6th Infantry Division). Only this first volume and Part I of *Volume IV*, 5th Infantry Division History, include separate sections for lessons. The latter section consists of just two pages out of the 131 of that part and of the 293 pages of the whole volume.[19] Thus, it would seem there were additional reasons for their writing this study.

The army's reasons for writing the *Record of the Rebellion* were multifaceted, as were the reasons why the Irish Command had 'failed' in Ireland. In some ways, the study was an attempt to shift the blame for this failure to the Cabinet and government. They had fought a war of paradoxes they did not understand.

Their actual mission in Ireland was not to prevent Irish independence; Irish independence was the law of the United Kingdom since 1914, and while it may not have taken the form the republicans wanted, this did not change the technical reality.[20] The army's mission was not to defeat the IRA, but rather to prevent them installing a revolutionary republican government. The army's mission was not to defeat Sinn Féin, but to assist in the establishment of what is now called 'stability' and to maintain it.

The suppression orders against the IRA were meant to give the army legal standing to operate against them in aid of civil authority. Their prosecution of the conflict belied their understanding of their mission. Part of the reason for this was that the government never really defined the army's mission. For just as the IRA did not have doctrine or a strategy to achieve their end state, neither did the British army. Without a clear mission, the army was left without the fundamentals necessary to the formulation of strategy and doctrine.

With this understanding, it is important to note that one of the true missions of the Irish Command was to restore order by mostly acting in 'aid of civil authority'. The law of the land was still home rule; thus Ireland's freedom was already guaranteed, at least until repealed. So, in a strange way, the army and RIC were fighting to stabilize Ireland long enough to grant some form of independence, while the rebels' war was over the form that independence would take.

For the Irish Command, this history served as a codified record of what they did and why. Further, since it was the Cabinet and Irish administration who, with their inability to formulate a plan and stay with it, stymied the army's attempts, seemingly at every turn, to instil order, this was meant to be vindication while pointing fingers at government, the republicans, and, sometimes, even the RIC. This study reads very much like an explanation of how the 'loss of Ireland' was not the army's fault.

Leaving aside that the Irish Free State's status in 1922 remained similar to what had been promised in September 1914, the army could not see this change of power as anything but a defeat. That the Cabinet decided to end it made the army's sacrifices seem worthless. The Irish Command, and one must assume the Imperial General Staff, if not also the War Office, since it was a collaboration, seems to have wanted to go on the record to justify how and why the army had not been *permitted* to win. Yet, *The Record of the Rebellion* cannot define what 'success' was, or how they were to know whether they were successful or not. There are just the instinctual reactions that the Truce, the Treaty and establishment of the Irish Free State and its grant of dominion status equalled defeat. So in large measure, they set out to establish a record demonstration they were not at fault.

The original vision for these volumes appears to have come from General Sir Nevil Macready, General Officer Commanding-in-Chief, British Forces, Ireland, sometime in late 1921 or early 1922 when plans 'were drawn up in Ireland immediately after the Treaty was signed, so that an accurate official history of the military aspect might exist in concise form'.[21] The actual writing, however, had begun sometime in the summer of 1920 when Col W. J. Maxwell-Scott, a General Staff Officer 1st Grade (GSO-1) with the 5th Division, began writing its history in Ireland, apparently of his own accord. Later, he and Maj J. S. Drew, the GSO-1 from the staff of the Dublin District, writing its history, began working in conjunction with each other. After the war, GHQ assigned Lt-Col J. E. S. Brind to lead the Irish Command's effort and the Imperial General Staff (IGS) assigned GSO-1 Lt-Col H. E. R. R. Braine as overall project co-ordinator. In the early autumn of 1920, Capt C. H. Peck of the Directorate of Military Operations and Intelligence (MO&I) of the IGS, working for Braine, asked Maj-Gen Sir E. P. Strickland to edit the 6th Infantry Division history, a draft of which already existed. It is unclear who originally penned it, but Strickland was keen to participate in its editing and may very well have been the author. Braine worked with the three editors and Brind while also co-ordinating with a GSO-1, Lt-Col P. J. Macksey, in the War Office. The actual compiler appears to have been Peck in London.[22] It seems that a draft copy of the first two volumes, on operations and intelligence respectively, were printed by the summer of 1922.[23] Shortly thereafter, they produced the first galley proofs of the Divisional histories.

In mid-April 1922, Brind had sent a copy of each of the drafts of the 5th Infantry Division, 6th Infantry Division and Dublin District histories to Braine in MO&I at the IGS asking them to print enough copies to hand out one to each unit that served in Ireland during the conflict. The copies went to MO&I sub-directorate, the Administration and Special Duties Section (M.O.3). Braine wrote back asking how many units had served in Ireland during the period under review. Interestingly, it was easier for M.O.3 to write to the Irish Command's general staff than to attempt to find the information in the IGS, who should have already had a list considering that the MO&I was responsible for sending these units.[24]

General Macready personally responded, sending his letter directly to the Secretary of State for War, H. Creedy[25], rather than having his staff respond at their level to their counterparts on the IGS. This was a bit unusual. Macready wanted sixty copies each for the two divisions and fifty for the Dublin District. He intended to provide six to the division headquarters, three to cavalry and infantry brigade headquarters, two to the artillery brigade headquarters, and one to each cavalry regiment, infantry battalion, armoured car company and tank battalion. Finally, he wanted sufficient copies printed to have some left over 'as cases will undoubtedly arise where additional copies would be of value'.[26]

While Macready wanted to provide a work that would detail the history of the war from the view of the army, he wanted also to pay tribute to his men, as well as provide lessons for future conflicts. So the general was 'quite anxious' to get the document out for presentation to his command.[27] This did not happen.

Don't Offend the 'Frocks'

When Braine forwarded the drafts to the office of the Deputy Director of MO&I, he explained that his office had already read and marked the errors. He also mentioned that the wording 'will want careful editing to avoid any criticism of government action, [and] that we can see to that before proofs are made. A first note of corrections necessary has already been taken.'[28] These they sent back to the Irish Command.

Unfortunately, these typed drafts have apparently not survived, but there are some lists from Braine that provide some clues.[29] In the 6th Infantry Division volume, then *Volume VI*, they noted some 'statements regarding Michael Collins' that were likely to be derogatory. Considering that Collins was one of the leading Free State government and military officials, it would not do to allow the army to insult him in an official publication.[30]

The Irish Command authors did not reserve their venom for just republican figures like Collins; they criticized liberals in general, government, and parliament too. For instance, they criticized the English Labour Party during the Munition Strike of May to December 1920, saying that they were 'willing and eager to assist with their tongues and pens, turned a deaf ear to all appeals to their pockets, or to requests for direct action which was likely to lead to their own inconvenience'.[31] They did not stop there. In tone and language, the authors were highly critical of the government. On one line, they decided to delete the phrase 'the Government's lethargy', and later seven more 'criticism[s] of Government' that Braine found. These were likely references to what the Irish Command felt was slowness and indecision that seemed to typify the Irish administration's and the Cabinet's reactions. They also criticized Parliament, saying that many of their problems stemmed from having to answer questions in the Commons 'instigated by some of the leading rebels themselves'.[32]

The vehemence of some of what they cut was surprising. The Dublin District's *Volume VII* was most direct, saying that 'The political policy in August [1921] may be described as one of drift, so far as the British Government were concerned.' A little later, they were more insulting with a statement that 'By September, the weakness of the Government, in permitting the rebels to transgress the terms of the truce, was becoming a danger.'[33] These references to the Truce expressed the haphazard manner of implementing it, as well as the resistance of the Government to use the established protocols in the Truce agreement to redress violations with the republican leadership. Furthermore, such a statement skirted the boundaries of acceptable criticism of policy by going further in suggesting that the Government was the threat. Such wording from serving officers would have been acceptable, if provocative, in private, but was wholly unacceptable in an official publication. What is interesting is that these types of comments appeared only in the 6th Infantry Division and the Dublin District histories, not Jeudwine's 5th Infantry Division. Perhaps it was a matter of the 5th Infantry Division operating in areas of lower overall violence. While this may have been what they actually experienced or how they felt, the leadership was not going to let the 'Frocks', as late CIGS Field Marshal Wilson had called them, see it, so they expunged these types of statements.[34] But there were other obstacles to be overcome as well.

Maps and the Price of History

There were two factors that affected the cost of the study: the number of copies, and the number and clarity of maps. Originally, the authors of the Divisional and Dublin District histories wanted to use several maps apiece, but the details required a higher resolution than they could afford to print economically. Indeed, the 'cost of 350 copies of each of the three maps is £46. Each additional 100 copies of the three, if printed at the same time as the 350 is £3/15/-.'[35] Their first answer to this problem was to suggest using existing Ordnance Survey maps of one inch to ten miles resolution, and issue one map of Ireland with each volume. These were inexpensive and in good supply, but did not have the overlay information and details that an actual headquarters or command post map would have on it. Thus, the maps would lose much of their utility.[36] They therefore decided to use 'traced' maps in the end, which were essentially just rough sketches by hand. Ultimately, only the 6th Infantry Division history used graphics, albeit in relatively small numbers: six maps, one illustration and four charts. Still, these added value.

Form of the Volumes

Originally planned as a seven-volume work, the new Secretary of State for War, Lord Derby[37], reduced it to four volumes by combining the three volumes of the 5th and 6th Infantry Divisions and Dublin District into one, three-part *Volume IV*. The original plan called for a separate volume for personnel and administration and another on supply and logistics.[38] When these were cancelled is unclear, and no draft copies appear to have survived, but they would have to have been struck off some time in the summer or early autumn of 1922 at the latest. The last draft form of the work came to:

Volume I: Operations
Volume II: Intelligence
Volume III: Law
Volume IV: 5th Infantry Division, 6th Infantry Division and Dublin District

The decision to publish the individual histories in one volume was not based on cost; there was a negligible difference, but mostly for ease of use for the readers. Each volume had its own appendices.

Interestingly, the 1st Infantry Division in the north was hardly mentioned in the history. While they existed for only about a year, their input would have been interesting indeed. The IRA conducted operations in Ulster, both in the counties forming the Northern Irish State as well as the three remaining. The formation of the 1st Infantry Division was somewhat an admission of the failure of policy in the north. The Ulster Special Constabulary was billed as a force that could replace the army units in the north by relieving the need for them to remain, and thereby freeing them to fight in the south. The heavily sectarian nature of the force quickly precluded such a move to the south. Thus, the Irish Command formed the northern brigades into the 1st Infantry Division on 7 August 1920. They felt the situation in the north to be sufficiently distinct to require its own command structure. Although their constituent brigades remained after re-absorption into the rest of the Command after the disbanding of the 1st Infantry Division in June 1921, the units in the north of Ireland had no history of their own in the document, merely becoming mentioned in the 5th Infantry Division history. Was this a question of apprehension over what the army might say about Northern Ireland, or did they simply not have enough to say?

Over the past decade and a half, numerous books and studies on this era of Irish history have mentioned the *Record of the Rebellion in Ireland* in some manner, and yet, when doing so, virtually all of the historians have used the copies that exist in the Jeudwine and Strickland papers in the Imperial War Museum rather than the draft copies housed in the National Archives at Kew. In part, this is due to the latter being released in April 2001. Interestingly, the Jeudwine and Strickland versions are drafts of their division's histories only, rather than a draft of the complete fourth volume. Hart's edited second volume on Intelligence[39] from 2002 used a draft copy from the Imperial War Museum as well, while Sheehan's as *Hearts & Mines* (2009) and *Fighting for Dublin* (2007) both used the drafts at Kew. Patrick McCarthy of the Military History Society of Ireland has edited Part II of *Volume IV*, the 6th Divisional history using the Strickland copy in the Imperial War Museum. Finally, prior to this author's *Ambushes and Armour*, he had only seen one reference, other than Sheehan's of course, to the existence of the complete four volumes at Kew, in Meda Ryan's *Tom Barry: Freedom Fighter*; Ryan did not, however, cite from those volumes, but rather used the Imperial War Museum copies.

Considering that the only extant copies of the *Record of the Rebellion* are housed in the National Archives and in the Jeudwine and Strickland Papers in the Imperial War Museum, why the study was never published and released is a good line of inquiry. At least some 240 draft copies of *Volume I* were printed; how many were distributed for comment is unclear. It would seem that there are few records to hint at what happened.

One hint comes from a mid-January 1946 note from the Records directorate of the IGS, forwarded the file of this study to the office of the Assistant Undersecretary of State for War, G. W. Lambert[40], for determination about whether its classification should be downgraded, since 'There appears to be no purely military reason why this downgrading should not be allowed but in view of the P.U.S.'[41] remarks [only he could authorize release] I feel your concurrence should be obtained...' but that this 'would not in any sense release the report to the general public'. The response eight days later revealed that they still had a stock of 122 copies, with none 'in circulation', and closed by adamantly refusing, saying that 'this paper should <u>not</u> [emphasis original] be downgraded'.[42] No reason was given, although one might well imagine the effect of the relations between the Free State and the United Kingdom at the time as being a significant part of the reasoning. Nevertheless, as a result of the release of this volume, along with Ferguson's *Volume III*, when combined with the several other volumes already published, the full record is now available. The Irish Command's concept of the several ground truths in Ireland is accessible to all, without having to go to London.

Original Foreword

This record of the operations of the Military Force employed in the Rebellion in Ireland during the years 1920–21 has been compiled at General Headquarters, the Forces in Ireland. It contains a general account of the military measures taken, and of the police on which these measures were based.

It is considered that the military history of these operations, carried out under unusual conditions of great difficulty, will be of value to any military commander who may in the future be faced with a similar problem.

GENERAL STAFF
WAR OFFICE
March, 1922.

Original Introduction

In the following pages an attempt has been made to record a faithful and accurate account of the more important events which have taken place in Ireland during the years 1920–21, and to show how the various lines of action adopted by the Government have been applied, in so far as affected by them, by the military authorities. The various volumes and records have been compiled by the branches of the Staff, who, during the period of activity, were responsible for dealing with the particular subjects recorded.

It is hoped that this record may be of use in the event of similar situations arising in any part of the Empire, and in order that the reports of the different branches of the Staff may be available and easily referred to, no attempt has been made to compile the different records into one volume.

Reference has been made in almost all cases to the period prior to 1920, and in one or two of the reports events which took place as far back as the Rebellion of 1916[42] have been briefly referred to.

It may be claimed that in a record of military activities reference to political aspects and action is out of place. It is, however, pointed out that in the case of Ireland under review political and military activities were so closely interwoven that it is impossible to disentangle them. Further, it is hoped that the record may not be entirely without value to any government which may have to deal with a somewhat similar situation in future years.

NOTES

1   HMSO, *Statistics of the Military Effort of the British Empire During the Great War, 1914–1920* (first published, HMSO, 1922 reprinted by Naval And Military Press, 1999), pp. 88–9. For more on the effects of the First World War and Ireland, see, K. Jeffery, *Ireland and the Great War* (2000) and A. Gregory and S. Pašeta. *Ireland and the Great War: 'A War to Unite Us All'?* (2002).

2   This was the British army, not the Indian army.

3   The classic study of this is K. Jeffery, *The British Army and the Crisis of Empire, 1918–22* (1984), while, for criticism of the lack of imperial context in most studies on Ireland of the era, see his 'The road to Asia, and the Grafton Hotel, Dublin: Ireland in the "British world"', Irish Historical Studies, xxxvi, no. 142 (Nov. 2008), pp 243–56; J. aan de Wiel, *The Irish Factor 1899–1919: Ireland's Strategic and Diplomatic Importance for Foreign Powers* (2011) provides imperial and European context.

4   The other significant outlet for them was *The Army Quarterly*, but there were actually just a few articles on Ireland between 1920 and 1939.

5   The Fighting Stories series consisted of: J. White, ed. *Dublin's Fighting Story, 1913–21: Told by the Men Who Made It* (Tralee: The Kerryman, LTD., 1947); M. Keegan, ed. *Rebel Cork's Fighting Story, from 1916 to the Truce with Britain* (Tralee, Co. Kerry, The Kerryman, 1947); *Kerry's Fighting Story, 1916–21: Told by the Men Who Made It* (Tralee: The Kerryman, 1942); Col J. M. McCarthy, ed. *Limerick's Fighting Story: From 1916 to the Truce with Britain* (London: Anvil Books, N.D.). To this list could be added *With the I.R.A. in the Fight for Freedom: 1919 to the Truce* (Tralee: The Kerryman, 1955) and National Association of Old IRA, *Dublin Brigade Review* (Dublin: Cahill & Co., 1939).

6   Field Marshal Sir Henry H. Wilson (b.1864–d.1922) was CIGS until February 1922. He supported Ulster unionism wholeheartedly. In June 1922, two London assassins who were IRA members claiming to be supporting Northern Ireland's Catholics murdered him. Suspicion has fallen on Michael Collins, but Hart said there is no evidence of Collins' complicity, P. Hart, *Mick: The Real Michael Collins* (2005), pp, 396–7. For more on Wilson, see K. Jeffery, *The Military Correspondence of Field Marshal Sir Henry Wilson, 1918–1922* (1985) and K. Jeffery, *Field Marshal Sir Henry Wilson: A Political Soldier* (2006) and B. Ash, *The Lost Dictator: A Biography of Sir Henry Wilson, Bart, GCB, DSO, MP* (1968).

7   See, F. Costello, *The Irish Revolution and Its Aftermath, 1916–1923: Years of Revolt* (Dublin: Irish Academic Press, 2003); J. Augusteijn, *The Irish Revolution, 1913–1923* (London: Palgrave Macmillan, 2002); M. Hopkinson, *Irish War of Independence* (2004); C. D. Greaves, *The Irish Crisis* (New York: International Publishers, 1974); B. Grob-Fitzgibbon, *Turning Points of the Irish Revolution: The British Government, Intelligence, and the Cost of Indifference, 1912–1921* (Palgrave, 2007); Fanning, Ronan. *Fatal Path: British Government and Irish Revolution, 1910–1922* (2013); D. Fitzpatrick, *Politics and Irish Life, 1913–1921* (1977); N. Mansergh, *The Irish Question 1840–1921* (1965); and K. Matthews, *Fatal Influences: The Impact of Ireland on British Politics 1920–1925* (2004).

8   See; *1916: Easter Rebellion Handbook* (Mourne River Press, 1998); B. Barton, *From Behind a Closed Door: Secret Court Martial Records of the 1916 Easter Rising* (Belfast: Blackstaff Press, 2002); T. Coates, *The Irish Uprising: Papers from the British Parliamentary Archive* (London: The Stationery Office, 2000); G. Doherty and D. Keogh, eds, *1916: The Long Revolution* (Dublin: Mercier Press, 2007); F. McGarry, *The Rising: Ireland: Easter 1916* (Oxford University Press, 2010) and *Rebels: Voices from the Easter Rising* (Dublin: Penguin Books, 2011); K. Jeffery, ed., *The Sinn Féin Rebellion as They Saw It* (Dublin: Irish Academic Press, 1999); K. Jeffery, *The GPO and the Easter Rising* (Dublin: Irish Academic Press, 2006); R. Taillon. *When History Was Made: the Women of 1916*, (1999); W. I. Thompson, *The Imagination of an Insurrection: Dublin, Easter 1916: A Study of an Ideological Movement*

(New York: Harper Colophon Books, 1972); C. Townshend, *Easter 1916: The Irish Rebellion* (Chicago: Ivan R. Dee, 2006).

9   See S. O'Mahoney, *Frongoch: University of Revolution* (1987) and L. Ebenezer, *Fron-Goch and the birth of the IRA* (2005). For more on the transition to violence, see J. Augusteijn, *From Public Defiance to Guerrilla Warfare: The Experience of Ordinary Volunteers in the Irish War of Independence, 1916–1921* (1998).

10 Clausewitz, Carl von, *On War*, trans. Sir M. Howard and P. Paret (1984), p. 486.

11 Ibid., p. 89.

12 Probably one of the earliest uses of 'information operations' in the U.S. military was with Field Manual (FM) 100–6, *Information Operations* (27 August 1996). The latest iteration of this is FM 3–13 *Information Operations: Doctrine, Tactics, Techniques, and Procedures* (28 September 2003).

13 See E. Morrison, 'Kilmichael Revisited: Tom Barry and the "False Surrender"', *Terror in Ireland, 1916–1923*, D. Fitzpatrick, ed.; W. Kautt, *Ambushes & Armour* (2010); M. Ryan, *Tom Barry: Freedom Fighter* (2005); P. Hart, *The IRA & Its Enemies* (1998) for modern views on this ambush.

14 See Townshend, *Political Violence*, p. 359.

15 *The Record of the Rebellion,* Volume IV '5th Division History', pp. 40, 54–5.

16 Ibid., Appendix XXI 'Interpretation of the "Agreement" of 11th July 1921, by GOC 5th Division', p.120.

17 Ibid, pp. 133–226 and 227–82.

18 P. Hart, *British Intelligence in Ireland: The Final Reports*, 'Irish Narratives' (2002), p. 2 and W. Sheehan, ed., *Hearts & Mines: The British 5th Division, Ireland 1920–1922* (2009), p. xvii.

19 *Record of the Rebellion*, Vol. IV, pp. 73–4.

20 Most now argue the Government of Ireland Act, 1914, the so-called 'Third Home Rule Bill', was not going to be implemented regardless of the law. See, Fanning, *Fatal Path*, pp 105–53.

21 Chief, Imperial General Staff (Lord Cavan) to Secretary of State for War (Lord Derby), 18 April 1923, National Archives, Kew, WO 141/93/57.

22 Col W. B. R. Tandy to Lt-Col H. E. R. R. Braine, 21 October 1922; Lt-Col W. J. Maxwell-Scot to Capt C. H. Peck, No. 2/72634.G., 27 September 1922; Capt C. H. Peck to Maj-Gen Sir E. P. Strickland, B.M. No. 17 (m.o.3), 28 September 1922; Capt F. C. Murphy, GHQ, Ireland to Lt-Col P. J. Mackesey, M.O.3, War Office, No. 2/62197.G., 11 August 1922; Lt-Col P. J. Mackesey to Capt F. C. Murphy, No. G.M./M.O.3./17., 15 August 1922, NAUK WO 141/93/41a, 42a, 34a, & 35a respectively.

23 Braine to DDMO&I, Min No., 8 May 1922, NAUK WO 141/93/5, pp. 1–2.

24 Brind to D.M.O., Memo No. 2/62197/G, 13 April 1922 and Braine to GOCinC, The Forces in Ireland, Memo No. M.O.3.B.M. No. 17, 20 April 1922, NAUK WO 141/93/1A and 2A respectively.

25 Sir Herbert Creedy (b.1878–d.1973), KCVO, GCB.

26 GOCinC (Macready) to The Secretary, War Office (Creedy) Memo No. 2/62197/G, 26 April 1922, NAUK WO 141/93/4.

27 Braine to DDMO&I, 8 May 1922, NAUK WO 141/93/5, p 1.

28 Handwritten note from Bartholomew to D.M.O.&I., on memorandum from Braine, IGS to D.D.M.O.&I., 11 May 1922, NAUK WO 141/93/6.

29 There is a corrected copy of the third proof in WO 141/94. It is the version of the document from July 1922, the one already corrected.

30 M.O.3 to GHQ, Irish Command, '6th Divisional Record: Points requiring editing before circulation', 21 April 1922, NAUK WO 141/93.

31 *The Record of the Rebellion*, Vol. I, 'Operations', proof copy No. 3, attachment to Macready to Director, M.O., Min. No. 2/62197, 4 May 1922, NAUK WO 141/94/1A, p 16.

32 M.O.3 to GHQ, Irish Command, '6th Divisional Record: Points requiring editing before circulation', 21 April 1922, NAUK WO 141/93 and *The Record of the Rebellion*, Vol. I, 'Operations', proof copy no. 3, attachment to Macready to Director, M.O., Min. No. 2/62197, 4 May 1922, NAUK WO 141/94/1A, p 45.

33 M.O.3 to GHQ, Irish Command, '6th Divisional Record: Points requiring editing before circulation', 21 April 1922; M.O.3 to GHQ, Irish Command, 'Record of 5th Division', 25 April 1922; and M.O.3 to GHQ, Irish Command, 'Necessary Amendments, Vol. VII', N.D., NAUK WO 141/93.

34 They also removed a remark about the Royal Navy in which they said: 'Representations made to the Admiralty on the subject of the inadequacy of naval resources in Ireland had met with little response before the cessation of activity on 11th July, 1921.' *The Record of the Rebellion*, Vol. I, 'Operations', proof copy no. 3, attachment to Macready to Director, M.O., Min. No. 2/62197, 4 May 1922, NAUK WO 141/94/1A, p. 44.

35 M.O.3. to M.I.4., 30 May 1922 , NAUK WO 141/93/16 and M.I.4 to M.O.3, 19 June 1922, NAUK WO 141/93/18. The cost of the first 350 maps in 2008 pounds Sterling is £7,410, while each of the additional 100 maps is £602, see Lawrence H. Officer, 'Five Ways to Compute the Relative Value of a UK Pound Amount, 1830 to Present,' MeasuringWorth, 2008 (measuringworth.com).

36 Maxwell-Scott to M.O.3 (Lt-Col P. J. MacKenny), 8 June 1922; P. J. MacKenny to I.C. GHQ (D. J. C. K. Bernard), 1 August 1922; M.O.3. to Col W. J. Maxwell-Scott, Dublin District GHQ, Memo No. B.M./M.O.3/17, 1 August 1922; Capt F. C. Murphey to Bt.Lt-Col P. J. Mackesy, Memo No. 2/62197.G., 11 August 1922; M.O.3. to F. C. Murphy, Memo No. B.M./M.O.3./17, 15 August 1922; Murphey to Mackesy, Memo No. 2/62197.G., 19 August 1922; M.O.3. (Capt C. H. Peck) to Henderson, Memo No. B.M. No. 17 (M.O.3.). 26 September 1922; Maxwell Scott, GHQ Ireland to Peck, Memo No. 2/72634.G., 27 September 1922; Peck to Strickland, Memo No. B.M. No. 17 (M.O.3), 28 September 1922 , NAUK WO 141/93/17A, 30a, 31a, 34a, 37a, 40a and 41a.

37 Edward G. V. Stanley (b. 1865–d.1948), 17th Earl of Derby.

38 Chief, Imperial General Staff (Lord Cavan) to Secretary of State for War (Lord Derby), 18 April 1923, NAUK WO 141/93/57.

39 This work is an excellent resource because it juxtaposes Volume II with the final report of Brig-Gen Sir Ormond de L'Épée Winter, chief of police intelligence in Ireland.

40 Guy William Lambert (b.1889–d.1984).

41 Permanent Undersecretary of State for War, probably Sir Herbert Creedy, who served from 1920 to 1939 in that position.

42 M.O.1. (Records) to A.U.S., Min. No. 79/Irish/966, 14 January 1946 and A.U.S. to M.O.1. (Recs), 22 January 1946, NAUK WO 141/93.

43 24–29 April 1916.

CHAPTER I

The Situation in Ireland at the end of 1919 to April 1920

Situation end of 1919.—By the end of 1919[1] the rebel movement in Ireland had made considerable headway throughout the country. The organization of the Irish Volunteers had been considerably elaborated on the lines of a rebel army, of which the controlling force was the old-standing secret society, the Irish Republican Brotherhood.[a] The Sinn Fein[b] leaders had also inaugurated a system of rebel civil administration; Sinn Fein Arbitration Courts[c] sat and dealt with claims arising out of agrarian disputes, and with persons accused of acting to the detriment of the rebel cause. The Irish Members of Parliament[d] who refused to sit at Westminster had formed themselves into an "Irish Republican Parliament," known as Dail Eireann[e], which held secret sessions and issued decrees.

[a]   The IRB was founded c.1853 by James Stephens (b.1824–d.1901) and John O'Mahony (b.1816–d.1877), and did not control the 'rebel movement', by which they meant 'republican movement', in Ireland. The IRB, by 1919, under the leadership of Michael Collins, had few assets of their own, but frequently used the assets of other organizations and generally tried to exert influence on them. This clearly demonstrates that the Irish Command still did not understand the basic structure of the republican movement after the war.[2]

[b]   Sinn Féin ('Ourselves Alone'), was an amalgamation of multiple nationalist groups between 1905 and 1907. Amongst these groups were Cumann na nGaedheal, Inghinidhe na hÉireann and the Dunganon Clubs. John Sweetman (b.1844–d.1936) was the first president, with Arthur Griffith (b.1872–d.1922)[3] and Bulmer Hobson (b.1883–d.1969)[4] as vice presidents.

The party was not very popular before the Rising, but, since the press and the British blamed them for the Rising, the Irish Volunteers returning from internment took it over in 1917 and turned it into a militant republican party.[5]

[c] The Arbitration Courts were established under the auspices of the Dáil Éireann in 1919 to mediate agrarian disputes and, since voluntary, were legal until specifically proscribed in 1920. They did not hear cases outside their remit.[6]

[d] Sinn Féin won seventy-three of the 105 Irish seats in Parliament in the December 1918 General Election. The returned republican MPs met at the Mansion House in Dublin and declared themselves the Dáil Éireann, or 'Assembly of Ireland' on Tuesday, 21 January 1919. At this meeting, they formed a provisional republican government.

[e] Dáil Éireann—original spellings and misspellings are original to the text and maintained throughout.[7]

Information regarding rebel activities was very meagre, owing to the fact that during the Chief Secretaryship[f] of Mr. Birrell[g] the Secret Service[h] had ceased to exist, and Sinn Fein had had every opportunity of planning and organizing in security. The Irish Volunteers[i] had begun to be used by the Sinn Fein leaders as an armed instrument for the establishing of a Republic, and at this period the two main objects of their activities were the destruction of the Royal Irish Constabulary[j], as being the principal instrument of British authority, and the domination of the civilian population. The first of the objects Sinn Fein attempted to attain by means of the cold-blooded murder[k] of constables whenever they could be found singly or in very small numbers. The second object was being rapidly accomplished by means of armed intimidation; forced to join the 'Volunteers,' ex-soldiers and their families were persecuted, and every effort was made to terrorize local people into silence regarding outrages committed in their districts.[l] In addition, the Dublin and Provincial newspapers had been enlisted on the side of Sinn Fein, and published virulent rebel propaganda[m], while Sinn Fein emissaries in foreign countries, especially in America, were busy doing the same thing.[8]

[f] The Chief Secretary for Ireland was the day-to-day governmental administrator of Ireland, working under the Lord Lieutenant or viceroy, but usually answering to the Cabinet.

g Augustine Birrell (b.1850–d.1933), Chief Secretary for Ireland, 1907–16.[9]

h Birrell disbanded the Secret Service in Ireland in 1917.[10]

i The Irish Volunteers were the primary militant republican force, which eventually became known as the Irish Republican Army. Formed in November 1913 under Eoin MacNeill (b.1867–d.1945), they had conducted the Easter Rising. The Irish Volunteers' relationship to Sinn Féin was not as simple as the army thought. Sinn Féin was the dominant republican political group after 1918 and led the Dáil. While most of the senior Volunteer leaders tended to be Sinn Féin members, the party did not control the Volunteers. The Volunteers were more independent than most revolutionary armies because they were founded before Sinn Féin became republican as well as the Dáil. Normally, the political movement pre-exists the militant group.

j The Royal Irish Constabulary was the national police force of Ireland. Founded in 1836, the RIC held primary responsibility for policing throughout the country. By the time of the conflict, they were the only armed police force in the United Kingdom. The Dublin Metropolitan Police was also founded in 1836, was unarmed and responsible for policing the City of Dublin, although a substantial RIC presence was posted in the City– about 400 men at the RIC Depot, a Reserve Force of almost 270 and some 100 men manning the three RIC stations in the Phoenix Park District.[11]

k Between January and December 1919, sixteen RIC members were killed as a result of political violence, while during the same period the Dublin Metropolitan Police lost four men.[12]

l Although somewhat emotional, this description is essentially correct. The RIC boycott was meant to get the men to quit the force, but took on a larger role as a means of social and political control. Given Sinn Féin received only a plurality (46 per cent) of the popular vote in the General Election of 1918, they could not validly claim the 'support of the people of Ireland', nor claim a 'mandate' from them for separation from the Empire. Although they had a strong position politically, they needed to consolidate political power to move forward. To do this, they needed to ensure the support of the people, willing or unwilling. Anyone considered a threat, policemen and soldiers and their families, veterans, judges and justices of the peace, anyone who spoke against Sinn Féin or the Irish Volunteers or their actions was liable to be targeted. Since there was not uniform support throughout the country, there were not uniform responses to actions or threats; what was acceptable in one location might not be in another.

m Propaganda was critical to this campaign of recruitment of men, education of supporters and intimidation of enemies.[13]

Police force.—For the suppression of this lawlessness the Government, up to the end of 1919, still relied upon the police forces, directed and controlled by the Civil Administration at the Castle.[n] The Dublin Metropolitan Police were in a very awkward position. The personnel for the most part, when coming off duty, went back to their own homes, where they became easy victims for any rebel sympathizer.[o] The Detective Division[p] had been so reduced by murder or resignation that there were barely half-a-dozen men who could even identify the leading rebels, and the police officer, Mr. Redmond[q], who was appointed to reorganize the Detective Division, was murdered in a street in Dublin in January, 1920.[14] In these circumstances little was to be expected from the D.M.P.[r], except ordinary point duty in the streets by day.

n A reference to Dublin Castle, seat of the British administration in Ireland.[15]

o The RIC were under boycott since 1918, which meant that, in those areas where support for boycott was strongest, no one could conduct trade with, talk to, be seen with or have any contact with boycotted persons or their families.

p A reference to 'G' Division, which also investigated political crimes and served as the intelligence arm of the DMP from whom the government received most of their intelligence about the City of Dublin. This included information about the Dublin IRA Brigade, the pro-republican groups normally headquartered in the City, along with the Dáil, and the Irish Volunteers General Headquarters and its departments. Targeted directly by Michael Collins's 'Squad', the G-men suffered terrible losses during the war. Of the twelve DMP men who were killed during the war, ten were serving in intelligence duties; but this was not all. Of the men of G Division in 1919 and 1920, three officers retired early, five men were assassinated, five transferred on their own request, and one man was so severely wounded that he was fit only for office duty. This left five men remaining, all of them young and inexperienced. The 'Squad' had destroyed G Division's capabilities.[16]

q   Mr William Charles Forbes Redmond (b.1872), Assistant Commissioner, DMP, who formerly had headed G Division, was shot by the 'Squad' at the Standard Hotel, Dublin, 21 January 1920. By the time he was killed, there was little reason to do so other than to target the senior police leadership to degrade DMP leadership and capabilities. His assassins were helped by information from Redmond's secretary, Jim McNamara.[17]

r   Prior to the Easter Rising, when they lost three men killed-in-action and seven wounded, the DMP had not lost a man in the line of duty since the 1870s.[18]

The R.I.C. were at this time distributed in small detachments[s] throughout the country, quartered in "barracks," which consisted, in the vast majority of cases, of small houses adjoining other buildings, quite indefensible and entirely at the mercy of disloyal inhabitants. The ranks of the force had been depleted by murders, and many men, through intimidation of themselves or more often of their families, had been induced to resign. Although, in the main, a loyal body of men their moral had diminished, and only two courses were open to their detachments; to adopt a policy of *laisser faire* and live, or actively to enforce law and order and be in hourly danger of murder.

s   Barracks were the offices and billeting for the RIC. Such structures were usually houses converted for this purpose. Larger barracks obviously housed more men and had higher ranking men in charge, such as a head constable or an officer (district inspectors ranked in classes 3 through 1 and county inspectors above them). Smaller barracks might be under charge of a sergeant. There were also smaller RIC establishments, or 'stations', with only three or four men under an acting sergeant. There were also 'huts', which usually supported a larger barracks and were typically no more than raised wooden platforms with four walls and a roof. Since they were designed as outlying observation posts, huts were essentially indefensible and policemen were reluctant to man them.[19]

The head[t] of the police force complained, not unnaturally, that, while the D.M.P. and R.I.C. were opposed to an ever-increasing rebel force and a population which, through inclination or intimidation, was hostile to them, there was a large body of troops in the country who were not called upon to render any assistance (except the ordinary limited duties in aid of the civil power)[20], shared none of the responsibilities[u], and were exposed to little of the danger. Loyal and law-abiding members of the community also complained bitterly that they received no protection, and that, as there was no inducement to continued loyalty, large numbers of the population were adopting the line of least resistance[v] and accepting the rebel domination.

[t] This refers to the RIC Inspector-General, Brig-Gen Joseph Aloysius Byrne (b.1874–d.1942); Assistant I-G Robert G. C. Flower (b.1861–d. unknown); and Assistant I-G Henry D. Tyacke (b.1859–d. unknown); and DMP Chief Commissioner Lt-Col Sir Walter Edgeworth-Johnstone, KBE (b.1863–d.1936).

[u] British governmental opinion remained that this was a criminal enterprise, and that it should therefore be the purview of the police forces. There were several reasons for this policy choice beyond the issue of criminality. Common law did not recognize a state of rebellion and, thus, did not accept any of its actions as legitimate. Further, the law and the constitution did not permit the use of military force in aid of civil power except under rare and extraordinary circumstances. This use of force had to be proportional to the threat and had to be justifiable in criminal court, to the authority of which the forces were subject. The law did not envisage an armed, organized and determined group threatening the Government, and so there were inadequate mechanisms in place to deal with the threat.[21]

This meant that the RIC and the DMP became the primary agents of the government's plan. So, when the republicans began their boycott of the RIC in 1918, and when the Irish Volunteers began to target the police throughout 1919, it was due to the very real threat they posed to the movements through intelligence gathering and arrest. The protests came primarily from Byrne and Edgeworth-Johnstone; the former throughout the last months of 1919 and into 1920, and the latter in March of 1920, when he said that the situation in Dublin had 'long been beyond the powers of any Police Force to cope with effectually. The D.M. Police are a civil body, unused until lately to the use of arms and were never intended to cope with an armed disciplined body of desperate, well-directed fanatics such as the Irish Volunteers'.[22]

ᵛ The issue of support amongst the Gaelic Catholic and Protestant communities in southern Ireland for government or for home rule was mostly irrelevant after a nearly a decade of violent political struggle. Only recently have researchers asked whether there was more support for home rule and/or government than previously assumed.[23]

Intervention of military forces, January, 1920.—This was, briefly, the situation when in January, 1920, the Government decided that the police forces by themselves were no longer able to cope with the rebel campaign of terrorism and outrage, and that the troops must be called upon to assist. The methods of the rebels had recently become more audacious, *e.g.*, the attempt to assassinate the Lord Lieutenant[w] on the 19th December, 1919, and the murder of Mr. Redmond on 21st January, 1920.

ʷ Field Marshal, John Denton French (b.1852–d.1925), 1st Viscount of Ypres and of High Lake (1916) and 1st Earl of Ypres (1922). Lord Lieutenant of Ireland, 1918–21.[24]

ˣ*Troops, January, 1920.*—The distribution of troops in Ireland at the beginning of 1920 was as follows:—

Unit	OC	Locations
5th Infantry Division	Lt-Gen. Sir H. S. Jeudwine	Curragh
13th Infantry Brigade	Brig-Gen T. S. Lambert, GOC[y]	Westmeath, Longford, Roscommon, Galway, & South Leitrim
1st East Surrey	Lt-Col C. C. G. Ashton	
1st Leicestershire	Lt-Col E. L. Challenor	
1st East Yorkshire	Lt-Col T. A. Headlam	
2nd Border Regiment	Lt-Col G. de la P. B. Pakenham	Mayo
14th Infantry Brigade	Brig-Gen P. C. B. Skinner, GOC	Carlow, Kildare, King's County, Queen's County & part of Wicklow
1st Cameronians (Scottish Rifles)	Lt-Col J. G. Chaplin	The Curragh

2nd King's Shropshire Light Infantry	Lt-Col G. Meynell	The Curragh
1st Prince of Wales' North Staffordshire	Lt-Col T. A. Andrus	The Curragh
15th Infantry Brigade ('Ulster Brigade')	Brig-Gen G. T. C. Carter-Campbell, GOC	Ulster counties & Counties Donegal, Cavan, Monaghan, Louth, Sligo and North Leitrim
1st Duke of Cornwall's Light Infantry	Lt-Col J. H. P. Price	Ballyshannon
1st Dorsetshire	Lt-Col C. C. Hannay	Londonderry
1st Norfolk	Lt-Col F. C. Lodge	Dublin
1st Somerset Light Infantry	Lt-Col P. M. Wardlaw	Holywood
Divisional Artillery		
33rd Bde RFA	Lt-Col H. G. Lloyd	Dundalk
36th Bde RFA	Lt-Col A. Hinde	Kildare
41st Bde RFA	Lt-Col C. St. L. G. Hawkes	Kildare
Vth Reserve Bde RFA	Lt-Col C. St. M. Ingham	Athlone
6th Infantry Division	Maj-Gen Sir E. P. Strickland, GOC[z]	Cork
16th Infantry Brigade ('Fermoy Brigade')	Brig-Gen C. H. T. Lucas, GOC	Waterford, Wexford, Kilkenny & South Tipperary
1st Lincolnshire	Lt-Col R.H.G. Wilson	Tipperary
2nd Yorkshire (The Green Howards)	Lt-Col Geoffrey Brouncker de Maries Mairis	Tipperary
1st Royal East Kent (The Buffs)	Lt-Col R. McDoual	Fermoy
2nd Highland Light Infantry	Lt-Col J. C. Grahame	Ennis, Co. Clare

[x] As the authors did not have all the official documents to hand when writing, the Orders of Battle are drawn from several sources.[25]

[y] Col Thomas Stanton Lambert (b.1871–KIA1921).

[z] Sir (Edward) Peter Strickland KCB, KBE, CMG, DSO (b.1869–d.1951).

17th Infantry Brigade ('Cork Brigade')	Brig-Gen H. W. Higginson, goc	Cork and Kerry
1st Essex	Lt-Col F. W. Moffitt	Kinsale
2nd Hampshire	Lt-Col C. M. French	Cork
1st Machine Gun Corps	Lt-Col J. F. R. Hope	Ballyvonare
2nd Oxfordshire and Buckinghamshire Light Infantry	Lt-Col E. R. Clayton	Cork
2nd East Lancashire*	Lt-Col E. C. da Costa	Buttevant
18th Infantry Brigade ('Limerick Brigade')†	Brig-Gen C. Coffin, goc	
2nd South Lancashire	Lt-Col H. C. Herbert	Dublin
2nd Royal Welch Fusiliers	Lt-Col O. de L. Williams	Limerick
1st Northamptonshire	Lt-Col H. R. H. Drew	Templemore
1st Oxfordshire & Buckinghamshire Light Inf	Lt-Col F. N. Stapleton	Ballyvonare
Divisional Artillery		
1st Bde rfa	Lt-Col J. Farquahar	Kilkenny
2nd Bde rfa	Lt-Col F. W. Mackenzie	Fermoy
42nd Bde rfa	Lt-Col D. W. L. Spiller	Fermoy
The Cavalry Brigade	Brig-Gen G. A. Weir, goc	Curragh
1st Royal Dragoons		Ballinasloe
12th Lancers	Lt-Col H. Sadler	The Curragh
15th Hussars	Lt-Col F. C. Pilkington	Marlborough Barracks, Dublin

* Additional, listed in 'Composition of Headquarters of the Forces in Ireland' of March 1920.
† The 6th Divisional history lists the Green Howards as being in the 18th Infantry Brigade, but the 'Composition of Headquarters of the Forces in Ireland' of March 1920 lists them in the 16th Infantry Brigade, replacing them with the 2nd S. Lancs.

Dublin District had recently[aa] been converted from a brigade of the 5th Division into a district, under the command of a Major-General[bb].

[aa] January 1920.

[bb] Maj-Gen Sir Gerald Farrell Boyd (b.1877–d.1930), GOC.

By the end of January this consisted of two infantry brigades, viz.:—

Unit	OC	Locations
24th (Provisional) Infantry Brigade	Brig-Gen R. F. Oldman, goc	Dublin City north of the River Liffey, and, later, County Meath
1st South Wales Borderers	Lt-Col A. J. Reddie	
2nd West Riding	Lt-Col R. N. Bray	
1st Wiltshire	Lt-Col B. T. Buckly	
2nd Worcestershire	Lt-Col H. A. Carr	
25th (Provisional) Infantry Brigade	Brig-Gen C. C. Onslow, goc	Dublin City south of the River Liffey, & part of County Wicklow
1st Royal Lancaster	Lt-Col B. D. L. G. Anley	Dublin
1st South Lancashire	Lt- Col D'O. B. Dawson	
2nd Welch	Lt-Col H. J. B. Span	
2nd Royal Berkshire	Lt-Col W. B. Thornton	
1st Cheshire	Lt-Col B. A. Chetwynd Stapylton	

There were also in the country:—

Six young soldier[cc] battalions.		Ulster
3rd Cavalry Bde	Brig-Gen G. A. Weir	Curragh
1st Royal Dragoons	Lt-Col H. Sadler	
12th Lancers	Lt-Col C. Fane	
15th Hussars	Lt-Col F. C. Pilkington	
4th Bde, rha	Lt-Col A. B. Forman	
12th Bde rga	Lt-Col C. E. Philips	
13th Bde, rga	Lt-Col A. Ellershaw	

[cc]   The Training Reserve Battalions were reorganized in May of 1917 into fourteen 'Young Soldier Battalions', which provided basic training to recruits who were eighteen years old; and twenty-eight associated 'Graduated Battalions', two per Young Soldier Battalion. The recruits were assigned

to the latter once they passed out of basic training with the former. This reorganization realigned these battalions to specific regiments to which the men would be assigned once sufficient numbers were available in the Graduated Battalions. The six battalions mentioned were the battalions that fed men into the 36th (Ulster) Division, but were not part of the Training Reserve, but since they served the same function, were probably mistaken for Young Soldier Battalions.[26]

Royal Engineers		
12th Field Company		Limerick
38th Field Company		Moore Park, Fermoy
17th Field Company		The Curragh
59th Field Company		The Curragh
No. 613th (Fortress) Company		Belfast
5th Armoured Car Company	Lt-Col D. R. Pratt	Dublin
No. 11 (Irish) Wing, RAF	Grp-Cpt. A. V. Bettington	36 aeroplanes total
No 2 Squadron (Bristols)	Sqdn-Ldr L. F. Forbes	RAF Station Fermoy: Flights, A & B
C Flight (Bristols)		RAF Station Organmore
No. 100 Squadron (DH-9s)		RAF Station Baldonnel: Flights, A, B,C & D (one detached)
Detached Flight (Bristols)		RAF Station: Castlebar
1 Flt, No. 4 Squadron (Bristols)		RAF Station Aldergrove

Government policy, January, 1920.—The new policy inaugurated by the Government in January, 1920, was an attempt to deal with the situation without having recourse to Martial Law. The arguments for and against the declaration of Martial Law had been propounded for a long time, and the Government had always shown a strong disinclination to adopt such a course. It was asserted by the Law Officers of the Crown[dd] that the powers existing under the Defence of the Realm Act[ee] provided all that was necessary and that such powers could be administered by the Competent Military Authority[ff] without incurring the odium which would attach to a Military Governor enforcing Martial Law. It was, therefore, decided to make this final attempt to deal with the situation before declaring Martial Law.

dd The Attorney General of Ireland, Sir Denis Stanislaus Henry (b.1864–d.1925), 1st Baronet (1923), KC, and the Solicitor General, Daniel Martin Wilson, KC (b.1862–d.1932).

ee Of 1914, amended 1915.[27]

ff Usually, the senior military officer in a defined geographical area. In this case, they were the various brigade commanders.

Briefly, the policy was to transfer to the Competent Military Authority the powers, previously vested in the police authorities and magistrates, of instituting and organizing action against the perpetrators of outrage and the organizers of lawlessness, and to deport and intern under D.R.R.[gg] 14b, such persons on a warrant signed by the Chief Secretary for Ireland. Secondly, the Competent Military Authority was to be empowered to search individuals and buildings for arms, explosives and seditious literature.

gg Defence of the Realm Regulations (derived from the Defence of the Realm Act of 12 August 1914).[28]

Instructions to Divisions.—In order to put this policy into effect, instructions to the following effect were issued to Divisions on 7th January, 1920. G.Os.C. Divisions were instructed to prepare lists of "Commanders," "Officers" and prominent members of the Irish Volunteers, and other individuals responsible for the prevalent outrages and terrorism.

Warrants for the arrest and deportation to England of these individuals were to be obtained from the Chief Secretary and forwarded to G.Os.C. Divisions, to whom the power to effect the arrest was delegated. Whenever an outrage occurred, Competent Military Authorities (*i.e.*, G.Os.C. Divisions and such subordinate Commanders as were deputed by them to act as such) were empowered to arrest from among the individuals for whom they held warrants, a number corresponding to the seriousness of the outrage. Individuals so arrested were to be deported to England as soon as possible, but in the event of evidence of an offence against D.R.R. being discovered against any of them, such persons were to be handed over to be dealt with by the civil power in Ireland.

The actual arrest was, if possible, to be carried out by a police constable, one or two of whom were to accompany every party of troops employed for this purpose; instructions were issued by the Police Authorities to their subordinates that orders issued were issued by Competent Military Authorities were to be carried out accordingly. The action was to be perfectly open, and the names of the arrested men, together with their believed appointments in the Irish Volunteers, were to be forwarded at once to G.H.Q. for communication to the press.

With regard to the searching of individuals and buildings a wide latitude was given to Military Commanders with the main object of preventing disloyal persons from going about armed. Competent Military Authorities were authorized to employ, if necessary, the whole of their troops for this purpose at any time, day or night, but stress was laid upon the necessity for existing the greatest care and consideration for law-abiding people, women and children.[hh] The actual search of an individual was, where possible, to be conducted by civil police, otherwise by an officer. In the event of it becoming necessary to search a woman, female searchers[ii] were to be employed, and troops were forbidden to arrest a woman.

[hh] One wonders how considerate armed men can be when holding people at gunpoint in the middle of the night, having turned them out from their homes in order to search. Still, one must recognize the requirement to perform necessary duties and the attempt to reduce the negative effects on the civilian population as much as was possible. It is difficult to say how this more noble idea worked in actual practice.

[ii] Female searchers were hired from police forces in Britain and brought over for this purpose.[29]

Persons arrested by troops for offence against D.R.R. were to be handed over to the civil police with a statement showing the reason for the arrest, the name of the person making the arrest, and a list of the property found on the arrested person.

8th January, 1920, G.Os.C. authorized to arrest dangerous persons.—On 8th January authority was given to G.Os.C. Divisions to carry out the arrest of individuals as soon as warrants were received, in respect of outrages which had recently taken place, and which would have been dealt with under these instructions had they been in force at the time. The total number of persons for whom Divisions might apply for warrants were, in the first instance, fixed at: 5th Division, 80; 6th Division, 200; Dublin District, 120. It was also pointed out to G.Os.C. Divisions that the applications for warrants should be restricted to really important and dangerous persons. The date on which the initial arrests were to be made was synchronized in all Divisions[jj], and was fixed for the night 23rd/24th January.[30]

> [jj] It is quite clear from these statements that the army and the rest of the Government did not understand the implications of what would be seen as an arbitrary abuse of rights. The illogical republican position complaining of the unfairness of a Government violating the laws the republicans had already rejected as illegitimate notwithstanding, the 'average person' saw these measures as unjustified. This was where they could have lost the battle for the support of the populace. Shaw's brief details the justifications for taking this action as being beyond the powers of the police.

21st January, 1920, changes of Government policy.—On 21st January, however, the Government decided that all action based on this new policy was to be suspended until further notice. Subsequently the Government decided that no warrants should be issued previous to arrest, but that persons suspected of complicity in an outrage might be arrested by Competent Military Authorities under D.R.R. 55[31], and detained under a "Detention Order." If evidence of an offence was forthcoming against individuals so arrested, they were to be dealt with by the civil power.[kk] If no evidence was obtained, but it was required to intern them as dangerous persons, then application was to be made for warrants to deport and intern them.

> [kk] Shaw's memorandum accompanying this document, although somewhat hyperbolic, praised the Irish Volunteers in their training, organization, intelligence, communications and discipline, saying: 'The system which they have built up is a remarkable one…' and they are 'commanded in a manner which would be creditable to highly trained Military experts…'. Shaw, perhaps exaggerating to justify his advice, said clearly what needed to be done: 'The time of leniency and "sympathy" has gone past, and it is only by the most drastic and repressive action that we can hope to deal with this situation.' How could this be seen as other than oppressive?[32]

26th January, 1920, instructions to Divisions.—Instructions to this effect were sent to G.Os.C. Divisions on 26th January, and the night 30th/31st January was fixed for the arrest of the individuals selected. It was at the same time decided that as soon as action on these lines had been taken, the second part of the new policy regarding the search of individuals, buildings, &c., was to be put in force.

30th/31st January, 1920, first arrests by military authority.—On the night of 30th/31st January, action was taken in all division areas as arranged. Out of a total of 74 individuals whose arrest was attempted, 57 were arrested. In addition 7 persons, known to the police as dangerous, were arrested, amongst whom was R. C. Barton[ll], who had been charged with incitement to murder but had escaped from Mountjoy[mm] in March, 1919.[nn] Of this total of 64 individuals, 61 were deported to England for internment on 8th, February, 1920.[33]

[ll]   Robert Childers Barton (b.1881–d.1975).

[mm]   Mountjoy Prison, Phibsboro, Dublin.

[nn]   Interestingly, there are no comments about these arrests in *An t-Óglác*.

The success of which attended this first series of arrests was apparent from the outcry in the Irish Press, which had almost entirely been enlisted on the side of Sinn Fein for propaganda purposes; and there is no doubt that considerable alarm was caused amongst leading rebels who had imagined that they were working for Sinn Fein under impenetrable camouflage.[34]

Seizure of arms.—The second part of the new policy was also now put into force with a view to the seizure of arms and suppression of outrages. Military patrols accompanied the police in the streets of large towns and assisted in searching individuals and houses and in making arrests in co-operation with the police. In the first instance these activities caused a certain amount of open hostility, but this soon disappeared and military patrols became a normal procedure.

Need for military intelligence.—It became apparent very early that arms would not be found on individuals searched in the streets, although it is probable that many rebels had been in the habit of carrying revolvers before these searches were instituted.[oo] It was also evident that raids on houses on insufficient information raised resentment for which the results obtained did not compensate. The lack of a thorough intelligence system was gravely felt, and it was decided that the best course would be to develop the Military Intelligence Section in all formations.[pp] The gradual development of this gave excellent results which were soon evident. The raids on houses, which had previously been carried out on the information supplied by the police, now came to be conducted as the result of evidence pieced together from captured documents, and from the reports of law-abiding people who at this time occasionally came forward.[qq]

oo   Arms carried in urban environments were almost entirely pistols due to both their concealability and disposability. Truly random searches of individuals and establishment of checkpoints never really occurred; once rebels recognized the patterns, they avoided them easily.

pp   Birrell's disestablishment of the Secret Service in Ireland in 1917 was certainly a blow to the intelligence capabilities there, but does not alter the fact the Irish Command had resources available in Ireland that they did not employ. The RIC had their Crime Special Branch and the DMP had G Division. While the army complained that these did not meet their needs on several levels, they did not try to mitigate this by using policemen highly experienced in army intelligence. Lieut-Col Ivon Henry Price, BA, LLD (b.1866–d.1931), and Maj. Philip Armstrong Holmes (b.1876–KIA1921), both served as army intelligence officers in the Great War; Price was Chief Intelligence Officer of the Irish Command during the war. These men, and probably others, would have been able to help facilitate the exchange of information since they knew both sides. The situation did not improve until the establishment of the military intelligence system that coincided with the Irish Command's creation of divisional structures in 1919. It took some considerable time for the requisite officers to complete their training and arrive.[35]

qq   Brig-Gen Sir O. Winter became chief of police intelligence in 1920. In his reforms, he established the Raids Bureaus to collate and analyse captured documents in what is today called 'document exploitation' or 'DOCEX'. Unfortunately for the British, they had insufficient time before the end of the war for their intelligence work to tell.

Practical difficulties of the new policy.—There were, however, certain difficulties which proved a handicap in carrying out this new policy. All applications for deportation warrants had to be examined and recommended by the legal advisers at Dublin Castle. Considerable delay was caused in this way and the arrested men in the meantime had to be kept in prisons or regimental guardrooms. The whole essence of the policy was that leaders must be made to take the onus of outrages committed in their areas, and that suspicion of complicity was a sufficient reason for their internment under D.R.R. 14b[rr]. In practice, however, the legal advisers based their decisions on the known past character of the arrested men. Very often all that was known of these men was that they held a position in the I.R.A.; their actual complicity in previous crime was, in the then state of the police intelligence system, not likely to be on record. In consequence, a large number of warrants were refused and the arrested men had to be released.[ss]

rr   Provided for internment.[36]

ss   The issue of 'catch and release' tended to embolden rebel leaders and demonstrate weakness of policy and decision-making to the people. It also frustrated military leaders and hurt police morale because their hard work was nullified by political decisions.[37]

Further delay was caused in the cases of arrested men against whom there appeared to be evidence of an offence for which they might be tried. Such cases also were reviewed by the legal advisers at Dublin Castle; weeks and sometimes months, elapsed before a decision was given. These facts aggravated the situation in that an outcry was raised against the prolonged detention of men without trial or internment, and odium attached to military commanders for ordering the arrest of individuals for, it judged in the light of their subsequent release, no reason.

The searching of houses also had its drawbacks, and Sinn Fein supporters, both in Ireland and England, were not slow to take the opportunity offered to them of inventing and publishing propaganda. Exorbitant claims for damages were submitted by the owners and occupiers of the premises searched, and a good many false accusations were made against the behaviour of these officers and men of the search parties. These claims were in the large majority of cases grossly exaggerated, and the accusations were almost invariably unfounded.[tt] The public were misled to believe that houses were broken into by troops indiscriminately, whereas in fact good grounds always existed for believing that the owner or occupier was hiding arms, ammunition or seditious documents, or harbouring law-breakers. The fact that, in a great many cases, nothing incriminating was found in the searched houses, was largely due either to information of an impending search having leaked out, or to the inexperience of the troops, at this time, in conducting searches.

tt   There was always a problem of intelligence being sufficient for military action, but not for trial. This issue still confounds governments. This issue of propaganda is difficult in that the army was searching for and causing damage. Not all claims were exorbitant, nor were they all false. At the same time, the existence of an exorbitant or false claim did not always indicate pro-republican sympathies, but mere greed. Finally, there were instances of Unionists making such claims against the authorities.

The trial of the arrested men presented very great difficulties, for witnesses were afraid to come forward to give evidence in the civil courts against the perpetrators of outrage, and Courts Martial were empowered to try offences against the Defence of the Realm Regulations only, which did not include the crime of murder. For this reason it was impossible to get a conviction against many of the men arrested, and consequently the rebel propaganda was able to make capital out of the fact that large numbers of men had been arrested and not brought to trial.[38]

Result of policy.—In spite of difficulties, however, the policy was a great advance on the previous procedure, and for a time placed the rebels on the defensive. The loss of leaders in the I.R.A. caused some confusion in the organization of the rebel forces, for at the time efficient substitutes were not forthcoming. Suspicion and mutual distrust also grew up in the ranks of the I.R.A. owing to doubts as to the source of the information on which the raids were made.[39] The immediate result of the arrests was a decrease in the number of outrages for a short period, and loyal people, thinking that a strong line was taken with rebellion and outrage, began to take heart, and information concerning outrages began to come in rather more freely.[uu] It was not long, however, before the rebel leaders began to take measures to counteract the advantage temporarily gained by the Crown forces. Their action took the form of an intensified terrorism designed to impress the general public with their power[vv], and to raise the moral of their supporters. Large operations were not attempted, but the murders of individual policemen[ww] increased, as did also threatening letters written to any law-abiding person who had any dealings with the police or the Government. [xx] Isolated police barracks were also attacked wherever the position of the barracks and the weakness of the garrison seemed likely to give success with little risk to the attackers. The consequent withdrawal of the more isolated police detachments gave the rebels the opportunity for a perfectly safe form of advertisement by burning down the vacated barracks.[yy]

[uu] As with the previous statement regarding suspicions, there is little evidence to support this assertion; the RIC I-G Monthly Confidential Reports contain no such observance. Considering the volume of army operations conducted based on 'information obtained from civilians',

instead of those from documents captured, one can only conclude that there were considerable numbers of informants in Ireland. With the exception of the 5th Infantry Division, which did not normally mention sources, these informants were most active in the 6th Infantry Division.[40]

vv   There appears to be stronger evidence of this; the introduction to the February RIC I-G Monthly Confidential Report began by saying 'I have to report that, as a result of the Sinn Fein republican pretensions, the Provinces remained in a very unsettled and unsatisfactory state. The campaign of assassination and outrage against the police, who are regarded with bitter hostility by the republicans as the chief obstacle to realization of their political aspirations, was secretly and ruthlessly carried on.' It went on to say that there was an increase of indictable offenses of 10 per cent.[41]

ww   There were nine policemen killed between 12 February and 19 March 1920. They were: Const. Michael Neenan (12 February), Allihies RIC Barracks, Co. Cork; Const. John M. Walsh, DMP (20 February), Suffolk & Grafton Streets, Dublin; Const. John Martin Heanue (4 March 1920), Bouladuff, Co. Tipperary; Const. Thomas Ryan (10 March), Hugginstown RIC Barracks, Co. Kilkenny; Sgt George Neazer (10 March), Rathkeal, Co. Limerick; Const. Timothy Scully, (11 March), Glanmire, Co. Cork; Const. Charles Healy (17 March), Toomevara, Co. Tipperary; Const. James Rocke (19 March), Toomevara, Co. Tipperary; Const. Joseph Murtagh (19 March), Pope's Quay, Cork.[42]

xx   The killing of policemen came in two forms: battle, and targeted assassinations. Battles came in the form of raids against barracks (see below) and ambushes. The latter were of two varieties: deliberate attacks, and hasty or 'encounter' battles. In the former, rebel forces exploited local intelligence by attacking police patrols (foot, bicycle or motor vehicle) and convoys that used the same routes over and again. The hasty attacks or encounter battles were more meetings of chance, and were considerably more dangerous for the attacker than the pre-planned ambushes.[43]

Assassinations were targeted killings of individual policemen. They usually targeted specific policemen, but there were attacks where the particular individual did not matter as long as he was a policeman. One could hardly describe most of these incidents 'combat', because the policeman usually faced multiple armed attackers who struck while he was most vulnerable. While considering the moral propriety of such attacks, one should bear in mind two important realities: guerrilla warfare is an asymmetric strategy of the weak against the strong, and it is foolhardy for the guerrilla to attack his enemy's strength. While one may question the morality of such killings, one cannot dispute their effectiveness. The killing of men with valuable information and experience could hardly have a positive effect within the police forces and the Government.

[yy] Attacks against RIC barracks were certainly nothing new; they had occurred with increasing frequency since 1918, reaching their pinnacle in 1921, but continuing even into the Civil War. According to the Inspector-General reports, there were at least four barracks attacks in 1918, thirteen in 1919, ninety-eight in 1920 and 172 in 1921.[44]

Curfew, 22nd February, 1920.—In Dublin the murders of police constables[zz] and other lawless acts in the streets during the hours of darkness led to the first imposition of curfew. On 23rd February, 1920, a Proclamation was issued by the G.O.C., Dublin District, on instructions received direct from the Lord Lieutenant, requiring all persons not in possession of a permit to be within their houses between the hours of 12 midnight and 5 a.m. The order caused a good deal of protest in the Press and from disloyal public bodies. People whose business required them to be at work during the curfew hours refused, in many cases, to apply for permits, and the Dublin Corporation decided to turn off all lights in the city during these hours. In time, however, these attempts to stultify the effect of the proclamation were dropped, and the curfew order became a matter of satisfaction to law-abiding people. Individuals arrested by curfew patrols were brought before a magistrate each morning and either fined, or, in the case of a first offence, let off with a caution.[45]

[zz] As mentioned above, there was an increase in police fatalities during this period: by 22 February, 1920, only two members of the DMP had been killed: Asst-Comm Redmond and Const. Walsh. Thus, this argument is somewhat spurious. That said, the increase of DMP deaths that occurred after 22 February was dramatic. The slain were: D/Con Const. Henry Kells (b.1878–KIA 14 April, 1920), Upper Camden and Pleasants Street, Dublin; D/Con Laurence Dalton, (b.1893–KIA 20 April, 1920), Mountjoy Street, Dublin; Const. Michael McCarthy (b.1891–KIA 23 April, 1920), Clonakilty, Co. Cork. D/Cons Kells and Dalton were members of G Division and were targeted for assassination by Collins's Squad; McCarthy was home on leave.[46]

Curfew orders were not until later imposed in Cork or other towns, as it was considered that the troops were too fully employed to find sufficient patrols to enforce it, and also, in country districts, outrages were usually carried out before the hours of darkness.[a3]

[a3] While the full effects of the curfew are questionable, it certainly became a factor for rebel planning; they had to consider how to get around it and work with it while not being caught. Of course, the police and military had an easier job in some respects because the 'average' person was not on the streets, thus it partially removed an obstacle to their hunt for rebels.

Sinn Fein methods.—Some idea of the methods employed by the rebels in what the hostile Press described as a "War for Freedom" may be gathered from the notes to this chapter showing some typical instances of outrages committed from the latter part of Jánuary to the end of April. These are only a few of the crimes committed during this period, and in the majority of cases were due to the deliberate policy of the Sinn Fein leaders to intimidate the police and loyal civilians. In addition, there were numerous cases of police constables being fired at and killed or wounded, of the posting of notices threatening death to anybody having dealings with the police or their families[b3], and the robbery of mails and old-age pension money from country postmen.

[b3] This was the active part of the RIC Boycott by the republicans against all police.[47]

Brigade commandants	27
Brigade staff	13
Battalion commanders	16
Battalion officers	116
Other prominent officials	145
Total	317

During this period over 20 police barracks were attacked by large bodies of men, but in all three cases the small police garrison succeeded in driving off their assailants. More than 240 vacated police barracks were maliciously burnt during the same period, most of them at Easter, 1920.[c3] But, although outrages were numerous, the policy of arresting leaders and of organized searches for arms had had considerable effect in raising the moral of the R.I.C. and in upsetting the organization of the I.R.A. The arrests which resulted up to 14th April numbered as follows:—

c3 From January 1919 to June 1920, the rebels burnt 351 vacant and 15 occupied RIC barracks, while damaging 105 of the former and 20 of the latter.[48]

May, 1920.—By the beginning of May over 250 rebel leaders had been deported to England for internment. The arrest of so many "brigade commanders" at this period (more than ever taken subsequently) was due to the capture in Dublin of certain documents which gave the names of the brigade commanders or important members of their staffs in each country. With the approval of the Government, steps were taken to arrest these men, with a view to internment, before news of the capture of the documents containing proof of their complicity could reach the individuals concerned.

Murder of MacCurtain.—Among the men whose arrest were ordered was one Thomas Curtin, commander of the 1st Mid-Cork Brigade, who was the same individual as Thomas MacCurtain[d3], the Lord Mayor of Cork. The G.O.C., 6th Division, at Cork queried the instructions to arrest this man, though he was well aware of his connection with the Irish Volunteers, because it happened that His Majesty's judges were then holding the Assizes at Cork, and he feared retaliation against them. It was decided that as the judges were protected the arrest was to take place that night before Curtin could go "on the run."[e3] The party detailed to carry out the arrest arrived too late, the Lord Mayor having been murdered an hour or two previously.

d3 Tomás MacCurtain (b.1884).

e3 According to Florey O'Donoghue, MacCurtain 'considered it beneath the dignity due to his office that he should evade arrest'.[49]

It has never been definitely established by whom the murder was committed. The Coroner's jury brought in a verdict against the police, but as a very large proportion of the jury were reputed to be officers of the Irish Volunteers or leading Sinn Feiners, their finding can hardly be considered impartial. There is no doubt that the discipline and restraint of the R.I.C. had been strained almost to the breaking point by the murders of their comrades and by the failure of themselves and the Government to bring one single murderer to justice. On the other hand, it was reliably reported that MacCurtain had recently made himself very unpopular in Sinn Fein circles by his action in denouncing the murders and assassinations that had been committed by his followers.[f3]

[f3] The Irish Volunteers believed that the RIC killed MacCurtain and held the District-Inspector of Cork City North, DI Oswald Ross Swanzy (b.1881), responsible. Collins sent B Company, 1st Cork IRA Bn intelligence officer, Lt Seán Culhane to Lisburne, Co. Antrim to kill him, where Swanzy was reassigned in June 1920. Linking up with Belfast IRA Bde men Culhane shot Swanzy on Market Street just after he exited Christchurch Cathedral on Sunday, 22 August 1920.

Moral and strength of troops.—The strain put upon the troops during these months was very considerable. The battalions were much below their proper strength. The men were, for the most part, very young and inexperienced, and their training had been greatly curtailed by the number of guard duties which they were called upon to perform. No military establishment was safe without a guard, and in addition many public buildings had to be guarded; escorts for arrested men moving about the country to ports of embarkation added to the duties, and there was an ever increasing demand for detachments to support outlying police stations. All these duties had to be performed in addition to incessant searches and patrols. The situation was further complicated by the fact that during February and March, 1920, the young soldiers battalions in Ireland were demobilized. This, together with the despatch of drafts for foreign battalions, made a serious reduction in the number of troops available for dealing with the situation. The Commander-in-Chief[g3] had stated that he considered 25,000 bayonets as essential, and by the middle of March the numbers fell short of this by, roughly, 5,000 men.[50] Application was made to the War Office for additional troops. The War Office replied that they hoped to make good the deficiency by the end of March by means of drafts of 3-month recruits, and by utilizing surplus personnel of the Royal Artillery. By the end of March, however, the number of drafts received had not been adequate, and the Royal Artillery personnel had not become available. The shortage of troops had led to the necessary depletion of force in certain areas, and lawlessness had consequently increased. This was particularly the case in Counties Galway, Mayo and Kerry.

g3   Lt-Gen Sir Frederick Charles Shaw (b.1861–d.1942), Commander-in-Chief, 1918–20.

Reinforcements, April to May, 1920.—In view of this unsatisfactory situation, an application was made to the War Office at the beginning of April for an additional four battalions each 800 strong. The War Office were unable at the time to make four battalions available, but agreed to send four cavalry regiments instead. Three of these (the 10th Hussars, 17th Lancers and 1st Dragoons) arrived during April, and the fourth (the 9th Lancers) arrived in May. Two infantry battalions (the 1st Bn. Lancashire Fusiliers and 1st Bn. Manchester Regiment) were also sent to Ireland during April and allotted for duty in Dublin and the 6th Divisional Area (Munster) respectively.

Commencement and effect of hunger strike, April, 1920.—In the second week of April the rebels who were detained in Mountjoy Prison in Dublin, both those awaiting trial and those awaiting deportation, began a hunger-strike. Ostensibly their grievance was one of their treatment as ordinary prisoners instead of political prisoners.[h3] In fact, they were receiving the treatment of unconvicted prisoners, and the strike was ordered by the rebel headquarters as a means of rousing the sympathy of the Irish people and of the uninformed public in England and abroad. It was intended to act as a lever to compel the Government to give up its policy of arresting leaders and deporting them, and most unfortunately this result was attained. The hunger-strike became the burning question throughout Ireland and in the English Press. The whole affair was cleverly engineered by those who knew how to work upon the feeling of all classes of Irishmen. Crowds assembled daily outside Mountjoy Prison, kneeling and reciting the Rosary, singing hymns and waving handkerchiefs. The situation in the neighbourhood of the prison became so critical that on 11th April the Chief Commissioner, Dublin Metropolitan Police, requested the G.O.C., Dublin District, to send troops to reinforce the military guard at Mountjoy, and to assist the police in clearing the streets round the prison.

h3   This decision was taken on 22 March, 1920.[51]

In response to this request, a company of the 1st Bn. Lancashire Fusiliers, with two tanks, were sent to Mountjoy Prison at 2.40 p.m. on the same day. Later in the afternoon this party was reinforced by a company of the 1st Bn. Wiltshire Regiment. The troops had orders to clear the streets round the approaches to the prison. The clearing of the streets was a very difficult operation; the crowd had swelled during the afternoon to enormous proportions and were at first not disposed to move. The officer commanding the troops spoke to them through a megaphone repeatedly, and at length by means of threats of bayonet charges the crowd was induced to clear back, and by 11.30 p.m. the situation had become normal. The result had been achieved without a single casualty, thanks to the patience, tact and discipline of the troops and their officers. The troops were retained in their position for some days and the same crowds spent their time daily in the streets near the prison, without any disturbance occurring. The leaders of the Irish Transport and General Workers' Union, which ever since the days of Jim Larkin[13] had been a formidable organization on the side of disorder and rebellion, decided or were induced by the rebel leaders to throw their weight into the balance in favour of Sinn Fein.

[13]   James Larkin (b.1876–d.1947), Irish labour leader, founder of Irish Transport and General Workers' Union in 1907.

General strike in Dublin.—In consequence a general strike was declared in Dublin to begin on 13th April and continue until the hunger-strikers were released. The demand for release was taken up by several newspapers in England and by the Labour Party in the House of Commons. The general strike duly began on 13th April and involved every trade. All shops were closed, railways and tramways ceased work, and the docks closed down. Special precautions against riot and disturbance were taken by the G.O.C., Dublin District.[52] This entailed additional guards on all military establishments, the protection of important civil installations, such as power stations, petrol stores, docks and railway stations, and the patrolling of the city in co-operation with the police.[53] For 2 days the general strike continued. Rumours were rife that some of the hunger-strikers, having refused food for 7–14 days were on the point of death, and a very tense situation prevailed.

Release of hunger-strikers, 14th April, 1920.—On 14th April the Government decided to release the hunger-strikers. It was originally intended that the only men to be released should be such of the untried prisoners, as the doctors certified to be in danger owing to their hunger-strike, and that the release should be "on parole." In the end, however, owing to a misunderstanding of instruction by the civil authorities, all the hunger-strikers, including many men who had been tried and convicted of serious crimes, were released. This result was, not unnaturally, hailed as a great victory by Sinn Fein leaders and their supporters throughout Ireland, England and abroad.[54]

Change of Commander-in-Chief, April, 1920.—On 14th April General Sir Nevil Macready[j3] took over the appointment of Commander-in-Chief of the Forces in Ireland from Lieut.-General Sir Frederick Shaw. In view of the fruitless efforts made by the military authorities subsequently to induce the Government to improve their propaganda methods, it is interesting to note that the last document signed by the retiring Commander-in-Chief was an appeal to the Lord Lieutenant for greater publicity.

[j3] Gen Sir Cecil Frederick Nevil Macready, 1st Bart, (b.1862–d.1946).

Change of Chief Secretary.—Within the next few weeks several changes took place at Dublin Castle. A new Chief Secretary, Sir Hamar Greenwood[k3], replaced Mr. Ian Macpherson[l3]. An additional Under Secretary, Sir John Anderson[m3] was appointed to share the duties of Mr. James MacMahon[n3], who for some months had been in semi-retirement. Mr. Cope[o3] replaced Sir John Taylor[p3] as Assistant Under Secretary.

[k3] Hamar Greenwood (b.1870–d.1948), Chief Secretary for Ireland, 2 April 1920–19 November 1922; 1st Bart. of Holborn 1915, 1st Viscount Greenwood 1937.[55]

[l3] (James) Ian Stewart Macpherson (b.1880–d.1937), Chief Secretary for Ireland, 10 January 1919–2 April 1920; 1st Bart of Banchor, 1933, 1st Baron Strathcarron, 1936.

[m3] Sir John Anderson (b.1882–d.1958); 1st Viscount Waverley, 1952.

[n3] James MacMahon (b.1865–d.1954).

[o3] Sir Alfred (Andy) Cope (b.1877–d.1954).

[p3] Sir J. (John) J. Taylor.

Change of Government policy. Attempt at conciliation.—In accordance with the policy outlined in his election speeches at Sunderland[q3], Sir Hamar Greenwood did his utmost to initiate a policy of conciliation, and it was hoped, by some at any rate, that the concessions made by the release of the hunger strikers, &c., would produce some slight sign of reciprocal good feeling on the part of the rebels.

[q3] For which Greenwood was MP, 1910–1922.

3rd May, 1920.—The release of the hunger-strikers was followed very soon (on 3rd May, 1920) by an order from the Government cancelling the powers granted in January to Competent Military Authorities to arrest rebel leaders for presumed complicity in outrages committed in their districts. The power to search individuals and houses for arms and to arrest persons actually found committing outrages, or against whom evidence was sufficiently strong to bring them to trial, was, indeed, allowed to remain, but this power was to a large extent neutralized by the terrorism which the rebels exercised over any person who was likely to be a witness at such trials.

The effect of this cancellation of the previous policy upon the R.I.C. was very marked. During the period January–April, 1920, the R.I.C. had considerably increased their activities in regard to the suppression of lawlessness. The influence of the force had acquired a fresh impetus by reason of the co-operation of troops, and the spread of rebel domination had been for a time held in check. The extent of the success attained may be judged from the following extract from *An T'Oglac*[r3], the official organ of the Irish Volunteers:—

"In some areas things are in a decidedly unsatisfactory condition. It is only fair to remember that many districts have been hard hit through capture of their best officers by the enemy...We wish to point out that those places where guerilla warfare against the enemy has been waged with great activity and effectiveness represent only a small portion of the country. In some other parts there has been a marked inactivity...There is a war on in which some portions of our Army are not fitting themselves to take part."[56]

[r3] *An t-Óglác: The Official Organ of the Irish Volunteers*, the bi-monthly, later weekly, journal.

The release of the hunger-strikers and the cancellation of policy, however, nullified the effect of the efforts made by the Crown forces during the three preceding months. The situation reverted to that obtaining in January, 1920, and was further aggravated by the raised moral of the rebels, brought about by their "victory," and a corresponding loss of moral on the part of the troops and police, accompanied by a natural irritation at seeing the release of men who had been engaged in cowardly outrages, and whose arrest had entailed untiring efforts, attended by considerable hardship and loss of life.

Effect on Sinn Fein.—Up till May, 1920, the rebel movement had been engineered by a comparatively few extremists, who, by enlisting the more desperate young men of the country and stiffening their ranks with professional "gunmen," had succeeded in terrorizing certain districts and in gaining adherents to their policy of systematic outrages.[57] The complete domination of Sinn Fein had, however, not been brought about at this time. There was still a considerable portion of the community, notably the farmers and tradesmen, who only desired peace, and who looked upon the I.R.A. rather than the Crown forces as being the obstacle to peace. But for the unfortunate lack of troops, and the ease with which a few armed men can terrorize Irishmen of moderate views, it is possible that, had the Government policy of January, 1920, been vigorously pursued, the inhabitants might have been relieved of this armed terrorism, and a situation in time created when a political solution might have had a reasonable chance of success on lines which the majority of Irishmen, unterrorized, would have approved.

Such a result was, however, in any case, rendered impossible by the release of the arrested leaders from Mountjoy, and the reversal of the January policy. Law-abiding people recognized that the Government had receded from the strong position which it appeared to be taking up, and that, as the combined activities of troops and police had been curtailed, the domination of Sinn Fein, backed by an ever-increasing membership of the I.R.A., would be able to intimidate them into acquiescence in a political demand for which they had no particular wish, and even into open and armed hostility to the forces of law and order.

What would have been the result of a refusal to release the hunger-strikers, and a continued enforcement of the policy of arresting leaders, it is difficult to say. But it is significant that any really strong action taken against lawlessness in Ireland, although raising a tremendous outcry in the Press and amongst disloyal people in the first instance, soon comes to be accepted and has a quieting effect. The imposition of curfew, which at the time was considered very drastic, the motor restrictions, and, later, the introduction of the capital penalty for bearing arms in the martial law area, and the refusal to release McSwiney[s3] are all instance where strong action has had a good effect without causing any irrepressible counter-action.[t3]

[s3] Terence McSwiney (b.1879), IRA leader. Deputy Lord Mayor of Cork when Lord Mayor Thomas MacCurtain was murdered. Arrested 12 August, 1920, died after a seventy-four-day hunger strike.

[t3] Joe Murphy (b.1895–d.25 Oct 1920) and Michael Fitzgerald (d.17 Oct 1920) started hunger strikes at the same time, and also died.

Loss of initiative by Crown forces.—The resultant situation in May was that the Crown forces were thrown back on to the defensive, and although competent military authorities retained the power to order arrests for offences committed against D.R.R., the troops were practically restricted to the old position of carrying out duties in aid of the civil power.

Notes to Chapter I

Typical instances of outrages during January—May, 1920.

19.i.20.—At Kilkenny a taxi-driver was held up by armed rebels who bound the driver and threw the car into the river.[u3]

[u3] Why this particular incident was worth reporting next to the killing of Redmond or of the half-dozen raids conducted at the same time is unclear. The incident is not reported in the RIC I-G Monthly Confidential Report for January 1920.

21.i.20.—Mr. Redmond, Assistant Commissioner of Police, was waylaid in a crowded street in Dublin and murdered, his murderers running away unpursued.[58]

24.i.20.—A large body of armed rebels attacked a few R.I.C. constables in their barracks at Baltinglass (Co. Wicklow). A little girl was employed to right the bell and hand in newspapers while a rebel shot the constable[v3] who opened the door. Although great preparations had been made for the attack by blocking all roads, the rebels ran away on the first volley being fired by the police. Two constables were wounded.

[v3] Const. James Joseph Malynn (b.1890).[59]

14.ii.20.—The R.I.C. barracks at Ballytrain (Co. Monaghan) were attacked by a large body of rebels who blew in the walls with explosives and overcame the small garrison.[60]

12.ii.20.—At Allihies (Co. Cork) an attempt was made by a large body of armed rebels to capture the R.I.C. barracks in order to obtain the keys of the explosives magazine. A prolonged fight ensued in which the small party of police, although two of their number were wounded and the building was partially destroyed, succeeded in driving off the rebels.[61]

17.ii.20—An officer driving in a motor car, and accompanied only by his chauffeur, came across a large party of rebels in motor cars stationary on a road at Inagh (Co. Clare). The rebels ran away and left some arms in their cars which the officer seized and drove away, being fired at from the hedges beside the road.

19.ii.20.—Two officers in a motor car were held up by a party of armed rebels near Tipperary. The car having been stopped by a barricade, the officers were called on to put up their hands. The officers got behind the car and fired their revolvers, whereupon the rebels fired one volley and fled.[w3]

[w3] They were attacked near Dundrum.[62]

20.ii.20.—A constable on duty in a Dublin street was shot dead by a rebel who had stopped to speak to him.[x3]

[x3] Dublin Metropolitan Police Const. John Walsh (b.1882); Sgt James Dunleavy (b.1883) was also wounded in the attack.[63]

25.ii.20.—At Mountpleasant (Co. Cork) 100 armed rebels attacked the R.I.C. barracks garrisoned by a few police. The approach of the rebels was observed and the police were ready. The rebels, therefore, contented themselves with firing a few shots from a distance and running away.

4.iii.20.—Two R.I.C. constables buying goods in a grocer's shop in Thurles (Co. Tipperary) were fired at by three armed rebels; one of the constables was killed.[y3]

[y3] Const. John Martin Heanue (b.ca.1896) was mortally wounded at Bouladuff, Thurles (Co. Tipperary).[64]

10.iii.20.—At Rathkeale (Co. Limerick) a party of armed rebels broke into the room of a serjeant and constable, R.I.C., at an hotel, murdering the serjeant and wounding the constable.[z3]

[z3] The policemen, Sgt George Neazer (b.1877), who was mortally wounded and Const. Garret Doyle (b.1886), also wounded in the attack were escorting an 'enemy civilian'. IRA Cmdt. Seán Finn approached with a group of the battalion flying column, whereupon, the IRA men claim, Neazer fired on them in the hotel.[65]

13.iii.20.—At Toomevara (Co. Tipperary) two constables[a4] were shot dead in the public square.

[a4] This actually occurred on 17 March 1920. The victims were Const. Charles Healy (b.1896) and Const. James Rocke (b.1893).[66]

18.iii.20.—At Cahirdamel (Co. Kerry) in order to gain possession of five police bicycles housed in the Courthouse, a party of armed rebels shot the caretaker[b4] dead.

[b4] The caretaker was Cornelius Kelly. [67]

18.iii.20.—At Castlegrove (Co. Galway) 200 armed rebels attacked the police barracks. In spite of the fact that the barracks were partially demolished by explosives, the small police garrison eventually drove off the attackers.

25.iii.20.—At Ballyheigue (Co. Kerry) the house of a R.I.C. constable was raided by six armed rebels who stole his South African medal and six other articles, and directed his wife to leave the locality.

26.iii.20.—At Gortatlea (Co. Kerry) a large armed party of rebels took possession of a house from which they poured paraffin over a hut at the railway station, used by the R.I.C., and set it on fire, firing into it with rifles from all sides. Only after three of the six constables had been wounded did the R.I.C. evacuate the hut.[68]

26.iii.20.—Mr. Alan Bell[c4] (Resident Magistrate) was dragged from a tram car in Dublin by a gang of armed men and murdered there and then on the pavement.

[c4] Alan Bell (b.1858) Resident Magistrate of Banagher, Co. Offaly. He was in Dublin serving on a committee on the proposed amalgamation of the DMP with the RIC. He was also a former RIC officer and was on the Lord Lieutenant's intelligence committee.[69]

5.iv.20.—At Mohigeela (Co. Cork) a woman employed at the R.I.C. barracks was fired at in her own house.

9.iv.20.—Near Newport (Co. Tipperary) three R.I.C. constables were fired on by a gang of 20–30 men. Two of the constables were killed.[d4]

^{d4} This attack on a three-man bicycle patrol occurred at Lackamore Wood, Rearcross, Newport. Const. William Finn (b.1896) and Const. Daniel McCarthy (b.1894) were killed; also wounded was a Const. Byrne.[70]

11.iv.20.—At Aughamore (Co. Roscommon) two R.I.C. constables were fired at and wounded at a dance.

14.iv.20.—A constable, D.M.P., was murdered as he was leaving his home in Dublin to go on duty.^{e4}

^{e4} DMP Det. Const. Henry Kells, 10119 (b.1878). This was an assassination on the corner of Upper Camden and Pleasants Streets by Paddy Daly of Collins's Squad; Kells was working for G Division.[71]

17.iv.20.—Near Waterville (Co. Kerry) a R.I.C. constable^{f4} was murdered while on leave.

^{f4} Const. Martin Clifford (b.1899).[72]

20.iv.20.—A R.I.C. constable^{g4} was murdered in a street in Dublin.

^{g4} DMP Det. Const. Laurence Dalton (b.1893).[73]

17.iv.20.—At Bruff (Co. Limerick) armed rebels entered the house of a civilian and took his two daughters, who were in their night attire, outside the house, where they made them kneel down, gagged them, and informed them that they were condemned to death for walking with policemen. The raiders then cut the hair off the heads of the two girls.

22.iv.20.—At Lackenoola (Co. Cork) a R.I.C. constable^{h4} was murdered while on leave and working on his father's farm.

^{h4} The victim was DMP Const. Michael McCarthy (b.1891).[74]

25.iv.20.—At Innishannon (Co. Cork) a R.I.C. serjeantⁱ⁴ and constable were murdered by a number of armed rebels lying in ambush.

ⁱ⁴ Sgt Cornelius Crean (b.1872) and Const. Patrick McGoldrick (b.1861).[75]

NOTES

1   For a British Army view of the situation in Ireland up to 1919, see Maj C. J. C. Street, *The Administration of Ireland, 1920* (1921), pp. 14–34. For the best explanation of the British conduct of the war, see C. Townshend, *The British Campaign in Ireland, 1919–1921: The Development of Political and Military Policies* (1975). For civil government, see T. Jones, *Whitehall Diary. Vol. III, Ireland, 1918–1925*. Keith Middlemas ed. (1971).

2   Street, *Administration of Ireland*, pp. 63–7. For nationalism generally, see D. G. Boyce, *Nationalism in Ireland* (1995); R. English, *Irish Freedom: The History of Nationalism in Ireland* (2006); T. Garvin, *Nationalist Revolutions in Ireland, 1858–1928* (1987) and T. Garvin, *The Evolution of Irish Nationalist Politics* (2005). For the IRB, see L. O'Broin, *Revolutionary Underground: The Story of the Irish Republican Brotherhood* (1976) and O. McGee, *The IRB: The Irish Republican Brotherhood, from the Land League to Sinn Fein* (2007).

3   P. Colum, *Arthur Griffith* (1959); R. Davis, *Arthur Griffith* (1976); B. Maye, *Arthur Griffith* (1997).

4   B. Hobson, *Ireland Yesterday and Tomorrow* (1968) and M. Hay, *Bulmer Hobson and the Nationalist Movement in Twentieth-Century Ireland* (2009).

5   M. Laffan, *The Resurrection of Ireland: The Sinn Fein Party, 1916–1923* (1999).

6   See M. Kotsonouris, *Retreat from Revolution: The Dáil Courts, 1920–1924* (1994) and *The Winding Up of the Dáil Courts 1922–1925* (2004); and L. Ó Duibhir, *The Donegal Awakening* (2009), pp. 134–61.

7   For republican development of the Dáil, see B. Farrell, *The Founding of Dáil Éireann: Parliament and Nation Building* (1971) and A. Mitchell, *Revolutionary Government in Ireland: Dáil Éireann, 1919–22* (1995).

8   For more about the issues of American public opinion see F. M. Carroll, *American Opinion and the Irish Question, 1910–23* (1978); C. C. Tansill, *America and the Fight for Irish Freedom* (1957); and A. J. Ward, *Ireland and Anglo-American Relations 1899–1921* (1969). For a treatment of the Irish Diaspora in Canada, see R. McLaughlin, *Irish Canadian Conflict and the Struggle for Irish Independence, 1912–1925* (2013).

9   L. Ó Broin, *The Chief Secretary: Augustine Birrell in Ireland* (1969).

10 For more, see M. Walsh, *G2: In Defence of Ireland: Irish Military Intelligence 1918–45* (2010); P. McMahon, *British Spies and Irish Rebels: British Intelligence and Ireland, 1916–1945* (2008); E. O'Halpin, *Decline of the Union: British Government in Ireland, 1892–1920* (1987); Brig.-Gen Sir Ormonde de L'Epée Winter, *Winter's Tale: An Autobiography* (1955); K. Jeffery, 'British Military Intelligence Following World War I' in *British and American Approaches to Intelligence*, ed. K. G. Robertson (1987), pp. 55–84; *British Intelligence in Ireland, 1920–21: The Final Reports*, P. Hart, ed. (2002); C. Andrew, *Her Majesty's Secret Service: The Making of the British Intelligence Community* (1986); M. Foy, *Michael Collins's Intelligence War* (2006) and D. Kostal, 'British Military Intelligence-Law Enforcement Integration in the Irish War of Independence, 1919–1921', *Can't We All Just Get Along? Improving the Law Enforcement-Intelligence Community Relationship*, T. Christenson, Ed. (2007), pp. 117–42.

11 See 'RIC Nominal Returns for Depot and County Dublin, January 1921' National Archives, (hereafter NA), Kew, HO 184/62, cited in D. Leeson, 'Death in the Afternoon'.

12 See J. Herlihy, *The Royal Irish Constabulary: A Short History and Genealogical Guide* (1999) (hereafter *The RIC*), p. 151 and Herlihy, *The Dublin Metropolitan Police: A Short History and Genealogical Guide* (2001) (hereafter *The DMP*), p. 210. See also, D. M. Leeson, *The Black and Tans: British Police and Auxiliaries in the Irish War of Independence, 1920–1921* (2012), pp. 9–10, 40 & 134–41 and E. McCall, *The Auxiliaries: Tudor's Toughs, A study of the Auxiliary Division Royal Irish Constabulary 1920–1922* (2010), p. 262.

13 See D.G. Boyce, *Englishmen and Irish Troubles: British Public Opinion and the Making of Irish Policy, 1918–1922* (1972); L. Curtis, *Ireland, the Propaganda War: The Media and the "Battle for Hearts and Minds"* (1983); I. Kenneally, *The Paper Wall: Newspapers and Propaganda in Ireland, 1919–1921* (2008); B. P. Murphy, OSB, *The Origins and Organisation of British Propaganda in Ireland, 1920* (2006); and M. Walsh, *The News from Ireland: Foreign Correspondents and the Irish Revolution* (2008).

14 See Statement of D. Breen, (Military Archives [hereafter MA] , Dublin WS 1739), p 29; Statement of P. Daly, WS 387, pp. 22–4; Statement of Joseph Dolan, WS 663, pp. 1–2; and Statement of Joe Leonard, WS 547, p. 7.

15 For contemporary comment see, Street, *The Administration of Ireland, 1920* (1921) and *Ireland* (1922) and M. Sturgis, *The Last Days of Dublin Castle: The Mark Sturgis Diaries*, M. Hopkinson, ed. (1999). See also L. W. McBride, *The Greening of Dublin Castle: The Transformation of Bureaucratic and Judicial Personnel in Ireland, 1892–1922* (1991); E. O'Halpin, *The Decline of the Union: British Government in Ireland, 1892–1920* (1987); C. Magill, ed., *From Dublin Castle to Stormont: The Memoirs of Andrew Philip Magill, 1913–1925* (2003) and B. A. Follis, *A State under Siege: The Establishment of Northern Ireland* (1995).

16 See Herlihy, *The DMP*, pp. 122–53; E. Malcolm, *The Irish Policeman, 1822–1922: A Life* (2006), pp. 167–8; M. Scanlon, *The Dublin Metropolitan Police* (1998), pp. 31–6. See T. Ryle Dwyer, *The Squad: and the Intelligence Operations of Michael Collins* (2005) and D. Nelligan, *The Spy in the Castle* (1968).

17 See McMahon, *British Spies & Irish Rebels*, p. 31; Herlihy, *RIC Officers*, p. 262 and Abbott, *Police Casualties*, pp. 52–4.

18 See Herlihy, *DMP*, pp. 166–8 & 175.

19 See, J. A. Gaughan, *The Memoirs of Constable Jeremiah Mee, RIC* (2012), pp. 79–82 and 99–100. See also, J. Augusteijn, *The Memoirs of John M. Regan: A Catholic Officer in the RIC and RUC, 1909–48* (2007).

20 For more on contemporary opinions, see B. C. Denning, 'Modern Problems of Guerilla Warfare', *Army Quarterly* (January 1927), pp. 347–54.

21 See also S. Hare, 'Martial Law from the Soldier's Point of View', *Army Quarterly*, vol. VII (October, 1923 and January, 1924), pp. 289–300; C. Townshend, *Britain's Civil Wars*, pp. 19–27; K. Jeffery, 'Colonial Warfare', pp. 35 and 36; J. Pimlott, 'The British Experience', p. 17; and 'The Record of the Rebellion', vol. IV, p. 40.

22 'Uniform Force', report to Committee, March 1920, NAUK CO 904/24/5.

23 For home rule, see A. O'Day, *Irish Home Rule, 1867–1921* (1998); J. Smith, *Britain and Ireland: From Home Rule to Independence* (2000); M. Wheatley, *Nationalism and the Irish Party: Provincial Ireland 1910–1916* (2005); and S. M. Duffy, *The Integrity of Ireland: Home Rule, Nationalism, and Partition, 1912–1922* (2009). For the questions about support, see J. Borgonovo, *Spies, Informers and the 'Anti-Sinn Féin Society': The Intelligence War in Cork City, 1920–1921* (2007); P. Hart, *The IRA & Its Enemies* (1998); and W. Sheehan, *A Hard Local War* (2011).

24 R. Holmes, *The Little Field Marshall: Sir John French* (1981) and J. French, *The Life of Field-Marshal Sir John French, First Earl of Ypres* (1931).

25 Appendix 'A' to 5th Division Order No. 1, 13 January 1920, Appendix III, *The Record of the Rebellion in Ireland*, Vol. IV, 'A History of the 5th Division in Ireland, November, 1919–March 1922', NAUK WO 141/93, pp. 83–4; 'Composition of Headquarters of the Forces in Ireland', March 1920, WO 35/215, pp. 6–7; The Army List, 1920.

26 For more, see Mitchinson, *Defending Albion: Britain's Home Army, 1908–1919* (2005), pp. 147–8; R. Robertson, *From Private to Field-Marshal* (1921), pp. 305 & 363; and B. Chappell, *The Regimental Warpath 1914–1918* (2008), p. 13.

27 See Additional Appendices for full text.

28 Provided for internment. See Additional Appendices.

29 See Commandant M. Allen, OBE, *The Pioneer Policewoman* (1925).

30 See Shaw, 'The Military Situation in Ireland', 25 March, 1920, NAUK WO 32/9519/4–6.
31 'Special Police and Fire Brigade Areas.' See Additional Appendices.
32 See Shaw, 'The Military Situation in Ireland', 25 March 1920, NAUK WO 32/9519 and Shaw to Churchill, Memorandum Nº. 95400g, 27 March, 1920, WO 32/9519/p. 1.
33 See *Irish Bulletin*, contained in Aubane Historical Society, *Irish Bulletin: a full reprint of the official newspaper of Dáil Éireann giving news and war reports*, Vol. i, 12 July, 1919–1 May, 1920 (2012).
34 See Hart, *Final Reports*, pp. 20–21; Hopkinson, *Irish War of Independence*, p. 28 and Townshend, *British Campaign*, p. 59.
35 See Abbott, *Police Casualties*, pp. 189–91; Herlihy, *RIC Officers*, pp. 169 & 258 Hart, *Final Reports*, pp. 4–5; Townshend, *British Campaign*, pp. 50–52; Ormonde Winter, 'Report on the Intelligence Branch of the Chief of Police, Dublin Castle, from May 1920 to July 1921', WO 35/214 (contained in Hart, *Final Reports*, p. 65).
36 See Additional Appendices for text of regulation.
37 For Irish Command discussion of this, see *The Record of the Rebellion*, Vol. II, 'Intelligence', pp. 20 & 27.
38 For more on the courts and new laws see S. Enright, *The Trial of Civilians by Military Courts* (2012) and C. Campbell, *Emergency Law in Ireland 1918–1925* (1994).
39 See Hart, *Final Reports*, pp. 10–11.
40 See *The Record of the Rebellion in Ireland*, Vol. IV, pp. 144–7, 154, 158, 161, 164, 170–74, 177, 185–6 & 190–91. For a discussion of informers, see J. Borganovo, *Spies, Informers and the 'Anti-Sinn Fein Society'*.
41 RIC Inspector-General Monthly Confidential Reports (hereafter RIC I-G Report) CO 904/111/271–3. See also, Hart, *Final Reports*, pp. 13 & 15; *The Record of the Rebellion*, Vol. II, 'Intelligence', pp. 21, 24–5, 28 & 47–9; Ormonde Winter, 'Report on the Intelligence Branch of the Chief of Police, Dublin Castle, from May 1920 to July 1921', WO 35/214, contained in Hart, *Final Reports*, pp. 66, 72–4, 77–8 & 82.
42 Abbott, *Police Casualties*, pp. 60–64.
43 For more, see Abbott, *Police Casualties*; Kautt, *Ambushes & Armour*; and D. Leeson, *Black and Tans*, pp. 141–6.
44 See RIC Inspector-General Monthly Confidential Reports in general, NAUK CO 904/103–113.
45 See, for instance, Statement of Mrs S. Beaumont (Née Maureen McGavock), Mil Arch, Dublin, WS 385, p. 6; Statement of R. Walsh, WS 400; Statement of V. Byrne WS 423; Statement of T. Flynn, WS 429; Statement of C. Dalton, WS 434; Statement of J. O'Connor, WS 487, p. 40; Statement of S. MacEoin, WS 1716, p. 62; Statement of R. Brennan, WS 779, §3, p. 600; and Statement of S. Prendergast, WS 755, §3, pp. 440–43.
46 Abbott, *Police Casualties*, pp. 69–73.
47 See RIC I-G Reports, 1920 in general, NAUK CO 904/111–113.
48 Abbott, *Police Casualties*, pp. 55–6.
49 See F. O'Donoghue, 'The Greatness of Tomás MacCurtain,' *Rebel Cork's Fighting Story, 1916–1921: Told by the Men Who Made it* (2009), pp. 46–61; see also, F. MacCurtain, *Remember It's for Ireland: A Family Memoir of Tomas MacCurtain* (2008); F. O'Donoghue, *Tomas MacCurtain Soldier and Patriot: A Biography of the first Republican Lord Mayor of Cork* (1971); P. Hart, *The IRA & It's Enemies*, p. 79; M. Hopkinson, *Irish War of Independence* (2004), p. 156; and T. P. Coogan, *The Man Who Made Ireland: The Life and Death of Michael Collins* (1992), p. 149.
50 See Shaw to Secretary, the War Office, Memorandum Nº. 95400G, 27 March, 1920 and Shaw, 'The Military Situation in Ireland', 25 March, 1920, NAUK WO 32/9519/2–6.
51 Street, *Administration of Ireland, 1920*, pp. 39–40.
52 For counter-plans see, 'Suggested Permanent Organization for Meeting Strikes', 10 November, 1919 NAUK CAB 24/92 CP97; and 'Minutes of Food Committee Conference', 3 January, 1919, 31 January, 1919, 27 March, 1919 and 17 December, 1920 NAUK CO 904/158.

53 For details, see, P. B. Leonard, 'The necessity for de-anglicizing the Irish nation: boycotting and the Irish war of independence', PhD Thesis, University of Melbourne, 2000 and W. H. Kautt 'Logistics & Counter-Insurgency: Procurement, Supply & Communications in the Irish War of Independence, 1919–1921', PhD Thesis, University of Ulster at Jordanstown, 2005.

54 See Directorate of Intelligence (Home Office), 'Report on Revolutionary Organizations in the United Kingdom', 20 May, 1920, NAUK CAB 24/106/110, pp. 8–9 and 'Report on Revolutionary Organizations in the United Kingdom', 27 May, 1920, NAUK CAB 24/106/190, p. 10. See also, Hart, *Final Reports*, p. 11; *The Record of the Rebellion*, Vol. II, 'Intelligence', pp. 24–5; Ormonde Winter, 'Report on the Intelligence Branch of the Chief of Police, Dublin Castle, from May 1920 to July 1921', WO 35/214, contained in Hart, *Final Reports*, p. 65.

55 See Street's discussion of Greenwood's appointment, *Administration of Ireland, 1920*, p. 38–9.

56 *An t-Óglác*, vol. II, Nº. 10, 1 May, 1920, p. 85.

57 For demographics of the IRA, see P. Hart, *The IRA At War: 1916–1923* (2003), pp. 110–37.

58 See T. R. Dwyer's account of the killing in *The Squad and the Intelligence Operations of Michael Collins* (2005), pp. 70–82.

59 See R. Abbott, *Police Casualties in Ireland, 1919–1922* (2000), pp. 55–6.

60 See RIC I-G Report for February 1920 NAUK CO 904/111/273 and P. J. O'Daly, 'Monaghan Men's Baptism of Fire at Capture of Ballytrain RIC Post', in *With the IRA in the Fight for Freedom, 1919 to the Truce* (2010), pp. 91–100.

61 RIC I-G Report for February 1920. NAUK CO 904/111/274.

62 See ibid. NAUK CO 904/111/275.

63 See Abbott, *Police Casualties*, p. 62 and Jim Herlihy, *The Dublin Metropolitan Police: A Complete Alphabetical List of Officers and Men, 1836–1925* (2001) (hereafter *DMP List*), pp. 72 & 249.

64 Abbott, *Police Casualties*, p. 62.

65 Abbott, *Police Casualties*, p. 63; Herlihy, *The RIC*, pp. 173–211; and 'Volunteer', 'The IRA Campaign in West Limerick—Shooting of RIC in Rathkeale Hotel', *Limerick's Fighting Story, 1916–1921: Told By the Men Who Made It* (2009), pp. 257–8.

66 Abbott, *Police Casualties*, p. 63 and Herlihy, *The RIC*, pp. 186 & 220.

67 See S. Joy, *The IRA in Kerry, 1916–1921* (2005), p. 64.

68 See republican account by 'Volunteer', 'Attacks on Gortatlea, Scartaglin and Brosna Barracks', in *Rebel Cork's Fighting Story* (2009), pp. 211–17.

69 McMahon, *British Spies & Irish Rebels*, p. 31; Street, *Administration of Ireland, 1920*, p. 38; 'Uniform Force', report to Committee, March 1920 NAUK CO 904/24/5); see T. Ryle Dwyer, *Tans Terror and Troubles: Kerry's Real Fighting Story, 1913–23* (2001), p. 182.

70 Abbott, *Police Casualties*, pp. 68–9 and Herlihy, *The RIC* pp. 177 & 200.

71 Abbott, *Police Casualties*, p. 69 and Herlihy, *DMP List*, p. 130

72 Abbott, *Police Casualties*, p. 69; Herlihy, *The RIC*, p. 165; Herlihy, *RIC List*, p. 67; Dwyer, *Tans Terror and Troubles*, p. 189.

73 Abbott, *Police Casualties*, p. 72 and Herlihy, *DMP List*, p. 53.

74 Abbott, *Police Casualties*, p. 73 and Herlihy, *DMP List*, p. 160.

75 Abbott, *Police Casualties*, p. 73 and Herlihy, *The RIC*, p. 203.

CHAPTER II

Policy and Leadership Changes, May to August 1920

E*ffect of change of policy, May to August, 1920.*—During the period May to August, 1920, the arrest of persons found actually committing outrages, combined with searches for arms in co-operation with the police, constituted the main activity of the Crown forces. This was unlikely to be productive of any great results, owing to the fact that information again began to be scarce, and witnesses could not be persuaded to give evidence which would secure convictions.[a] In consequence, the month of May and the succeeding months proved an invaluable period for the Sinn Fein leaders and from this time dates the rapid increase in the organization of the rebel forces and the assumption of civil administration by Dail Eireann and subordinate illegal bodies.[b]

[a] Coercion is frequently necessary in any revolution as the revolutionaries vie with the Government for the adherence of the people. The revolutionaries will accept assistance, willing or unwilling. In certain situations, they may have to settle for merely preventing assistance to the enemy through coercion. This is critical to their success.

[b] The Dáil Éireann was declared illegal by Dublin Castle on 10 September, 1919.

The important men in the rebel movement lost no time in making use of this period of comparative immunity. They were able to move about at will, to raise and organize units of I.R.A. and to inaugurate Sinn Fein Courts[c], and, although by this time a large number of them were known to the Military Intelligence

Section[d], they were secure from arrest so long as they did not take part in the actual outrages. Illegal organizations such as the Gaelic League[e], the Cumman Na MBan[f] (the women's branch of the I.R.A.) and the I.R.A.[g] itself openly held meetings which were reported in the newspapers and their suppression by force had become a matter beyond the now limited powers of the Crown forces.

[c] Sinn Féin courts, also called Arbitration Courts, were established by the Dáil Éireann in June 1919. Their purview was limited, and was technically legal since they were not coercive. These were followed by criminal courts a year later. The ideas behind both courts were the delegitimization of British rule by attacking its ability and right to enforce law.[1]

[d] The description of them being 'known to the Military Intelligence Section...' is questionable, given that the pre-existing section was reorganized in early May 1920 with an officer, Bvt. Maj S. S. Hill Dillon, Royal Irish Rifles, assigned. Shortly thereafter, the 5th and 6th Infantry Divisions received additional help. They got an additional officer at the division staff and each brigade was allotted an officer for intelligence work. The battalions each had an intelligence officer, but it would appear that this was an additional duty of one of the officers already assigned.[2]

[e] Founded by Douglas Hyde on 31 July, 1893.

[f] Cumann na mBan was founded by Kathleen Lane-O'Kelley (née Shannahan) at Wynne's Hotel, 35–39, Lower Abbey Street, Dublin, 5 April, 1914. It was independent of Sinn Féin and the IRA, but worked alongside both.[3]

[g] The Irish Volunteers declared themselves the 'Army of the Irish Republic' in the inaugural issue of *An t-Óglác*[4], but the term 'IRA' did not become commonplace until 1920. The Dáil Éireann did not officially accept their status until April 1921, although the Volunteers swore an oath of allegiance to the Dáil in August 1920.

Increase of outrages.—Outrages increased almost immediately after the release of the hunger-strikers[h] and the cancellation of the January policy, and from now onwards all classes in the country were gradually subjected by inclination, force of circumstances or armed intimidation, to the domination of a party which a few months before had been a minority in the country.[i]

h   Dublin Castle was concerned about the implications of the hunger strike. Sturgis said in his diaries that it was 'the hourly worry'.[5]

i   Although a bit melodramatically stated, the statement is essentially correct, with one proviso: Sinn Féin ceased to be a 'minority party' in the 1918 General Election, when they gained a plurality of the popular vote and a majority of the seats.[6]

Sinn Fein propaganda.—Every effort was made by skilful propaganda of a most unscrupulous kind in newspapers and by means of emissaries abroad to represent the bands of armed civilians as an army waging a legitimate war against a foreign power. *An T'Oglac* published its instructions to the I.R.A. fortnightly (and later weekly), maintaining that the shooting of policemen was an act of war, and that the murder of an officer in his house was recognized form of guerilla warfare known as "cutting off stragglers."[j]

j   There were no specific references to 'the murder of an officer in his house...[as a] recognized form of guerilla warfare known as "cutting off stragglers"' in *An t-Óglác* in 1920, but there were two instances of mentioning attacking 'stragglers'. This theme showed up again the next year in three issues.[7]

More intensive campaign against R.I.C.—Although, in spite of some rumours to the contrary, a general rising was not considered likely, and was probably never contemplated by the rebels, the outrages committed during May and the succeeding months were in some cases on a somewhat more ambitious scale. The main objective of the outrages still remained the R.I.C. in continuation of the rebel policy of reducing this force to impotence, but troops, as a result of their co-operation with the police[k], were also subjected to attackers where they could be engaged by very superior numbers. In the more rigorous prosecution of this "guerilla warfare" the following new or elaborated methods were employed. Ambushes consisting of men purporting to be peaceful labourers were laid on roads were it was known that small police patrols were likely to move. Roads were blocked by felled trees or stone walls in order to hold up lorries conveying small bodies of troops. Telegraph and telephone wires were cut, and trains held up and boarded by armed and masked men who stole the mails. Civilians opposed to Sinn Fein were systematically subjected to more dastardly outrages. Ex-soldiers and their families[l] and anybody suspected of friendliness with the

Unit	Aug 1918	Dec 1918	Sep 1919	Mar 1920	Sep 1920	Feb 1921
Irish Command	Maj R.B. Gooden	Capt E.H. Howard	Capt R.A.R. Neville	Capt S.S. Hill Dillon	Maj S.S. Hill Dillon	Lt P.W. Amor Capt C.P.C. Daneill Lt W. Vaughan Lt F. O'Driscoll Capt N. Gilvary
5th Inf Div	NA	NA	NA	Capt L.S. Mallory	Vacant	Maj J.C.M. Miller Lt F.A.S. Gibson
15th (Ulster) Bde	NA	NA	NA	Maj C.deM. Leathes	NA	NA
13th (Athlone) Bde	NA	NA	NA	Lt C. H. Gairdner	Lt C. H. Gairdner	Lt C.O.I. Tully Lt C.H. Gairdner
14th (Curragh) Bde	NA	NA	NA	Lt J. Bockett	Lt J. Bockett	Lt J. Bockett
Galway Bde	NA	NA	NA	NA	Capt A.J. Elwick-Harrison	Capt A.J. Elwick-Harrison
6th Inf Div	NA	NA	NA	Capt C. Kelly	Capt C. Kelly	Capt C. Kelly Lt J.C. Stephen
16th (Fermoy) Bde	NA	NA	NA	Vacant	Lt L.C. Gates	Lt L.C. Gates
17th (Cork) Bde	NA	NA	NA	Lt J.B. Harvey	Lt J.B. Harvey	Lt H Hammond
18th (Limerick) Bde	NA	NA	NA	Vacant	Lt H.A. Davies	Lt H.A. Davies
Kerry Bde	NA	NA	NA	NA	Vacant	Lt F.C. Sherwood
Dublin District	NA	NA	NA	Capt F.H. Jebena	Capt F.H. Shove	Lt P.W.H. Carpenter
24th Bde (Prov)	NA	NA	NA	NA	Capt C.H.R. Barnes	Capt C.H.R. Barnes
25th Bde (Prov)	NA	NA	NA	NA	Lt L.P. Hodson	Lt L.P. Hodson
1st Inf Division	NA	NA	NA	NA	Maj C.deM. Leathes	Maj C.deM. Leathes
15th Bde	NA	NA	NA	NA	Vacant	Lt P.E.E. Chappell
Londonderry Bde	NA	NA	NA	NA	Vacant	Lt R. Francis

Table 2.1 Intelligence Officers Assigned to the Irish Command, 1918–1921.

police were boycotted[m], intimidated into leaving their homes, and in some cases murdered; and women who associated with any of the Crown forces were seized and had their hair cut off.[n] Concurrently with these outrages the murder of individual policemen, the attacks on isolated police barracks, the burning of vacated police barracks and raids[o] on private houses for arms, and on post offices and postmen[p] for funds for the I.R.A. continued as before.

[k]   The policemen were targeted because they were symbols and enforcers of British Government power. They were also a good source of weapons and ammunition.

[l]   There is growing debate about the extent to which the IRA targeted veterans solely due to their status as military veterans. At the same time, it was not unusual for the IRA to target police pensioners. Yet again, it is not entirely clear what association these men had with the struggle, since policemen who resigned were largely left alone. Of course, some of these resignees joined the movement. It is also more likely that veterans tended to be pro-Government or, at least, home rulers, and were thus in opposition to the rebels, or seen to be. There are no empirical studies demonstrating veterans to be more likely to be informers or spies.[8]

[m]   See the previous chapter for the RIC boycott.

[n]   Attacks against women were not uncommon, depending on location. Young women spending time with policemen or soldiers in areas where republicans were active risked being targets of retaliation. Strippings, beatings and shearing, what Ward has labelled 'symbolic humiliation', were methods of boycott going back forty years. Sociologist Louise Ryan says that 'There is also evidence to suggest sexual violence was used as a weapon of war.'[9] While generally frowned upon by GHQ, it was not possible to eliminate communal retribution inherent within Irish secret societies. Crime against women during this era remains insufficiently studied.[10]

[o]   Raiding private houses was proscribed by IRA GHQ and communicated many times in General Orders as well as in *An t-Óglác* throughout 1920, but these orders appear to have had little effect.[11]

[p]   The subject of attacks on postal employees deserves greater study, especially since the Royal Mails were heavily infiltrated by republicans.

The notes to this chapter give a few of the numerous outrages occurring during the period May—July, 1920.

The attacks on police barracks, although the rebels were always at a numerical advantage of anything from 10 to 1 upwards, were not a great success, and the attackers suffered a considerable number of casualties, although the attacks were seldom pressed home.[q] Probably as a result of these casualties, and of the more rapid assistance which was forthcoming from troops and other bodies of police, the attacks on police barracks to decrease towards the middle of June, and individuals murders, entailing less risk to the I.R.A., increased.[r]

[q] Attacks against police barracks were rarely successful due to lack of offensive capability amongst the Volunteers. After the harassment of 1919, indefensible positions were either fortified or abandoned. During this period of the war the rebels lacked sufficient explosives to breach the defences of all but the weakest barracks. Police reports make frequent reference to outrageous numbers of attackers, where, in fact, the actual numbers tended to be considerably smaller. Likewise, the claim the police inflicted heavy losses is demonstrably incorrect. Indeed, a remarkable feature of this war is the relatively light casualties inflicted by both sides. For all the shooting, few got hit. The exceptions are noteworthy due to their rarity, although casualty rates were climbing.

Hopkinson reports 624 British dead and 752 civilians (including IRA). Abbott lists 430 police dead from 1919 to 1921 and *Last Posts* lists 585 republican dead.[12]

[r] While the RIC and army created excellent response capabilities, rebel ambush skills likewise increased.

Kidnapping military officers, 26th June, 1920.—On the 26th June the rebels, for the first time, started the kidnapping of military officers. Brig.-General C.H.T. Lucas[s], commanding the 16th (Fermoy) Infantry Brigade, was on short leave with Lieut.-Colonel Danford,[t] R.E., and Lieut.-Colonel Tyrell[u], R.E., at a fishing cottage near Kilbarry, Co. Cork. On returning to the cottage these officers discovered the caretaker bound and a party of armed rebels in possession. The rebels seized the three officers, and placing them in motor-cars, drove away. On the way Lieut.-Colonel Danford attempted to jump from the car, and was at once shot at and wounded. He was left beside the road with Lieut.-Colonel Tyrell, General Lucas being carried off to an unknown destination. For over a month General Lucas was detained until, on 30th July, 1920, he succeeded in escaping.[13]

[s] Brig-Gen Cuthbert Henry Tindall Lucas (b.1879–d.1958).[14]

[t] Lt-Col B. W. Y. Danford, DSO, RE, Commanding Royal Engineer, 16th (Fermoy) Brigade. He survived and retired from the army on 29 April 1930.[15]

[u] Bvt. Lt-Col W. G. Tyrrell, DSO, RE. After serving in Ireland, he served in India, retiring from the army on 15 November, 1937. 'Tyrrell' is the correct spelling of his name.[16]

Increase in attacks on military.—About the middle of July outrages directed against troops became more frequent, and information was received that the rebel leaders had inaugurated a systematic attempt to irritate troops into troops into retaliation.[v] Propaganda in the Press was to assist in this by representing all future outrages committed by the I.R.A. as just counter-action. The success with which the newspapers in Ireland and England, with very few exceptions, played this rôle, is a sure indication either of the gullibility, or the fear of personal violence, of their staff, and of the feebleness of the counter-propaganda by the Government.[w]

[v] There is little to suggest that this was the case.

[w] This direct criticism of the Government is unusual in *The Record of the Rebellion*. The Public Information Branch was responsible for British propaganda efforts and headed by Sir (Thomas) Basil Clarke, KBE (b.1879–d.1947), and really were as feeble as described.[17]

Murder of Colonel Smyth, 17th July, 1920.—On 17th July one of the most cold-blooded of all the murders committed by the I.R.A. was perpetrated in Cork. A party of armed rebels[x] entered the Country Club, and walking into the room where Colonel Smyth[y], R.I.C., was sitting, shot him dead, and wounded County Inspector Craig[z], R.I.C., who was with him. Colonel Smyth had a distinguished war record. He was unable adequately to defend himself as he had lost an arm in the late war.[18] Following this murder further disturbances took place in Cork City during the night, and one man was shot by the troops during a fracas in which he and others attacked a patrol. On the following evening about 500 civilians man-handled unarmed soldiers in the town, and indulged in a good deal of indiscriminate firing. An armed party of about 50 men was at once sent out from barracks. This party was fired at on reaching the principal street. This fire was returned at once and a considerable number of casualties inflicted, and after two or three hours' patrolling, during which fire was opened on them from side streets and a few bombs thrown, they restored order completely in the city. The troops suffered no casualties, but inflicted severe loss on their attackers. The exact number was never discovered, but was believed to be about 25. The Press was almost silent on the subject, so it is probable that they included no women or children, or persons about whom Sinn Fein propaganda could have protested. After this affair there was no serious disturbance in the city for some months, and armed parties of troops were never interfered with.[aa]

---

[x] Led by Daniel 'Sandow' [O']Donovan (b.1890–d.1975).[19]

[y] Lt-Col Gerald Brice-Ferguson Smyth (b.1885). Born in the Punjab, to an Anglo-Irish family, he passed out of Woolrich in July 1905 a second lieutenant of Royal Engineers. By 1908 he was promoted to lieutenant and posted to Gibraltar. In 1913, he went to the 17th Field Company at the Curragh and participated in the 'mutiny' in 1914. He deployed with the BEF in August and served in the rearguard of the retreat. He was wounded at the Aisne in October, losing his left arm at the elbow. Promoted to captain in Oct 1914, he returned after his convalescence in April 1915 and was posted to the 90th Division. He assumed command of the 90th Field Company at Loos and was brevetted to major. In Nov 1916, after returning from convalescence, he was given command of the 6th Bn KSOB. He was made acting lieutenant colonel in Jan 1918, and was serving with Tudor as his division commander. In October 1918, he was made a temporary brigadier general. In 1919, he relinquished his general officer rank and reverted to his highest brevet rank, lieutenant colonel. He had been wounded five times, mentioned in despatches at least seven times, promoted four times (skipping colonel altogether), received two brevet ranks, the DSO and bar. When he returned to Ireland in June 1920 to command the 6th Infantry Division's 12th Field Company, Tudor seconded him to the RIC as Divisional Commissioner for Munster.[20] He was also the impetus for the 19 June, 1920 'Listowel Mutiny', in which fourteen members of the RIC refused to hand over their barracks to the army.[21]

[y] County Inspector George Fitzgerald William Craig (b.1869–d.1956).[22]

[aa] The IRA suffered no casualties from this that are recorded in the standard references.

The intensifying of the "guerilla warfare" against the troops led inevitably to more strained relations between the soldiers and the civilian population. An attempt to boycott the troops was, however, a failure, partly because trade with the troops formed the shopkeepers' chief source of income, and partly because when tradespeople refused to supply the troops, the goods required were requisitioned.[bb]

[bb] Revolutionaries must always strike a balance between controlling a population and harming it in the process. To do too much damage would harm the local economy, which could backfire on them. Controlling too much of a community's affairs would make the IRA appear too overbearing, and not too different from their enemies.

Curfew extended.—At the end of July the state of Cork and some other towns in Munster became such that it was decided to impose curfew restrictions, which had a good effect.

Labour troubles.—Another scheme of the Sinn Fein leaders seriously embarrassed the military situation. Having realized the advantage gained by co-operation with the Irish Transport and General Workers' Union[cc] in the demand for the release of the Mountjoy hunger-strikers, the rebels made further use of this powerful organization for a form of military boycott at the docks and on the railways. About the middle of May the dock labourers refused to handle military stores, and struck work whenever a ship arrived carrying such stores.[dd] The result of this was that all military stores had to be conveyed in Government vessels and landed at the Government Quay at Kingstown, being off-loaded and conveyed to their destinations by military labour. This naturally greatly increased the already heavy duties of the troops.

[cc] Founded by Larkin in 1908, it was an omnibus union covering all trades. It remained a force in Irish labour and politics for decades.

[dd] On 20 May, 1920, the dockers at North Wall Quay spontaneously refused to offload a ship, starting what became known as the Munition Strike, which lasted from May to December 1920. They refused to handle military or police cargo, or to convey troops or police. The workers amended this to armed troops or police later.[23]

June, 1920.—Following this action of the dockers, the railway employees on all southern Irish lines, about the middle of June, refused to handle military stores on the railways.[24] Here, again, it became necessary to employ military labour, and to send armed escorts on the trains with all consignments. The railway employees then refused to work trains carrying armed soldiers or police, and, later, they also refused to carry unarmed parties going on leave. To counter this action armed parties of troops and police were detailed to enter trains at various stations daily. These parties took rations with them, and, if the driver refused to work the train, they continued to sit in the train until it was cancelled or preceded on its journey. This procedure led to a good deal of dislocation of the railways, but no attempt was ever made to eject the armed force from a train.[ee] That it should be necessary for His Majesty's forces to have recourse to such undignified methods in order to deal with the open defiance of constituted authority is eloquent testimony of the ineffectual powers that were given to the Commander-in-Chief for dealing with the situation.

[ee] One remarkable aspect of the Munition Strike was its non-violence, and yet its crippling effect on military and police transportation for the rest of the year, especially heavy transport.

This method was obviously very wasteful in man-power, and subsequently an arrangement was come to with the railway companies that they should dismiss every engine-driver or guard who refused to work a train carrying Crown forces. This arrangement was, for the most part, loyally carried out by the railway companies, and, ultimately, though not for over six months, the strike was broken by this means. Another factor in breaking the strike was the lack of funds for supporting the dismissed railway employees. The Irish Transport Union, misjudging the situation, had counted on financial assistance from the general public and the English Labour Party. There is no doubt that the majority of railway employees acted under compulsion in refusing to work the trains, and that they were only too glad when the strike ended.[ff] No objection, therefore, was raised when the railway companies decided to reinstate the dismissed men. With a typical misrepresentation of the facts, and a cynical disregard for the perspicacity of the public, the hostile Press represented the end of the strike as a great victory of the railway over the Government which had sought to ruin the railways of Ireland.[gg]

[ff] The contributions collected were probably given freely. While there were isolated reports of coercion early on, there is no indication that the majority of strikers were anything but volunteers. They ended their strike due to the

burden of insufficient funds. Although the strike was popular in the south, it was less so amongst the northern railway workers.[25]

gg The Munition Strike forced the police and military to use the inadequate roads with the insufficient numbers of motor vehicles. Considering Gen Macready's description of the situation as a 'railway paralysis', it is clear that the Strike created severe transportation difficulties for the British forces.[26]

Cattle driving.—Another illegality which was overcome by an ingenious method, failing the power to adopt more open and drastic means, was the agrarian trouble caused by driving cattle from the land of loyalists or of the Congested Districts Board, and replacing it by the cattle of Sinn Fein supporters. To deal with this certain enclosures were erected in various parts of the country and were legalized as "pounds." As soon as cattle were driven on to land where it had no right it was driven into the "pound," by the troops or police, and notices were posted to the effect that the owners could have the cattle at the expense of becoming known to the police, and liable to prosecution, or of having their cattle sold. This procedure proved to be quite successful in putting an end to this particular form of lawlessness.

Sinn Fein Courts.—During June and July Sinn Fein courts were established in the majority of districts in Ireland. These courts were ostensibly arbitration courts, and as such not illegal. In fact, however, they "tried" all kinds of cases and passed sentence. Civilians were made[hh] to bring their cases to these courts by means of intimidation, and the "offences" dealt with were frequently not offences known to law, but merely lack of disloyalty. The ordinary magistrates' courts were boycotted and individuals who intended to appear before these in any capacity, sometimes the magistrates themselves, were kidnapped and detained.[27] These courts also "tried" and "condemned to death" individuals, for the most part members of the R.I.C. The trials were a mere farce, as the "offender" was not present at them, and the "execution of the sentence" was brought about by cold-blooded murder, either by kidnapping the victim or by laying in wait for him.[ii] The sentence of death on two R.I.C. constables was captured, and proved to be confirmed by Terence McSwiney, Lord Mayor of Cork and Commandant, 1st Cork Brigade, I.R.A.[28]

hh It appears that the resort to these 'courts' was usually voluntary, although this is hard to gauge from just republican sources. According to Cmdt Liam Haugh, 'Sinn Fein Courts were accepted without any demur by the mass of the people.' But he then went on to describe the enforcement of the decisions using theft of livestock, and after this 'Sinn Fein Court edicts were no longer questioned.'[29]

ii Most sentences consisted of fines. There are many BMH Witness Statements that describe the fairness of these courts and their decisions, including some by judges.[30]

The sittings of the Sinn Fein courts, in which civil cases were dealt with, were much advertised in the Press in pursuance of the rebel policy of demonstrating that Dail Eireann was administering the country. An Irish Republican Police Force[jj] was inaugurated, and endeavoured on all occasions to usurp the functions of the D.M.P and R.I.C., and to bring persons to trial at Sinn Fein courts.

jj Originally, the IRA performed police functions, and detailed men to perform these functions. In the late spring of 1920, the republicans founded a police force to assume these policing duties of the IRA and some of the IRA men became republican police. Their eventual leader was Simon Donnelly (b1891–d.1966), who led the force to the end of the War.[31]

Increased use of troops.—The increasing difficulty of the situation during the period succeeding the release of the hunger-strikers had placed many additional duties upon the troops. Patrols were increased and the number of detachments throughout the country were multiplied in order to give further support to the R.I.C. in country districts; guards were numerous and all stores sent by train required an escort. Owing to the weakness of the 30 battalions in the country they were unable to perform all the duties without excessive strain, while the small number of nights in bed was a serious drain on the health of the young and immature troops.[kk] In these circumstances it was considered[ll] necessary to apply for additional battalions from England.

kk The IGS investigated the claims of violations of King's Regulations, that during peacetime troops were to be given the three consecutive nights of sleep in barracks prior to standing guard for one night. The response from the IGS was that they were at war. When troops complained that they were not getting the entitlements authorized in wartime, such as extra rations, the IGS said that they were not at war.[32]

ll   General Macready opposed this plan in writing. Interestingly, the memorandum generated debate about Macready's use of the word 'proletariat' rather than about the serious problems outlined therein.[33]

Reinforcements, May to June, 1920.—In May the War Office were asked to send four additional battalions to Ireland from the eight battalions which were held as a reserve in England for duty in Ireland when necessity arose. The 6th Division area was the most lawless, and required two of these battalions, the other two were required to deal with the areas outside Dublin.

During May and June four battalions arrived and were distributed as follows:—

Unit	OC	Division
2nd Bn. Cameron Highlanders	Lt-Col C. G. M. Sorel Cameron	6th Infantry Division
1st Bn. Devonshire Rgt	Bvt. Col E. D. Young	6th Infantry Division
1st Bn. Cheshire Rgt	Lt-Col B. A. Chetwynd	5th Infantry Division[mm]
1st Bn. South Wales Borderers	Lt-Col A. J. Reddie	5th Infantry Division[nn]

In addition, the following reliefs were carried out during June and July:—

mm   The Cheshires actually went to the Dublin District.

nn   The Borderers actually went to the Dublin District.

Relived	OC	Relieving	OC	Div
1st Bn. East Surrey Rgt	Lt-Col R. H. Baldwin	2nd Bn. Duke of Wellington's Rgt	Lt-Col H. A. Carr	Dublin
2nd Bn. S Lancashire Rgt	Lt-Col D'O. B. Dawson	2nd Bn. Welch Rgt	Lt-Col A. Derry	Dublin
2nd Bn. Highland Light Inf	Lt-Col J. C. Grahame	2nd Bn. Royal Scots	Bvt. Lt-Col H. E. P. Nash	6th

The necessity for employing lorries for the rapid movement of patrols led to a demand for additional mechanical transport. This was gradually provided by the War Office and became the normal method of patrol work in the country areas, and, to a certain extent, in towns.[34]

The next addition to the troops in the country was the result of serious riots which broke out in Londonderry towards the end of June.[oo] These riots beginning with faction fights spread to such an extent as to be beyond the control of their leaders, and the troops were in insufficient strength to suppress them. The 12th July, "Orange Day," celebrations in Belfast being imminent, and the general situation in the north being critical, it was considered necessary to ask for additional troops for that city also. As a result of these demands the following battalions arrived at the end of June and early July:—

Unit	OC	Posted
1st Bn. The Queen's Royal[pp]	Lt-Col H. W. Whinfield	Londonderry
2nd Bn. Rifle Brigade	Lt-Col W. E. Davies	Belfast
1st Bn. Bedfordshire & Hertfordshire Rgt	Lt-Col E. I. de S. Thorpe	Belfast

[oo] This is the only mention of the considerable sectarian strife against Roman Catholics in *The Record of the Rebellion*. There were two separate riots here. The riot at the beginning of June began in Londonderry, killing some nineteen people, mostly Catholics. In Belfast, the Twelfth celebrations reached a fever pitch with anti-Sinn Féin and anti-republican sentiments running high. The murder of Lt-Col Smyth in Cork presaged the coming fight. The arrival of his body in Banbridge on 20 July, and subsequent funeral on the 21st, initiated rioting there and in Dromore. Rioting in Belfast also began on the 21st.[35] This strife was one reason why the creation of the Ulster Special Constabulary did not free troops posted in the north.[36]

[pp] Officially, the Royal West Surrey Regiment.

Unit	OC	Posted
1st Bn. King's Liverpool Regiment	Lt-Col L. M. Jones	6th Div
1st Bn. Royal Fusiliers	Lt-Col C. J. Hickie	6th Div
2nd Bn. Argyll & Sutherland Highlanders	Lt-Col W. J. B. Tweedie	5th Div

Reinforcements, July, 1920.—In order to carry out this policy a further addition was required to the number of troops in Ireland. Two battalions and an additional infantry brigade headquarters were asked for the 6th Division, and one battalion and an additional infantry brigade headquarters for Co. Galway in the 5th Division. The additional brigade headquarters became necessary owing to the increase of troops and the abnormal extent of the brigade areas.

New formations.—The Kerry Infantry Brigade was formed on 13th July, 1920, and included the Co. Kerry and a portion of Co. Cork transferred from the 17th Infantry Brigade. The Galway Infantry Brigade was formed in September, 1920, and included Co. Galway and Co. Mayo, transferred from the 13th Infantry Brigade.

Before the end of July it was found necessary to ask for an additional divisional headquarters for Northern Ireland, up to now controlled by the 15th Infantry Brigade of the 5th Division. This area comprised the six Ulster Counties together with Cos. Sligo, North Leitrim, Donegal, Monaghan, Cavan and Louth; it was decided to divide this into two infantry brigade areas, making an additional infantry brigade headquarters at Londonderry. These proposals were agreed to by the War Office, and on 7th August, 1920, the headquarters of the 1st Division was established at Belfast. On 14th August the Londonderry Brigade was established comprising Cos. Donegal, Londonderry, Tyrone, Cavan, Fermanagh, North Leitrim and Sligo, the 15th Infantry Brigade retaining its headquarters at Belfast, and consisting of Cos. Antrim, Armagh, Louth, Down and Monaghan.

Unit	GOC / OC	Location
1st **Infantry Division**	**Maj-Gen Sir E. G. T. Bainbridge**	**Ulster**
15th Infantry Brigade	Brig-Gen G. T. C. Carter-Campbell	Belfast
1st Bn Norfolk Rgt		Belfast
1st Bn Somerset Light Infantry		Holywood
1st Duke of Cornwall's Light Infantry		Ballykinlar
Londonderry Brigade	Brig-Gen W. H. L. Allgood	Londonderry
1st Royal West Surrey Rgt		Londonderry
1st Bn Dorsetshire Rgt		Londonderry
2nd Bn Rifle Bde		Glenties
1st Bn Bedfordshire & Hertfordshire Rgt		Finner Camp
5th **Infantry Division**	**Jeudwine**	**The Curragh**
Galway Brigade	Brig-Gen J. G. Chaplin	
2nd Bn Border Rgt		Castlebar

2nd Bn Argyll & Sutherland Highlanders		Claremorris
6th Dragoon Guards		
1st Royal Dragoons	Lt-Col H. A. Tomkinson	Athlone
13th Infantry Brigade	Brig-Gen T. S. Lambert	
1st Bn East Yorkshire Rgt		Mullingar
1st Bn Leicestershire Rg		Athlone
		Athlone
14th Infantry Brigade	Skinner	Curragh
1st Bn Cameronians (Scottish Rifles)		Curragh
2nd Bn Shropshire Light Infantry		Curragh
1st Bn North Staffordshire Rgt		Curragh
12th Lancers		Curragh
6th Infantry Division	**Strickland**	**Cork**
18th Infantry Brigade	Brig-Gen A. R. Cameron	Limerick
2nd Bn The Royal Scots		Ennistymon
2nd Bn Yorkshire Rgt		Rath Keale
2nd Bn Royal Welch Fusiliers		Limerick
1st Bn Oxforshire & Bukinghamshire Light Inf		Limerick
1st Bn Northamptonshire Rgt		Templemore
CAV RGT		
Kerry Brigade	Brig-Gen R. O'IL Livesay	
1st Bn King's Liverpool Rgt		Bantry
2nd Bn East Lancashire Rg		Tralee
17th Infantry Brigade	Brig-Gen H. W. Higginson	
2nd Bn Hampshire Rgt		Cork
2nd Bn South Staffordshire Rgt		Cork
1st Bn Essex Rgt		Kinsale
1st Bn Manchester Rgt		Ballincollig

2nd Bn Cameron Highlanders		Queenstown
17th Lancers		Buttevant
16th Infantry Brigade	Brig-Gen J. Steele replaced Lucas	Fermoy
1st Bn The Buffs (East Kent Rgt)		Fermoy
1st Bn Royal Fusiliers		Kilworth
1st Bn Lincolnshire Rgt		Tipperary
1st Bn Devonshire Rgt		Waterford
Dublin District		
15th Hussars		Marlborough Barracks
24th (Provisional) Infantry Brigade	Oldman	Dublin
1st Bn Lancashire Fusiliers		Dublin
2nd Bn Worcestershire Rgt		Dublin
2nd Bn West Riding Rgt		Collinstown
1st Bn Wiltshire Rgt		Dublin
1st Bn South Wales Borderers		Dollymount
25th (Provisional) Infantry Brigade	Onslow	Dublin
1st Bn Royal Lancaster Rgt		Dublin
1st Bn South Lancashire Rgt		Dublin
2nd Bn Welch Rgt		Dublin
2nd Royal Berkshire Rgt		Dublin
1st Bn Cheshire Rgt		Rathdrum

This gave a total of 40 battalions and 7 cavalry regiments; the battalions, however, were extremely weak.

Situation, August, 1920.—These additional troops enabled a closer support to be given to the R.I.C. in country districts, while military lorry patrols were able to move over more extended areas. This had a good effect, outrages on a large scale became less frequent, and the number of attacks on troops and police barracks were reduced to a very low figure.[qq]

qq   This is a rather odd claim, given that the barracks attacks reported for August 1920 were more than twice as many as for July.[37]

The situation was, however, far from satisfactory. Intimidation of law-abiding people, raiding of private houses and individual murders continued. And, although a considerable number of arrests had been made, convictions were few as courts martial, which were the only courts where conviction was likely, were not empowered to deal with offences other than those against the Defence of the Realm Regulations. Sinn Fein courts were for the most part unmolested as the Competent Military Authority had no power to act against them.[38]

Moreover, the weapon of the hunger-strike still remained, and there is no doubt that these strikes were ordered from I.R.A. headquarters, and that prisoners would have refused to strike only at the risk of their lives when their sentence expired.[rr] A complete stultification of all efforts to suppress lawlessness might thus have been brought about had it not been for the firm stand made by the Government in the case of the Lord Mayor of Cork.

rr   No evidence to support this conclusion has come to light. It would appear that once the hunger strike began, one would not be permitted to end it, but the strikes were called off after MacSwiney's death.

Arrest and death of McSwiney, 7th August to 25th October, 1920.—On 12th August, as a result of a captured document, the arrest was effected at Cork on 12 important I.R.A. officials, including Terence McSwiney, Lord Mayor of Cork and Commandant of the 1st Cork Brigade, I.R.A. The building in which their meeting took place was surrounded and entered, and many seditious documents were found in McSwiney's possession, including an order to start a bomb factory, and the key of the police cipher.[ss] McSwiney was also the confirming authority in a "sentence" of death by virtue of which two members[tt] of the R.I.C. had been murdered.[tt]

ss   Possibly supplied by Siobhan Lankford (née Creedon), who worked for MacSwiney.[39]

tt   These were Sgt Denis Garvey (b.1873) and Const. Daniel Harrington (b.1876) on 11 May 1920; Garvey was 'prominent' at MacCurtain's inquest, and was deliberately targeted.[40]

These 12 rebels[uu] went on hunger-strike as soon as they were arrested. McSwiney was tried and convicted on 16th August. During his trial he threatened that all officers who took part in the trial would be arrested by the rebel forces. He was transferred to England on 17th August and continued his hunger-strike in Brixton Prison. His case became a *"cause célèbre."* For weeks he lingered on, far beyond the period that was believed possible. The majority of the English papers and a large and hysterical portion of the British public, forgetting the fate of the victims of his crimes, took up his case, wrote and spoke of him as a hero and a martyr, and clamoured for his release. Crowds organized by the Irish Self-Determination League in London assembled outside the prison and recited the Rosary. The Government, however, remained firm and refused to give way from the position they had taken up. Long before the end came McSwiney was said to be at his last gasp, but rallied repeatedly. Rumours were rife that he was being surreptitiously fed by his visitors, but whether this was a fact has never been discovered.[vv] At any rate, he reduced himself to such a state that at last, on 25th October, after a fast of 75 days, he died. A tense situation had existed in Cork and Dublin for some time and rumours had spread of the awful reprisals which would follow his death. Nothing serious, however, happened. It is significant that amongst the papers found when the office of the "Chief of Staff," I.R.A.[ww] was raided in Dublin, was a letter from Miss Mary McSwiney[xx] requesting that her brother might be permitted to give up his strike.[41] The firmness of the Government proved the death knell of hunger-striking. No prisoner ever seriously attempted this again and so a very difficult complication was removed from the situation.

[uu] Of the men who went on the hunger strike, Michael Fitzgerald (d.17 October, 1920) and Joseph Murphy (b.1895–d.25 October, 1920) also died. O'Farrell lists the following men as participating in that hunger strike: Michael Burke, John Crowley, Peter Crowley, Thomas Donovan, Sean Hennessy, Joseph Kelly, Joe Kenny, Con Neenan, Michael O'Reilly, John Power and Christopher Upton. Of these men, Sean Hennessy left a BMH Witness Statement (WS 1090).

[vv] The British were giving the hunger strikers albumin in their water from the beginning of their strike, but this was leaked by the RAMC physician at the Cork gaol in late August 1920. No evidence has come to light to show that MacSwiney received any sustenance during his hunger strike. The rumours that he did, however, have existed at least since the time of his death.[42]

ww   Richard Mulcahy (b.1886–d.1971); the raid occurred on Friday, 19 November, 1920.

xx   Mary MacSwiney (b.1872–d.1942).

Coal strike in Great Britain, August, 1920.—In August the industrial situation in England, owing to the strike of coalminers, was so critical that orders were received to hold 10 battalions in Ireland in readiness to proceed to England at a few days notice.[43] Ten battalions were detailed, four of them from the 1st Division, three from the 6th Division, two from Dublin District and one from the 5th Division. Had it been necessary to despatch these battalions the situation in Ireland might have been seriously affected. The rebels would probably have taken advantage of the decrease in troops in the country to carry out more extensive outrages.[yy] The plan which it had been intended to follow had the battalions been withdrawn, was to abandon certain distant areas rather than to create dangerously weak detachments in order to continue to occupy them. For 3 months these 10 battalions continued to be held on short notice to move and the loss of their activities for this period, though unavoidable, was a serious waste of valuable time.

yy   There is no indication that the IRA was aware that anything out of the ordinary was planned. It is, however, most probable that they would have exploited any decrease in British troop strength in Ireland wherever possible.

November, 1920.—Finally on 5th November, the coal strike broke down, and the battalions reverted to their normal duties.

Restoration of Order in Ireland Act, 13th August, 1920.[zz]—There had been a growing feeling during June and July amongst whose duty brought them into collision with the rebels that their efforts were neutralized by the failure to bring to justice large numbers of murderers, whose capture had involved risk to life and limb. But for some time an Act of Parliament had been in preparation with a view to giving the competent military authority larger legal powers for dealing with the situation. Early in August, 1920, the Act was passed, and on 13th August it came into operation. This Act was known as the "Restoration of Order in Ireland Act," and regulations were made as sanctioned by the Act.

zz   See Additional Appendices.

Notes to Chapter II

Some Typical Methods of the Rebels during the Months
May to July, 1920.

Intimidation.—On 2nd May, at Graiguenamanagh (Co. Kilkenny), 3 tons of hay belonging to a prominent anti-Sinn Feiner were maliciously burnt.

On 7th May, a horse belonging to a man who supplied the police with milk, was shot dead at Newceston (Co. Cork).[a3]

[a3] See Extra Appendix for IRA instruction on killing animals.

On 10th May, at Newport (Co. Tipperary) a shopkeeper and his daughter each received a letter signed "Officer I.R.A. Commanding the District," threatening them with bodily harm, if the daughter continued to talk to policemen's wives.[b3]

[b3] This appears to be typical of an RIC boycott action against a more prominent family, and one that could not be attacked without giving due warning.

On 10th May, at Broadford (Co. Limerick), an armed gang of 80—100 men entered the shop of a tailor who made police uniforms. Having assaulted the tailor and his son, the gang made off with 400*l*. The same gang having then proceeded to the house of a R.I.C. pensioner, having pulled his 16-year old son out of bed and into the street, stripped him naked and compelled him to swear never to speak to a policeman again.

On 11th May, near Causeway (Co. Kerry), the Resident Magistrate whilst driving to Petty Sessions was held up and fired at by a party of armed men, who, however, ran away when the Resident Magistrate fired one shot from his revolver.

On 21st May, at Timoleague (Co. Cork), threatening notices were received by the members of the coroner's jury which returned a verdict of wilful murder at the inquest on a R.I.C. serjeant.[c3]

[c3] This was probably an inquest on RIC Sgt John Flynn, who was killed on 10 May, 1920 near Trimoleague along with Constables William Brick and Edward Dunne. The attack was conducted by the Bandon Battalion under Charlie Hurley, then Battalion Vice OC. Constable Arthur Grimsdell was also wounded in the attack.

On 2nd June, at Thomastown (Co. Kilkenny), the landlord of a house received a letter threatening his life for letting his house to a District Inspector, R.I.C.

On 6th June, at Midleton (Co. Cork), the club premises of the Comrades of the Great War[d3] was maliciously destroyed by fire.

[d3] Comrades of the Great War was a conservative veterans' organization founded in 1917; it later joined several other groups to form the British Legion.[44]

On 16th June, at Castletownroche (Co. Cork), two R.A.F. officers were held up by 15 armed rebels who burnt their motor cycle and side car, and cut the hair of the heads of two ladies in the house where the officers had been visiting.

On 1st July, at Tralee (Co. Kerry), 15 armed rebels dragged a girl of 17 out of her house, cut off her hair and tarred her head, because two of her brothers were in the R.I.C.

On 3rd July, at Clonakilty (Co. Cork), the house of a lady was entered by armed rebels, who dragged her daughter, aged 19, from the house, and held a pistol to her head while they cut off her hair. The girl is the daughter of a soldier and two of her brothers served in the late war.

On 9th July, the son of a Justice of the Peace at Cragganock (Co. Clare), was kidnapped by armed rebels. The J.P. received a notice that his son would be released when the J.P. resigned his commission.[e3] This was done.

[e3] This was Christopher P. Kelly, J.P., and his nineteen-year-old son Patrick J. Kelly.[45]

On 11th July, at Ballyshannon (Co. Donegal), two men who were to have appeared as witnesses for the Crown in the Assizes, were kidnapped and taken to an unknown destination.

On 14th July, at Newpallas (Co. Limerick), the house of an ex-soldier whose wife was employed as a barrack servant, was raided and searched by 100 men.[f3]

[f3] This is an example of the typical exaggeration in these reports. One can hardly picture a hundred men raiding one house.

On 16th July, at Arklow (Co. Wicklow), bombs were placed in two shops which supplied troops.

The following attacks were made on R.I.C. barracks:—

On 8th May, at Cloyne (Co. Cork), by 230 rebels armed with rifles, shot guns, and bombs. The police defended gallantly, but owing to the building catching fire were ultimately forced to surrender.[g3]

[g3] The 4th Bn. East Cork, under Commandant Michael Leahy, attacked the three-storey structure on the town's main street at about 23.00 hours. The RIC fired a Verey light, usually a signal for help, but none appears to have been despatched. After about two hours of sporadic firing, the Volunteers breached the walls on the second floors of the two houses on either side of the barracks, poured in petrol and ignited it, whereupon the RIC surrendered and were released after being disarmed.[46]

On 10th May, at Newtownhamilton (Co. Armagh), by about 300 armed rebels. After 4 hours' fighting, the building was set on fire, but the police refused to surrender.

On 11th May, at Shevry (Co. Tipperary), an attack on the R.I.C. barracks was contemplated by a large body of rebels, who, however, ran away when the police threw a few bombs.

On 12th May, at Hollyford (Co. Tipperary), by a large body of rebels armed with rifles and bombs. The building was set on fire but the police eventually drove off the attackers.[h3]

[h3] This occurred on the night of 10/11 May. The attack was commanded by Tadgh Dwyer, OC 2nd IRA Bn, South Tipperary Bde. Among those present were Dan Breen, Ernie O'Malley, Seamus Robinson and Seán Treacy.[47]

On 30th May, at Ferns (Co. Wexford), an attack on the R.I.C. barracks was frustrated by the arrival of a party of troops, at whose approach the rebels fled in all directions.

On 1st June, at Geashill (King's County), the rebels withdrew after 3–4 hours, as they were unable to face the police fire.[i3]

[i3] The RIC vacated the barracks a few weeks later, whereupon it was burnt by the IRA.[48]

On 2nd June, at Feakle (Co. Clare), attack lasted for 2½ hours, when the rebels were driven off.[49]

On 4th June, at Cappawhite (Co. Tipperary). After more than 2 hours' fighting the rebels were repulsed. Heavy casualties were reported to have been inflicted on the rebels.[j3]

> [j3] There is only a brief account in the RIC reports. There were no casualties reported in *The Last Post*.[50]

On 9th June, at Carrigadrohid (Co. Cork). The attack lasted 5 hours, and a portion of the barracks was wrecked, but the police drove off the rebels.[51]

On 17th June, at Cookstown (Co. Tyrone). The rebels effected an entrance, surprised the guard, and disarmed the constables. The head constable with remaining police drove out the rebels and released the guard.[52]

On 18th June, at Brosna (Co. Kerry). The attack lasted 2 hours, and roads were blocked for a radius of 15 miles. The police drove off the rebels.[k3]

> [k3] There was no mention of this incident in *Kerry's Fighting Story*, but they did recount the attack on the Brosna RIC Barracks of 5 June, 1920, in which they blocked the roads, but claimed that they withdrew due to the arrival of a superior military relief.[53]

On 2nd July, at Brookeen (Co. Galway), the R.I.C. barracks was set on fire, but the police, who held out for 3 hours, drove off the attackers.[54]

On 11th July, at Rathmore (Co. Kerry), a large body of rebels was forced to withdraw after 3 hours' fighting.[l3]

> [l3] This action was a feint in support of a larger operation; the main effort was called off at the last minute, but this attack and a similar one at Broadford went ahead because the cancellation orders did not arrive in time.[55]

On 11th July, at Rearcross (Co. Tipperary), a large body of rebels set the R.I.C. barracks on fire. The police were forced to evacuate the building, after having forced the rebels to retire.[56]

The following attacks on troops were made:—

On 6th June, at Midleton (Co. Cork), a cyclist patrol, 11 strong, were attacked and disarmed by a large party of rebels, who pretended to be playing a game by the roadside and thus effected a surprise. The troops had only just arrived in the country.[57]

On 4th July, at Midleton (Co. Cork), a party of rebels attempted to attack the military billet. The troops opened fire with a Lewis gun, whereupon all the rebels ran away.[m3]

[m3] Abbott says that this occurred on 11 July. Const. Alexander Will (b.1896) was killed in the fighting; he was the first 'Black and Tan' to die.[58]

On 22nd July, at Ennistymon (Co. Clare), two military officers were attacked by 15 rebels, who attempted to deprive them of their revolvers. After a severe struggle the officers dispersed the mob, killing one of their assailants and wounding several others.[lix]

[n3] The day before, the Volunteers captured a group of seven soldiers and took their weapons. On this day, only three men tried to hold up the two officers, who were not going to give up without a fight. One of the officers fired, killing Volunteer Michael Conway and wounding Volunteer Seámus McMahon.[59]

On 19th July, in Dublin City, a large party of rebels overpowered and disarmed a military guard and set fire to some military stores loaded in trucks at the G.S. and W. goods station. The rebels were disguised as railway workmen and thus effected surprise. The Dublin Fire Brigade arrived and though they prevented the fire from spreading they refused to save the military stores.[o3]

[o3] The operation, by D Coy, 1st Bn., 1st Dublin IRA Bde, occurred at 10.30 a.m. The rebels claimed to have taken nine rifles, 1,000 rounds of .303 rifle ammunition and one revolver.[60]

On 20th July, at Ballyvourney (Co. Cork), a military lorry patrol was ambushed by rebels. An officer was fatally wounded[p3], two soldiers were also wounded.

[p3] They were: Capt. James Airey, Sgt. Nicholson, Ptes McEwen and Barlow of the 1st Manchesters and Driver Ball, RASC; Barlow died of wounds later.[61]

On 21st July, at Mitchelstown (Co. Cork), a military lorry patrol was fired on by rebels. The troops returned the fire, killing two of their assailants.[q3]

q3   The account of this in *Rebel Cork's Fighting Story* (2009) states that the troops fired on a group of young men and women without warning, killing two: McGrath and McDonnell.[62]

On 23rd July, in Cork City, a military patrol was fired on by rebels. The troops returned the fire, wounding one civilian and arresting 13 others.[r3]

r3   This occurred on the evening of the 18th.[63]

On 25th July, in Cork City, a mixed party of troops and police were fired on. The fire was returned, one rebel being killed and two wounded.

On 25th July, at Bandon (Co. Cork), a corporal[s3] was shot dead by a rebel.

s3   This was L/Cpl Maddox, Essex Regiment, who was killed on 27 July, 1920 at Bandon, Co. Cork.[64]

On 28th July, at Ballingeary (Co. Cork), two military lorries, which broke down, were attacked by rebels, who burnt the lorries and disarmed the escort. Five rebels were arrested.[t3]

t3   The I-G Monthly report does not contain this incident, primarily because of the multiple killings it recounts, including DC Smyth.

On 29th July, in Dublin City, a party of 11 military foot police, including five unarmed, were attacked by a large number of rebels armed with revolvers. The serjeant in command of the police wounded several assailants before being himself wounded. Two rebels on searching one of the police and finding him unarmed deliberately fired at him, hitting him in the chest.

On 29th July, at Bruree (Co. Limerick), a mixed patrol of eight soldiers and police was ambushed, one soldier being killed.[u3] Reinforcements dispersed the rebels, killing two of them.

u3   Interestingly enough, the account of what appears to be this incident in *Limerick's Fighting Story* states that it occurred on 4 August, and that the Limerick Flying Column killed a Pte. W. Rogers. Strangely, the British have no record of a soldier named Rogers killed in Ireland in all of 1920, and no record of any soldier dying in Limerick in July or August 1920.[65]

On 30th July, at Oola (Co. Limerick), a military mail lorry was ambushed by rebels, who threw a bomb into the lorry, wounding four men.[v3] The serjeant in command dispersed the rebels by fire from a Lewis gun.

[v3] This was the military lorry that Brig-Gen Lucas encountered on the morning after his escape from the rebels. Meanwhile, Seán Treacy had already decided to ambush the regular lorry, and Lucas was in it when the ambush commenced. Killed in the attack were Pte Daniel Verey Bayliss (b.ca.1902) and L/Cpl G. B. Parker, 1st Bn. Ox and Bucks.[66]

In addition to the above numerous vacated police barracks and a considerable number of Inland Revenue offices were burnt during this period. Raids for explosives were also made on Coastguard stations.

NOTES

1 M. Kotsonouris, 'The Dáil Courts in Limerick', *The Old Limerick Journal* (Winter, 1992), pp. 37–40; M. Kotsonouris, *Retreat from Revolution: The Dáil Courts*, pp. 17–27.

2 The Record of the Rebellion, Vol. II, 'Intelligence', p. 9 and Hart, *The Final Reports*, pp. 21–2.

3 For more, see C. McCarthy, *Cumann Na mBan and the Irish Revolution* (2006); for wider studies, see A. Matthews, *Renegades: Irish Republican Women 1900–1922* (2011); M. Ward, *Unmanageable Revolutionaries: Women and Irish Nationalism* (1995) and *In Their Own Voice: Women and Irish Nationalism* (2001); K. Steele, *Women, Press, and Politics During the Irish Revival* (2007); and S. McCoole, *No Ordinary Women: Irish Female Activists in the Revolutionary Years 1900–1923* (2003) and *Guns and Chiffon* (1997).

4 Vol. I, No. 1, 15 August, 1918, p. 1.

5 Sturgis Diaries, 22 August and 24 August, NAUK, PRO 30/59/1, pp. 47–9.

6 See 'Outrages against Police', NAUK CO 904/148–50 in general.

7 See *An t-Óglác*, vol. II, No. 5, 15 January, 1920, p. 61 and vol. II, No. 6, 1 March, 1920, p. 69 'Minor Activities', vol. III. No. 2, April 1, 1921, pp. 152–3; 'Opportunities for Sniping' vol. III, No. 10, 27 May, 1921, p. 3; and 'Cutting Off Stragglers', vol. III, No. 13, 17 June, 1921, p. 4.

8 See Eve Morrison, 'Kilmichael Revisited: Tom Barry and the "False Surrender"', *Terror in Ireland* (2012), pp. 158–80 and Borgonovo, 'Revolutionary violence and Irish historiography', *Irish Historical Studies*, vol. xxxviii, No. 150, pp. 325–31.

9 M. Ward, *Unmanageable Revolutionaries: Women and Irish Nationalism* (1995), p. 143 and L. Ryan, ' "In the line of fire": representations of women and war (1919–1923) through the writings of republican men', L. Ryan and M. Ward, eds. *Irish Women and Nationalism: Soldiers, New Women and Hags* (2004), p. 48 and Ryan, Louise, '"Drunken Tans": Representations of Sex and Violence in the Anglo-Irish War (1919–21)', *Feminist Review* Nº. 66 (Autumn 2000), pp. 73–94. See also, S. McCoole, *No Ordinary Women: Irish Female Activists in the Revolutionary Years 1900–1923* (2003); C. Woodcock, *Experiences of an Officer's Wife in*

Ireland (1994)—(originally published in *Blackwood's Magazine*, No. MCCLXVII. Vol. CCIX, May 1921, pp. 553–98); and L. Ryan, and M. Ward, eds. *Irish Women and Nationalism: Soldiers, New Women and Hags* (2004).

10 For instances listed in Witness Statements, see Statements of George F. H. Berkeley, (WS/821 p. 123) describing an accusation of rape by British forces; Seamus Fitzgerald (WS/1737 p. 30) describing evidence of rape by Black and Tans; Frank Henderson (WS/821 p. 65–7) describing a civil trial conducted by the Dublin Brigade of a man accused of rape; and James Maloney (WS/1525 p. 22) describing republican women fearing rape by British troops. In none of these instances was any evidence provided. For more on crimes against women during the conflict, see A. Matthews, Renegades: *Irish Republican Women 1900–1922*.

11 See 'General Notes', vol. II. N°. 5A, February 1920, p. 68; 'General Notes', vol. II. N°. 6, 1 March, 1920, p. 71; 'We Must Not Fail', vol. II. N°. 7, 15 March, 1920, p. 73; 'Our Work', vol. II. N°. 9, 15 April, 1920, p. 81; and 'General Notes', Vol. II. N°. 11, 15 May, 1920, p. 92.

12 Hopkinson, *Irish War of Independence*, p 201; Abbott, *Police Casualties*, pp 298–310; *Last Post*, pp 98–130.

13 For republican accounts of this incident, see G. Power, 'The Capture of General Lucas', pp. 82–7 in *Rebel Cork's Fighting Story* (2009) and 'Volunteer', 'The IRA Campaign in West Limerick—Captivity of General Lucas', *Limerick's Fighting Story* (2009), pp. 267–9.

14 See RIC I-G Report for Cork ER & City for June 1920 NAUK CO 904/112/19–20; F. O'Donoghue, *No Other Law* (1954), pp. 75–87; G. Power, 'The Capture of General Lucas', in *Rebel Cork's Fighting Story* (Anvil Press edition), pp. 73–7. For the British view of this incident, see the file 'Whether Officers in Ireland are on Active Service', NAUK WO 32/4309. See also, Townshend, *British Campaign*, pp. 88 & 96.

15 'Composition of Headquarters of the Forces in Ireland', March 1920, p. 11, NAUK WO 35/215 and *The London Gazette*, 29 April, 1930, N°. 33601, p. 2647.

16 See *The London Gazette*, 20 September, 1921, N°. 32464, p. 7445; 30 September, 1927, N°. 33316, p. 6192; 21 November, 1930, N°. 33663, p. 7416; 16 November, 1937, N°. 34455, p. 7185.

17 Kenneally, *The Paper Wall*, pp. 85–7.

18 For republican accounts of this incident, see Fr. J. A. Gaughan, *Memoirs of Constable Jeremiah Mee, RIC* (2012); The American Commission on Conditions in Ireland, *Interim Report* (1921), pp. 68–71; Abbott, R. *Police Casualties*, p. 97; 'Lee-Sider', 'Caused Mutiny in Listowel, Shot in Cork', *Rebel Cork's Fighting Story*, P. Hart, ed. (2010), pp. 126–30 & 'Lee-Sider', 'Caused Mutiny in Listowel Shot in Cork', *Kerry's Fighting Story 1916–21: Told by the Men Who Made It* (2010), pp. 220–27; C. Casey, 'Shooting of Divisional Commissioner Smyth', *Rebel Cork's Fighting Story* (Anvil Press edition), pp. 77–80; T. Ryle Dwyer, *Tans, Terror and Troubles*, pp. 209–14; A. Ryan, *Comrades: Inside the War of Independence* (2008), pp. 104–08; and I. Kenneally, *The Paper Wall*, pp. 85–7.

19 See U. MacEoin, *Survivors: the story of Ireland's struggle*, (1987), p. 255.

20 J. Murland, *Departed Warriors: The Story of a Family in War* (2008), pp. 191–211 and *London Gazette*, 19 January, 1917, Issue 29910, p. 812; 17 May 1918, Issue 30692, p. 5968; 5 July, 1918, Issue 30782, p. 8018; 12 November, 1918, Issue 31009, p. 13410; and 9 November, 1920, Issue 32119, p. 10917. See also Street, *Administration of Ireland*, pp. 81–3.

21 See Statement of Jeremiah Mee (MA WS/379); Mee Contemporary Documents (MA CD 117); *Freeman's Journal,* 10 September, 1920.

22 See Herlihy *RIC Officers*, pp. 107–8.

23 See C. Townshend, 'The Irish Railway Strike of 1920,' *Irish Historical Studies*, Vol. XXI, N°. 81 (March 1978), pp. 265–82; E. O'Connor, *A Labour History of Ireland* (1992); Street, *Administration of Ireland, 1920*, pp. 40–42; J. McKenna, *Guerrilla Warfare in the Irish War of Independence, 1919–1921*, pp. 70–72; E. MacLysaght, 'Larkin, Connolly, and the Labour Movement', *Leaders and Men of the Easter Rising: Dublin 1916*, F. X. Martin, ed. (1967), p.

132; P. Yeates, 'Irish craft workers in a time of revolution 1919–1922', pp. 37–56 *Saothar 33*, 2008, pp. 37–54 and K. Jeffery and P. Hennessy, *States of Emergency: British Governments and Strikebreaking Since 1919* (1983).

24 'Munitions Strike', Papers on Munitions Strike (NLI MS 17134) and Statement of Captain T. J. Fyans, Infantry Officer's Course, Collins Papers (MA A/0800/XI).

25 See Cuman na mBan directive 'Munitions of War Fund', n.d. [summer 1920] (NLI MS 8786). Townshend. 'The Irish Railway Strike of 1920' and Street, *Administration of Ireland*, pp. 87–97.

26 Macready Memorandum of 26 July, 1920 NAUK CAB 24/110 C.P. 1750. For greater discussion of the effect of the strike on British military transport, see Kautt, *Ambushes & Armour*, pp. 57–62.

27 See 'Extracts of War Committee Meeting 49A', (Appendix), 25 August, 1920, NAUK CAB 23/21/23. There is one book by a magistrate during the war, C. P. Crane, *Memories of a Resident Magistrate 1880–1920* (1938).

28 See L. O'Broin, *W. E. Wylie and the Irish Revolution 1916–1921* (1989), p. 46; F. Campbell, *Land and Revolution: Nationalist Politics in the West of Ireland 1891–1921* (2008), pp. 248–57 & 272–81; F. Costello, 'The Republican Courts and the Decline of British Rule in Ireland, 1920–1921', *Éire-Ireland* (Samradh/Summer 1990), pp. 36–55; Nicholas Mansergh, *The Irish Free State: Its Government and Politics* (1934), pp. 292–327; M. Kotsonouris, 'The Dáil Courts in Limerick', *The Old Limerick Journal* (Winter, 1992), pp. 37–40; M. Kotsonouris, *Retreat from Revolution: The Dáil Courts*, pp. 17–27.

29 Statement of Cmdt Liam Haugh (MA WS/474, pp. 9–11). See 'Official letters re the submission of a case to the Sinn Fein courts, by George O'Grady, J.P.', from August 1919 to April 1920 (NLI MS 7326).

30 For examples, see Statement of Conor A. Maguire (MA WS/708, pp. 5–7); Statement of Patrick Moylett (WS/767); Statement of Kevin R. O'Sheil (WS/1770); Statement of John Shouldice (WS/679, p. 22) and Statement of Cahir Davit (WS/993).

31 See IRA General Order Nº. 9 'Police' (New Series), 19 June, 1920 (NLI Ms 900); Statement of Cahir Davit (WS/993, generally); Statement of Sgt Bryan Doherty (WS/1292, p. 14); Statement of Simon Donnelly (WS/481); Statement of Laurence Flynn (WS/1061, p. 9); Statement of Garda John Grant (WS/658, generally); Statement of Michael Healy (WS/1064, p. 17); Statement of Samuel Kingston (WS/620, p. 4); Statement of John McCoy (WS/492, pp. 111–14); Statement of James McGuill (WS/353, p. 63); Statement of Gilbert Morrissey (WS/874, p. 7);Charles J. O'Grady (WS/282, p. 8); Statement of Patrick Ormond (WS/1283); Statement of Seán Prendergast (WS/755 pt II, generally); Statement of Oscar Traynor (WS/340, p. 45); Statement of John Walsh (WS/966, generally); SIC 'Weekly Survey of the State of Ireland', 4 July, 1920 and 19 July, 1920, NAUK CAB 27/108; Jones, *Whitehall Diary*, July 1920, p. 24.

32 See 'Memorandum on the Present Military Situation', and 'General Proposals in Ireland to Troops During the Coming Winter', 26 July, 1920, p. 2; J. C. C. Davidson to E. H. Marsh (posing Bonar Law questions), 15 October, 1920, NAUK WO 32/9540; Lt-Col Braine to Secretary of State (in answer to Bonar Law questions), 18 October, 1920, WO 32/9539 Report from Macready, 8 January, 1921, CAB 24/118 CP 2456.

33 See 'Memorandum on the Present Military Situation, and General Proposals in Ireland to Troops During the Coming Winter', 26 July, 1920, p. 3–5 and Creedy to Macready, 9 August, 1920, NAUK WO 32/9520.

34 See 'Supply of Motor Transport', NAUK WO 32/9539 and 'Increase in Mechanical Transport in Ireland', WO 32/9540. See also, Kautt, *Ambushes & Armour*, pp. 60–76 and G. Barndollar, 'British Military Use of Armoured Cars, 1919–1939', Ph.D. Thesis, Oxford, 2011.

35 For the rioting, see J. McDermott, '*Northern Divisions. The Old IRA and the Belfast Pogroms 1920–22*' (2001); R. Gallagher, *Violence and Nationalist Politics in Derry City, 1920–1923* (2003); for a polemical treatment, see G. B. Kenna (Fr John Hassan). *Facts and Figures of the Belfast Pogrom, 1920–1922* (1922).

36 R. Lynch, *The Northern IRA and the Early Years of Partition, 1920–1922* (2006), pp. 25–31 and Murland, *Departed Warriors*, pp. 210–11. Lynch cites multiple BMH Witness Statements so there is no need to do so here. For northern nationalists, see P. Bew, *Ideology and the Irish Question: Ulster Unionism and Irish Nationalism* (1998); E. Staunton, *The Nationalists of Northern Ireland 1918–1973* (2001); L. Ó Duibhir, *The Donegal Awakening: Donegal & the War of Independence* (2009); and M. Harris, *The Catholic Church and the Foundation of the Northern Ireland State* (1994). For more on the Ulster Special Constabulary, see M. Farrell, *Arming the Protestants – the formation of the USC and the RUC 1920–5* (1983); for a more polemic view, see P. Lawlor, *The Outrages 1920–1922: The IRA and the Ulster Special Constabulary in the Border Campaign* (2011). For studies of other counties and regions, see CONNAUGHT: F. Campbell, *Land and Revolution: Nationalist Politics in the West of Ireland 1891–1921* (2008); M. Farry, *The Irish Revolution: 1912–23: Sligo* (2012); D. Price, *The Flame and the Candle: War in Mayo 1919–1924* (2012); M. O'Callaghan, *For Ireland and Freedom: Roscommon's Contribution in the Fight for Independence* (2012). MUNSTER: T. R. Dwyer, *Tans, Terror and Troubles: Kerry's Real Fighting Story, 1913–23* (2001); S. Joy, *The IRA in Kerry, 1916–1921* (2006); J. O'Callaghan, *Revolutionary Limerick: The Republican Campaign for Independence in Limerick, 1913–1921* (2010); P. Óg Ó Ruairc, *Blood on the Banner: The Republican Struggle in Clare* (2009).
37 See RIC I-G Monthly Reports for July and August 1920 NAUK CO 904/112/272–556.
38 See RIC I-G Monthly Reports for July and August 1920 NAUK CO 904/112/272–556.
39 See Lankford Pension Claim and Evidence from Sean Culhane in support of Pension Claim (dated 24 January, 1938), Siobhan Lankford Papers (Cork Archives Institute (CAI) U169A). For another instance of postal employees providing information, especially for ciphers, see Collins Papers (MA A/0362/27–8 and A/0394/7).
40 See Abbott, *Police Casualties*, p. 76.
41 A republican account of these events is found in C. Harrington, 'Arrest and Martyrdom of Terence MacSwiney', *Rebel Cork's Fighting Story* (2009), pp. 62–75. See also B. Flynn, *Irish Hunger Strikes 1912–1981: Pawns in the Game* (2011), pp. 39–69; D. Hannigan, *Terence MacSwiney: The Hunger Strike that Rocked an Empire* (2010); and F. J. Costello, *Enduring the Most: The Life and Death of Terence MacSwiney* (1995). In addition, see S. O'Mahony, *The First Hunger Striker: Thomas Ashe* (2001) and S. Mcconville, *Irish Political Prisoners 1848–1922: Theatres of War* (2003). P. O'Farrell, *Who's Who in the Irish War of Independence and Civil War, 1916–1923* (1997), p. 72.
42 See Sturgis Diaries, 26 August and 28 August, for the albumin, PRO 30/59/1, pp. 52–4; 5 October regarding MacSwiney getting food; 17 October for the death of FitzGerald, the first to die; 25 October for MacSwiney's death and 26 October for the death of the last; Street, *Administration of Ireland*, pp. 45–50; Murphy, PRO 30/59/2, pp. 30, 43, 48–50.
43 See K. Jeffery and P. Hennessy, *States of Emergency: British Government and Strikebreaking Since 1919* (1983), pp. 51–6 and Directorate of Intelligence (Home Office), 'Report on Revolutionary Organizations in the United Kingdom', 26 August 1920, CAB 24/111/55–6, pp. 2–3.
44 See RIC I-G Report for Cork for June 1920 NAUK CO 904/112/20.
45 See RIC I-G Report for Clare for July 1920 NAUK CO 904/112/19 & 285. The Kellys are listed in the 1911 Census transcriptions as 'Keely'.
46 See P. O'C 'The East Cork Brigade in Action—Capture of Cloyne Police Barracks', *Rebel Cork's Fighting Story* (2009), pp. 225–7.
47 See Abbott, *Police Casualties*, p. 91; Hopkinson, *The Irish War of Independence*, p. 120; D. Breen, *My Fight for Irish Freedom* (1964), pp. 107–110; and E. O'Malley, *Raids and Rallies* (1982), pp. 11–26.
48 See RIC I-G Report for King's Co for June 1920 NAUK CO 904/112/11.
49 See RIC I-G Report for Co Clare for June 1920 NAUK CO 904/112/19.
50 See RIC I-G Report for Tipperary, WR, for June 1920 NAUK CO 904/112/24 and Breen, *My Fight for Irish Freedom*, p. 116 and O'Malley, *Raids and Rallies*, p. 59.

51 See RIC I-G Report for Cork ER June 1920 NAUK CO 904/112/20.

52 Abbott, *Police Casualties*, pp. 137–8.

53 M. Harnett, *Victory and Woe* (2002), pp. 54–6; 'Volunteer', 'Attacks on Gortatlea, Scartaglin and Brosna Barracks', *Kerry's Fighting Story* (2009), pp. 215–6.

54 See RIC I-G Report for Galway ER for July 1920 NAUK CO 904/112/282.

55 See P. Óg Ó Ruairc, *Blood on the Banner: the Republican Struggle in Clare* (2009), pp. 136–8 and RIC I-G Report for Clare for June 1920 NAUK CO 904/112/19.

56 See Abbott, *Police Casualties*, pp. 92–4; Breen, *My Fight*, pp. 116–22; O'Malley, *Raids and Rallies*, pp. 41–65.

57 'P. O'C', The East Cork Brigade in Action—The Cameron Highlanders Attacked at Whiterock', *Rebel Cork's Fighting Story* (2009), pp. 227–8 and P. Cashman, 'A Clever Ruse Leads to Disarming of Highlanders near Midleton', *With the IRA*, pp. 117–24.

58 Abbott, *Police Casualties*, p. 91.

59 See Ó Ruairc, *Blood on the Banner*, p. 142; *The Last Post*, p. 101; and RIC I-G Report for Clare 1920 NAUK CO 904/112/285.

60 See Statement of Captain T. J. Fyans, Infantry Officer's Course, Collins Papers (MA A/0800/XI); 'Weekly Survey of the State of Ireland', SIC 28, 26 July 1920, NAUK CAB 27/108/13; Statement of Michael Burke, Mulcahy Papers (UCD AD PR/6/39); Statement of Patrick McCrea (MA WS/413) and Statement of James Slattery (MA WS/445).

61 See RIC I-G Report for Cork WR for July 1920 NAUK CO 904/112/286; see also 'History: 1919–1945', Museum of the Manchester Regiment (www.tameside.gov.uk/museumsgalleries/mom/history/1919-1945#1st [accessed 20 April 2010]). See also, T. Sheehan, *Lady Hostage (Mrs. Lindsay)* (1990), p. 70 and S. O'Callaghan, *Execution* (1974), p. 26–7.

62 See P.J. O'B, 'Campaigning in the Mitchelstown Area', pp. 259–60.

63 See RIC I-G Report for Cork ER 1920 NAUK CO 904/112/286.

64 See RIC I-G Report for Cork, WR for Jul 1920 NAUK CO 904/112/287.

65 See 'Volunteer', 'Ballinahinch and Bruree Ambushes', p. 175; Commonwealth War Graves Commission (http://www.cwgc.org) and The War Graves Photographic Project (http://twgpp.org).

66 See Breen, *My Fight*, pp. 123–6.

CHAPTER III

A New 'Campaign', September 1920

Good effect of R.O.I.R.—The additional powers granted by R.O.I.R. soon began to have effect. The number of convictions steadily increased, running into 50–60 per week. The result of this was that the number of men "on the run" grew week by week. The moral of the troops was greatly raised, and they began to show a good deal more cunning in dealing with attacks, in which the rebels suffered considerable casualties.[a] The recruiting of the R.I.C. also increased greatly, and during September there was a general feeling that things were improving.[b] Outrages grew less[c] and were mainly confined to raids on mail trains, which inconvenienced the civil population much more than the troops, as a mail service by destroyers, aeroplanes and motor-cars had been formed for official correspondence. The effect upon the rebel moral was just the reverse. It became known that many of the rank and file of the I.R.A. were anxious to give up their activities[d], and an indication of the state of moral of some of their units was provided by the following two instances which occurred near Dublin:—

[a] As the IRA was constantly growing, there were greater numbers of men to arrest. It is hardly surprising that soldiers' morale rose with the increase in arrests in September 1920; for soldiers, action was always preferable to inaction. With captures of men, there were also, now, tangible results. While there appears to be some increase in IRA KIAs beginning in September 1920, it is difficult to know if this is related to increased British forces' activity or not. This does correspond with an increase in IRA operations, especially combat operations, and a 50 per

cent increase in police casualties in September, 12 per cent increase in October and a 30 per cent increase in November. But this is hardly conclusive, as any increase in operations is likely to increase casualties. Yet casualties are not necessarily a good indicator, as there was a 40 per cent decrease in police casualties in December 1920, which then jumped 52 per cent the first month of 1921 and another 34 per cent the next.[1]

[b]   The statement about recruiting was most likely based on assumption, as it does not take into account demographics. The records of the various recruiting versus the resignations, retirements, expulsions and deaths in the regular RIC indicated otherwise: there was a steady decline in the number of Irishmen joining the force. At the same time, by the last week of September 1920, when 229 men joined, of that number, only seven were Irish. The numbers of 'foreigners' (non-Irishmen) joining the force brought the total strength to just over 10,000.[2]

[c]   Based on an examination of the RIC reports, there appears to have been a considerable decrease in IRA attacks on RIC Barracks after August 1920. From January 1920 to the end of August, there were some 77 IRA attacks on RIC Barracks. The IRA attacked Trim RIC barracks on 30 September 1920, the only one that month. Yet, as noted above, there were increases in RIC deaths.

[d]   There is little to support this statement, as is evident from the example given.

September, 1920.—On 19th September, 35 rebels, engaged in bombing practices, surrendered to a party of police after a single shot had been fired over their heads. On 21st September, 15 rebels mounted on bicycles surrendered to a small military patrol.

Increase of terrorism by I.R.A.—As frequently occurred, however, the leaders of the I.R.A., realizing that lawlessness was declining, and fearing to lose their grip and power of terrorism, urged on their supporters to fresh outages, and, towards the end of September, several serious outrages were committed, amongst which were the following:—

On 22nd September, at Milltown-Malbay, five R.I.C. were ambushed and were murdered as they lay wounded on the road. A patrol of troops which arrived on the scene was also attacked, but, on the arrival of more troops, the rebels ran away.[e]

^e This was the Rineen Ambush in Co. Clare. The victims were: Sgt. Michael J. Hynes (b.1891), Constables Reginald Hardman (b.1899), Michael Harte (b.1892), John Hodnett (b.1889), Michael Kelly (b.1884) and John McGuire (b.ca.1900). The accusation of shooting wounded men is supportable in that Const. Harte and Sgt Hynes were shot after being wounded. Harte was wounded by the opening attack of two grenades. He dismounted when the lorry halted, and he tried to crawl to safety towards the strand to the west. Volunteers Tom and Donal Lehane found him and shot the unarmed man. Hynes, also wounded in the opening attack, ran to the east towards the Volunteers' positions and was gunned down. Hynes was armed, and thus was still a threat when he was shot. He died of wounds on 24 September after he was found by British forces lying in the road. The 53 men of the rebel force, under command of their 4th Bn, Mid-Clare Bde, commandant Ignatius O'Neill, conducted a proper and orderly withdrawal on the arrival of considerably larger army and police forces.[3]

On 24th September, an attempt was made to murder General Strickland[e] in his motor-car in Cork. He returned the fire, and one rebel is believed to have been shot. He escaped injury, though several bullets pierced the car. A rebel report of this incident was afterwards captured, from which it transpired that the rebels had carefully planned the outrage and been waiting their opportunity for a long time. With this report was also captured a letter from the Chief of Staff, I.R.A.[f], expressing his sympathy with the would-be murderers for their failure.

^e Maj-Gen Sir E. (Edward) Peter Strickland, (b.1869–d.1951), GOC, 6th Division.[4] The republican sources state that there were two attempts on Strickland on 20 September rather than the 24th. In the second of these, at Killacloyne Bridge, Co. Cork, Strickland mortally wounded Vol. Seán Deasy, who died later that day.[5]

^f Richard Mulcahy.

Beginning of retaliation.—With the renewal of outrages on a larger scale, there arose again the difficulty of dealing swiftly and drastically with the perpetrators, or with known leaders who organized them. Even with the additional powers granted by R.O.I.R., it was extremely difficult, owing to intimidation, to obtain any evidence against the actual perpetrators of outrages. The results of this was that although a considerable number of rebels in whose houses arms or seditious literature were found during the searches had been sentenced to long terms of penal servitude men who had committed murder and arson went free, and many prominent rebels in various areas lived unmolested in their houses.

This was a situation which was beyond the power of comprehension of the junior officers and men, both of the Army and of the police force, who, having borne the brunt of the outrages with great patience for a long time, began to show a tendency to take the law into their own hands.[g] Several cases of retaliation had occurred amongst the R.I.C., and, although the Army was practically free from this taint, there had been two or three cases amongst the troops. After the kidnapping of General Lucas some troops had wrecked some shops in Fermoy; at Queenstown, as a result of a rebel attack on some unarmed soldiers dismantling a hut, some soldiers had broken out of barracks and done damage in the town; and at Mallow, after the cavalry barracks had been attacked in the absence of most of the garrison and a serjeant had been murdered, retaliation took place.[h] These lapses of discipline did not spread, and in each case the troops were quickly got back into barracks, but the attack on General Strickland brought prominently into view the difficult situation which might have arisen in Cork had the attack been successful, and no arrest or conviction resulted. General Strickland's immediate action in ordering the arrest of 12 prominent Sinn Feiners in the City of Cork probably saved an outbreak on the part of the troops.

[g] The first reprisal to which the Government admitted was Tuam in July 1920.[6]

[h] Rebels under Liam Lynch (b.1893–d.1923) and Ernie O'Malley attacked the 17th Lancers, killing Sjt W. G. Gibbs on 28 September, 1920. Soldiers burnt several buildings in Mallow in reprisal; Hopkinson noted that it was the local ADRIC company that stopped the soldiers from doing worse.[7]

Commander-in-Chief's memorandum, 27th September, 1920.— On 27th September the Commander-in-Chief wrote a strongly worded memorandum to the Chief Secretary on the subject. In this it was pointed out that the inadequate measures adopted by the Government for dealing with the rebels was likely to put a strain upon young soldiers which might lead them to break the bonds of discipline. As to the R.I.C., it was admitted that they had been far more highly tried than the troops, nearly 100[i] of their comrades having been murdered, and the murderer having paid the penalty in no single case. Although retaliation could not be tolerated, the fact remained that the effect on the rebels was most marked, and that, for the most part, the sufferers from retaliation were instigators or abettors, if not the perpetrators, of the outrages. In view of this it was strongly urged that, in order to do away with the cause for retaliation, some drastic measure for dealing with crime should be introduced by the Government. Two alternative courses were suggested—

(a) The declaration of Martial Law throughout the country, and its application in areas as and where thought necessary by the authority administering it.

    One great advantage claimed for this was that the troops and the police would be under one controlling authority.

(b) The Government to acknowledge publicly that a state of insurrection exists in Ireland, that organized rebel forces were in active opposition to the Government, and that peace could not be restored without military measures such as would be taken under Martial Law.

> [i] A total of 156 RIC had been killed since Soloheadbeg in 1919; 105 in 1920.

The effect which it was claimed would result from this course was that the public would be warned of the Government's intention to take into custody, in those areas where outrages were committed, or where there was good reason to apprehend outrage, such persons as were reasonably suspected of belonging to rebel organizations, and intern them under conditions similar to those of prisoners of war, until such time as the conditions of the country admitted of their release. Arrested persons against whom charges could be substantiated would be brought before courts martial, the remainder would be treated as prisoners of war. Those who disclaimed any connection with the I.R.A. and kindred associations would be called upon to sign a declaration to that effect, and to find two sureties for their good behaviour. They would then be released. It was further claimed that this procedure would not be open to defeat by a hunger-strike, as was the case when a somewhat similar method was adopted in March, 1920, because every arrested person would be either tried as a member of an illegal body, or released on signing a declaration to the contrary. This assumed that a convicted prisoner would not be released on account of hunger-striking.

To this memorandum was attached the outline of the action it was proposed to take in the event of the second alternative being sanctioned. The first essential was to seize the initiative which, except for a brief period between the January, 1920, policy and the release of the Mountjoy hunger-strikers, had hitherto been with the rebels. Objectives for attack were selected, and these, in the first stage, were to be the I.R.A. organizations in important towns, in which every member of the I.R.A. was to be arrested and dealt with in accordance with the foregoing letter. The second stage was to be clearing of areas bordering on the main lines of essential railway communications.[i] Thirdly, to concentrate against active hostile organizations in country districts, and, finally, to deal with any remaining troublesome towns and districts.[j]

[i] This was inherently part of the Munition Strike since, by this point, it made railway traffic virtually impossible for British forces throughout most of Ireland except parts of Ulster.

[j] The problem with these recommendations was that the first forced the Government to admit that it was not wholly in control of the political situation in Ireland. This, effectively, would be an admission of defeat and was unacceptable to the Government. The second suggestion was unworkable because common law did not recognize a state of insurrection, thus the Government could not act in this manner. This was the reason for raising the Ulster Special Constabulary, the Black and Tans and the ADRIC. At its base was the legal opinion that the 'Government doesn't make war on His Majesty's subjects'.

The scheme rather assumed that the rebel forces having been so far organized in battalions and brigades, would act as units, or at any rate remain in their districts. The infinite capacity of the officers and men of the I.R.A. for going on the run and staying there, was perhaps not fully foreseen at this time. It was not suggested now, or at any other time that any military action could finally pacify the country or solve the Irish problem. All that was claimed was, that given sufficient powers and numbers, the Crown forces could in course of time produce a situation in which a political solution might be offered with reasonable chance of acceptance.[k]

[k] Such an attitude demonstrated an advanced understanding of the nature of counter-insurgency operations. Indeed, this is a point that took the better part of the past century to work its way into counter-insurgency doctrine, training, and practice in most armies around the world. Despite this, the response from the army was not always measured, and proved surprisingly volatile.

Commander-in-Chief's memorandum, 17th October, 1920.[8]—No answer having been received to this memorandum, the Commander-in-Chief wrote, on 17th October, to the Chief of the Imperial General Staff[l], to whom a copy of the original memorandum had been sent. In this letter it was reiterated that the existing situation, where troops did their difficult and dangerous task cheerfully, but saw that outrages could be carried out with impunity, was straining the patience of the troops to such a point, that the bonds of discipline might be broken, and retaliation take place in a manner beyond anything that had happened heretofore. Retaliation, it was explained, although for the sake of discipline and the honour of the Army it must at all costs be suppressed, had, in the few cases where it had occurred, produced such a quelling effect upon the lawless, and such a corresponding peaceableness in the district concerned, that its sudden and drastic suppression, which was being enforced, would, in the absence of some compensating Government policy, lead to a more vigorous campaign of murder and outrage on the part of the rebels and renewed incitement to retaliation on the part of the Crown forces.

[l]   Field-Marshal Sir Henry Wilson (b.1864–d.1922).

[m]   At the same time, Macready said that 'a regiment that did not try to break out when a story – however untrue – was told them e.g. that one of their comrades had been chucked into the Liffey and shot at in the water, was not worth a damn…'. Street went out of his way to defend reprisals.[9]

It was also suggested that, should the Government not be prepared to declare Martial Law throughout Ireland, a policy of authorized punishments should be instituted on the following lines:—

Whenever a house or houses are burnt or destroyed by rebels, the house of a prominent member or officer of the I.R.A. in the immediate vicinity should be destroyed.

Where shots are fired or bombs thrown from houses, those houses should be destroyed.

Where, as was often the case, ambushes were laid for troops in the vicinity of houses, whose inhabitants must be well aware of the presence of the ambush, those houses should be destroyed.

Certain restrictions were laid down as to the authority who should have power to order such action.[n]

[n] Brigade commanders were eventually given authority to order reprisals.[10]

In the case of cold-blooded individual murders, it was advocated that half-a-dozen prominent members of the I.R.A. should be at once arrested and interned, being held at all costs until Ireland returned to a normal state of peace, and all arms were handed in.

Lastly, it was explained that orders were about to be given for the carrying of one or two prominent local members of the rebel organization in every lorry in districts where attacks were probable.[o]

[o] The carrying of hostages, although not specifically proscribed, was a violation of Article 50 of the 1907 Hague Conventions with regard to the treatment of enemy populations. Yet, under the laws of war in force at the time, the 1899 and the 1907 Hague Conventions, applied only to international wars rather than internal struggles.[11] The British held the conflict was a rebellion and thus outside the purview of the treaty. Of course, the republican counter to this was the people of Ireland freely elected the Dáil, which declared independence. While this is true, it is also irrelevant, as the Dáil was not recognized by any sovereign state until July 1921 at best.

The British army took great pains to justify their denial of belligerent status, and thus protection under the Hague Conventions. In the *Record of the Rebellion*, they rejected the American example of the U.S. Army granting belligerent status to the Confederate forces during their Civil War (1861–5), arguing the Confederate forces met the four criteria for belligerents. Adopted by the Hague Conventions, they are:

To be commanded by a person responsible for his subordinates;
To have a fixed distinctive emblem recognizable at a distance;
To carry arms openly; and
To conduct their operations in accordance with the laws and customs of war.[12]

The British army argued that, while the Volunteers had commanders, they did not wear uniforms or emblems, bear arms openly or follow the laws of war.[13] By these standards, the British army was right. It is important to note, however, the Government made the possession of arms or ammunition a capital offense and criminalized membership in the Volunteers or wearing uniform. This, along with the point that the Volunteers obeyed the laws of war and fulfilled each of these requirements during the Rising, but were subject to trial and death, gave the Volunteers little incentive to obey the laws of war. Lastly, it is important to note the Volunteers usually obeyed the laws of war, especially in the countryside.

Formation of Auxiliary Division, R.I.C., September, 1920.—During September[p] the Auxiliary Division of the R.I.C. was formed, and companies began to be distributed to areas. This force was formed of ex-officers[q], and was intended to stiffen the R.I.C. by the infusion of companies composed of men of experience and proved capability. The force was commonly spoken of as the "Black and Tans," although the term was originally applied to the recruits of the regular R.I.C., from the fact that they were originally clothed partly in khaki and partly in black R.I.C. uniform.[r] The efficiency of the companies varied a great deal, according to the character of their company commander, and although the discipline was at first not good, there is no doubt that they played a great part in the quieting of the districts where they were stationed. The outcry which was raised against them in the Press and by certain members of Parliament, though ostensibly based on certain excesses, really had its origin in the fear which they instilled into the rebel terrorists, who failed to terrorize them.[s]

[p] Advertised on 10 July, 1920, the first ADRIC cadet, Harold C. Pearsons, arrived in Ireland on 27 July, 1920. The first four companies were operational 'by the end of August'.[14]

[q] There were a large number of former RAF officers.[15]

[r] The phrase 'Black and Tans' was originally applied to the non-Irishmen recruited into the RIC as constables starting in February 1920. There were insufficient regular dark-green RIC uniforms, so the temporary constables were issued one khaki uniform and one RIC uniform; to differentiate themselves from the Army, they mixed the uniforms. This situation lasted for just a few weeks, but the name stuck.

[s] This is classic misdirection on the authors' part; the ADRIC's poor discipline had nothing to do with what the rebels thought of their operational capabilities. The ADRIC were variously capable, depending on the company commander, as stated. The only systematic examination of the police atrocities is Leeson's masterful *The Black & Tans* (2011).

Rebel flying columns, October, 1920.—About the middle of October the rebel leaders devised a scheme for making use of the numerous "officers" of the I.R.A. and others who were "on the run."[t] Some of the units of the I.R.A. had for a time been reduced to comparative inaction by the absence of the leaders. A scheme of flying columns and active service units was, therefore, inaugurated. Flying columns were formed from men on the run. These columns moved about, billeting themselves on the inhabitants of various areas, and requisitioning supplies without payment. Their role was to ambush Crown forces and dominate whatever district they were it. The active service units were formed as training establishments for "officers" I.R.A. These "officers" were not necessarily all "on the run." The role of the active service units was much the same as that of the flying columns. The areas where both flying columns and active service units[u] located themselves, as a rule, were not those occupied by the troops or police. These bodies existed right up to the end in varying numbers, and were difficult to deal with, because after being roughly handled on several occasions when met with, they ceased to go about as a military force, but hid their arms and became apparently peaceful civilians, except when an outrage was undertaken.[v]

[t] Interestingly, the Irish Volunteers credited the British with the first use of flying columns in Ireland, in *An t-Óglác* in June 1920, saying this was a change from the 'passive defence of their posts', which failed. The Volunteers also noted that this new threat was considerable, and recommended pressing attacks harder and blocking roads to counter them more effectively. The Volunteers discussed their own flying column operations openly in October 1920.[16]

Most of the men in the flying columns were not on the run beforehand, although they were not able to move about freely once they became known. Part of the undercurrent in this paragraph was the Truce-era frustration of having to deal with IRA officers as equals.

[u] Active Service Units stemmed from the IRA realization that not every Volunteer necessarily wanted to fight, or indeed was capable of fighting. The ASUs were formed to act as the combat arm of the Volunteer battalions. Technically, the ASU was part time and generally mobilized for patrols, attacks and in support of the full-time brigade flying columns when operating near their battalion area. These were the official differences between them, but in practice the terms 'ASU' and 'flying column' were frequently used interchangeably.[17]

[v] This latter characterization was true for some of the Volunteer companies that fought as companies, but the flying columns relied on stealth, support network from the populace and sheer fighting abilities to move or retreat.

Situation in November, 1920.—Up to the middle of November there was no further change in the methods of the rebels, or in the policy of the Government. The number of outrages varied from week to week.[w]

[w] The IRA tactics did not change much during the period of August to December 1920, primarily because their tactics were effective. They did not change until the British army introduced armoured vehicles in large numbers at the New Year.

The rebel flying columns carried out occasional attacks on a fairly large scale without much success, while other units of the I.R.A. confined themselves mostly to small affairs involving little risk.[x] The troops were still for the most part compelled to restrict their activities to searching houses for arms or arresting men actually engaged in outrages. The powers granted by the R.O.I.R. enabled suitable punishments to be awarded for crimes, and there was some indication that this was having a depressing and disorganizing effect upon the rebel forces, but anything in the nature of an offensive against the I.R.A., or wholesale arrest of rebels, militant or political, formed no part of the Government policy. Indeed, neither at this time nor any other did the Government ever give to the military authorities any enunciated policy.[y] The Commander-in-Chief was left to devise the best means he could for quelling lawlessness and crime with whatever powers, or handicaps, he derived from the Act of Parliament for the moment in force, and without authority to control the police force, which continued to be under the civil government and a chief of police.[z]

[x] The Longford flying column, under Seán MacEoin (b.1893–d.1973), defeated an attempted British reprisal at Granard, Co. Longford, on 2 November 1920.[18]

[y] The army's clear frustration was a result of the ambiguity of their mission in Ireland. Their roles and responsibilities were rarely clear, while their authority was rarely defined except in terms of what they could not do. This nebulous mission was irksome. Street commented at length, in much the same terms, regarding Governmental policy.[19]

z   From November 1920, the RIC Inspector-General position was vacant. Sir Thomas J. Smith (b.1863–d.1939), the Deputy I-G who had replaced Brig-Gen Sir Joseph Aloysius Byrne (b.1874–d.1942) in March 1920, retired in November of that year. The police advisor to the Lord Lieutenant was Lt-Gen Sir Henry Hugh Tudor (b.1871–d.1965), who effectively had control of the RIC from his appointment in March 1920.[20]

The troops remained merely a military police force, and action against the rebels was mostly a question of a search party acting on some local information regarding a suspected house, or a subaltern and his platoon rounding up an ambush laid by the rebels for a lorry patrol. A letter to the Irish Government advocating the arrest and trial for conspiracy to treason of De Valera[aa] and Arthur Griffith[bb] met with no result, and, in fact, when De Valera returned to Ireland from America in 1921 the Government gave instructions that he was not to be arrested.

aa   Éamon de Valera (b.1882–d.1975).[21]

bb   Arthur Griffith (b.1872–d.1922).

Towards the end of November, however, events occurred which enabled the military authorities to obtain sanction for a change of policy.

Dublin murders, 21st November, 1920.—At about 9 a.m. on the morning of Sunday 21st November, 1920[22], there occurred in Dublin a series of murders committed by the I.R.A. which, if the rebels had perpetrated no other outrage, would have marked them for ever as the most cold-blooded and cowardly of murderers. Eight houses in the south-eastern part of the city were entered by gangs of armed men who murdered seven officers, three ex-officers, two R.I.C. cadets and two civilians.[cc] In addition four officers[dd] and one civilian were shot but not killed. At least two other houses were entered but the officers escaped. Most of the officers were in bed or dressing at the time, and they were either murdered in their beds or dragged from their rooms and murdered. Some were murdered in the presence of their wives, and in one case an officer's wife[ee] was fired at, while in another case the officer, who had lost a leg, was in bed, with his artificial leg off. With the exception of one wounded man[ff] the murderers escaped.[23]

cc   The dead were: civilian Thomas Herbert Smith (b.1873) and Capt. D. L. MacLean (b.1889) at 117 Morehampton Rd; ADRIC Cadets Cecil A. Morris (b.1898) and Frank Garniss (b.1886) on Northumberland St;

Maj Charles Milne Cholmeley Dowling (b.1891), Bvt. Lt-Col Hugh Ferguson Montgomery (b.1880–died-of-wounds: 10 December 1920) and Capt. Leonard Price (b.1885) at 28 Upper Pembroke St; Lt Henry James Angliss (b.1893) at 22 Lower Mount St; Lt Peter Ashmunt Ames (b.1888) and Lt George Bennett (b.1882) at 28 Upper Mount St; Capt. Patrick J. McCormack (b.1877) and W. A. Wilde (b.1891) at the Gresham Hotel; Capt. John Fitzgerald, RIC (b.1898) at 28 Earlsfort Terrace; Capt. Geoffrey Thomas Baggally (b.1891) and Capt. William Frederick Newbury (b.1875) at 92 Baggot St.[24]

dd These were John Caldow (b.1898–unknown), Capt. Brian Christopher Headlam Keenlyside (b.1889–d.1941), Lt Randolph George Murray (b.1897–d.1938) and Lt-Col Wilfrid James Woodcock (b.1878–d.1960).

ee Mrs Carolyn Woodcock at Upper Pembroke St.

ff Volunteer Frank Teeling (b.1900–d.1976) was captured, having shot Lt McMahon, and was about to be summarily executed when saved by Brig-Gen Frank Crozier (b.1879–d.1937), commander of the ADRIC.[25]

Immediately after the murders patrols and armoured cars were sent into the streets, and all motor cars were searched and sent back to their garage.[gg] No train was allowed to leave Dublin. These restrictions were kept in force until the afternoon of 22nd November. All officers living out were ordered into barracks, and from now onward were accommodated in barracks or requisitioned hotels protected by guards. From this time onwards, the lives of all officers were constantly in danger. They were instructed not to go about singly, and an automatic pistol was issued to every officer, which he was never to be without.[hh]

gg Volunteer Cmdts Peadar Clancy (b.1888) and Richard McKee (b.1893) were killed by the RIC at Dublin Castle, along with Conor Clune (b.1893), on the evening of 21 November 1920. It is unclear whether Clune was a member of the IRA or not, and there were persistent rumours that all three were tortured before being murdered.

hh All officers' wives and children were sent to Britain.[26]

It is believed that subsequent arrests included 13 of the murderers, but owing to the difficulty in obtaining identifications to satisfy the impartiality of the Courts

Martial who tried the cases, only five were convicted of murder, and only two were actually hanged.[ii]

[ii] Volunteers Thomas Whelan (b.1898) and Patrick Moran (b.1888) were hanged by John Ellis at Kilmainham on Monday, 14 April, 1921. There was considerable evidence presented in their defence that they had been elsewhere during the killings. Hanged with them were: Volunteers Thomas Bryan (b.1897), Patrick Doyle (b. 1892), Frank Flood (b.1901) and Bernard Ryan (b.1900).[27]

Croke Park, 21ˢᵗ November, 1920.—On the afternoon of the same day a football[jj] match took place at Croke Park, Dublin, between teams from Tipperary and Dublin. As it was considered that this match might have been used, as was often the case, for the introduction into the city of a gang of murderers amongst the crowd, it was decided to search the spectators. It was arranged that troops should surround the ground, and that the police should carry out the search, after the crowd had been warned through a megaphone that they must keep their seats and afterwards leave by a particular exit, where they would be searched. The police arrived before their time so that the cordon of troops was not in position, and, consequently, no warning was given. Shots were fired at the police as they drew up, and the police returned the fire. A stamped ensued in which the crowd broke down a paling. As a result about 10 civilians were killed and about 65 wounded or injured, chiefly as a result of the stamped.[kk] The suspicion that the crowd contained gangs of men who had come to Dublin for the committal of outrages would seem to have been justified, as, although the majority of the people left without being searched, some 30 to 40 revolvers were picked up afterwards on the ground.[ll]

[jj] Gaelic football.

[kk] The dead were: Jane Boyle, James Burke, Daniel Carroll, Michael Feery, Thomas Hogan, Michael Hogan (player), James Matthews, Patrick O'Dowd, Jerome O'Leary (aged 10 years), William Robinson (aged 11 years), Thomas Ryan (shot while rendering aid to M. Hogan), John Scott (aged 14 years), James Teehan, Joseph Traynor.

There is little in this apologia to correspond with the truth. This would appear to be a rather weak attempt to justify what occurred. The first two civilians killed were the two youngest boys (O'Leary and Robinson), who were watching the match from two trees just in front of the south entrance. They were likely mistaken for lookouts. The ADRIC began shooting almost immediately, but there is no evidence that they received any fire. In all, the police expended 228 rounds in about two minutes. The only people to die of something other than gunfire were Teehan and Traynor, who died from cardiac arrest due to the stampede; the rest were shot. The rest of the 'injured' were chiefly wounded by gunfire.[28]

ll   This was obvious fabrication on the part of the authors; no firearms were found according to the official British records of the event.[29]

Attempts were made, not only by the hostile Press, but by supposedly reputable English newspapers, and by members of Parliament, to interpret the unfortunate loss of life at Croke Park as a deliberate retaliation for the murders of the morning. As a fact, however, the discipline of the troops in Dublin in face of this provocation was exemplary, and a General Order of the Day was issued on the subject, a few days later. (*Vide* Appendix III).[mm]

mm   As this was a police action, this is one of the few truthful statements. Two courts of inquiry ordered by Maj-Gen Boyd, GOC, Dublin District; found that the shootings were unwarranted and unjustifiable.[30]

Arrest of Arthur Griffith, 26ᵗʰ November, 1920.—Mr. Arthur Griffith was arrested on 26ᵗʰ November, 1920, an action which greatly helped to control and to cool the heated spirits of the troops, although it was criticized by the Government.

NOTES

1   Herlihy, *History of the RIC*, p. 152.
2   See '"Outrage" Summaries', NAUK CO 904/148–51.
3   Abbott, *Police Casualties*, pp.123–6; Herlihy, *The RIC*, pp. 185–98; Hopkinson, *The Irish War of Independence*, p. 130; Kautt, *Ambushes & Armour*, pp. 91–5; Leeson, *Black and Tans*, pp. 170–72; P. Lynch, 'A Fighting Rearguard Saved IRA in the Retreat after the Rineen Ambush',

With the IRA, pp. 131–49; O'Malley, *Raids and Rallies*, pp. 64–90; Ó Ruairc, *Blood on the Banner*, 156–70; and Townshend, *British Campaign*, p. 115.

4   See 'P. O'C.', 'The East Cork Brigade in Action—Waiting for General Strickland', *Rebel Cork's Fighting Story* (2009), pp. 228–9; *The Last Post*, p. 103 and O'Farrell, *Who's Who*, p. 105.

5   Hopkinson, *The Irish War of Independence*, p. 109 and 'P. O'C.', 'The East Cork Brigade in Action—Waiting for General Strickland', *Rebel Cork's Fighting Story* (2009), pp. 228–9.

6   See RIC I-G Reports for Co. Kerry for July 1920, for Co. Sligo for October 1920 and for Co. Longford for September 1920, NAUK CO 904/112–3.

7   See Hopkinson, *Irish War of Independence*, p. 80 and P. Lynch, 'Capture of Mallow Military Barracks', *Rebel Cork's Fighting Story* (Anvil Press edition), pp. 95–102 and 'The Only British Military Barracks Captured by the IRA was at Mallow', *With the IRA*, pp. 150–62.

8   Macready to Secretary of State for War, Memorandum No. 2/26908(a) 1 September 1920, NAUK WO 32/9537. The text refers to an additional letter sent, which received a reply from Creedy to Macready on 19 October 1920, WO 32/9537/8. See copy of original memorandum in Additional Appendices.

9   Sturgis Diaries, 19 August, 1920, Vol. I, p. 45 and Street, *Administration of Ireland*, pp. 108–16.

10 'General Officer, Commanding-in-Chief, Ireland, Weekly Situation Report', 1 January 1921, SIC NAUK CAB 27/108.

11 See Hague I, 1907, preamble and Part I to V, Articles 1–97.

12 Hague IV, 1907, Annex to the Convention Regulations Respecting the Laws and Customs of War on Land Section I on Belligerents, Chapter I, The Qualifications of Belligerents, Article 1.

13 See chapter 8, 'Note on Belligerency'.

14 Abbott, *Police Casualties*, pp. 106–109. See Leeson, *Black and Tans* and McCall, *Tudor's Toughs*.

15 See A. D. Harvey, 'Who Were the Auxiliaries?', *The Historical Journal*, vol. 35, No. 3 (1992), pp. 665–69.

16 'Flying Columns', *An t-Óglác*, Vol. II, No 12, (1 June 1920) pp. 94–5 and 'Notes from Headquarters', Vol. II, No. 12 (15 October 1920), p. 130.

17 See Maj-Gen Donnocha O'Hannigan, 'The Flying Column Originated in East Limerick', *Limerick's Fighting Story*, pp. 165–73. For other accounts of columns, see T. Barry, *Guerrilla Days in Ireland: A Personal Account of the Anglo-Irish War* (1995); D. Begley, *The Road to Crossbarry: The Decisive Battle of the War of Independence* (1999); Ewan Butler, *Barry's Flying Column* (London: Leo Cooper, 1971); and Jim Maher, *The Flying Column: West Kilkenny, 1916–21* (1988).

18 See M. Coleman, *County Longford and the Irish Revolution, 1910–1923* (2003), pp. 123–4.

19 Street, *Administration of Ireland*, pp. 137–51.

20 Leeson, *Black and Tans*, p. 233, n67.

21 For a pro-de Valera biography, see Earl of Longford & T. P. O'Neill, *Eamon de Valera* (1974); for a less complimentary work, see T. P. Coogan, *De Valera – Long Fellow, Long Shadow* (1993); for the most balanced biography to date, see D. Ferriter, *Judging Dev: A Reassessment of the Life and Legacy of Eamon de Valera* (2007).

22 For new appraisals of the events that day, see J. Leonard, '"English Dogs" or "Poor Devils"? The Dead of Bloody Sunday Morning', and E. O'Halpin, 'Counting Terror: Bloody Sunday and The Dead of the Irish Revolution', *Terror in Ireland* (2012).

23 For republican and other versions of what occurred, see Dwyer, *The Squad*, pp. 170–99; M. Foy, *Michael Collins's Intelligence War: The Struggle between the British and the IRA, 1919–1921* (2006), pp. 141–77; and J. Gleeson, *Bloody Sunday: How Michael Collins's Agents Assassinated Britain's Secret Service in Dublin on November 21, 1920* (2004).

24 See Statement of Vincent Byrne (MA WS/423); O'Farrell, *Who's Who*, pp. 4–94; Abbott, *Police Casualties*, p. 152; Statement of Col Charles Dalton (WS/434); Statement of James Doyle (WS/771). See also Ernie O'Malley, 'Bloody Sunday', *Dublin's Fighting Story, 1916–1921: Told By the Men Who Made It* (Cork: Mercier Press, 2009), pp. 283–94 and Street, *Administration of Ireland*, pp. 59–62.

25   See R. Bennett, *The Black and Tans: The British Special Police in Ireland* (New York City: MetroBooks, 2002), p. 130; Dolan, 'Killing and Bloody Sunday, November 1920', *The Historical Journal*, Vol. 49, No. 3 (2006), pp. 789–90, 801 and Crozier, *Impressions and Recollections* (London: T. Werner Laurie, 1930), pp. 256–9.

26   Woodcock, Caroline, 'Experiences of an Officer's Wife in Ireland', *Blackwood's Magazine*, Nº. MCCLXVII Vol. CCIX (May 1921), pp. 553–98 (also published by Galago Books, 1994).

27   See O'Farrell, *Who's Who*, pp. 12, 30, 35, 71, 91 and 101.

28   For an excellent survey of the events and the courts of inquiry, see D. Leeson, 'Death in the Afternoon: The Croke Park Massacre, 21 November 1920', *Canadian Journal of History* (April 2003), pp. 43–68; for more of the British Army's view of this incident, see Street, *Administration of Ireland*, p. 59.

29   See Major E. L. Mills, ADRIC to Adjutant ADRIC, 22 November, 1920, 'Mater Hospital Inquiry', 8 December, 1920. NAUK WO 35/88B. Maj Mills was the ADRIC on-scene commander.

30   'Findings of Mater Hospital Inquiry', 8 December, 1920. NAUK WO 35/88B.

CHAPTER IV

Introduction of Martial Law

Arrest of I.R.A. leaders sanctioned, 21ˢᵗ November, 1920.—The murders of 21ˢᵗ November brought about a new policy. Within a few hours of the crimes having been committed, the Irish Government had given sanction for the arrest of all known "officers" of the I.R.A. and their internment at Ballykinlar Camp, Co. Down.[1] All divisions at once made arrangements to arrest the "officers" whose names were on their selected list. This was greatly facilitated by the fact that a short time previously an office of the I.R.A. had been raided in Dublin, and papers found which confirmed the Order of Battle which had been compiled from intelligence already received.[a]

In Dublin permission was given to arrest known members of the I.R.A. even if they were not known to be "officers." In Dublin alone, 87 arrests were made within 48 hours, and during the week the number of arrests throughout Ireland had reached over 500.[b]

[a]   This refers to the raid on Irish Volunteer Chief of Staff Richard Mulcahy's office on Friday, 19 November, 1920.

[b]   The most important of these were the arrests of Peadar Clancy and Richard McKee.[2]

The initial arrests were accomplished without any difficulty. Such action was evidently not contemplated by the rebels, and many were no doubt ignorant of the fact that they were known as "officers" of the I.R.A. The troops during the days on which these first arrests were made, enjoyed a comparative immunity from attack; the generally submissive demeanour of the arrested rebels, and the absence of active opposition seemed to indicate that the rebels feared that their recent action had at last roused the Government to stern measures.[c] The rate at which arrests were made naturally decreased as the weeks went on, owing to the fact, that leaders who feared arrest left their homes and districts.

[c] It is likely that the Dublin Volunteers had no plan to deal with the aftermath of the attacks. This is remarkable given that the attacks were led by Squad members leading Dublin Brigade Volunteers, all of it orchestrated by Collins.

Effects of military activity—Initiative regained.—From this time the initiative may be said to have passed to the Crown forces for the first time since May, 1920. Rebel leaders were being perpetually hunted, and, although only a few arms were captured during the arrests, information regarding arms and other matters began to come in from unexpected sources. The success of these united operations and the difference in the atmosphere which was brought about for a time by the assertion of authority showed what might be effected if an objective continued to present itself for the troops. It was even thought at this time that moderate opinion, consequent on the removal of many of the leading terrorists might assert itself, and tentative "peace" proposals were actually spoken of.[d] Moderate men, however, did not come forward, and nothing resulted from the tentative "peace" proposals. This was probably due to the fact that the number of leaders and extremists arrested was not sufficiently large to remove the risk of death to anybody who seemed likely to take action which would thwart the rebels plans.

[d] It is hard to reconcile this paragraph's claims with the realities in Ireland in the last six weeks of 1920. Although Dublin was in shock after the killings, the rest of the country was not. The various Volunteer operations would continue as before. Indeed, in Co. Cork, the violence levels continued to climb with Barry's flying column conducting an ambush at Labacally on Friday, 26 November, two days before the infamous Kilmichael Ambush on Sunday, 28 November. The remainder of November and the first eleven days of December saw violent attacks in Cork, culminating with ADRIC'S K Company burning part of Cork City on Saturday, 11 December. In the process, K Company also killed Jeremiah Delaney, and perhaps his brother Con, in their home that night.[3] The violence had increased, and more IRA leaders were in captivity, but new leaders would come forward and IRA operations did not suffer outside of Dublin as a result.

Sea transport difficulties, December, 1920.—By 10th December internment orders had been applied for in respect of over 800 "officers" or prominent members of the I.R.A., and of these, 600 had already been interned at Ballykinlar.[e] The rapidity with which the arrested men could be conveyed to Ballykinlar for internment was greatly affected by the shipping facilities. The ships available were too few in number and unsuitable in design. Destroyers were used for 100 internees, but this was a larger number than the Admiralty considered suitable, and on 5th December information was received from the Senior Naval Officer, Kingstown, that the Admiralty objected to the use of destroyers for internees and that they could not provide any other ships for the purpose. The Admiralty had also instructed the Admiral, Queenstown[f], to request the military and police authorities to reduce their demands for ships. As a result of this lack of shipping, the question of arrested men in divisional areas, more especially in the 6th Division, became serious. A telegram was sent to the War Office on 8th December explaining the Admiralty's attitude and asking for the provision of two ships, each capable of carrying one hundred internees. On 10th December the Admiral received instructions to meet the military requirements in shipping, for which purpose a minesweeper and a sloop had been placed at his disposal. The capacity of these two vessels combined was only for 100 internees. Later, a light cruiser was made available for a time. The shortage of shipping was, however, a source of some difficulty for a long time.

[e]   They had also discussed their desire to place prisoners on the Isle of Man.[4]

[f]   This was the Admiral Commanding-in-Chief, Western Approaches, Adm Sir Reginald Godfrey Otway Tupper (b.1859–d.1945), who served in this capacity from January 1919 to May 1921.

It was also foreseen that additional internment camps would soon be required. The original camp at Ballykinlar had a capacity for 1,000 internees; orders were issued for a second camp at the same place of similar capacity, and for a third camp at Bere Island in the 6th Divisional Area.[g]

[g]   Officially known as 'Military Prisons in the Field'; rebels were interned at Spike Island; Bere Island; Ballykinlar; Sligo Prison; Detention Barracks, Cork; and the Cork Male Gaol.[5]

System of internment.—The system of internment was as follows:—
Divisions submitted to G.H.Q. lists of men they wished to intern, giving
their believed rank in the I.R.A. These lists were examined at G.H.Q. and
forwarded to the Chief Secretary with applications for internment warrants.
Owing to delay in the issue of warrants and the congestion which would
have occurred in divisional areas had the arrested men been retained until
the warrants were received, divisions were authorized to ship to Ballykinlar
batches of men whose internment had been approved, as and when shipping
facilities became available, the internment warrants were then sent direct
from G.H.Q. to the Commandant of the internment camp.[h] This system,
although possibly the best which could be improvised at short notice and
with nothing but the ordinary military staff to carry it out, was obviously
open to serious disadvantages. After the first batch or two of arrests, the
arrested men became merely obscure individuals and the correct description
of their names and addresses was a great difficulty. Consequently, some
internment warrants bore the wrong Christian name, and confusion arose in
the internment camps through the difficulty of fitting the warrants received
from G.H.Q. to the individuals received from divisions. On the whole,
however, the policy was a success, and it certainly caused satisfaction to the
law-abiding people and to troops and police, who saw at last some results
of their ceaseless efforts.

[h]   The Commandant of Ballykinlar Internment Camp was Colonel
Richard George Hely-Hutchinson (b.1871–unknown) of the Royal
Dublin Fusiliers; he was well regarded for his humane treatment of
internees.[6]

As was to be expected, after the first shock of the arrests the rebel
leaders who had escaped internment urged on the I.R.A. to new efforts. It
was not long before substitutes were provided for the lost leaders, and the
flying columns received an impetus from the influx of the greatly increased
number of rebels who found it necessary to go "on the run."

Macroom outrage, 28th November, 1920.[i]—On the 28th November an
outrage of a particularly atrocious kind occurred in Co. Cork. Two lorries[j]
containing 16 auxiliary police were proceeding along the Macroom—
Dunmanway road when they were stopped by a rebel[k] dressed as a British
soldier and wearing a steel helmet. This man said that he belonged to a party
of soldiers whose lorry had broken down, and wanted help. The police who at
once went to give assistance were led straight into an ambush. The rebels, many
of whom were dressed in British uniform[l], fired a volley which disabled most

of the police immediately. Those who were lying wounded on the road were deliberately murdered, and their bodies bore the marks of having been hacked with axes.[m] Only one[n] of the 16 police[o] escaped.[p]

---

[i] This was the Kilmichael Ambush of Sunday, 28 November 1920.

[j] Known widely as Crossley 'Tenders', officially it was the 'Type J' Lorry.

[k] Cmdt Tom Barry (b.1897–d.1980).

[l] Barry stated that he was the man who stepped into the road and was wearing a Volunteers shirt under a trench coat and steel helmet. In the dark, these could easily have been taken for British military items. There is no evidence that any of the rebels spoke to the Auxiliaries before attacking.

[m] The only evidence of this was the marks on the bodies, but these marks could have come through other means.[7]

[n] T/Const. F. H. Forde (b.1896–d.ca.1980). Forde was badly wounded in the head, suffering brain damage and was a quadriplegic for life.

[o] The victims of the ambush were: D.I. F. W. Crake (b.1893), Cadets W. T. Barnes (b.1894), C. J. W. Bayley (b.1898), L. D. Bradshaw (b. 1898), J. C. Gleave (b.1899), P. N. Graham (b.1889), S. Hugh-Jones (b.1893), F. Hugo (b.1880), A. G. J. Jones (b.1897), E. W. H. Lucas (b.1889), W. Pallester (b.1895), H. O. Pearson (b.1899), F. Taylor (b.1898), C. Wainwright (b.1884), B. D. Webster (b.1890) and T/Const A. F. Poole (b.1899). Cadet Guthrie escaped the scene, and was captured by the IRA and shot two days later.[8]

[p] Three Volunteers were also killed; Michael McCarthy (b.1895) and Jim O'Sullivan (b.1894) were killed-in-action and Patrick Deasy (b.1904) later died of wounds. In addition, Jack Aherne (b.1901–d.1973), Jack Hennessy (b.1899–d.1970), John Lordan (b.1892–d.1930) and Jack Roche (b.1902–d.1973), were wounded.

This atrocity emphasized the lawless state of Co. Cork and the surrounding counties, and the inadequacy of the existing powers to deal with the situation there.[q]

---

[q] This statement betrays the paradox of the British understanding of the revolutionary aspects of the war. They understood they could not solve a

political problem with military force, but at the same time they attributed political violence to simple crime. While there is no consensus today about the nature of political violence, there is clearly a difference between ordinary crime and political crime. These distinctions determine the best means of dealing with such problems.

Discussion on Martial Law, 1ˢᵗ December, 1920.—On 1ˢᵗ December the Chief Secretary visited G.H.Q., and, in the absence of the Commander-in-Chief, saw the Brigadier-General[r], General Staff. He stated that the Government was greatly concerned about the murders in Dublin and the outrage near Macroom, and that they were anxious to proclaim Martial Law in Co. Cork and Co. Kerry. At a subsequent conference on the same day, the Chief Secretary asked General Jeudwine[s], who was acting as Commander-in-Chief in the absence of General Macready, to consider the following points and report his decision:—

(1) Were the military authorities prepared to enforce Martial Law?
(2) *Was it considered advisable to proclaim Martial law throughout Ireland or only in the most lawless parts?
(3) Would additional troops be required?

[r] (Temp) Brig-Gen. John Edward Spencer Brind (b.1878–d.1954).

[s] GOC, 5ᵗʰ Infantry Division.

5ᵗʰ December, 1920.—On 5ᵗʰ December, after consultation with Divisional Commanders[t], General Jeudwine informed[9] the Chief Secretary[u]—

(1) That he was prepared to undertake the enforcing of Martial Law.
(2) That Martial Law should be proclaimed throughout Ireland, it being left to the Military Governor to intensify it in defined areas as and when considered desirable.
(3) That in the first instance four extra battalions would be required, with three more held in England in readiness to proceed to Ireland when necessary.

---

* The views of the Military Authorities regarding the manner of imposing Martial Law are given in Appendix IV.

The general lines on which it was proposed to impose restrictions under Martial Law were also mentioned.

> [t]   Maj-Gen.s Bainbridge of the 1st Division, Strickland of the 6th and Boyd of the Dublin District.
>
> [u]   Sir Hamar Greenwood.

These included—

The formation of a Press Censorship.
A system of Passports.
Registration of inhabitants of houses.
Institution of Identity Cards.

It was also pointed out that internment camps outside Ireland would be desirable, and that a considerable increase in shipping facilities for the removal of internees would be necessary.[10]

9th December, 1920.—On 9th December the Commander-in-Chief attended a Cabinet meeting in London, at which the Government decided to proclaim Martial Law in Co. Cork, Co. Kerry, Co. Tipperary and Co. Limerick only. The Commander-in-Chief urged that Co. Waterford should be included so that the whole of Munster (south of the River Shannon) should be under Martial Law. This suggestion was not, however, agreed to, but it was intimated that if found necessary an extension of Martial Law could be made later on the recommendation of the Commander-in-Chief to the Chief Secretary.[11]

Martial Law proclaimed, 10th December, 1920.—On the afternoon of 10th December a Proclamation was issued by the Lord-Lieutenant, declaring Martial Law in Co. Cork, Co. Kerry, Co. Tipperary and Co. Limerick, and appointing the Commander-in-Chief as Military Governor-General. On 12th December the Commander-in-Chief, as Military Governor-General, issued the necessary Proclamations. The main points were—

(1)   The appointment of the Generals or other Officers Commanding the 6th Division, 16th, 17th, 18th and Kerry Infantry Brigades as Military Governors.

(2)   Surrender of all arms, ammunition and explosives by unauthorized persons by 27th December, after which date any unauthorized person found in possession of them to be liable to suffer death after trial by a military court.

(3) Any unauthorized person wearing the uniform of His Majesty's forces or similar uniform calculated to deceive, to be liable to suffer death, after trial by a military court.

(4) A state of armed insurrection was declare to exist and any person taking part in, or aiding and abetting this, to be liable to suffer death, after trial by a military court.

(5) All Law Courts, Corporations, Councils and Boards were to continue to carry out their functions, until otherwise ordered.

(6) The forces of the Crown in Ireland were also declared to be on active service.

The declaration of Martial Law in four counties[v] only had great disadvantages. In the first place it seemed probable that in order to avoid the penalties incurred by carrying arms in the Martial Law area, parties of rebels would make their way to adjoining counties. To prevent this it would be necessary to guard the boundaries, and there were not sufficient troops to do this. Secondly, the demand for the surrender of arms was not likely to be complied with in the Martial Law area where extremists were in a majority, and the moral of the I.R.A. was therefore such as to encourage defiance of the order; whereas in areas less terrorized such an order might have produced the desired result and gradually spread. Thirdly, had Martial Law been proclaimed throughout Ireland the control of all Crown forces would have been centred in one head—the Military Governor-General. This would have ensured co-ordination of effort and unification of policy. Whereas partial Martial Law led to an anomalous position, the police in the proclaimed counties being under the local Military Governors, while divided control existed throughout the rest of Ireland.[w]

[v]   Cork, Kerry, Limerick and Tipperary.

[w]   The issue of martial law was contentious, as is evident from the discussion here. A proclamation of martial law did not relieve the military of responsibilities under civil law. Thus, a soldier could be held subject to criminal laws while acting in his official duties and still be subject to military law at the same time. A soldier ordered to fire on 'rebels' could be held criminally liable for doing so, even though failure to obey a lawful order would constitute a crime under the Army Act. The way around this

potential legal nightmare was for Parliament to pass an Act of indemnity to coincide with the proclamation of martial law. This was not, however, done during the War of Independence, and was not passed by either side until 1923.

Again, two separate forms of trial were necessary. In the Martial Law area trials were by a Military Court, whereas in other areas they were by Court Martial, and a similar offence was liable to a death penalty in one place and not in a place a few miles away.[x]

[x] British military authorities expressed reservations, particularly about the fairness of the application of martial law under such circumstances.[12]

Also, the newspapers were a great source of strength to the rebel cause; had it been possible to control these all over Ireland, as it was in the Martial Law area, the cause of Law and Order would have gained an advantage which is incalculable.

Proclamations under Martial Law.—The proclamation of the Commander-in-Chief as a Military Governor-General was followed by a series of proclamations issued by the G.O.C., 6th Division, as Military

Governor of the Martial Law area. These dealt with the following subjects:—

Proclamation No. 1.

Made all crimes into offences punishable by Martial Law
    Made tampering with official notices and proclamations an offence.
    Required owners of occupied buildings to keep a list of the inmates posted on the door.
    Required owners of hotels and boarding-houses to keep a register of guests and supply it to the police.

Proclamation No. 2.

Prohibited all meetings and defined a meeting as consisting of six people or more.
    Prohibited loitering in the streets.
    Prohibited sending telegrams in code or cipher.

Made the possession of wireless instruments or carrier pigeons an offence.

Proclamation No. 3.

Required anyone having knowledge about rebels or their goings immediately to give information.

Warned people who damaged or destroyed Government property that the property of such persons was liable to be confiscated or destroyed.

As a result of the declaration of Martial Law, the police in the four counties concerned came under the orders of the Military Governors in their respective areas, under the following conditions:—

There was to be as little interference as possible with the normal necessary routine of police patrols and duties.

Military Governors were to issue their orders to the police through the senior police official in their area, except in case of emergency, when it might be done direct.

Military Governors were to hold Divisional Commissioners, R.I.C., responsible for the discipline of the police.[y]

The police were to continue to be disciplined and administered by their own officers.

No bodies of police or companies of the Auxiliary Divisions, R.I.C., were to move into Martial Law area, nor change their permanent location in that area, without the sanction of Military Governor, Martial Law area.

Owing to a certain amount of difficulty experienced by the Military Governor, Martial Law area, with regard to orders for moves being issued to police from the police authorities in Dublin, a Divisional Commissioner was at a later date appointed, at the Commander-in-Chief's request, to be attached to the 6th Division Headquarters as advisor on police matters.

[y] How exactly they would control policemen was unstated. The regulations governing the RIC were administrative, and had no provision for punishing a man beyond fines, demotion and dismissal.

Extension of Martial Law area, 5th January, 1921.—As was anticipated, the proclamation ordering the surrender of arms by 27th December had no effect, and several conflicts with large bodies of rebels near the eastern boundary of

Tipperary confirmed the expectation that parties of rebels would cross the Martial Law limits.[z] Before the end of December, therefore, the Government were informed that it was considered necessary to extend Martial Law so as to include Co. Clare, Co. Kilkenny, Co. Waterford and Co. Wexford. This was done by proclamation on 5th January, and the Martial Law area then coincided with the 6th Divisional area.[13]

[z] It is not entirely clear to which actions this refers. There was an attack on 16 December, 1920 at Kilmacommon, Co Tipperary where four members of the RIC were killed: Patrick J. Haford (b.1893), Ernest F. Harden (b.1899), Albert H. Palmer (b.1896) and Arthur Smith (b.1898). There was another attack at Glenbower, Co Tipperary, where RIC Sgt Thomas Walsh (b.1880) was killed.[14]

Motor Restrictions Order, December, 1920.[15]—During December certain restrictions other than Martial Law were put into force. Of these the most important was the Motor Restriction Order. It had for some time been apparent that motor vehicles were being largely used to facilitate the committal of outrages and the escape of the perpetrators. To trace a motor car was practically impossible owing to the fact that Irishmen were not in normal time accustomed to take out licences for their cars, and consequently, the police had no reliable record of the cars and their owners in any district. It was decided, therefore, to introduce a system of military permits for all motor vehicles. The terms set out in a proclamation issued by the Commander-in-Chief as Competent Military Authority, came into force on 1st December. Briefly the restrictions were as follows:—

No person was allowed to be in possession of or use a motor vehicle without a permit signed by a Competent Military Authority.

On all permits the place at which the vehicle in question was to be garaged was specified, and no motor vehicles might be garaged elsewhere.

With the exception of doctors, nurses, &c., no motor vehicle was allowed to circulate between the hours of 8 p.m. and 6 a.m.

No motor vehicle might be used outside a radius of 20 miles from the place of garage specified on the permit.

"Special" permits were issued by the Competent Military Authority for cars whose owners were granted, temporarily or permanently, exemption from any of these restrictions.

Certain regulations regarding the letting out of motor vehicles for hire, and the registration of cars permitted to be garaged at public garages were included in the order.

The troops and police combined to enforce these restrictions by mean of patrols, examining posts and the visiting of garages, in order to check the vehicles. In theory it should have been possible at any given time, between 8 p.m. and 6 a.m., to account for every motor vehicle other than those in respect of which special permits had been issued. In practice this ideal was not attained, and cars were no doubt still used on occasions for the conveyance of arms, or of persons engaged in an outrage. The restrictions, however, proved of good value, and enabled the troops and police to exercise a control over the movement of disloyal persons, which they had not previously possessed.

In addition to the restrictions on motor vehicles, Competent Military Authorities were authorized to restrict the use of pedal bicycles in districts where an outrage had been committed.

Restriction of Fairs and Markets, December, 1920.—Outrages and the destruction of roads, a practice which, towards the end of December, 1920, was just beginning, were met by proclamations by the Competent Military Authority of the area forbidding fairs and markets to be held within a certain radius of the scene of outrage. This had a very marked effect in setting farmers against the rebel extremists, and, since the restrictions were removed when a district became quiet, law-abiding people and farmers' sons, who had been forced into the I.R.A., had an inducement to endeavour to curtail rebel activity in the district concerned.[aa]

[aa] There is little to suggest that the closing of fairs, markets and creameries turned the people against IRA operations other than the claim made herein. It is difficult to know who did and did not provide wholehearted support to the IRA, since proclaiming oneself to be against them was decidedly dangerous in many areas. There have been no studies of popular support during the war. Claims of support must be taken with caution and examined with rigour.

Curfew restrictions.—The imposition of curfew restrictions had by December become a recognized method of counteracting disorder in towns. Local Competent Military Authorities had the power to impose curfew by proclaiming, but such an order could only be withdrawn again by sanction from G.H.Q.[bb]

bb Again, there is little to suggest that this had any positive influence on the populace, as it prevented their safe freedom of movement, inconveniencing the rebels only slightly. The actual effect of this curfew was to endanger anyone who stepped outside during the targeted times as one was liable to be shot. The one effect on the rebels was to eliminate their ability to 'fade into' the crowd, but as there would be few crowds out during the hours of the curfew anyway, it really made little difference.

Sinn Fein leaders carried in lorries, 18th December, 1920.—On 18th December, in the Martial Law area, the system was adopted of carrying leaders of the I.R.A. in every lorry convoy. The object of this was to prevent attacks on lorries, and the fact that Sinn Fein leaders were to be so carried was made public by notices and in the Press.cc

cc There is mixed information regarding the effectiveness of carrying hostages. It appears to have prevented attacks in some cases and not to have in others. According to J. M. MacCarthy, a meeting of the Cork, Limerick and Tipperary Brigades on 6 January 1921 'decided that the fact of the enemy carrying hostages will not prevent our attacking them (unless otherwise ordered by G.M.Q.)'. The BMH Witness Statements seem to indicate that the hostages were treated poorly by the troops.[16]

Official punishments.—The most important of the methods which came into force as a result of the Declaration of Martial Law was the system of "Official Punishments." This system raised a storm of protest from many quarters, and under the name of "Reprisals," it was made a catch-word to revile the Crown forces, not only by rebel propagandists, but by certain public men and newspapers in England, who saw in it a good opportunity for embarrassing a Government to which they were opposed, and even by honest men who were not in possession of the facts. The idea was prevalent, and was widely circulated and believed, that "reprisals" were carried out indiscriminately by troops and police without control or authority, that the houses destroyed were those which happened to be most ready to hand, and that acts of destruction were undertaken with a brutality resulting from blind fury. These facts were very different. Official punishments were never permitted outside the Martial Law area, and the orders for carrying them out were most explicit, and were only put into practice after a warning had been given in Proclamation No. 3 issued by the Military Governor of the Martial Law area.dd dd The illogical nature of such actions truly does not seem to have occurred to the officers engaged in these activities. The idea that one could stop troops' indiscipline by destroying homes 'by the numbers' has an almost Prussian ring to it, but was certainly not going to slake any need for vengeance. As Townshend has noted, 'the I.R.A. could win an arson competition easily'. Worse still, most of the homes likely to be destroyed were rented properties. This fell right into the republicans' hands.[17] They appear to have believed the people of Ireland would not see this as arbitrary.

The following rules were laid down:—

Punishments, included confiscation, or, if necessary, destruction of houses and property, may be carried out against any person or persons who may be considered to be implication in or cognizant of outrages against Crown forces. Such outrages to include ambushes, attacks, &c.[ee]

Punishments will only be carried out on the authority of the Infantry Brigade Commander, who, before taking action, will satisfy himself that the people concerned were, owing to their proximity to the outrage, or their known political tendencies, implicated in the occurrence, and will give specific instructions in writing or by telegram to the officer detailed to carry out the operation.

The punishment will be carried out as a military operation, and the reason why it is being done will be publicly proclaimed.

Full particular will be notified immediately to divisional headquarters.

Great stress was laid upon the necessity for the most rigid adherence to these instructions.

ee One could take great exception to 'rules laid down', as the first paragraph makes it quite clear *anyone* with knowledge of a pending IRA operation was liable for 'punishments'. The problem was there was no due process, no form for appeal, or any guarantee there was any means open for a person to report, if so inclined.

Infantry Brigade Commanders were forbidden to delegate their authority in the matter, and were ordered to satisfy themselves that the outrage was of sufficient gravity to justify the punishment, and that the persons concerned were implicated in the crime. The owners of the houses selected were always given notice in writing setting out the reasons for the punishment. Time was given for the removal of valuables. In the destruction of houses explosives only were used, it being forbidden to set fire to a house.

Later it became the practice to inflict fines instead of destroying property, except in very serious cases.

The campaign against "reprisals" was conducted in complete ignorance of the above facts, and left out of account the number of houses of loyalists and of Government buildings which were destroyed by the rebels. These, up to the end of May, 1921, included, in the Martial Law area only, 236 police barracks, 70 country houses and 101 other buildings. The statement which was sometimes made that "reprisals" (meaning "official punishments") had devastated areas, was a travesty of the facts. In the Cork district in which most of the punishment had been carried out, the destruction of houses by all sources, did not exceed one per cent.[ff]

[ff] While truthful in fact, this statement again demonstrates the duality of British Army thought on counterinsurgency. On the one hand, they knew they were fighting for the support of the people; while on the other, they usually acted with either emotion, thus missing their objective, or with cold calculation. The latter demonstrates their ignorance of their enemy. They understood the upper and upper middle classes well enough, but did not grasp the aspirations of the revolutionaries of the primarily middle and working classes. Their calculated, reasoned approach was lost entirely on the people caught in the middle, who merely wanted to be left alone.

The system of "official punishments" lasted for about 6 months, when, under instructions from the Government, it was stopped. It was admittedly difficult to convince the general public of the justification for the system, especially in view of the failure of Government propaganda, but it was a method of dealing with individuals whose complicity in outrages was well known locally, but in the abnormal circumstances impossible to prove owing to refusal of persons to give evidence. The system, while it lasted, had considerable effect in restraining any but the most extreme rebels, and its withdrawal in no way lessened the rebel burnings which had been undertaken as "counter-reprisals."[gg]

[gg] As with many statements, there is no evidence these actions had any influence on curbing IRA activity.

Reinforcements, December, 1920.—The introduction of Martial Law, and the necessity for compensating for the withdrawal of drafts for foreign service battalions, led to a considerable increase of battalions in Ireland during December, 1920. On 7th December the 2nd Bn. King's Royal Rifle Corps arrived at Belfast and took over various outlying detachments from the 1st Bn. King's Royal Rifle Corps. The latter battalion, which had been added to the Irish Command in September, 1920, was sent to guard the internment camp at Ballykinlar. Later in December the 3rd Bn. Rifle Brigade and the 1st Bn. Gloucestershire Regiment arrived, and were allotted to Dublin District and the 6th Division respectively. At the end of December, 1920, and during January, 1921, the following battalions arrived[18]:—

Unit	OC	Location
2nd Bn. King's Royal Rifle Corps	Lt-Col H. C. R. Green	Belfast
1st Bn. King's Royal Rifle Corps	Lt-Col R. G. Self	Internment Camp, Ballykinlar
3rd Bn. Rifle Brigade	Lt-Col J. Harington	25th Infantry Bde (Prov)
1st Bn. Gloucestershire Regiment	Bvt. Col F. C. Nisbet	16th (Fermoy) Infantry Bde
1st Bn. Royal Warwickshire Regiment		6th Division
2nd Bn. Suffolk Regiment	Lt-Col A. S. Peebles	13th (Athlone) Infantry Bde, 5th Division
2nd Bn. King's Own Yorkshire Light Infantry	Bvt. Col J. B. G. Tulloch	Londonderry Bde, 1st Division
1st Bn. Royal Scots Fusiliers	Bvt Lt-Col H. E. P. Nash	18th (Limerick) Infantry Bde, 6th Division
2nd Bn. The Loyal Regiment	Lt-Col R. E. Berkeley	Kerry Bde, 6th Division
2nd Bn. King's Own Scottish Borderers	Lt-Col H. D. M. McLean	17th Infantry Bde, 6th Division
2nd Bn. East Surrey Regiment	Lt-Col R. H. Baldwin	24th Provisional Infantry Bde, Dublin District[19]

This raised the number of battalions in Ireland to 51, but the actual number of troops in the country was not very largely increased, owing to the reduced state of the battalions which had provided drafts and the weakness of the battalions arriving from England.

Armoured cars, 1920.—The organization of armoured cars had been developed during the latter part of 1920. Originally these armoured cars consisted of 16 Austins and 20 Jeffrey Quads, with a few Peerless. They were armed with Hotchkiss guns. The Austins were manned by the 5th Armoured-Car Company, which consisted of Tank Corps personnel. The Jeffrey Quads and Peerless were manned by infantry crews drawn from local battalions.[20]

During September additional Peerless cars had been demanded for the protection of the mail service. The Austins and Jeffrey Quads gradually became derelict owing to lack of spare parts[21], but Peerless armoured cars were sent from England, and by the beginning of 1921 there were in Ireland 54 of these and 2 Rolls-Royce armoured cars. These were eventually increased to 70 Peerless and 34 Rolls-Royce by the spring of 1921. The cars were distributed to divisions, and by them to brigades as and were considered necessary, and were used for escort to patrol lorries or convoys, and for quelling disturbances or taking part in raids for arms. Their moral effect was very great, and, up to the end of 1920 at any rate, no ambush was attempted against a patrol accompanied by an armoured car.[22][hh]

[hh] The reason for this, rather than fear, as implied by the text, was that the IRA had no armour-piercing weapons. It thus became an issue of means, need and opportunity. They lacked the means to attack armoured vehicles at first, but did not need to attack them as there were sufficient targets elsewhere.

The Tank Corps personnel of the 5th Armoured-Car Company took over the manning of Rolls-Royce or Peerless as the Austins became derelict, but the crews of the great majority of the cars had still to be provided by infantry or cavalry. The wide dispersion of the cars made organization, administration and maintenance a difficult matter, especially as the Tank Corps officers of the 5th Armoured-Car Company[23] were the only experts available to advise and inspect. It was in these circumstances found necessary to ask the War-Office for sanction to improvise four armoured-car company organizations, one for each division. The War Office were also asked to provide from the Tank Corps personnel in England, a battalion headquarters and four company commanders and staff to command the improvised companies.[24]

Although the discussion regarding the proposed organization went on for some time, a cadre tank battalion headquarters with a small staff was all that the War Office would sanction. This, however, proved of great value in advice and administration. As Rolls-Royce cars increased, the 5th Armoured-Car Company personnel took them over, and the infantry crews manned the Peerless. In spite of the lack of technical personnel to assist, the improvised organization did most valuable work and the infantry crews picked up the work well.

Armoured tactical lorries.—During November and December, 1920, tactical lorries used by patrols were armoured.[ii] The first 150 sets of armouring obtained were rifle-proof[jj], and subsequently a revolver proof[kk] pattern was supplied by the War Office. The despatch of the armouring from England and the fitting of it to lorries in Ireland took a long time, but by the end of 1920 sets of plates for some 80 lorries had been supplied. Eventually, practically every lorry and Crossley was armoured with either rifle or revolver proof plates. In large towns, such as Dublin or Cork, where rebels armed with revolvers could approach close to the lorries and get away again in the crowd, the armouring was of great use, but in country districts, where a larger proportion of the rebels were armed with rifles, the usefulness of these lorries was not so great. Only a small percentage of them were fitted with rifle-proof plates and the speed of armoured lorries was considerably reduced. Also, as the training of lorry patrols insisted on the necessity, when attacked, of getting quickly out of the lorry, the armouring ceased to be of much value after the rebels had fired the first volley.[25]

[ii] The tactical lorries referred to Crossley tenders fitted with about 3,000 to 7,000 pounds of steel plate encasing the engine, driving compartment and cargo areas. The armouring of these lorries was done at the Inchicore Railway Yard in Dublin. The first of these vehicles was delivered in October 1920.

[jj] These plates were one-inch thick steel plates of varying lengths.

[kk] The plates were one-half inch thick steel plates, similar to the rifle-proof pattern.

NOTES

1   L. Ó Duibhir, *Prisoners of War: Ballykinlar Internment Camp 1920–1921* (2013) and L. Walsh, *'On my keeping' and in theirs: A Record of Experiences 'on the run', in Derry Gaol, and in Ballykinlar Internment Camp* (1921).

2   For the arrests, see Hopkinson, *War of Independence*, pp. XIV and 91 and Dorothy Macardle, *The Irish Republic 1911–1925* (1937), p. 406.

3 *The Last Post* only lists Jeremiah, while O'Donoghue says that Con was also killed. *The Last Post*, p. 111 and F. O'Donoghue, 'The Sacking of Cork', *Rebel Cork's Fighting Story* (2010), pp. 100–101.

4 General Staff, HQ, Irish Command, War Diary, 3 July 1920, wo 35/93/p 4. See 'Military Prisons in the Field', NAUK WO 35/141/4; 'Detention Barracks & Soldiers Detained', WO 35/50/1; and 'Report of the QMG', WO 35/50/6.

5 The NAUK WO 35/50/1 and WO 35/141/4.

6 See Louis J. Walsh, *'On my keeping' and in theirs: A Record of Experiences 'on the run', in Derry Gaol, and in Ballykinlar Internment Camp* (1921), pp. xiii–xiv, 48 and 98.

7 See Morrison, 'Kilmichael Revisited', *Terror in Ireland*; Kautt, *Ambushes and Armour*, pp. 99–117, for discussion of the action at Kilmichael; see also Ryan, *Tom Barry* and Peter Hart, *The I.R.A. & Its Enemies*, pp. 22–9. For Barry's account, see Tom Barry, *Guerrilla Days*, pp. 41–2 and 'Auxiliaries wiped out at Kilmichael in their first clash with the IRA', *With the IRA*, pp. 225–40. For recent provocative views, see McCall, *Tudor's Toughs*, pp. 101–109 and E. Browning, *Slaughtered Like Animals: A detailed examination of the killing of 17 members of the Royal Irish Constabulary Auxiliary Division by the IRA at Macroom, County Cork on 28th November 1920, and similar notorious incidents in that period* (2011), pp. 150–57 & 165–246.

8 Abbott, *Police Casualties*, p. 157 and Leeson, *Black and Tans*, pp. 50, 101, 111, 129, 152–6.

9 See Jeudwine to Greenwood, 5 December 1920, The Nat. Arch., Kew CO 904/232, pp. 1–4. See Additional Appendices.

10 See also 'Draft Conclusions of a Conference of Ministers held at 10 Downing Street, S.W.1, on Thursday, 2nd December 1920', NAUK CAB 23/23/161–6.

11 See Conclusions of a Meeting of the Cabinet, held at 10 Downing St, S.W.1, on Thursday, December 9, 1920, NAUK CAB 23/23/203–4, pp. 1–2.

12 See 'Notes on the Administration of Martial Law', 1921, Strickland Papers IWM EPS 2/2; see also, Jeudwine Papers IWM 72/82/2. For acquittals, see 3 August, 1920 and 'Report on the Situation in Ireland by General Officer Commanding-in-Chief', 8 August, 1920 NAUK, CAB 27/108/13; and 'Weekly Summary of the State of Ireland' CAB 27/108/15 SIC 26/27.

13 See 'Weekly Survey of the State of Ireland', 4 January, 1921, NAUK CAB 24/118/74–5 CP 2419.

14 Abbott, *Police Casualties*, pp. 165–6.

15 See, 'Report by the General Officer Commanding-in-Chief on the Situation in Ireland for the Week Ending January 15th, 1921', NAUK, CAB 24/118/391–2.

16 See Statement of J. M. MacCarthy (WS/883), appendix G; 'War Diary of the General Staff, GHQ Ireland', p. 13, 19 December, 1920, NAUK WO 35/93A and Sir N. Macready, *Annals of an Active Life*, Vol. II (1925), pp. 503 and 525 for the British side. See, for instance, Witness Statements of C. Brown (WS/873, p. 36); Col. S. Conway (WS/440, p. 14); S. Donnelly (WS/481, p. 18); P. Kearney (WS/444, p. 6); D. Lordan (WS/470, p. 22); M. O'Sullivan (WS/793, pp. 12–13); Dr P. O'Sullivan (WS/878, pp. 15–16); and Capt S. Sexton (WS/396, p. 15) for instances of attacks proceeding with hostages known to be present. S. Moylan (WS/838, pp. 162–3); M. O. Laoghaire (WS/797, p. 56); A. Reidy (WS/1021, p. 15) and J. Walsh (WS/966, p. 25) for instances of planned attacks being halted for the presence of hostages.

17 Townshend, *Political Violence*, p. 352 and M. F. Seedorf, 'Defending Reprisals: Sir Hamar Greenwood and the "Troubles", 1920–21', *Éire-Ireland: A Journal of Irish Studies*, (Geimhreadh/Winter 1990): 77–92.

18 Table not original to text.

19 The Royal Warwickshire was left out of the headquarters listing, but appeared in the Order of Battle of the 6th Division in Table 3. 'Showing Units Stationed in South of Ireland on July, 1921, and Detachments Found by Them', Appendix II 'Showing Distribution of Troops in South of Ireland. March, 1920, to July, 1921', Volume IV of *The Record of the Rebellion*. It was assigned to the 18th (Kerry) Infantry Bde and had detachments at Newcastlewest, Rathkeale, Abbeyfeal and Foynes (p. 218).

20 Notes of General Officer Commanding's Conference Held at Dublin District Headquarters, 3 June, 1920, NAUK WO 35/90/1/5, p. 3.
21 See various correspondence between Irish Command, the War Office, the Imperial General Staff and the Quartermaster General regarding the problems of spare parts and vehicle non-mission capable rates from May to Dec 1920, NAUK WO 32/9522.
22 See 'Steps to Meet the Requirements of the Irish Command in Regard to Armoured Cars', NAUK WO 32/9534.
23 Lt-Col D. H. Pratt, OC, Dublin.
24 See, 'Supply of Motor Transport', NAUK WO 32/9539; 'Increase in Mechanical Transport in Ireland', WO 32/9540 and 'Mechanical Transport, Armoured Cars and other forms of Protection for Troops in Ireland', WO 32/9541.
25 For a full discussion of the armoured vehicle issues, see Kautt, *Ambushes and Armour*, pp. 61–72 and G. Barndollar, 'British Military Use of Armoured Cars, 1919–1939', D.Phil Thesis, Oxford University, 2011.

CHAPTER V

Elections for Northern and Southern Parliaments, December 1920

Situation, December, 1920, to July, 1921.—From December, 1920, until July, 1921, there was no further change of policy. With the additional battalions which arrived in December and January, the increase in the R.I.C.[a] and Auxiliary Divisions[b], Martial Law in Munster, R.O.I.R.[c] in force throughout Ireland, the power of arrest and internment in the hands of Competent Military Authorities, and restrictions of motor vehicles, fairs and markets, and the curfew available where necessary, it was, perhaps, not surprising that the Government and the general public should imagine that the Crown forces would be capable of stamping out lawlessness and suppressing outrages.

[a] This actually referred to the non-Irishmen who entered into the RIC as constables starting in March 1920, commonly referred to as 'Black and Tans'; Recruitment of Irishmen into the RIC declined throughout the war.[1]

[b] Auxiliary Division, RIC; there were seventeen companies designated 'A' through 'Q'.[2]

[c] Restoration of Order in Ireland Regulations.

Military difficulties.—The problem with which the troops were confronted, however, was full of difficulties, which had long been recognized by the military authorities in Ireland, but which had become accentuated as a result of the spread of armed terrorism over the population during the past year.

In the first place, Ireland consists of some 30,000 square miles, in every part of which lawlessness and disorder might and did occur. The 51 battalions which at this time were in Ireland, even with the addition of the R.I.C. and Auxiliary Division, were obviously insufficient for dealing rapidly with the whole of this area, especially as the battalions were very weak, averaging, roughly, 250–300 men for offensive action after deducting barrack guards and other essential duties. The rank and file and many of the officers were very young, and their training in the ordinary military duties had been greatly curtailed.[d] The conditions were entirely unlike any preconceived ideas of military operations, and called for very special alertness, vigilance, resource, patience and forbearance. The necessity for regarding every civilian with suspicion as a potential enemy was extremely difficult to instil into the men. There was a perpetual antagonism between the sound military policy of concentration of force and the political requirements which demanded a considerable dispersion in detachments for the purpose of protecting and putting heart into loyal or law-abiding inhabitants and bolstering up the influence of the R.I.C.[3] [e]

[d]   This is one of the dangers of demobilization. As one demobilizes, one loses talent and experience, while usually still requiring these for active operations.

[e]   This highlights one of the paradoxes of counterinsurgency: the dual necessities of 'concentration of force', as the British principles of war call it, while being simultaneously omnipresent. The British Army recognized that they were trying to gain popular support from the people of Ireland, but were never able to produce the security necessary for the potential supporters to come forward safely. To accomplish this, the Army and police needed to be omnipresent in the towns and villages of Ireland. This would prove impossible if they could not defeat the IRA, which required this concentration of force. To provide the concentration and sufficient dispersion to create security probably required at least twice the number of men as they had available.

There was no objective for operations; there was no defined theatre of war, since non-combatants and loyal persons were intermingled with rebels in every district; there was no "front line" or "No Man's Land," and the only secure base for any body of troops was inside its own barrack walls. The troops were, in fact, living inside the enemy's lines, where their every movement was known as soon as begun, and in many cases was betrayed even before that. No means of communication were safe except by armoured cars; telegraphs, post offices and railways were almost entirely staffed by men and women who were either confessedly rebels or intimidated into aiding and abetting them.[4] The rebels, on the other hand, had everything in their favour. They were indistinguishable from harmless civilians until they had fired, and consequently they had little difficulty in carrying out ruses upon sentries and small bodies of troops. A group of men playing the Irish national game of pitch and toss by the roadside is so common a sight that it was a simple matter for a party of rebels intent on attacking a small patrol to camouflage themselves in this way. Men apparently engaged at work on the land could without difficulty form themselves into an ambush along the hedges on the approach of troops being signalled by a scout. The murder of individuals in the streets of a town required no courage when the murderer was covered by half a dozen accomplices who could successfully intimidate any passers-by from raising the alarm or following the criminal. Even the weapons with which the murder was committed could be quickly disposed of by handling them to women confederates, who were always considered by the troops, with perhaps a mistaken chivalry, to be exempt from search.[f]

[f] This brings up another of the paradoxical dualities of counterinsurgency: the coexistence of its military and criminal characteristics. By the time the insurgents are conducting operations with dozens of men, they have passed out of the realm of merely constituting a criminal threat; such a force requires the military to defeat it. Military forces are usually ill suited to policing civilian communities. Thus, the army's mission in Ireland was to defeat the IRA in strength, co-ordinate operations with the RIC to protect it from larger guerrilla bands, while establishing conditions in which the police could gather intelligence for future military operations, as well as arrests and prosecutions at the lower scale. Synchronizing these activities is difficult now; then, without modern communications, it was next to impossible. Finally, COIN theory was embryonic, so it is no wonder the army did not always understand its mission.

Neither did the more ambitious projects of the I.R.A., such as attacks on small detachments of troops or police, require any great skill in the preparation, or courage in the execution. The principle military difficulty in beating an enemy in detail is the successful and secret concentration of superior force at the given time and place. To the rebels, having no uniform[g] and able to move into a locality without molestation in twos and threes, there was no difficulty in assembling in force in houses adjoining their objective, or in positions of ambush near a road. There was practically no chance of information being given to the troops; the case of Mrs. Lindsay[h] and hundreds of others was a perfectly sufficient deterrent. Moreover, the rebels' plans seldom entailed the attack of more than 10 to 12 troops or police, and, even so, they did not attempt to attack unless they could count on tremendous odds in their favour. In the attack on Kilmallock [Co. Limerick] police barracks on 28th May, 1920, where two R.I.C.[i] were burnt alive, the odds were 200 to 1; 500 men actually attacked while 1,800 blocked roads and provided covering parties. The R.I.C. post numbered 10 men.[j] On the other hand, when considering the number of occasions on which troops were surprised, ambushed and overwhelmed by rebels, it must not be forgotten that the I.R.A. were perpetually on the look out for favourable opportunities for attack with little attendant risk, and that cases were undoubtedly very numerous where the excellence of the tactical precautions taken by commanders of troops frustrated any attempt. In such cases the pitch-and-toss players or the pseudo-farm labourers remained in their assumed rôles, and nothing was ever heard of an intended attack.[k]

[g] This complaint is disingenuous, considering that the authorities made the wearing of the Volunteer uniform an offense in 1916 under the DORR and under the 'Restoration of Order in Ireland Regulations', Section 9AA punishable with up to life imprisonment.

[h] Mrs Mary Lindsay and her driver were killed by the IRA in retaliation for her having informed the police about the Dripsey Ambush on 28 January, 1920.[5]

[i] They were Sgt Thomas Kane (b.1871) and Const. Joseph Morton (b.1872). The policemen were repeatedly called upon to surrender, but refused; there were conflicting reports about whether the two men died of wounds or burned to death.[6]

[j] The numbers given here are simply beyond credulity, and were a source of great humour to the veterans of the IRA. There is no doubt that the enemy massed and attacked in force, but the IRA could not muster such great numbers of armed men for such a small operation. One should remember that Barry's flying column numbered around 100 men, and still lost three

men killed and five wounded (about 8 per cent) when attacking twenty ADRIC at Kilmichael. These were by no means 'safe' operations.

k   This is the very nature of small wars; it is, fundamentally, asymmetric method of the weak against the strong. The only realistic way to defeat it is to separate the guerrilla from the people somehow. To accomplish this, the counterinsurgent could move the populace as in the Second South African War, (1899–1902), but this brings with it a host of other problems. It is not realistic to hope to be omnipresent, as mentioned above, without being oppressive. In all, the counterinsurgents must understand that their role is to *serve* the people whom they are protecting, otherwise they will fail.

If these conditions are compared with a legitimate form of war, where the enemy are recognizable by their uniforms, and can be attacked wherever and whenever seen without the necessity of waiting for their identity to be disclosed by a hostile act, it will be realized that the troops and their commanders were placed in a particularly anomalous position, and that their superiority in arms and equipment was to a large extent neutralized. Some of these difficulties admittedly exist in ordinary guerilla warfare, but the many points of difference inherent in the situation which confronted the troops in Ireland were evidently not appreciated by the writers of articles in the English Press nor by individuals, well-meaning and otherwise, who from time to time offered suggestions. The most common suggestion was that the troops should "treat it as a war" and avail themselves to the full of their superiority in armament and training; but this ignores the fact that the main difficulty of offensive action was the lack of an objective.[l] Other suggestions realized this difficulty and proposed the plan of blockhouse lines and drives as in the South African war. This again left out of account the impossibility of identifying large numbers of rebels, the unlikelihood of finding arms on the men searched, and the hardship which would have been inflicted on loyal or law-abiding non-combatants.[m] The withdrawal of all troops to the coast, followed by an economic blockade, gained a good deal of support in unofficial circles. This suggestion, however, was open to insurmountable objections. It ignored the question of loyalists and the fact that the presence of troops was the only safeguard against an even more oppressive intimidation than already existed. The economic blockade would have raised an outcry in England and America long before it had achieved results, the troops would then have been required to return to their original stations, where they would have found their barracks burnt, and a state of armed terrorism even more difficult to deal with than before.

[l] While their angst is understandable, to argue that guerrilla warfare was not legitimate, a common feeling up to the present, must be the charge against the Duke of Wellington, or at least some of his Spanish allies, in his Peninsular War. Further, this complaint was actually obfuscation, an attempt to draw attention away from their failure to recognize, to accept and to adapt to their situation. Merely complaining that the rebels were using these tactics and the press were aiding in turning public opinion did not fix the problem. The army could not accept this problem, and thus could not adapt to it until relatively late in the war. These protestations demonstrate that not everyone did accept it, even after the war. It is only appropriate to acknowledge that the British forces, especially the Army, became more adept in this type of war during the last few months of the fighting. Although one cannot blame the army for not developing effective counters to the IRA, indeed, they created the first counterinsurgency school, this does not change their failure to recognize and accept their situation.

[m] For the British to claim a desire to prevent unnecessary suffering amongst the civilian population in Ireland, while at the same time invoking the memory of the Boer War, is not without irony. Although fairness requires one to admit that their atrocities against the Boer civilians were largely unintentional, it does not remove their horrific crimes against them, nor does it remove culpability once the effects were known. Even so, relations between the British and the Irish at the time were strained.

A further great handicap under which the Crown forces, and those who controlled them, laboured, was the licence which was allowed to the Press. The large majority of the newspapers in Ireland were openly and avowedly bitterly hostile to British rule in general and the Crown forces in particular. No libel was too gross, and no lie too obvious, for them to print. They were used freely by the rebel leaders as a medium for circulating propaganda, and the part which they played in poisoning the public mind both in Ireland and abroad, belauding the outrages of the I.R.A., and vilifying the Crown forces, amounted to nothing less than incitement to murder. As an instance, the murder of Colonel Smyth[n], Divisional Commissioner, R.I.C., in Cork, on 17th July, 1920, followed on a series of attacks upon him of a most virulent and provocative nature in a well-known Dublin newspaper. All attempts to suppress these hostile papers failed. Before the end of 1919 one of them had been suppressed, but in January

1920 the Government ordered the printing plant to be returned, and the paper reappeared on even more scandalous lines than before. Later, resort was had to prosecution of papers for publishing misstatements, and in December, 1920, the conviction of the *Freeman's Journal*[o] was secured and sentence was passed involving a heavy fine, and the imprisonment of the owner and editor.[p] This was subsequently quashed.

[n] Lt-Col Gerald Brice-Ferguson Smyth (b.1885), late of the King's Own Scottish Borderers and Royal Engineers. Appointed RIC Divisional Commissioner for Munster July 1920; his brother, Maj George Osbert Stirling Smyth (b.1890), was killed leading a raid in Dublin on the morning of 12 October 1920.[7]

[o] Founded in 1763 by Charles Lucas (b.1713–d.1771).

[p] On 25 November 1920, Martin Fitzgerald (b.1867–d.1927) and Hamilton Edwards, directors, and the editor Patrick J. Hooper (b.1873–d.1931), were found not guilty of four charges revolving around making false statements to spread or likely to spread 'disaffection'; they were found guilty of 'spreading a false report' and one intending to cause 'disaffection' with the monarch.

Rebel Press propaganda, March, 1921.—In March, 1921, the Commander-in-Chief in a letter to the Chief Secretary stated as his opinion, after a year's experience, that the time had come for the suppression of the *Freeman's Journal* and the *Independent*[q], that these papers were nothing less than daily propaganda of rebellion, that prosecution was quite ineffective, and that, as being responsible for the good behaviour and good name of the troops, he gave it as his emphatic opinion that drastic action should be taken. The reply to this letter was that, owing to the pressure which would be put upon the Government by English newspapers, if the papers in question were suppressed, the Chief Secretary[r] did not consider it advisable. The Commander-in-Chief registered his protest against this decision. The hostile Press remained to the end as one of the strongest weapons in the hands of the rebels.

[q] The *Irish Independent*, founded by William Martin Murphy (b.1844–d.1919); ironically, the republican community viewed this newspaper as being largely anti-IRA.

[r] Greenwood.

It was not, however, the openly hostile Press of Ireland only which was increasing the difficulty of the cause of law and order.[s] The correspondents of a good many English papers, some even reputable papers, also sent home exaggerated accounts of rebel "daring," and libellous statements concerning the troops. The truth was that the terrorism of the "gunmen" was such that no journalist could travel about Ireland, and get "copy" and live, unless he adopted Sinn Fein sympathies, or at any rate a colour neutrality. Representations were frequently made to the War Office and to the Government regarding the increased difficulties which were experienced by the refusal of the Press in England to use its influence in the cause of the Crown forces.[t] Nor did public men attempt to enlighten the public, or to learn the truth themselves. On the other hand, many of them were willing to use their influence to cast aspersions on the Crown forces, and some actually in direct correspondence with leading rebels.

[s] This comment is telling in several respects. By seeing this as nothing but 'law and order', the authors betray their ignorance of the situation. They were social elites, and were satisfied with the status quo as constituting a natural order that everyone, in good conscience, should accept. They did not understand the revolutionary desire to change this system, and anyone who wanted to do so was 'Bolshie'; this comes out repeatedly in their descriptions of the IRA.[8]

They did not understand the revolutionary nature of the World War; the aristocracy had suffered enormous losses and this, combined with the exponential expansion of the Army, created a need for officers that the aristocracy could not fill. As a result, they commissioned many who would not otherwise have had such an opportunity. Yet after the war, with overly rapid demobilization, the Army returned to the old order and debated what to do with these 'temporary gentlemen', ultimately forcing them out. One reason why the ADRIC held relatively high rank, as officer cadets equal to sergeants, and high pay of £1 per day, was in recognition of their skill and status.[9]

Of course, the British army leadership in Ireland formed an interesting group, as Boyd, Jeudwine, Strickland and Tudor were not destined for general officer rank before the war. Bainbridge and Macready were the only general officers of them prior to the war, yet neither was very distinguished. The war made their careers.

Yet these authors could not see that there were others in society who had the same skills and background, yet were irritated with a system preventing their advancement in society. The leaders of the republican movement were overwhelmingly middle class and well educated, with few notable exceptions in either direction. Combined with Irish nationalism, second-class citizenship as middle class, Irish and Catholic, revolution was the natural outlet to break the glass ceiling.

Although most people in Ireland had the basic necessities in life: food, clothing and shelter, they wanted courtesy and respect. These officers, intellectually dishonest, could not admit that Ireland rarely received courtesy and virtually never respect. The perfect example of this, writ large, was from the viceroy and the Chief Secretary, and sometimes to lower levels; Ireland was rarely governed by Irishmen. This was the message spurring the home rule movement. Of course, one need only look to how Parnell and Redmond were treated by the British establishment. The authors' inability to admit any legitimate complaint explains their seeing any criticism of the Government's action as support for the rebels. Ironically, this failing gave support to the republican cause.

t The authors clearly did not understand the irony of their statements condemning the press for bias, and at the same time for not being biased. This is another demonstration of their myopia: to their minds, the papers should only report what the army believed, not what the rest of the country wanted.

Commander-in-Chief's report to Cabinet, November, 1920[10].—In November, 1920, the Commander-in-Chief in a report to the C.I.G.S. and the Cabinet stated—

One of the chief obstacles to further and more rapid improvement is the fact that a majority of newspapers in England, and many public men, use their influence and the freedom of speech which they enjoy on the side of organized opposition to authority in this country. The result is that the disloyal element in Ireland feel that they have a large backing in England.

Commander-in-Chief's letter to C.I.G.S., February, 1921.—And again in a letter to the C.I.G.S. in February, 1921—

The soldier and policemen in this country, unacquainted with the actual value of opinions expressed through the Press, are not encouraged by the campaign against them which is waged by politicians and journalists for their own ends and glorification at the expense of those who are endeavouring to carry out their duty to the Government, unpleasant and onerous though it may be.

Labour Party Commission, January, 1920.—A Labour Commission[u], including an ex-regular officer[v] came to Ireland twice to report on the state of affairs. On the first occasion, in January, 1920, members approached the Sinn Fein sympathisers only.

[u] The Committee's members were: Arthur Henderson MP; W. Adamson MP; J. Bromley; A. G. Cameron; F. W. Jowett; J. Lawson MP and W. Lunn MP. Additional members were Capt C. W. Kendall, Legal Adviser; Brig-Gen C. B. Thomson, Military Adviser; W. W. Henderson, Press Secretary; Arthur Greenwood, Secretary of the Commission.[11]

[v] Brig-Gen Christopher Birdwood Thomson, PC (b.1875–d.1930) 1st Baron Thomson (1924). He died in an airship crash in France.

December, 1920.—On the second occasion, in December, 1920, they came to General Headquarters and had matters explained to them, were shown many confidential documents, expressed themselves satisfied with the methods of the troops against whom they were much struck to have received no complaints during their tour. On return to England, however, individual members of the Commission spoke violently against the methods being employed in Ireland and against the conduct of the troops.[w] The troubles in Ireland were, in fact, used largely as a means of encompassing the discomfiture of political opponents.

The troops felt the lack of moral support from England very keenly, and it was only in June, 1921, when the Government had more drastic measures in contemplation, that the necessity of doing something to rouse the British public and obtain their support was realized.

Divided control of military and police.—In the absence of Martial Law all over the country, a further difficulty was the divided control of the forces of law and order and of civil administration. In the Martial Law area the police were under the orders of the Military Governor, and where this was recognized and acted upon it was possible to adopt some settled and co-ordinated policy decided on from time to time by the Military Governor of the Martial Law area, and issued by means of proclamation. Over the rest of Ireland responsibility for law and order rested with the civil administration, and the troops were theoretically called upon to assist in order to reinforce the police. In practice much of the information concerning the rebels was obtained by the Military Intelligence Section[12], and action was taken by troops by order of the competent military authority in virtue of his powers under R.O.I.R. But this did not obviate the difficulty of the two branches of the Crown forces being under different heads and carry out policies not necessarily similar.[x]

Effect of Martial Law, January, 1921.—Towards the end of January the Military Governor of the Martial Law area was able to report upon the general effect of Martial Law so far as could be judged. On the surface it did not appear that much progress had been made. Arms had not been handed in, and there had been a recrudescence of outrage and crime. These outrages were, however, mostly carried out in a half-hearted way, and were of a minor character. Attacks on police barracks were mostly in the nature of a demonstration, while protracted attacks were not attempted. There was some evidence, or, at any rate, a general impression, that the increased activity was ordered from the I.R.A. headquarters and was intended as an answer to the declaration of Martial Law, and to raise the moral of the rebels in that area.

[w] This misrepresents the Commission and its report. While not friendly, it was hardly a condemnation across the board. It admitted that, 'On the whole, few charges have been laid against the military forces in Ireland.' It does criticize the ADRIC and its lack of discipline, as well as the lack of command and control from the Government, but these same charges were levelled by their former commander, Frank Crozier. This type of hostility demonstrates the authors' wilful myopia.[13]

[x] Interestingly, Macready was offered command of the RIC in 1920 when he arrived, but refused, ostensibly on the grounds that it was too much work for one man, but probably also because he felt that there was little chance of success with the RIC.[14]

The fact that this appeal had not been answered with the same alacrity as heretofore was, it was thought, due to the fear of the penalties which Martial Law made possible. There had been a marked difference in the attitude of part of the population, and letters began to come in freely giving information and urging the military authorities to hunt down the murderers. Some of the information had led to the capture of a considerable number of arms in Fermoy, Cork and other places. This was apparently due to the fear of individuals whose houses had been used for the purpose. In short, although there had been an increase in rebel activity, a fact of which the hostile Press and *An T'Oglac* made the most, the general spirit apparent in the operations of the rebels had become one of timidity.[y]

Relations between police and military.—After two month's experience of Martial Law it was found that the co-operation of troops and police was much handicapped by two further difficulties. The first of these was the practice of the police authorities at Dublin issuing instructions direct to their subordinate police officials and commanders of companies of the Auxiliary Division, for the carrying out of operations, &c. This was contrary to the agreed arrangement for the Martial Law area, and led to lack of co-ordination and wasted effort. The second difficulty was that a different system of discipline, and of enforcing it, existed in the Police Force and the Army, although they were working side by side under single control of the Military Governors. This difficulty first became apparent the day before Martial Law was declared, when a big fire occurred in Cork City. The police were not at this time under the Military Governor, but the fire was attributed to members of the police by writers in the Press and others.[z]

[y] There was a decrease in the violent operations by the Irish Volunteers, but what the authors neglected to mention was that the rebels were reacting to the dramatic increase in armoured vehicles in Ireland. Beginning in May 1920, the British army tried to find a way to increase their firepower available in convoys, while at the same time providing protection for their men. The answer was to use armoured vehicles. They began by 'up-armouring' some of their existing fleet, primarily of Crossley 'Tenders', with half-inch and one-inch steel plates attached to the chassis by railway works in Dublin and Belfast. Half-inch plate stopped pistol rounds, while the one-inch plates stopped rifle bullets, as mentioned in the previous chapter. The increased weight on the chassis caused a 40 per cent non-mission-capable standing by December. The army also sent vehicles armoured by the vehicle manufacturers, the most famous of which was the Rolls-Royce Naval Pattern Armoured Car, but they also had the Jeffery Quads, Fords, and Austins. Thus, while there was a decrease in ambushes in the first six weeks of 1921, it was due to British forces using armoured vehicles. The rebel response, since they had no armour-piercing weapons, was to attack the roads and bridges to reduce British mobility. The IRA restarted their ambushes once they learnt effective counters.[15]

[z] This occurred the night of 11 & 12 December, 1920, after an attack on ADRIC in Cork City. The fires were set by K Company, ADRIC, who were proud of their actions. There is no doubt that the ADRIC set the fires in retaliation for the death of a comrade, as well as for almost continuous attacks since Kilmichael in November.[16]

The matter was taken up with the Government. It was strongly represented that Martial Law could only be effective, and that there was a possibility of friction occurring between the police and military authorities, unless it was quite clearly recognized that the police in the Martial Law area must look to the Military Governor as their immediate and only superior in everything except police routine of administration and interior economy. It was also requested that, although the police authorities were responsible for the administration of discipline of the police, the Military Governor should have the power of insisting on adequate punishment being inflicted where, breaches of discipline had taken place. Finally, it was asked that a senior police official not below the rank of Divisional Commissioner should be appointed as Police Advisor, attached to the staff of the Military Governor.[aa]

[aa] The senior police official was the Police Advisor to the viceroy. In the late spring of 1920, Lieut-Gen. Tudor was appointed to this position. That the army could not get the police to co-operate when the senior police official was an army general officer speaks to the dysfunctional relationship between the two organizations.

Increased rebel activities, February–March, 1921.—During February and March the activities of the rebels in the Martial Law area fluctuated without any definite change in the situation. Flying columns for a time became more daring and their activities on some occasions bore a resemblance to military operations, but as on such occasions they were usually worsted by the troops, a period of quiet would ensue, until the rebel moral was again sufficiently raised to become active. For instance, near Mourne Abbey, Co. Cork[17], on 15th February, rebels in ambush were surprised by a party of the Manchester Regiment. The rebels fled, but ran into a mixed party of the Lancashire Regiment and the police. In the fight which ensued 8 rebels were killed and 8 taken prisoners.[bb] Again, on 20th February, at Clonmult[18], Co. Cork a part of the Hampshire Regiment, 15 strong, came upon a party of rebels armed with Service rifles. Five of the rebels[cc] were killed and the remainder, 16 in number, were driven into a farmhouse and prevented from escaping until police reinforcements arrived, when the whole party was killed[dd] or captured[ee]. The result of the fighting was that 13 rebels were killed and 8 captured. Other examples of conflicts are shown in the notes to this chapter.

bb   Patrick Dorgan (b.ca.1899), Patrick Flynn (b.ca.1896) and Eamon Creedon (b.ca.1901) were killed-in-action, and Michael Looney (b.ca.1891) died of wounds. There were eight prisoners, of whom Patrick Ronayne, (b.ca.1897) and Thomas Mulcahy (b.ca.1903) were executed.[19]

cc   James Ahern, David Desmond, Michael Hallihane, Richard Hegarty and John Joe Joyce.[20]

dd   Jeremiah Ahern, Liam Ahern, Donal Denehy, Michael Desmond, James Glavin, Joseph Morrissey and Christy O'Sullivan.[21]

ee   Known as the Battle of Clonmult, it was the worst single defeat of the IRA during the war. All of the captives, Captain Higgins (WIA) and Vols. Terry, Walsh, Garde, Harty, Maurice Moore, Jeremiah O'Leary (WIA) and Paddy O'Sullivan were sentenced to death, but only Moore and O'Sullivan were executed (on 28 April, 1921 along with Ronayne and Mulcahy from Mourne Abbey).[22]

During the month of March, 1921, the attacks on Crown forces reached their height. This was probably due to a desire on the part of the leaders of the rebel forces to advertise their power in the country, and to counteract amongst civilians in the Martial Law area the undoubtedly growing feeling that the results attained by the action of the I.R.A. did not compensate for the inconveniences which resulted by the enforcement of Martial Law restrictions.

Murder of Colonel Cummings, 3rd March, 1921.—On the 3rd March, Colonel Cummings[ff], Colonel Commandant of the Kerry Brigade, whilst proceeding from Killarney to Rathmore with an escort in Crossley cars, and accompanied by an armoured car, was ambushed. The armoured car became ditched. Colonel Cummings and another officer were killed.[gg] During this month also a series of murders of ex-soldiers, Protestant farmers and others took place who were (generally quite without foundation) suspected of furnishing information to the police.[23] This form of outrage, in which men were dragged from their houses and butchered, became prevalent throughout the country about this time and continued up to the end. On 6th March, the Mayor[hh] and ex-Mayor[ii] of Limerick were murdered. An attempt was made in the Press to attribute these murders to the Crown forces, but the history of these two men throws a different light on the matter. It was, in fact, due to these two men and some influential priests that conditions in Limerick City had been peaceable for some months. The Mayor (Clancy) belonged to the first Limerick battalion,

I.R.A., which, largely owing to his influence, had the reputation of being unenterprising. The second Limerick battalion, therefore, seceded from the first battalion and became responsible for a number of outrages in the district. Considerable friction resulted between the two battalions owing to the peaceful nature of the first battalion. Documentary evidence of this exists.[jj]

[ff] Colonel Hanway Robert Cumming (b.1867). This is the correct spelling of his surname.

[gg] This was the Clonbanin Ambush, 5 March, 1921.[24]

[hh] George Clancy (b.1887).

[ii] Michael O'Callaghan (b.1879).

[jj] Despite the protestations herein, these men were mostly likely killed by the ADRIC; Clancy's wife, Mollie (née Kileen) was wounded in the hand during the attack on her husband. Clancy was a very active Irish Volunteer commander. The policemen also took one Joseph O'Donnoghue, who was found murdered on 7 March 1921.[25]

Attack on the Essex Regiment, 19th March, 1921.—Towards the end of March it was found that rebel flying columns were amalgamating into larger bodies, and on 19th March, near Bandon, Co. Cork, one of these rebel columns made an attack which was on a bigger scale than any previously attempted. A mixed party of the Essex Regiment and Hampshire Regiment with police having left their transport under escort were operating on foot. The rebel column attacked the transport and overcame the escort, doing considerable damage before the main body of the troops arrived. On the arrival of the troops the rebels stood to fight. A fierce fight ensued and finally the rebels withdrew. The Crown forces suffered 16 casualties, killed[kk] or wounded, of whom the majority were the transport party. Of the rebels 6 were killed, 6 captured and about 7 wounded.[ll]

[kk] The British soldiers killed were: Sjt Edward Watts, Pte.s Joseph Thomas Cafer, William Alfred Gray, S. W. Steward and William Wilkins.

[ll] The republicans called this the Battle of Crossbarry, and actually lost three men: Con Daly, Peter Monahan and Jeremiah O'Leary, while the British lost six wounded and nine killed. Although legend has overblown the results of this battle to ridiculous proportions, it was an example of

what the Irish Volunteers could do in extremely dangerous situations, what they were capable of when well led. It is probably safe to say this was Tom Barry's finest engagement.[26]

The British dead were: 1st Essex:

Pte Sidney Robert Cawley, Pte Joseph Thomas Crafer, Second Lieut G. T. Hotblack, Pte S. W. Steward, Sjt Edward Watts, Pte William Wilkins

RASC:

Pte H. Baker (DOW), Pte William Alfred Gray, Pte C. J. Martin (DOW).

Rebel concentrations in Kerry, March, 1921.—In Co. Kerry about the middle of March there was strong evidence that the rebels were concentrating, and it was believed that a rising was intended in that county. If this had occurred and had met with any success, as might easily have been the case in so remote a county, a very serious situation would have occurred, as it would probably have spread to other counties. Such a contingency would, however, have given the Army the opportunity of meeting large bodies of rebels and of asserting its superiority in arms and equipment. A telegram was, therefore, sent to the War Office asking for permission to make use of action from aeroplanes. This question had previously been raised in September, 1920, when it was not sanctioned.

Use of aeroplanes.—On this occasion sanction was given for the use of bombs and machine-gun fire from the air with certain restrictions. Action was to be taken only in country districts away from towns, and aeroplanes were only to carry armament on orders from a military officer not below the rank of Colonel Commandant.[mm] Arrangements were made for the despatch of reinforcements to Co. Kerry should necessity arise, but a rising was never attempted.[nn]

[mm] The rank of 'colonel-commandant' replaced that of 'brigadier-general' in the British army in 1921 for brigade commanders, and would later be changed simply to 'brigadier'.[27]

[nn] The guerrilla generally does not like enclosed spaces or large groups of his compatriots: the former is a trap, the latter a target. Having identified large concentrations of rebels in Kerry, and having received permission to use attack aircraft, the appropriate military response would have been to 'cordon and search', cut off escape from the affected districts and hunt the rebels therein. This is what the Essex tried at Crossbarry, but failed to close the cordon sufficiently. That the army did not attempt this in Kerry is telling, and calls into question either their military capabilities, or confidence in them, or both.

Situation in Martial Law area, April, 1921.—During April the number of attacks on Crown forces in the Martial Law area began to diminish and there was some indication that the rebels of the flying columns were becoming more averse from trying conclusions on a scale with armed bodies of troops. The Military Governor of the Martial Law area reported as follows regarding the situation in his area at the end of April:—

> The results of the 4 months Martial Law had, on the whole, been all that could be expected, bearing in mind the state of affairs that would have arisen in the absence of Martial Law, and the number of individuals who had probably been deterred from joining the rebel forces. A period of a month's comparative quiet during April, succeeding a period of intense activity on the part of the rebels, was attributed to reaction after losses which had undoubtedly been heavy, the desire of men "on the run" to return to their farms, and possibly instructions to keep quiet till after the elections to the Southern Parliament, which were due to take place in May. The flow of information which had begun at the initiation of Martial Law had fallen off during succeeding months. This was, it was thought, due to the large number of murders of suspected informers, but the more law-abiding civilians had gained heart, and in one instance at Roscarberry had actually turned out to drive a rebel party out of the village. The attitude and tone of the local Press in the Martial Law area had much improved thanks to firm control and power to enforce obedience.[28]

But although progress had been made and the Crown forces had a better grip of the situation in this area than in the rest of Ireland, the Martial Law which it was possible to enforce was not that which is ordinarily understood by the term. Civil administration to a certain extent continued to exist as well as military control, and disloyalty in the Civil Services, such as Post Offices, railways, and various county and town civilian administrative bodies was still able to complicate the situation. Whereas a quick punishment for offences is an important deterrent under Martial Law, appeals to the Civil Courts in Dublin were still permissible, and greatly delayed the carrying out of sentences passed by military courts. One thing had become quite clear, that the rigorous and continued enforcement of restrictions produced better results than any attempt at conciliation.[oo]

oo   This absolute belief in martial law is explicable only in terms of gut instinct; they had no other object data to use to judge the situation. The number of attacks on troops may have appeared to decrease, but casualties were higher than they had been the month before. Indeed, casualties continued to rise until July 1921 with the Truce. Republican forces were conducting ever more frequent and ever larger operations. There were no indications that the British forces were in any way 'winning' the conflict, which remained undefined. No one on the Government side defined what 'victory' meant. That said, the British army was not entirely out of its depth; their intelligence and responsiveness to fluid situations were improving. They had discovered that the same military answer to most problems; mobility through combined arms, worked against rebel forces too, and were acting to become more responsive.

Situation, rest of Ireland, January to April, 1921.—In the rest of Ireland, outside the Martial Law area, the situation during January to April, 1921, did not differ in any material particular from obtaining at the end of November, 1920. The policy of arrest and internment proceeded. The arrests had become fewer owing to the great difficulty in finding the wanted men, but by the end of April in all Ireland more than 3,300 officers or prominent members of the I.R.A. had been interned. Law of accommodation at one period led to a temporary decrease in the number of arrests made. Applications for internment camps outside Ireland had been refused, and a camp was, therefore, mode at the Curragh. There were then two camps at Ballykinlar, one at Bere Island, one at Spike Island, and one (afterwards two) at the Curragh.

The railway strike had come to an end by January and troops were able to travel by train, but the resumption of normal services led to numerous raids on trains for mails and military stores, and to various acts of sabotage involving sometimes attempts to wreck trains.pp

pp   The attacks by the IRA against trains were generally of two types: those against the mails and stores, as stated, and those against troops. The former were generally to obtain or deny to the enemy, while the latter were ambushes.[29]

Destruction of roads and bridges.—Early in the year the rebels began, in the 5th Divisional Area, a scheme which spread rapidly throughout the country, for hampering the movement of mechanical transport. Roads were cut by means of trenches or blocked by felled trees or improvised walls, and bridges were in many places blown up. This procedure was not apparently carried out on any regular system, but it had the effect of greatly restricting the roads which could be used for lorry patrols. The practice provided a safe way for the less bold spirits of the rebels to show some form of activity, and local units of the I.R.A. became responsible for this action in their respective areas. To counter this move several expedients were tried. Local inhabitants were impressed by the troops or police and compelled to fill in the trenches. Fairs and markets were prohibited for a fixed radius round the scene of road destruction, and creameries were closed in districts where the cases had been most frequent. This last restriction caused some considerable outcry, but in a great many cases, the managers of the creameries were prominent rebels, and sometimes the local creamery was the recognized meeting place, and distributing centre for the I.R.A. These restrictions had some result in that they were only removed when the roads had been repaired, but the greatest factor in reducing road destruction was the unpopularity in which such action was held by local farmers who were unable to get their goods to market. Latterly, farmers with local assistance used to fill in the trenches themselves, but although some districts became less obstructed, the practice continued up to July, 1921.[qq]

> [qq] While there is truth to the statement that attacking roads and bridges was a way for Volunteers who did not want to kill, at least not directly, to support the war, this interpretation as a means of avoiding danger is facile. Volunteers engaged in trenching roads and destroying bridges were in danger too, indeed there were many instances of Volunteers being captured while engaged in these activities, to the extent that IRA GHQ issued instructions for the protection of these operations. GHQ also ordered IRA units to ensure that local traffic could pass through the obstacles they created.[30]

Suggested Martial Law in Dublin.—After the declaration of Martial Law in Munster at the end of 1920 there was a short period of comparative immunity from outrage all over Ireland, but whether this was due to fear of the extension of Martial Law or to certain vague rumours of a settlement which were then in the air, it is not possible to say. As in the Martial Law area, however, so in the rest of the country activities were renewed on an increased scale about the middle of January. In Dublin particularly many outrages occurred. These mostly took the form of firing or throwing bombs at lorries carrying patrols in the streets. In some of these attacks the rebels suffered heavy casualties. On 19th January five rebels were wounded in an attack on a lorry at Terenure (Dublin)[31]; on 21st January auxiliary police captured six fully-armed rebels who had attacked a police lorry and Drumcondra (Dublin)[32]; on 29th January a lorry patrol was bombed in Dublin, one officer and eight other ranks were wounded[33].

Towards the end of January the question of Martial Law in Dublin was discussed, partly owing to the number of attacks on lorries in the streets, and partly because the headquarters of the I.R.A. were located in Dublin and it was thought that Martial Law might hamper the activities, or facilitate their capture and so cripple the rebel cause in the country. A letter was sent to the Chief Secretary asking his views. The Chief Secretary replied that he was not convinced, on the available evidence, that Martial Law would assist.

Searches in Dublin, February, 1921.—In February some extensive operations were carried out by troops and police in Dublin. Areas of the city were surrounded by cordons of troops and systematically searched. During one of these searches the office of the "Chief of Staff," I.R.A. (Richard Mulcahy), was discovered, and a great many very valuable documents were seized.[rr]

rr   Mulcahy's office was raided a second time on 22 March 1921.[34]

In the country, other than Martial Law areas and Dublin, there was no marked change in the situation during January and February, except that flying columns became rather more active during the beginning of February but with little success.[ss] The number of internments had broken up many local units, and a system of sending extremists into areas to stir up activity was adopted. As in the Martial Law area, so elsewhere, the month of March produced the largest number of attacks on Crown forces, though many of them were half-hearted. In April there was again a decrease in outrages, and in Dublin several important captures of arms were made, and, on 29th April, the meeting of a battalion of the I.R.A. was surrounded resulting in the capture of the battalion staff and 40 men together with some arms.[tt]

ss   The rebels were successful at the Clonfin Ambush on 2 February 1921, and at Ballyvourney on 25 March 1921, under Seán O'Hegarty.[35]

tt   According to the Dublin District history, this occurred on Blackhall Place, Dublin, on 19 April 1921, where: 'The 24th Brigade captured the Active Service unit of the 1st Bn. I.R.A., Dublin Brigade at Blackhall Place; some 40 men were taken without resistance. In addition, several dumps were discovered during this period. But our active offensive continued to be hampered in Dublin by congestion of prisoners, dating from the handing over of the Intelligence to the Police in December.'[36]

The tendency on the part of the rebels from now onwards was to refrain from outrages on a large scale and to confine themselves to minor outrages and the murder of loyalists in cold blood. This last form of outrage began at this time to increase greatly, and it became the custom for the murderers to pin labels on their victims bearing the legend "Convicted spy"; they were, as a rule, merely loyal individuals. This policy of avoiding risk was the usual rebel method for some time before the formation of flying columns. The latter had led to bigger operations for a short period, and the return to minor outrages, which was even advocated by *An T'Oglac* at this time, marks an improvement in the military situation, which was probably due to the ill-success of larger operations, to the fact that rebels were beginning to tire of being constantly "on the run," and that they were becoming unpopular with inhabitants who were compelled to billet and feed them without payment. Information regarding the movements of these columns was now very complete, and showed that they often gave up a projected attack for which they had moved into an area. In these circumstances an increase of individual murders might be calculated to enable the I.R.A. to retain its grip on the country with small exertion.[37]

Appreciation of the situation, February, 1921[38].—In the middle of February the Commander-in-Chief had written an appreciation of the situation to the Chief of the Imperial General Staff. In this he had called attention to the anomalous position existing owing to Martial Law being in force on only a portion of the country, and the fact that Dublin, the nerve-centre of the country from which the I.R.A. received the impetus for its activities, was exempt. At the same time he had stated that, unless compelled to do so, he should not wish to have Martial Law in Dublin unless it was also proclaimed over the rest of the country. The opinion was also expressed that, although there were no grounds for optimism, the military situation had improved, and that the large number of internments had for the time being upset the rebel organization and caused the disappearance of many Sinn Fein courts in the Martial Law area; and that certain sections of the population, including the Church in some areas, had gained sufficient courage to express disapproval of the rebels' campaign of murder and outrage.[39] The Commander-in-Chief further stated that he considered the policy of repression would in time succeed in wearing down the rebels, but that it would be a long time before this result was reached. It was emphatically stated, however, that if the existing policy of coercion was to be continued, steps must be taken to make it more intense without being more provocative to law-abiding people, and that this could only be done by instituting unity of command and by reorganizing the police force. Attention was particularly drawn to the cases of indiscipline and unauthorized reprisals carried out by the Auxiliary Division. Finally, the condition of the Army was reported to be excellent, the men being in good health, keen on their work, and well discipline.

Situation, April, 1921.—At the end of April this appreciation still held good, except that a little more progress had been made in dislocating the organization of the I.R.A. and restricting its activities. Divided control of the troops and police, however, still remained, and no extension of Martial Law had been proclaimed.[40]

Launches for inland waterways.—In the work of searching for arms and active rebels a difficulty had been experienced in regard to the inland loughs and navigable waterways. Numerous small islands existed in these loughs, and reports went to show that they were extensively used for concealing arms and ammunition and for other illicit purposes. The only facility for exploring these islands was the hiring of local boats, which were unsuitable for the purpose. As early as October, 1920, application had been made to the War Office for some suitable craft, and the motor boats used on the Rhine had been suggested. The matter was referred to the Admiralty, and it was finally decided that the best form of vessel was a steam harbour launch. In January, 1921, four of these had been applied for. It was intended that two should go to Athlone for work on Loughs Corrib and Erne and that two should remain in Limerick for duty with the 6th Division. It was suggested that a junior naval officer should command each launch, and that the small engine-room and navigating staff should be naval personnel, but that the personnel fighting the launches should be soldiers. The Admiralty in the first place objected to personnel of the Royal Navy being employed on this work, but after considerably correspondence an arrangement was made by which it was agreed that no operation should take place without previous conference between the naval and military authorities on the spot, and that the former should have the power to veto any proposed operation. In these circumstances the naval personnel was made available. The launches did not arrive in Ireland until June, 1921, and owing to difficulties in navigation of canals they were finally all concentrated on the Shannon at Limerick and were never used.[41] [uu]

[uu] Contrary to what is written here, motor launches were used by the army in several operations.[42]

Coal Strike in Great Britain, April to July, 1921.—At the beginning of April, 1921, on account of industrial troubles in England in connection with the threatened strike of the Triple Alliance, orders were received from the War Office to hold 10 battalions ready to embark for England at short notice.[43] These battalions were earmarked as follows:—

Four from the 1st Division and two from each of the 5th and 6th Divisions and Dublin district. The moves were to be by battleships and were worked out so that within 72 hours of the receipt of orders all 10 battalions could be ready to embark. On 4th April orders were received that the first two battalions were to proceed to Liverpool. The 1st Bn. Somerset Light Infantry from Belfast and the 2nd Bn. Duke of Wellington's Regiment from Dublin sailed on 6th April. The 2nd Bn. King's Shropshire Light Infantry from the Curragh and the 2nd Bn King's Own Yorkshire Light Infantry from Londonderry were at the same time ordered to concentrate at Kingstown and Belfast respectively. The 2nd Bn. King's Shropshire Light Infantry sailed on 7th April and the 2nd Bn. King's Own Yorkshire Light Infantry on 9th April. No further battalions were called upon.

Information was subsequently received that the prompt and unexpected arrival of these four battalions in Liverpool was a not inconsiderable factor in the solution of the difficulty. As the situation in Ireland was comparatively quiet at the time, the absence of the four battalions did not cause any serious inconvenience although it necessitated a lull in activities. All four battalions returned to Ireland between 9th and 11th May.

NOTES TO CHAPTER V

The following are some of the outrages committed or attempted in the Martial Law area during January and February, 1921:—

On 4th January, at Meelin, Co. Cork, an officer and 10 other ranks travelling in two Crossleys were ambushed by a large party of rebels, who had two machine guns. After a fight in which 17 rebels were seen to fall, the attackers fled. There were no military casualties.[vv]

[vv] Seán Moylan, commanding the Newmarket Battalion, conducted this attack. Neither side sustained any casualties.[44]

On 28th January, near Castle Island, Co. Kerry, two motor cars conveying a Divisional Commissioner, R.I.C., and six constables were ambushed. One policeman was killed, and all the rest of the party wounded. The Divisional Commissioner died of his wounds.[ww] The rebels used two machine guns.

[ww] This was the Toureengarriv (Tureengarriff) Ambush, under Seán Moylan. DC Philip Armstrong Holmes (b.1876) and Const. Thomas Moyles (b.1899) were killed. Also present were Sgt Arthur E. Charman, Const.s Francis Callery, James Hoare, Francis D. Calder and John H. Andrews, all of whom were wounded in action.[45]

On 3rd February, near Pallas Green, Co. Kerry, two police lorries were ambushed. Nine policemen were killed.[xx]

[xx] This was the Dromkeen, Co. Limerick ambush led by Donnocha O'Hannigan, OC East Limerick Bde flying column. Killed were: Constables Samuel Adams (b.ca.1900), George William Bell (b.ca.1900), John Joseph Bourke (b.ca.1891), Michael Doyle (b.ca.1890), Patrick Foody (b.ca.1876), William Hayton (b.ca.1900), William Kingston (b.1885), Sidney Millin (b.1887), Bernard Mollaghan (b.1877), Arthur Pearce (b.ca.1898) and Henry Smith (b.1898).[46]

On 11th February, at Millstreet, Co. Cork, a train conveying a small party of troops was held up and fired into by 200 rebels. One serjeant was killed and one officer and seven other ranks wounded.[yy]

[tt] Milstreet Battalion Column, Cork No. 2 Brigade, attacked the train at Drishaneberg near Rathcoole.[47]

On 15th February, at Upton Station, Co. Cork, a railway train which was carrying troops was fired into from both platforms. Five soldiers were wounded.[zz] The rebel fire killed five civilian passengers.

[zz] Cmdt Charlie Hurley led the attack; Volunteers killed were Batt Falvey and John Phelan; Patrick O'Sullivan later (18 Feb) died of wounds. Hurley and Sean Hartnett were wounded too. Six civilians were killed and five wounded. Vol. Dan O'Mahoney died of his wounds 'years later', according to Liam Deasy.[48]

On 28th February, in Cork, a series of attacks was made on unarmed soldiers in the streets. Seven soldiers were killed and five wounded.[a3]

[a3] Five soldiers were killed; they were: Cpl L. D. Hadnett (b.ca.1901), Pte Thomas Wise (b.ca.1891), Pte William Alfred Gill (b.ca.1901), Signaller B. Bowden (b.ca.1901) and L/Cpl J. Beattie (b.ca.1997). Hart accepted the claim that twelve were shot.[49]

NOTES

1   See Leeson, *Black and Tans*, pp. 23–6, 71–2, & 245 and 'Summary of Outrages', CO 904/149/ 4, 25, 43, 68, 84, 101, 119, 138, 173, 189, 203, 215, 228, 242, 253, 266, 279, 290, 299 & 308.
2   Leeson, *Black and Tans*, pp. 96–129 and McCall, *Tudor's Toughs*, pp. 178–262.
3   See Macready Memorandum to Cabinet, CP 1750, 26 July, 1920 NAUK CAB 24/110/263–4; see copy in Additional Appendix.
4   See, for instance, S. Lankford, *The hope and the sadness: Personal recollections of troubled times in Ireland* (1980) and 'Report by the General Officers Commanding-in-Chief on the Situation in Ireland', 29 November, 1921, NAUK CAB 24/131, CP 3521. There was concern with this going back to the time of the Rising, see 'Civil Servants in sympathy with Sinn Fein', the NAUK CO 904/26/1.
5   See *The Record of the Rebellion, The Irish Rebellion in the 6th Divisional Area*, Vol. VI, p. 75.
6   Abbott, *Police Casualties*, pp. 79–84; Leeson, *Black and Tans*, p. 142; J. M. McCarthy, 'History Repeated Itself in the Attack on Kilmallock Barracks in 1920', *With the IRA*, pp. 109–16; O'Reilly, *Rebel Heart*, pp. 49–51; and 'Volunteer', 'The IRA Campaign in West Limerick—The Attack on Kilmallock Barracks', *Limerick's Fighting Story*, pp. 260–61.
7   See 'Weekly Survey of the State of Ireland', 18 October, 1920, NAUK CAB 27/108/225 SIC 46.
8   See 'Intelligence notes from 1915–1919', NAUK CO 903/19; RIC I-G Report for August 1919, CO 904/109/153; RIC County Inspector's Report for Limerick for June 1920 CO 904/112; Record of the Rebellion in Ireland, Vol. IV, pp 19, 101 & 147.
9   Martin Petter, '"Temporary Gentlemen" in the Aftermath of the Great War: Rank, Status and the Ex-Officer Problem', *The Historical Journal*, Vol. 37, No. 1 (March 1994), pp. 127–52 and A. D. Harvey, 'Who Were the Auxiliaries?', *The Historical Journal*, Vol. 35, No.3 (1992), p. 668.
10   'Report of the Situation in Ireland by the General Officer Commanding-in-Chief for Week Ending 13th November, 1920', 22 November, 1920, NAUK CAB 27/108/275, p. 1. See copy in Additional Appendices.
11   See Street, *The Administration of Ireland, 1920*.
12   See *The Record of the Rebellion*, Vol II, 'Intelligence' or Hart, *The Final Reports*.
13   Labour Party of Great Britain. *Report of the Labour Commission to Ireland* (1921), p. 6.
14   See C. Townshend, *Britain's Civil Wars: Counterinsurgency in the Twentieth Century* (1986), p. 60; Hawkins, 'Dublin Castle', *The Irish Struggle 1916–1926* (1966), p. 172; and GOC Dublin District to Brigade Commanders, 29 September, 1920, NAUK, WO 35/180B/1.

15 For a full discussion of the armoured vehicle issues, see Kautt, *Ambushes and Armour*, pp. 61–72 and G. Barndollar 'British Military Use'.

16 See RIC I-G Report for December 1920 for Co. Cork ER and WR NAUK CO 904/113; Letter of an unidentified member of the Auxiliary Division, RIC cited in Coogan, *Man who made Ireland*, p. 165; Townshend, *British Campaign*, pp. 138–40; Bennett, *Black and Tans*, pp. 141–3; Leeson, *Black and Tans* p. 100; Minutes of War Cabinet Meetings, 14 January, 1921, 14 February, 1921 and 15 February, 1921; Seedorf, 'Defending Reprisals', p. 87–8; and Pimlott, 'British Experience', p. 31. See also, Crozier, *Impressions*, pp. 261–2.

17 See Kautt, *Ambushes & Armour*, pp. 237–40; for the British Army's analysis of this event, see 'The IRA (From Captured Documents Only)' NAUK WO 141/40, pp. 29–31.

18 For more, see, Hart, *The IRA and its Enemies*, p. 97; A. Ryan, *Comrades: Inside the War of Independence* (Dublin: Liberties Press, 2007), p. 87; Hopkinson, *The Irish War of Independence*, p. 111; 'P. O'G', 'The East Cork Brigade in Action—The Heroic Fight at Clonmult', pp. 232–41; T. O'Neill, *The Battle of Clonmult and the I.R.A.'s Worst Defeat* (Dublin: Nonsuch Publishing, 2006); and *The Irish Rebellion in the 6th Divisional Area*, pp. 84–5. See also, 'Cork's War of Independence: An account of the Irish War of Independence (or Anglo–Irish War) focusing on events in Cork city and county from 1918 to 1921' (http://homepage.eircom.net/~corkcounty/ index.html) accessed 28 July, 2010.

19 *The Last Post*, pp. 115–16.

20 *Ibid.*

21 *Ibid.*

22 *The Last Post*, p. 116 and 'Volunteer', 'Cork's War of Independence', 'Clonmult'.

23 See Borgonovo, *Spies, Informers*, generally; R. E. Fitzgerald, 'The Execution of "Spies and Informers" in West Cork, 1921', M. Murphy, 'Revolution and terror in Kildare, 1919–1923' and B. Hughes, 'Persecuting the Peelers', all in *Terror in Ireland*.

24 See Kautt, *Ambushes & Armour*, pp. 170–75; P. Lynch, 'British General Killed in Action Against Cork and Kerry IRA at Clonbanin', *With the IRA*, pp. 312–28 and 'Volunteer', 'North Cork from 1915 to the Truce—Clonbanin Ambush', p. 194.

25 See M. Daly, 'Gallant Cumann Na mBan of Limerick', *Limerick's Fighting Story*, p. 368; O'Farrell, *Who's Who*, pp. 16 & 78 and *The New York Times*, 8 March, 1921, pp. 1–6.

26 See Abbott, *Police Casualties*, pp. 210–11; T. Barry, *Guerrilla Days in Ireland*, pp. 122–3; Begley, *Road to Crossbarry*; F. Crowley, 'Encircling British Forces Taken on in turn and smashed at Crossbarry', *With the IRA*, pp. 329–41; Deasy, *Towards Ireland Free*, pp. 234–54; Hopkinson, *Irish War of Independence*, pp. 111–12; Hart, *IRA & Its Enemies*, p. 321; Kautt, *Ambushes & Armour*, pp. 138–48; T. Kelliher, 'Rout of the British at Crossbarry', *Rebel Cork's Fighting Story* (2009) p. 153–6; *The Last Post*, pp. 118–19; E. Neeson, *The Battle of Crossbarry* (2008); and Ryan, *Tom Barry*.

27 See 'Ireland—The Use of Aeroplanes', Conclusions of a Meeting held in Mr Chamberlain's Room, House of Commons', 24 March, 1921, NAUK CAB 23/24/192–3 and K. Hayes, *A History of the Royal Air Force and United States Naval Air Service in Ireland, 1913–1923* (1988).

28 See also, 'Report by the General Officer Commanding-in-Chief on the Situation in Ireland for Week Ending 23rd April, 1921', NAUK CAB 24/122/68–9; see copy in Additional Appendices.

29 See 'Volunteer', 'North Cork from 1915 to the Truce—Successful Train Ambush', *Cork's Fighting Story* (2009), pp. 89–92 and the RIC I-G Monthly Confidential Reports for the first quarter of 1921 in general for details on the train attacks.

30 See IRA GHQ Director of Engineering note, 'Pit for Overturning Military Motor Cars, etc.', 26 August, 1920 (MA A/0772/V) and IRA Engineering Circular No. 6, 2 April 1921.

31 See 'Operation Report', Dublin District Memorandum No. S/G.1.A., 20 January, 1921 NAUK WO 35/90.

32 See 'War Diary of General Staff, GHQ Ireland', p. 6, 21 January, 1921 NAUK WO 35/93a; 'The IRA (from Captured Documents Only)', p. 35, WO 141/40; *The Record of the Rebellion*, Vol. I, p. 39; and RIC I-G Report for Dublin for January 1921, CO 904/114 and 'Operation Report'

Dublin District Memorandum No. S/G.1.A., 23 January, 1921, WO 35/90; Hopkinson, *Irish War of Independence*, p. 102 and Kautt, *Ambushes & Armour*, pp. 194–6.

33 See 'Report on Patrol of the 2nd Bn. The Royal Berkshire Regt, Ambushed near Terenure Police Station on night of January 29/30, 1921', 31 January, 1921, Memorandum No. S/G88/A NAUK WO 35/90 and Kautt, *Ambushes & Armour*, pp. 196–202.

34 See Hopkinson, *Irish War of Independence*, p. 225n.

35 See Kautt, *Ambushes & Armour*, pp. 131–8 and 167–70.

36 See Dublin District history in vol. IV, p. 247.

37 See Borgonovo, *Spies, Informers and the 'Anti-Sinn Féin Society': The Intelligence War in Cork, 1920–1921* (2007).

38 For the 5th Division, '5th Division Area. Situation—February, 1921', see copy in Additional Appendices.

39 For more on martial law in general, see 'Report on the Situation in Ireland by General Officer Commanding-in-Chief', 18 December, 1920 NAUK CAB 27/108/21 SIC 64; Hare, 'Martial Law'; Judge Advocate General's Office to Secretary of State, 29 July, 1921 WO 141/53; 'Notes on the Administration of Martial Law', 1921, Strickland Papers IWM EPS 2/2; see also, Jeudwine Papers IWM 72/82/2; 'Record of a Meeting of the Irish Situation Committee', 16 June, 1921 CAB 27/107.

40 See Report by GOCinC, Ireland to CIGS, 23 April, 1921 NAUK CAB 24/122 CP 2872.

41 For discussion, see Sheehan, *Hearts and Minds*, pp. 66 & 117–18 and *The Record of the Rebellion*, Vol. IV Part I, 5th Divisional History, pp. 99–100.

42 See Appendix XIII, 'Ambush of Motor Boat Patrol Near Lough Ree, 17th October, 1920', *The Record of the Rebellion*, Vol. IV, pp. 99–100 and 37.

43 See K. Jeffery and P. Hennessy, *States of Emergency*, pp. 51–6.

44 A. Carroll, *Seán Moylan: Rebel Leader*, pp. 72–6; S. Moylan, *Seán Moylan in his own words: His memoir of the Irish War of Independence* (2004), pp. 86–7; O'Donnoghue, *No Other Law*, p. 129; 'Rebel Ambushes during January, 1921', *The Irish Rebellion in the 6th Divisional Area*, p. 74.

45 See Abbott, *Police Casualties*, pp. 189–91 and Herlihy, *RIC Officers*, p. 168 and *RIC History*, p. 208; Hopkinson, *Irish War of Independence*, p. 112; Kautt, *Ambushes & Armour*, pp. 122–5; P. Lynch, 'Quick on the Uptake: IRA Intelligence paved way to success at Tureengarriffe', *With the IRA*, pp. 279–85; and *Kerry's Fighting Story*, p. 299.

46 See Abbott, *Police Casualties*, pp. 195–7; Hopkinson, *Irish War of Independence*, p. 121; Leeson, *Black and Tans*, p. 27; LtCol J. M. McCarthy, 'Black and Tans Annihilated at Dromkeen', *Limerick's Fighting Story*, pp. 203–10 and 'Dromkeen Ambush Restored the Morale of the Local IRA and People', *With the IRA*, pp. 286–96.

47 See republican accounts of this in P. Lynch, 'Drishanebeg Train Ambush Yielded Fourteen Rifles to Millstreet Column', *With the IRA*, pp. 296–303 P. Lynch, 'Successful Train Ambush', *Kerry's Fighting Story*, pp. 296–8; 'Volunteer', 'North Cork from 1915 to the Truce—Successful Train Ambush', *Rebel Cork* (2009), pp. 189–92 and 'Train Ambushes', *The Irish Rebellion in the 6th Divisional Area*, pp. 79–82.

48 T. Barry, *Guerrilla Days*, pp. 93–4; L. Deasy, *Towards Ireland Free* (1973), pp. 219–23; and 'Train Ambushes', *The Irish Rebellion in the 6th Divisional Area*, pp. 81–2 and *The Last Post*, p. 115.

49 Hart, *The IRA & Its Enemies*, p. 99.

CHAPTER VI

Opening of Northern Parliament, May 1921

Elections, *May, 1921.*—In May, 1921, the elections for the Northern and Southern Parliament under the Act of 1920 took place. When it was learnt that the rebels in the south had decided to put up candidates, it was realized that they were making use of the election machinery merely to elect members to Dail Eireann, the Republican Parliament, and to render the 1920 Act inoperative. The success of the Republican candidates at the poll was never in doubt, because it was quite certain that it would be a "revolver election," and that it would be as much as anybody's life was worth to vote against the rebel candidates. It had been hoped by the Irish Government that candidates would have been forthcoming to stand against the rebels, even if their candidature had gone no further than nomination. There was, however, no single case in which there was a contest in the south. This was most unfortunate, because, had it been necessary for electors to go to the poll, even if the anti-Sinn Fein candidate had not polled a single vote, it is very probable that the total number of voters would have been a very small percentage of the electorate. In these circumstances the claim of the Republicans to represent the wishes of the entire country would have had no proof in fact. It is not likely that a candidate nominated to stand in opposition to Sinn Fein would have suffered violence, because the result of the contest was never in doubt, and the cause of the Republicans was best served by a quiet election.[1]

The nominations took place on 13th May, and resulted in Sinn Fein candidates being returned unopposed in every constituency in Southern Ireland except the four seats for Dublin University.[a] By an examination of the list of individuals nominated, the ascendancy of the "gunmen" was palpable.

Approximately 50 per cent. were prominent members of the Headquarters Staff of the I.R.A., or of brigades in the provinces. Leaders of flying columns and men in prison, internment or "on the run," figured prominently in the list, while more moderate men of the previous Dail, such as Father O'Flanagan[b] and John Sweetman[c], were omitted. Practically all the nominated representatives were men who had taken the oath of the I.R.B. or of the I.R.A. In the light of after events, when the Dail ratified the "Treaty" by only seven votes, it is important to remember the circumstances in which it members were elected, and the type of extremist from which they were drawn.

[a] There were 124 Sinn Féin candidates in addition to the four Trinity College, Dublin candidates.[2]

[b] Father Michael O'Flanagan (b.1876–d.1942), was vice president of Sinn Féin and gave the invocation at the First Dáil Éireann; he was not, however, an elected official at that time.

[c] Roger Sweetman (b.1874–d.1954) was returned for Wexford North and attended the First Dáil Éireann. John Sweetman, his cousin, was not elected in the 1918 General Elections.

The result showed a triumph of the methods of terrorism, and it was clear that moderate opinion would never come forward to discuss a reasonable settlement until the activities of the armed rebels had been reduced, and a determination displayed by the Government to take the most drastic steps towards this end. It was asked that a wide publicity should be given to the circumstances of the elections in order to counter the rebel propaganda, which declared that the elected "gunmen" represented the wishes of the entire Irish people. This publicity was never given.

The elections in Northern Ireland took place at the end of May.[d] All seats were contested, and the result showed an even greater majority for anti-Sinn Fein than had been expected. The hostile Press naturally attributed this result to intimidation, although the fact that Sinn Fein candidates could, without molestation, go about their areas and hold meetings, was an obvious contradiction of this assertion. It is, of course, inconceivable that any election in Ireland should take place without a certain amount of personation, and even intimidation, at the polls, but it is certain that in the north this was not on a large scale, and had no effect on the ultimate result. It was decided that troops should not be moved to protect polling stations, but where their quarters were conveniently situation they were available for assisting the police if necessary. Neither at the polling station in the north, nor during the nomination in the south, however, did any serious disturbance occur.[3]

^d 24 May, 1921, '40 Unionists, six Nationalists and six Sinn Féin candidates are elected' in Northern Ireland.[4]

Military situation, May, 1921.—The military situation in the country from May onwards showed little change in the methods employed by the rebels. Attacks on a large scale were infrequent, but minor outrages such as raids on mails, holding up of trains conveying military stores, cutting of telegraph wires, blocking of roads, and destruction of the property of loyalists, and, in some cases, of public buildings, continued. There was also an increase in the bombing of lorries containing troops in towns, and the shooting of transport horses had become prevalent.[5] More serious, however, was the large number of murders of individuals. These murders were not as a rule the result of a collision between rebels and the Crown forces, but were sheer cold-blooded assassinations, officers being murdered while travelling in trains or motor cars, but themselves or even with their wives, or kidnapped and "executed" by order of a Sinn Fein court, and civilians being dragged from their houses and done to death. During the Whitsuntide week-end (14th/15th May) no less than 11 outrages involving murder took place. Some of these crimes give an idea of the sort of "operations" which the rebel "forces" carried out, and which were hailed by their supporters as daring acts in a war for freedom.[6]

Murders of officials, May, 1921.—On 14th May a District Inspector, R.I.C.,[e] with a military officer,[f] a civilian[g] and two ladies were motoring in a private car. When near Newport they were fired on by about 25 armed rebels, the District Inspector being killed immediately. The officer returned the fire until his ammunition was expended, when, under heavy fire, he went for assistance. The rebels continued to fire at the unarmed civilian and ladies. One of the ladies[h] was killed and the other[i] wounded. The rebels refused assistance to the wounded lady, remarking "served her right."[j] They having fired into the dead body of the District Inspector they retired.[k]

^e District Inspector Henry 'Harry' Biggs (b.1894), late lieutenant (often mistakenly listed as 'major'), British army. He was an ADRIC cadet who became an officer in the RIC. Despised by the local republicans, he was marked for assassination. The party was ambushed at Coolboreen, Co. Tipperary.

[f] Lieutenant William Trevenen Trengrouse, (b.1898–d.1978) 1st Ox & Bucks.

[g] Former Major William Hampden Gabbett (b.1869–unknown), invalided out of the army in 1916.

[h] Miss Winifred Barrington (b.1897); the rebels claimed they mistook her for a man due to her manlike clothing.

[i] A Miss Coverdale.

[j] The rebel ambush team moved Barrington to a nearby house and sent for aid.

[k] Lieut Trengrouse's actions were controversial; he may or may not have fired on the rebels. Abbott said he did, but the rebels said he did not. The latter would seem to be correct, since he resigned from the army two weeks later for cowardice, having left the two ladies. He later died in Brazil.[7]

On 15th May a District Inspector, R.I.C., his wife, and two officers of the 17th Lancers, were leaving a private house in a motor car near Gort, Co. Galway, when they were surrounded by a party of armed rebels, who deliberately murdered all four of them.[l]

[l] Dist. Insp. Cecil Arthur Maurice Blake (b.1885); Lily Blake; Capt Fiennes Wykeham Mann Cornwallis (b.1890) (eldest son of Lord Cornwallis); Lieut Robert Bruce McCreery (b.1899); Mrs Lily Margaret Gregory (b.1884–d.1979) (neé Parry), widow of Maj William Robert Gregory and daughter-in-law to Lady Gregory, remarried to Vincent Gough in 1926.[8]

Six unarmed soldiers were set upon in Bantry by 30 armed rebels, who murdered three[m] of the soldiers and wounded the remainder.

[m] Pte John Alexander Hunter, Pte R. McMillan (b.ca.1902–d.1921), Pte D. Chalmers (b.ca.1900) of the 2nd Scottish Borderers.

On 19th May an officer[n] of the Worcestershire Regiment was motoring with three ladies near Dublin, when the car was held up by armed rebels. The officer was taken from the car, fired at and severely wounded. He was then put into the car and one of the ladies was compelled to drive to a lonely spot where the officer was again taken from the car and murdered.

n   Second Lieut Alfred Donald Hugh Breeze (b.1901), 2nd Bn, Worcestershire Regiment, was wounded in a struggle after surrendering to IRA men. The ladies dressed his wounds. He was then taken some distance and shot near Carrickmines Station in Dublin. He had ten-months' service. This actually occurred on 19 June.[9]

On the same day Colonel T. S. Lambert[o], Commanding 13th Infantry Brigade, was murdered by a party of armed rebels, who fired at the car containing also Mrs. Lambert and another officer[p] and his wife. The other officer's wife was also wounded.

o   Colonel Thomas Stanton Lambert (b.1871), former T/Maj-Gen, commanded the 32nd Division in the Great War. Like many officers, the post-war era saw him reduced to his highest permanent rank.

p   Colonel William Harold Carlisle Challoner, RE.

On 20th May, at Fethard, Co. Waterford, three officers, when out for a walk, were kidnapped. All three were subsequently discovered murdered.[q]

q   These were: Lt Walter George Cave Glossop, RFA; Lt R. F. Bettridge, RFA and 2nd Lt A. C. H. Toogood, 1st Lincolns.

Use of land mines[10].—The placing of land mines, fired mechanically, in roads became a new feature in the rebel methods during this period. These were not often successful, but on 31st May a musketry party of the Hampshire Regiment, marching along a road near Youghal, Co. Cork, were blown up by one of these mines. Seven soldiers were killed and 19 wounded, of the killed, four, and of the wounded, three were band boys[r].

r   The boys were: Frederick Evans (aged 17), G.W. Simmons (aged 15) and Fredrick William Hesterman (aged 14). The regular soldiers were: Cpl C. L. T. Whichelow, Bandsman. F. Burke, L/Cpl R. D. McCall and Pte F. Washington.

Destruction of Custom House, Dublin, 25th May, 1921.—The destruction of property during May and June included two serious cases of incendiarism. On 25th May, the Custom House, the finest building in Dublin, was rushed by about 100 armed rebels. The building was not under military guard. The rebels having shot dead an official who tried to give the alarm, poured petrol over everything and set the place on fire. Two companies of auxiliary police were quickly on the scene, and, as far as could be judged, practically all the raiders were accounted for. Seven were killed, 10 wounded and 70 captured.[s]

> [s] Only four were killed; they were: Volunteers Edward Dorrins, Daniel Head, Patrick O'Reilly and Stephen J. O'Reilly. Oscar Traynor commanded the force that burnt the Custom House.[11]

On 3rd June, a big fire occurred at the R.A.S.C. repair shop[t] in Dublin. The building was partially destroyed and about 40 motor vehicles were burnt. The fire, which was undoubtedly malicious, is believed to have had its origin in an incendiary bomb inside the building after it was closed for the day.

> [t] Officially known as the Motor Transport Depot, National Shell Factory on Parkgate Street. The attack destroyed ordnance stores and clothing, motor transport stores and vehicles, as well as private property, some £212,000 as well as £21,574 damage to structures.[12]

Attacks on troop trains, May–June, 1921.—Attempts to wreck troop trains was another rebel method which was begun during May and June.[u] These attempts were, as a rule, abortive, and on two occasions the rebels employed in these received sharp lessons. But a serious outrage took place at Adavoyle, Co. Armagh, on 24th June. A train conveying the King's escort of the 10th Hussars back from Belfast was derailed by means of explosives. Part of the train was hurled down an embankment. Three soldiers[v] were killed and four injured, while 51 horses were either killed or had to be destroyed.

> [u] These were not the first attacks against trains. The following were attacks on trains in motion:
> 11 February, 1921: Drishanebeg, Co. Cork
> 15 February, 1921: Upton, Co. Cork
> 21 March, 1921: Headford Junction (the British listed this as a train ambush); the train had stopped in the railway station.[13]
> 29 April, 1921: Ballylinch, West George Lennon and his Waterford Flying Column attacked a troop train.[14]
> 15 June, 1921: Meelick, Co. Clare[15]
> 23 June, 1921: Ambush of the 5th Hussars

ᵛ Sjt Charles Dowson (b.1893), Tpr. C. H. Harper (b.1897) and Tpr. William Henry Telford (b.1902).[16]

Restrictions of telegraph facilities.—The increasing number of cases in which telegraph and telephone offices were interfered with by rebels and the instruments stolen, and the extent to which the telegraph was used by them in connection with their outrages, led to an order being issued during June, giving divisional commanders authority to close down any offices which were not near police or military stations, and to take the instruments into military or police charge.ʷ This was done on a large scale, and had a good effect in hampering rebel communications. The offices closed were only re-opened after 11ᵗʰ July, 1921.

ʷ The components of telegraphs and telephones were also used to construct bombs by the various IRA bomb makers.

May, 1921.—In spite of rebel achievements in murders, incendiarism and raids on mails and telegraph wires, they practically had no important success from May onwards, and in several cases the rebels suffered considerably.

On 1ˢᵗ May, at Kidorreryˣ, Co. Cork, a mixed party of the Queen's Royal Regiment, the Green Howards and the R.I.C. were ambushed by armed rebels, of whom two were killed and five captured, with out casualty to the Crown forces.ʸ

ˣ Should be Kildorrery, Co. Cork.

ʸ The actual location was Shraharla, Co. Limerick. Mid-Limerick Bde OC, Liam Forde led a small group of Volunteers that was caught in the open by the military and police. In the fighting retreat, the Volunteers lost Capts Paddy Star, Tim Hennessy and James Horan. Volunteer Patrick Casey was captured, tried by FGCM, convicted and shot the next morning (2 May 1921).[17]

On 2ⁿᵈ May, at Lackelly, Co. Tipperary, 200 armed rebels attacked a patrol of 14 men of the Green Howards and R.I.C. The rebels lost seven killed, and a large number were wounded. Only two soldiers were wounded.ᶻ

ᶻ Only the following men were killed: Volunteers Seán Frahil, Thomas Howard, William O'Riordan and Patrick Ryan. Hannan added a Paddy Starr to the list in 'Winifred Barrington'.[18]

In Partry Mountains, near Toormakeady[aa], Co. Mayo, on 3rd May, a patrol of R.I.C. was ambushed by a large party of rebels.[bb] Four police[cc] were killed and two[dd] wounded. A mixed party of the Border Regiment[ee] and R.I.C., which came upon the scene, followed up and attacked the rebels occupied most favourable positions, they were routed. Several rebels were killed and wounded.[ff] A number of arms were captured.

[aa] This was the Tourmakeady Ambush, which was quite successful in that the rebels attacked and slaughtered the passengers of one vehicle of a two-vehicle convoy, and when attacked, conducted a fighting retreat with the aid of another flying column.

[bb] Bde. Cmdt Tom Maguire, South Mayo Brigade and its flying column.

[cc] Sgt John Regan (b.1874), Const. Christopher O'Regan (b.1894), T/Const. Herbert Oakes (b.1897) and Const. William Power (b.1882).

[dd] Constables Patrick Flynn and John Morrow.

[ee] 2nd Bn., Scottish Borderers.

[ff] Maguire was wounded, and his adjutant Michael O'Brien was killed in the fighting.[19]

On 18th May, at Kilmacthomas, a column of armed rebels was surprised by troops. Thirteen rebels were captured.[gg]

[gg] This was indeed a group of flying-column members, but they were returning from a funeral of one of their comrades, Patrick Keating, whom they were burying secretly at night. Keating died of wounds received in a train ambush on 7 May. The family and members of the column were returning when they ran into a patrol of the Devonshires. During the confused fumbling in the dark, several members of the column escaped into a bog, while the father, two brothers and two sisters of the deceased were amongst the captured and were apparently counted by the army as 'column' members.[20]

Drives, May-June, 1921.—During May and June it was decided to try the effect of "drives" on a large scale over a large area, using the cavalry for the purpose. Every male civilian was to be interrogated, and all who could be identified as members of the I.R.A. were to be detained, and houses were to be searched for arms. The first of these drives began on 5th May in the Mullingar—Tullamore district of the 5th Division. Four cavalry regiments were employed, assisted by local infantry units, and provided with mobile wireless sets. A different area was driven every day, the exits being blocked by infantry picquets. The Colonel Commandant[hh] of the 3rd Cavalry Brigade was in command of the operations and his column was self-contained as regards supplies, &c. A considerable number of individuals were arrested, and although only a small proportion were detained, these included 35 wanted men. The drive lasted 7 days, and no opposition was met with.

[hh] Colonel George Alexander Weir (b.1876–d.1951), CMG, DSO.

The second drive was in Co. Longford and Co. Leitrim of the 5th Division are and in Co. Monaghan, 1st Division area. It took place at the beginning of June and lasted about 3 weeks with a short interval in the middle. No conflicts occurred, but only a few wanted men were detained, although a very large number of individuals, over 1,500 in Co. Monaghan alone, were arrested.

On 6th June an operation on similar lines was carried out in Co. Kerry by infantry assisted by auxiliary police; aeroplanes also co-operated. Six columns were employed, numbering about 1,800 men, while the auxiliary police were used for blocking exits. The object of this operation was to discover whether there was any truth in the information received as to the concentration of large bodies of the I.R.A. and of arms, preparatory to a rising in Kerry. About 100 individuals were arrested, but nearly all released through lack of any evidence against them. It was, however, ascertained that the rumours of a concentration were unfounded.[21]

Although these drives had little result so far as arrests were concerned, they were useful operations. They provided good training for the troops who displayed excellent powers. The administrative arrangements were good, and the practicability of carrying out similar operations when more troops became available was proved. Also a good effect was produced in the districts, in some of which troops had never before been seen. The reasons that the visible success was not greater were in the first place that the identification of individuals was very difficult because the police, who had to be relied upon for this, were, in many cases, comparatively new to their areas, and in any case, were men who would be compelled to continue living in the district after the troops had left. Secondly, a larger number of troops per square mile and a longer time spent in each area would have been necessary in order to discover hidden arms. Lastly, such operations could only be really effective when it was permissible to detain and intern every young man arrested unless he could produce satisfactory evidence of his loyalty. There is no doubt that a large majority of the men released through failure to identify them were in fact connected with the I.R.A.

Lack of internment camps, June, 1921.—There were two difficulties which hampered the action of the Crown forces, and which had become more pressing as progress was made against the rebels.[22] The first of these difficulties was the internment camps. By the end of June more than 4,000 members of the I.R.A. were interned, and the camps in Ireland were practically full. Not only did these camps entail them, but the lack of sufficient accommodation had led to a curtailment in the number of rebels arrested; only the more important ones had to be released. Requests for the provision of camps in England were not sanctioned, and this had the effect of retarding the breaking up of the I.R.A.[23]

Importation of arms.—The second difficulty was the lack of ships in Ireland for the patrol of the coast. There were persistent rumours of gun-running, and although it was inevitably very difficult to obtain definite information of any actual case, it had been proved from records and material captured that arms, ammunition, &c., were finding their way into the country. Definite reports of landings of arms on the coast of West Donegal and at Kilkeel, Co. Down, had been received, whilst at several other places, and particularly on the Wicklow coast, landings were suspect. The ships at the disposal of the Admiral Commanding-in-Chief, the Western Approaches[ii], were 11 destroyers, 3 sloops, 10 trawlers, including vessels in dock and refitting, and of the destroyers, 2 and later 3 were necessarily and continuously employed on official mail services. This small force gave every assistance possible in patrolling the coast, estuaries, and mouths of rivers, but it was obviously inadequate to do more than stop and search a ship of which it had had previous warning.[ji]

[ii] RAdm Sir Ernest Frederick Augustus Gaunt (b.1865–d.1940) assumed command after Tupper retired in May 1921, and served in this position until 1922.

[ji] The rumours of gunrunning were true: Robert Briscoe and Charles McGuinness were in Germany smuggling arms through Britain and via ship to Ireland.[24]

The Customs officials did not, and could not be expected to, carry out their duties effectively unless they could be protected, which was not feasible with the troops available. At this time (May and June), when the troops were making much larger captures of rebel armouries than previously, it was a serious matter that the rebels should be in a position to replace the captured arms.

The Admiral Commander-in-Chief, Western Approaches, in order to make the most of his small resources, issued a scheme for concentrating vessels for intensive search in any area on information when received. The troops were to assist by passing on any information they received and by co-operating with search parties on the banks of rivers and estuaries which vessels could not reach.[25]

Re-organization of areas and formations, June, 1921.—In view of the result of the elections in the north, certain re-organization of the Ulster area was undertaken during June. This involved the abolition of the 1st Divisional Area which was reconstituted as the 13th Infantry Brigade Area. The Londonderry Infantry Brigade ceased to exist and a new infantry brigade, the 26th (Provisional) Infantry Brigade, was added to Dublin District, to included Cos. Monaghan, Cavan and Louth, which were to be transferred from the 1st Divisional Area. As a preliminary to this, Co. Sligo and the southern portion of Co. Leitrim had already been transferred from the Londonderry Brigade to the 13th Infantry Brigade (5th Division) and the remainder of the re-organization was carried out gradually in stages.

On 10th June the Londonderry Brigade was abolished, its area and troops being absorbed in the 13th Infantry Brigade. On 14th June the Colonel Commandant[kk] and staff of the late Londonderry Brigade spread their headquarters at Dundalk as the 26th (Provisional) Infantry Brigade consisting of Cos. Cavan, Monaghan and Louth. The brigade remained under the G.O.C., 1st Division until 24th June, when it was transferred to Dublin district; Co. Meath was subsequently added to this brigade. On 25th June the 1st Divisional Headquarters returned to Aldershot. From this time, therefore, the 13th Infantry Brigade consisted of the six Ulster counties with Co. Donegal, and came directly under G.H.Q.

[kk]   Lt-Col (t/Col Comdt) W. H. L. Allgood.

NOTES

1 'Report by the General Officer Commanding-in-Chief on the Situation in Ireland', 17 May, 1921', NAUK CAB 24/123/366–8, p. 2 CP 2948.

2 See O'Farrell, *Who's Who*, p. xviii.

3 See 'Report by the General Officer Commanding-in-Chief on the Situation in Ireland for Week Ending 9th April, 1921', NAUK CAB 24/122/102 CP 2828; Memorandum by Dr Addison, 'The Irish Elections and an Offer of a Truce', 13 April, 1921, CAB 24/122/110 CP 2829; Conclusions of a Meeting of the Cabinet, 'Ireland—Proposed Temporary Cessation of Military Activity', 12 May, 1921, Cabinet 39 (21), CAB 23/25/265.

4 O'Farrell, *Who's Who*, p. xviii and Hopkinson, *Irish War of Independence*, pp. 192–3. For more on the partition of Ireland, see D. Fitzpatrick, *The Two Irelands 1912–1939* (1998); F. Gallagher, *The Indivisible Island: The Story of the Partition of Ireland* (1957); T. Hennessey, *Dividing Ireland: World War One and Partition* (1998); M. Laffan, *The Partition of Ireland 1911–1925* (1983); and N. Mansergh, *The Unresolved Question: The Anglo-Irish Settlement and Its Undoing* (1991).

5 See IRA GHQ Operations Memorandum No. 1, 28 April, 1921; and *An t-Óglác*, vol. III, No. 5, 22 April, 1921 and No. 11, 3 January, 1921.

6 'Report by the General Officer Commanding-in-Chief on the Situation in Ireland for Week Ending 7th May, 1921', NAUK CAB 24/123/285–5 CP 2934; 'Report by the General Officer Commanding-in-Chief on the Situation in Ireland for Week Ending 14th May, 1921', CAB 24/123/366–8 CP 2948; and 'Report by the General Officer Commanding-in-Chief on the Situation in Ireland for Week Ending 21st May, 1921', CAB 24/123/458–64 CP 2974. See Additional Appendices for CP 2974.

7 See Abbott, *Police Casualties*, pp. 240–41; Herlihy, *RIC Officers*, p. 61; *London Gazette*, 32340, 31 May, 1921, p. 4368; 27730, 1 November, 1901, p. 7050; 26 May, 1916, 29596, p. 5209; Kevin Hannan, 'Winifred Barrington', *The Old Limerick Journal*, vol. 24, (Winter 1988–Barrington's Edition), pp. 107–113; and NAUK WO 339/26148.

8 See 'Report on the Ballyturin Tragedy', May 1921, pp. 1–5, NAUK CO 904/121/4/585–9.

9 See 'Operation Report', Dublin District Memo No. S/G.1.A., 20 June, 1921; 'Dublin District Weekly Intelligence Summary', No. 119, Copy 83 for week ending 19 June, 1921; and Appendix B, 'Dublin District Weekly Intelligence Summary', No. 119, Copy 83 for week ending 19 June, 1921, NAUK WO 35/91, p. 1 and Supplement to the *London Gazette*, 32005, 3 August, 1920, p. 8141.

10 For more on improvised explosive devices, see Kautt, *Ambushes & Armour*, pp. 152–84.

11 See *The Last Post*, pp. 124–5. See also, Costello, *The Irish Revolution*, pp. 134–5; Hopkinson, *Irish War of Independence*, pp. 134–5; O. Traynor, 'The Burning of the Custom House', *Dublin's Fighting Story*, pp. 313–21 and 'The Burning of the Custom House in Dublin Crippled British Civil Administration', *With the IRA*, pp. 405–13; and Townshend, *Military Campaign*, p. 180.

12 See War Office and Treasury inquiry files NAUK TS 46/87 and *An t-Óglác*, vol. III, No. 13, 17 June, 1921.

13 T. Ryle Dwyer, *Tans, Terror and Troubles*, pp. 289–95; 'Fianna', 'Military Ambushed at Headford Junction', *Kerry's Fighting Story*, pp. 255–9; E. Gallagher, 'Too Early Arrival of Train Robbed IRA of Fruits of Victory at Headford', *With the IRA*, pp. 342–55; Lynch, 'Drishanebeg Train Ambush Yielded Fourteen Rifles to Millstreet Column', *With the IRA*, pp. 296–303; and 'Train Ambushes', *The Irish Rebellion in the 6th Divisional Area*, p. 82.

14 T. O'Reilly, *Rebel Heart: George Lennon: Flying Column Commander*, pp. 138–44.

15 *The Irish Rebellion in the 6th Divisional Area*, p. 149.

16 See Kautt, *Ambushes & Armour*, p. 180.

17 See *The Last Post*, p. 122 and P. Maloney, 'With the Mid-Limerick Brigade, 2nd Battalion', *Limerick's Fighting Story*, p. 346.

18 *The Last Post*, pp. 108 & 122; see also, Hopkinson, *War of Independence*, p. 212.

19 See D. Buckley, *The Battle of Tourmakeady, Fact or Fiction: A Study of the IRA Ambush and Its Aftermath* (2008); E. Gallagher, 'Thirty IRA Men Defied 600 British Troops at Tourmakeady', *With the IRA*, pp. 388–93; and Kautt, *Ambushes & Armour*, pp. 243–50.

20 T. O'Reilly, *Rebel Heart: George Lennon: Flying Column Commander*, pp. 139–44.

21 'Report by the General Officer Commanding-in-Chief on the Situation in Ireland for Week Ending 14th May, 1921', NAUK CAB 24/123/366 CP 2948.

22 See Memorandum by the Secretary of State for War, 'Internment of Irish Rebels', 25 June, 1921, NAUK CAB 24/125/600 CP 3082.

23 General Staff, HQ, Irish Command, War Diary, 3 July, 1920, WO 35/93/p. 4. See 'Military Prisons in the Field', Nat. Arch. WO 35/141/4; 'Detention Barracks & Soldiers Detained', WO 35/50/1; and 'Report of the QMG', WO 35/50/6.

24 For more on arms smuggling, see C. D. Greaves, *Liam Mellows and the Irish Revolution* (1971); J. A. Pinkman, *In the Legion of the Vanguard* (1999); R. Briscoe, *For the Life of Me* (1958); and C. J. McGuinness, *Sailor of Fortune: Adventures of an Irish Sailor, Soldier, Pirate, Pearl-Fisher, Gun-Runner, Rebel, and Antarctic Explorer* (1935) also published as *Nomad* (1934).

25 See 'Draft Conclusions of a Meeting of the above Committee held in Mr Chamberlain's Room, House of Commons', 26 May, 1921, NAUK CAB 27/107 p. 5; CAB 24/125 and ADM 178/39 ('Résumé of Events Leading Up to Issue of Orders for Despatch of 8th R.M. Btn').

CHAPTER VII

Cessation of Active Operations

At the end of May, 1921, information had been received that as soon as the industrial troubles in England were definitely over, it was intended by the Government to utilize all available troops for service in Ireland with the object of stamping out the rebellion before the arrival of winter. The number of additional units which it was anticipated could be made available were 18-20 battalions, 3 cavalry regiments, with a proportion of armoured cars.[a]

[a] Such large numbers of forces would have permitted the army to guard important positions, while conducting a war of manoeuvre in the countryside. If conducted properly, there would be little the IRA could have done to counter such operations.

Commander-in-Chief's memorandum on moral of troops, May, 1921.— The Commander-in-Chief submitted two memoranda to the Chief of the Imperial General Staff relative to this proposal. The first memorandum[1] dealt with the state of the troops, and their ability in the existing conditions to carry out the work likely to be required of them. In this it was pointed out that the 'atmosphere' under which the troops were serving could not be appreciated by anybody outside Ireland. That the rank and file were in excellent health, keen on their work and under discipline, as evidenced by the fact that although the murder of officers and men was a daily occurrence[b], there had been during the last few months not a single instance of retaliation.[c] With regard to the feeling of the troops, it was explained that while the rank and file were in no sense discontented, there was a general feeling that their efforts and danger to which they were constantly exposed was not appreciated by people in Great Britain, and that the lack of anti-rebel propaganda, and the reports of

Parliamentary delegates and meetings presided over by influential people, were largely responsible for this feeling. The strain on officers was extremely great. Junior officers found themselves in command of detachments in a village where they were in hourly danger of assassination, and had to be prepared to come to sudden decision regarding the defence of their charge, or to go to assistance of the police, or to settle some libellous charge preferred by some rebel sympathizer.[d] The higher ranks and Divisional Commanders were working at even greater pressure, and the strain was correspondingly more intense. Finally, the Commander-in-Chief stated as his considered opinion that, although the troops could be counted upon to do their duty during the coming summer, he would not undertake that, if pressed too far by the campaign of outrage and murder against them, there might not be cases where they would take the law into their own hands, and that he was convinced in any case it would not be safe to leave the troops in Ireland for another winter under the conditions which obtained during the last.[e]

[b] However much the IRA may have wanted this to be the case, it is demonstrably false. The British army lost 261 men during the war. Hopkinson's analysis demonstrates that the casualty rates went up until the end. Thus, the soldiers certainly understood that the war was becoming more deadly, but the authors' statement was still hyperbole.[2]

[c] This was only true if one does not include the various groups of police. For instance, after the Rathmore Ambush on 4 May, they burnt five houses and the local creamery. It is clear that the authors intend to include only the army, but in such a situation this is disingenuous in the sense that what was important was the people's perception of the Government being responsible.[3]

Commander-in-Chief's memorandum on employment of troops, May, 1921.—The second memorandum[4] dealt with the lines on which it was proposed to employ the troops during the summer, on the assumption that the additional units mentioned were forthcoming, that the Government were prepared to take thorough and drastic steps in the direction of imposing Martial Law all over Ireland (outside the six counties of Ulster), and of instituting such a blockade as was considered necessary by the authorities in Ireland. The new units were in the first instance to be located at centres where they would have the opportunity of learning something of the prevailing conditions. Battalions would then be moved out to certain areas and distributed according to circumstances, but no detachment was to be less than a company. This distribution was based on the importance attached to "showing the flag" in districts where there was a considerable number of waverers likely to be influenced by evidence that the Government meant to "see the thing through."[f] A battalion would thus cover a large area by means of patrols sent out from each company, would get into touch with the inhabitants, assist in the re-occupation of stations vacated by the R.I.C., and despatch mobile columns to act against rebels who had been located. All movements were to be on foot, and accompanied by as little transport as possible. If the rebels took to the mountains it was intended to leave them there until the populated areas had been dealt with, when their rounding up would become a less difficult matter.[g]

[d] This statement is more accurate; the constant threat of harm by the IRA appears to have had a telling effect on the soldiers.

[e] There were two forces at work here. One was that the IRA were deliberately trying to make the conditions worse for the soldiers and police to undermine their morale. The other was the physical conditions that this imposed for safety. Thus, the barracks and fortified positions became uncomfortable and hard to live in.[5]

[f] A connexion with any potentially loyal populace would have to convince them that the Government was not going to abandon them.

[g] This distribution would make an effective occupation, but only as long as the Government was willing to continue to use such large numbers of the limited strength of the British army.

As regards the mounted troops, it was proposed to use three regiments in Munster as one force to carry out concentrated movements through certain districts as information dictated. In the 5th Division area the cavalry were to be divided into two brigades acting in the same way, and it might on occasions be necessary to use the whole of the cavalry in one large "drive."[h]

[h] The 'drive' was a large-scale, combined arms sweep through an area. Using horse-mounted cavalry, vehicle-mounted and foot-bound infantry, as well as aircraft, with logistical support from the RASC and Royal Engineers, the force moved relatively quickly through a district having cut it off. The

various types of transport for the men ensured that they could move faster, but without loss of search capacity. The logistical support allowed them to remain in the field for extended periods, while the engineers overcame counter-mobility obstacles.[6]

It was pointed out that as the policy must depend upon the circumstances and information existing at the time, it was not possible to give a more detailed appreciation, but that it must be recognized that troops would be operating with the same handicap as previously, namely, lack of a defined objective.[i]

[i] The issue of the military not having a clear objective is a constant theme throughout this work. 'Re-establishing order' is not a clear mission, and neither is merely ending political crime, when one has made the normal expression of political thought a crime. However advanced their understanding of counter-insurgency on a tactical and operational level, the British had not faced such a rebellion since the American Colonies and thus their counter-insurgent experience was against non-Europeans using levels of violence unacceptable against Europeans, regardless of the hypocrisy of it.

As a last point, it was urged that, if drastic measures were to be adopted, the Government should at the same time direct its efforts towards countering the rebel propaganda which was pursuing its course unchecked in the Press, at meetings presided over by prominent persons, and by certain members in both Houses of Parliament.

Reinforcements, June-July, 1921.[7]—During June and the early part of July the units for carrying out the Government's policy of drastic action arrived and were allotted as follows:— [j]

Date of Arrival	Unit	OC	Assignment
14 June	1st Bn. Northumberland Fusiliers	Lt-Col C. Yatman	5th Infantry Division
15 June	1st Bn. Royal Sussex Regiment	Lt-Col A. E. Glasgow	5th Infantry Division
16 June	2nd Bn. Royal West Kent Regiment	Lt-Col R. J. Woulfe-Flanagan	Dublin District
17 June	1st Bn. Middlesex Regiment	Lt-Col J. H. Hall	Dublin District

28 June	1st Bn. York and Lancaster Regiment	Lt-Col M. F. Halford	6th Infantry Division
28 June	1st Bn. Sherwood Foresters	Lt-Col J. C. Newman-Harding	6th Infantry Division
2 July	1st Bn. West Yorkshire Regiment	Lt-Col G. D. Price	6th Infantry Division
2 July	2nd Bn. Oxfordshire & Buckinghamshire Light Infantry	Lt-Col L. H. R. Pope-Hennessy	6th Infantry Division
2 July	1st Bn. Duke of Cornwall's Light Infantry	Lt-Col T. H. F. Price	Dublin District
2 July	1st Bn. King's Own Yorkshire Light Infantry	Lt-Col C. E. I. Brooke	5th Infantry Division
5 July	2nd Bn. Cheshire Regiment	Lt-Col A. B. Gosset	6th Infantry Division
5 July	3rd Bn. Royal Fusiliers	Lt-Col M. P. Hancock	6th Infantry Division
5 July	1st Bn. Highland Light Infantry	Lt-Col R. R. S. Prentice	6th Infantry Division
5 July	1st Bn. Loyal Regiment	Lt-Col F. W. Woodward	Dublin District
5 July	1st Regiment Royal Artillery Mounted Rifles		6th Infantry Division
6 July	4th Bn. Worcestershire Regiment	Lt-Col H. E. Gogarty	5th Infantry Division
6 July	2nd Bn. Gordon Highlanders	Lt-Col A. D. Greenhill-Gardyne	5th Infantry Division
7 July	1st Bn. Seaforth Highlanders		Dublin District
9 July	2nd Regiment Royal Artillery Mounted Rifles		6th Infantry Division

[j] Table not original to document.

In addition, it was proposed to send:—

One battalion Royal Marine Light Infantry,
One battalion Royal Marine Artillery,

Two companies Tank Corps organized as armoured-car companies
Additional signal personnel
Proportion of Royal Engineers
Proportion of Administrative services.

These additions had not arrived before 11th July, and so their despatch was cancelled. Before these units had finished arriving, events occurred which changed the situation.

King's speech at Belfast, 22nd June, 1921.[8]—On 22nd June, His Majesty The King opened the Northern Parliament at Belfast, and in the course of his speech he expressed a hope that the differences between Great Britain and Ireland, and between north and south, would be sunk, and a peaceful solution to the difficulties found.

Arrest and release of De Valera, 22nd June, 1921.[9]—On the same day during the search of a house at Blackrock, just outside Dublin, seditious literature had been found and the only male on the premises had, therefore, been arrested. This man proved to be De Valera.

Negotiations for a truce.[10]—On the following day, by the order of the Government, he was released and on the next day, 24th June a letter was sent by the Prime Minister to Sir James Craig and Mr. De Valera inviting them to attend a conference in London in order to attempt to find a solution to the Irish problem, in accordance with the wish expressed by His Majesty. This invitation was accepted by Sir James Craig, but Mr. De Valera replied that he wished to consult his colleagues. In the course of the next few days the Government released four leading Sinn Feiners from Mountjoy Gaol in order that they might confer with Mr. De Valera.

Release of extremists, June, 1921.[11]—The four selected were all extremists: Arthur Griffith, who had been in prison since November, 1920; Professor McNeill, who had in 1916 been Chief of Staff of the rebels, and who had expressed his approval of the murder of the officers in Dublin on 21st November, 1920; Michael Staines[k], an important member of the I.R.A. headquarters; E. J. Duggan[l], who at the time of his arrest had been Director of Intelligence, I.R.A. R. C. Barton was also released from Portland Prison[m], where he was carrying out a sentence of 3 years for incitement to murder. He had been "Minister for Agriculture" of the Dail Eireann and Commandant in the Wicklow Brigade, I.R.A. He had also been an officer in the British Army, employed at G.H.Q. (Ireland) during the 1916 rebellion.

k   Michael Joseph Staines (b.1885–d.1955), one-time IRA Quartermaster General and MP.

l   Edmund (Eamon) John Duggan (b.1874–d.1936). According to historian Katie Drake, his service as Director of Intelligence is likely to be incorrect.

m   HM Prison Portland, Isle of Portland, Dorset.

Further releases followed, and on 30th June it was noticed by the Government that, in view of the Prime Minister's letter to De Valera, communications were likely to pass between the leading Sinn Feiners, which the Government were bound to respect, and that, therefore, no raids or searches were to be made, for the time being, on premises occupied or frequented by persons of political importance. Orders to this effect were issued by G.H.Q. to all divisions. The discussions between De Valera and his colleagues and with Southern Unionists lasted for several days, but on 8th July he wrote accepting the Prime Minister's invitation.

Conferences at G.H.Q. and Mansion House, 8th July, 1921.[12]—On 8th July, Lord Midleton[n], with three colleagues representing the Southern Unionists[13], had an interview with the Commander-in-Chief at G.H.Q., at which was raised the question of easing down military activities in order to create an atmosphere in which peaceable proposals might be discussed. After Lord Midleton's visit the Commander-in-Chief held a conference at which were present the Chief of Police, Mr. Cope (Assistant Under Secretary) and the G.O.C., Dublin District.[o] As a result of this conference the Commander-in-Chief wrote to Lord Middleton stating that in the event of an agreement for cessation of "hostilities" being arrived at between the Government and Mr. De Valera, he was prepared, after consultation with the Chief of Police, to place certain limitations on the activities of the troops and police in consideration of certain guarantees required of Mr. De Valera. It was also requested that Mr. De Valera should nominate some person with whom the Commander-in-Chief could immediately get in touch in the event of reports being received of outrages being committed. Later in the day of 8th July the Commander-in-Chief, in order to explain more fully certain points, went to the Mansion House, Dublin, where Mr. De Valera was in conference with his colleagues. As a result of verbal discussion between the Commander-in-Chief and Mr. De Valera, certain terms of agreement were arranged. These terms were embodied in a second letter from the Commander-in-Chief to Lord Midleton.

ⁿ William St John Fremantle Brodrick, 1ˢᵗ Earl of Midleton, KP, PC (b.1856–d.1942), a leader of southern Unionists.

° Brig-Gen Boyd.

G.H.Q. communiqué on truce terms, 8ᵗʰ July, 1921.[14]—The terms were telegraphed to divisions on the afternoon of 8ᵗʰ July, and on the following morning they were issued to the Press in the form of a G.H.Q. communiqué as followed:—

Mr. De Valera having decided to accept the Prime Minister's invitation to confer with him in London, is issuing instructions to his supporters—

(a) To cease all attacks on Crown forces and civilians.
(b) To prohibit the use of arms.
(c) To cease military manoeuvres of all kinds.
(d) To abstain from interference with public or private property.
(e) To discountenance and prevent any action likely to cause disturbance of the peace which might necessitate military interference.

In order to co-operate in providing an atmosphere in which peaceful discussions may be possible, the Government has directed that—

(a) All raids and searches by military or police shall cease.
(b) Military activity shall be restricted to the support of police in their normal civil duties.
(c) Curfew restrictions shall be removed.
(d) The despatch of reinforcements from England shall be suspended.
(e) The police functions in Dublin to be carried out by the D.M.P.

In order to give the necessary time for these instructions to reach all concerned, the date from which they shall come into force has been fixed at 12 noon, Monday, 11ᵗʰ July, 1921.

On the morning of 9ᵗʰ July, Mr. Cope (Assistant under Secretary) brought to G.H.Q. two of Mr. De Valera's supporters, Messrs. E. J. Duggan and R. C. Barton. These two gentlemen took exception to the fact that the G.H.Q. communiqué referred to the instructions which Mr. De Valera was issuing to his supporters. It was explained to them that the instructions were those agreed to verbally by Mr. De Valera. After a discussion of the terms *serviatim* Messrs. Duggan and Barton left.

It was agreed that Mr. Duggan should be available as Mr. De Valera's representative for communication with G.H.Q. and that a representative should also be available as a liaison official with each division and brigade.

Irish version of truce terms, 9th July, 1921.—The evening papers of 9th July contained an extract from a special edition of the *Irish Bulletin*^p (a rebel paper secretly printed and circulated), in which the G.H.Q. communiqué was referred to as a "draft," and a different interpretation was placed on the terms of the agreement entered into by the Commander-in-Chief and Mr. De Valera. The terms as set forth in the *Bulletin* were as follows:—

On behalf of the British Army it is agreed as follows:—

(1) No incoming troops, R.I.C., and auxiliary police and munitions, and no movements for military purposes of troops and munitions, except maintenance drafts.
(2) No provocative display of forces, armed or unarmed.
(3) It is understood that all provisions of the truce apply to Martial Law area equally with the rest of Ireland.
(4) No pursuit of Irish officers or men or war material or military stores.
(5) No secret agents noting descriptions or movements, and no interference with the movements of Irish persons, military or civil, and no attempt to discover the haunts or habits of Irish officers and men. (NOTE.—This supposes the abandonment of curfew restrictions).
(6) No pursuit or observance of lines of communication or connection.
(7) No pursuit of messengers. (NOTE.—There are other details connected with Courts Martial, motor permits, and R.O.I.R. to be agreed to later.)

On behalf of the Irish Army it is agreed—

(a) Attacks on Crown forces and civilians to cease.
(b) No provocative display of forces, armed or unarmed.
(c) No interference with Government or private property.
(d) To discountenance and prevent any action likely to cause disturbance of the peace which might necessitate military interference.

^p   The Irish Bulletin was the mouthpiece of the rebel government. First edited by Desmond FitzGerald (b.1888–d.1947), then by Robert Erskine Childers (b.1870–d.1922) upon the former's arrest in March 1921.[15]

Although the general spirit of these undertakings was not considered to be greatly affected, there were certain obvious points of difference on which disagreement might and did subsequently occur.

In order to obviate future misunderstandings, a circular was issued to the troops explaining the discrepancy between the two documents. The circular was as follows:—

In order to avoid possible misconstruction of the terms referred to in G.H.Q. official statements and those issued as a supplement to the Irish Bulletin, it is notified for information that the wording of the G.H.Q. official statement is taken from the letter written by G.O.C.-in-C. to Lord Midleton (and agreed to in principle by Mr. De Valera), and is in no sense a draft. The wording as issued in the Irish Bulletin is their interpretation of the same terms issued after discussion at G.H.Q. in a form more acceptable to Mr. De Valera's adherents. The spirit of the two documents is identical.

A copy of this circular was sent to Mr. Duggan, but at the request of Mr. Cope who took exception to the wording, it was not issued to the Press.

Plans in case of breakdown of negotiations.[q]—During the lengthy negotiations which ensued, the chances of a final settlement resulting fluctuated from day to day, and it was necessary to continue to form a plan for employing the troops which had recently arrived from England, should the negotiations breakdown. The plan was based on the assumption that Martial Law would be universal outside Ulster, and the principles on which operations were to be carried out had been already outlined in the Commander-in-Chief's memorandum to the Chief of the Imperial General Staff on 23rd May. The principles had been further elaborated in a letter to divisions on 29th June which laid down—

(a) That our main object was to break up the Dail Eireann and the I.R.A. and capture the arms of the latter.

(b) That owing to the fact that members of the I.R.A. were indistinguishable from ordinary civilians, it was necessary to use methods involving identification of individuals, but that it should be on occasions possible to carry out operations against definite units and formations of the I.R.A. organization.

(c) That the most important objectives for military operations were the H.Q. of divisions, brigades and battalions, flying columns and active service units.

(d) That it was important to make the most of whatever remained of the summer months, and that operations when begun should be carried out with the greatest energy by day and night, the areas in the immediate proximity to our garrisons being the first to be cleared, then the intervening areas and those along our communications, the more distant areas being left till last.

(e) That as each area was cleared, police stations should be re-established and every effort made to restore confidence amongst the law-abiding.

(f) That all members of the I.R.A., and not only leaders, should be interned.

⁹ Few expected the Truce to be anything but a temporary ceasefire.

In order to facilitate the attainment of these objects it was proposed to take the following measures under Martial Law:—

The Dail Eireann, the I.R.A. and the I.R.B. to be declared illegal organizations, membership of which was treason.

After a date to be notified the possession of arms, ammunition or explosives without a permit to be punishable by death after trial by drumhead court.

The Press to be controlled.

A system of passports to be instituted to enter or leave the Martial Law area from Great Britain or abroad.

A system of identity cards to be introduced, which would be compulsory for any person living in defined areas in the proximity of military or police barracks, and for all persons travelling by train, motor vehicle, or pedal bicycle in any area.

Boycott of English or Belfast goods to be met by restrictions on export of Irish produce, and, if necessary, the closing of manufacturing establishments.

Destruction of Government property, animals, &c., to be met by requisition without payment on the area concerned.

All fairs, markets, race meetings to be stopped as required.

All ports, except Cork and Dublin to be closed.

All civil courts throughout the Martial Law area, except those considered necessary by Military Governors for trial of trivial cases, to be closed.

Persons of any nationality other than British to be required to produced certificates of nationality bearing a date not earlier than 1921.

All banks to be closed, and only re-opened in areas which have been cleared of I.R.A.

These proposals were submitted on 29th June to the Secretary of State for War for approval by the Cabinet and again with slight additions on 13th September.[16]

Proposed special enlistment of ex-soldiers, August, 1921.[17]—During August drafts had to be sent from battalions in Ireland to foreign service battalions. As a result it was proposed by the War Office that, should negotiations break down and the enforcement of Martial Law become necessary, battalions in Ireland should be made up in the first instance to 1,000, and subsequently to 1,200 by means of special enlistment of ex-soldiers in England. These numbers were in excess of the request submitted by G.H.Q., which had asked that all battalions should be made up to 800. Meantime, in order to make good the gaps left by the departure of drafts, the War Office agreed to send out recruits as soon as they had completed 12 weeks' training depôts, except in the Northern Command, where a certain experiment was being tried.

Proposed naval co-operation.—It had also been represented by the Commander-in-Chief that, in order to make effective the measures regarding the closing of ports, passport regulations, and restrictions on imports, which it was intended to impose, a large increase would be necessary in the naval resources available. A paper from the Cabinet stated the Admiralty had been instructed to place, so far as practicable, at the disposal of the Admiral Commander-in-Chief, Western Approaches[r], the force necessary to enable him to co-operate effectively with the military authorities.

[r] RAdm Gaunt. There were remarkably poor relations between the naval forces and the army during the war. Co-operation was negligible.

Time limit for ending truce.—It had been arranged by the Prime Minister with Mr. De Valera that should negotiations break down, 7 days' (afterwards 72 hours) notice should be given before the terms of the agreement of 11th July should cease to operate.

Rupture imminent, August–October, 1921.[18]—During the protracted correspondence between the Prime Minister and Mr. De Valera it was necessary to watch for chances of the negotiations coming to a sudden end. It had been arranged to warn divisions, by a system of code words sent by wireless, of any hitch in negotiations which called for special precautions. Such a contingency occurred on 16th August, when, at a meeting of Dail Eireann, De Valera bluntly refused the Government's offer.[19] A warning was sent out to all divisions to be prepared to put full protective and defensive measures in force. In October the fate of the negotiations again being in the balance, when De Valera's telegram to the Pope was sent, a letter was sent to the War Office in which it was pointed out that the means at the disposal of the Commander-in-Chief for taking energetic offensive action, should the negotiations break down, had been seriously diminished through the despatch of foreign drafts, and that the drafting into Ireland of the men destined to make up battalions to 1,000 strong must necessarily take some time, whereas the importance of assuming the initiative and striking at once would be imperative. To compensate for this situation it was suggested that the 4th Regiment, Royal Artillery Mounted Rifles, and the two battalions of Royal Marines should be concentrated ready for immediate despatch when required; that the 1st Bn. Loyal Regiment and 2nd Bn. North Staffordshire Regiment (which had recently left Ireland, being replaced by the 3rd Regiment, Royal Artillery Mounted Rifles, and 1st Bn. Duke of Wellington's Regiment) should be returned to Ireland, if they had not already sailed for abroad, or otherwise that the foreign service battalions which they were relieving should be sent; that the foreign service drafts on furlough in England should be returned to Ireland; and that the Army Reserve should be mobilized.

Commander-in-Chief's representations to the Secretary of State for War, October, 1921.[20]—At the same time the Commander-in-Chief wrote to the Secretary of State for War pointing out that no answer had been given to the two memoranda submitted on 29th June and 13th September respectively, in which were set forth the measures which it was intended to take under Martial Law should the negotiations break down. The Commander-in-Chief drew attention to the fact that, although steps had been taken as far as possible for putting these measures into force, even down to drafting the proclamations, it was impossible to complete the arrangements until the Cabinet decision was given. Further, the Commander-in-Chief stated that, in the absence of a Cabinet decision, he proposed at the end of the 72 hours' notice of the termination of the "truce" to take immediate and drastic action on the lines already proposed. Finally, it was requested that either the memorandum of 13th September should be answered, or that the Government should be prepared, in the event of a sudden emergency, to leave the situation entirely at the discretion of the Commander-in-Chief. No reply was received to this letter.

Truce begun 11th July, 1921.—Active operations as far as troops and police were concerned practically ceased on 11th July.

Casualties 1st April, 1920, to 11th July, 1921.—During the period 1st April, 1920, to 11th July, 1921, the following military casualties had occurred in Ireland:—

Killed: 43 officers and 113 other ranks.
Wounded: 35 officers and 307 other ranks.

Between 1st January, 1919, and 11th July, 1921, the police forces in Ireland had suffered a loss of 405[x] and 682[y] wounded.

[x] The RIC lost 503 men during this period.[21]

[y] While no exact figures appear to exist for RIC wounded, the RAMC treated 633 RIC for emergencies in 1921. Of this number, 61 died of their injuries.[22]

Decorations.[23]—In Appendix II. are shown some examples of actions in which the troops were engaged, and for which decorations were awarded to individual officers, non-commissioned officers and men. As will be seen from these examples, which are typical, the fighting in nearly all cases was carried out by a very small number of troops or police, who were seldom attacked except by greatly superior numbers of rebels.

NOTES

1   'Memorandum "B" by General Officer Commanding-in-Chief, Ireland', 23 May, 1921, NAUK CAB 24/123 CP 2965. See copy in Additional Appendices.

2   Hopkinson, *The Irish War of Independence*, pp. 201–02.

3   Abbott, *Police Casualties*, pp. 230–31; A. Carroll, *Seán Moylan*, p. 118; Hopkinson, *The Irish War of Independence*, p. 126.

4   'Memorandum "A" by General Officer Commanding-in-Chief, Ireland', 23 May, 1921, NAUK CAB 24/123 CP 2965. See copy in Additional Appendices.

5   See also 'Health of the Army in the UK', WO 35/179/3, NAUK RAMC 'Annual Reports of Sick for the Year 1921—Statistical Summaries', WO 115/1–2.

6 For the effectiveness of cavalry mobility against IRA counter-mobility operations, see Statement of Captain E. Gerrard (MA WS/348) and 'Proceedings from a Conference of Ministers', 8 June, 1921, NAUK WO 32/9522.

7 For Cabinet discussion, see Memorandum by the Secretary of State for War, 'Ireland and the General Military Situation', 24 May, 1921; CIGS to Secretary of State for War, memorandum unnumbered, 24 May, 1921; and C. Addison to Cabinet, 'Ireland', 31 May, 1921, NAUK CAB 24/123/427–613 CP 2964, CP 2965, CP 2999 respectively and 'Conclusions of a Meeting of the Cabinet held in Mr. Chamberlain's Room, House of Commons, S.W., on Tuesday, May 24th, 1921', CAB 23/25/288–9, Cabinet 41(21).

8 See copy of the speech in the Additional Appendices.

9 'Report by the General Officer-Commanding-in-Chief on the General Situation in Ireland for Week, Ending 25th June', NAUK CAB 24/125/641–2.

10 'Weekly Survey of the State of Ireland', 29 June, 1921, NAUK CAB 24/125/116–7 CP 3087; 'Report by the General Officer-Commanding-in-Chief on the General Situation in Ireland for Week, Ending 2 July 1921', CAB 24/126/66–7 CP 3109; 'Weekly Survey of the State of Ireland', 3 July, 1921, CAB 24/126/80 CP 3113; and 'Report by the General Officer-Commanding-in-Chief on the General Situation in Ireland for Week, Ending 9 July, 1921', CAB 24/126/283 CP 3134.

11 'Report by the General Officer-Commanding-in-Chief on the General Situation in Ireland for Week, Ending 2 July, 1921', NAUK CAB 24/126/66–7 CP 3109 & 'Weekly Survey of the State of Ireland', 3 July, 1921, CAB 24/126/79–80 CP 3113.

12 'Weekly Survey of the State of Ireland', 13 July, 1921, NAUK CAB 24/126/252–3 CP 3130 and 'Report by the General Officer-Commanding-in-Chief on the General Situation in Ireland for Week, Ending 9 July, 1921', CAB 24/126/274–5 CP 3134.

13 For more on Unionists in the south, see R. B. McDowell, *Crisis and Decline: The Fate of the Southern Unionists* (1998); A. Jackson, *The Ulster Party: Irish Unionists in the House of Commons, 1884–1911* (1989); for Unionist political aspirations generally; A.T.Q. Stewart, *The Ulster Crisis: Resistance to Home Rule* (1967) and T. Bowman, *Carson's Army: The Ulster Volunteer Force: 1910–22* (2007) for the Ulster Volunteer Force.

14 Appendix V, 'Report by the General Officer-Commanding-in-Chief on the General Situation in Ireland for Week, Ending 9 July, 1921', NAUK CAB 24/126/283–4 CP 3134. See Additional Appendices for copies of the GHQ IRA and GHQ Irish Command communiqués.

15 For more, see Kenneally, *The Paper Wall* and Murphy, *British Propaganda*.

16 'Ireland, Military Law, Committee Report', 1 August, 1921, NAUK CAB 24/126/602–04, CP 3185.

17 'Conclusions of a Meeting of the Cabinet held in Mr. Chamberlain's Room, House of Commons, S.W., on Wednesday, 29th June, 1921', NAUK CAB 23/26/92–3.

18 CIGS to Secretary of State for War, 16 August, 1921, NAUK CAB 24/126, CP 3236. See also Secretary of State for War Memorandum for the Cabinet, 'Irish Situation', 29 July, 1921, CAB 24/126/556 CP 3178.

19 See Appendix 'Conclusions of a Meeting of the Cabinet held in Mr. Chamberlain's Room, House of Commons, S.W., on Wednesday, 20th July, 1921', NAUK CAB 23/26/154–9 Cabinet 60 (21).

20 Macready to Secretary, War Office, Memorandum No. 2/493489, 17 October 1921, NAUK WO 32/9533.

21 See Herlihy, *RIC History*, p. 151.

22 See RAMC 'Annual Reports of Sick for the Year 1921 – Statistical Summaries', NAUK WO 115/1.

23 See also 'Recognition of the Services of Certain Officers under C-in-C Ireland', NAUK WO 141/42.

CHAPTER VIII

The Agreement of 11 July 1921
and the 'Treaty'

Terms of truce.—The agreement brought about at the expressed wish of the Government to create a peaceful atmosphere was in itself an illogical compact. On the one hand, the Crown forces agreed to refrain from action for the suppression of outrage, and, on the other hand, the rebels agreed to desist from acts which under any circumstances were crimes. The not unnatural result was that not only the rebels themselves, but the Press and a large section of the public, came to look upon any outrage committed by the rebels before the agreement as a legitimate act[a], or at least one to be condoned, while any action of the Crown forces taken for suppression of illegal acts after the agreement were regarded as "breaches of the truce."[b]

[a] The Truce was formal, reported to the League of Nations, and gave *de facto* and, one could argue, *de jure* legitimacy to the IRA, since one can only conduct a formal truce with an equal. This recognition was one of the many points to which the army took exception. That said, their analogy was illogical; mentioning IRA actions before the Truce had little to do with British forces' actions after it began.[1]

[b] The authors' anger is understandable considering their view of the conflict, but this does not negate the actions of their own Government. Further, while in effect, the army had to abide by the terms of it until cancelled. They clearly did not like this, but such is the nature of modern counterinsurgency.

General effect of truce terms.—The general tone of the Press, and of public utterances, appeared to imply that Mr. De Valera had demanded the cessation of military activity, and that this having been agreed to, be, as leader of the Republican Army, agreed to refrain from warlike action. The impression left on the mind was that Mr. De Valera had found himself, owing to the pressure exerted by the I.R.A., in a position to exact terms from the military authorities in Ireland, as a prelude to making demands from the British Prime Minister in London.[c]

[c] However much British officers did not like the Truce, this does not negate the essential truth of the situation. Regardless of what the realities on the battlefield may or may not have been, the truth was that the IRA fought their conflict until British *politicians* were ready to negotiate with them.

The troops and police viewed the situation brought about by the agreement with mixed feelings. On the one hand, there was a natural sense of relief from arduous and incessant work and danger, but, on the other hand, a feeling of humiliation was inevitable. The rebels who had been driven to hide in mountains and go "on the run" reappeared and openly paraded, sometimes in uniform. The troops and police were assailed in the streets with jeers and taunts by men, who, a few days before, would have run before them.[d] The papers flaunted the achievement of the I.R.A. in having vanquished the Crown forces, and this at a time when considerable progress had really been made, and even more drastic measures for dealing with the situation had been imminent. The troops and police, however, behaved with remarkable self-control under great provocation, and showed patience and loyalty to the spirit of the agreement.[e]

[d] One wonders if these men would have been the same if they were as pitifully armed and trained as the IRA normally were.

[e] By most accounts, this appears to have been true, although the claim of provocation was a bit overblown.

As regards the terms themselves, a difficulty was experienced due to the fact that there was no definite basis of agreement. In the absence of a clearly defined Government policy on the subject, the Commander-in-Chief had on 8th July made certain temporary arrangements with Mr. De Valera, but consistently refused to put his signature to any document, feeling that he was not empowered to do so without more definite instructions from the Government. The complications arising from such a situation were clearly shown in the different interpretations put upon the terms. For instance, complaints were received from liaison officials that troops continued to bear arms, and that fairs and markets were in some districts still closed. It was pointed out in reply that troops would continue to bear arms as part of their normal equipment, and that the re-opening of fairs, markets, &c., was dependent upon the repair of roads and bridges. By September practically all restrictions had been removed.[f]

[f] For the better part of two years, the army begged for clear and actionable policy from the Cabinet. When this policy finally came, in the form of Truce, negotiation and Treaty, they found it unpalatable for several reasons. They were Britons who certainly had opinions about the political condition and future of Ireland. Being under fire clarifies situations quickly and simply; the soldier, rightly or wrongly, develops plans quickly, so they thought that they knew what needed to be done. For a myriad of military, social and political reasons, the authors believed that the Government had made the wrong decision with its course of action. Knowing that the Cabinet's inaction for two years had cost lives, and worse, had 'lost' Ireland, was hard for them to accept. This explains their anger and the seeming pettiness in these statements.

Terms of truce ignored by rebels.—So far as concerned actual murder and outrage, the terms were well kept by the rebels, but otherwise no attempt was made to observe the spirit of the agreement. Illegal drilling with arms was openly carried out, I.R.A. training and musketry camps were prevalent all over the country, and every effort was made to re-organize much depleted units and raise shaken moral. *An T'Oglac* claimed openly that the period succeeding the agreement had not been wasted, but that much valuable training and equipping had been carried out. Sinn Fein courts, which had almost ceased to exist, sprung up again everywhere, and their proceedings were fully reported in the Press. The boycott of English and Belfast goods was intensified, forced collections for Sinn Fein or I.R.A. funds were made in many districts, houses were commandeered, and in some cases individual soldiers or policemen were attacked.[g]

[g] Considering the complaints given in the previous paragraph, this is rather petty. If weapons were a normal part of the British Tommy's kit, they were for the IRA too. Their complaint was that the Volunteers were not soldiers, but a formal truce negated that.[2]

Impotence of military under truce terms.—Military commanders were powerless to suppress these illegalities because the troops by the agreement were in a position in which they could take action only in aid of the civil power, and any attempt on their part to deal with these matters by force would certainly have been characterized as a "breach of the truce." The police, through ignorance of what their duties in the circumstances were, or from instructions received from superior authority, failed to take action against the rebels, and their function were largely usurped by the co-called Irish Republican Police.

August, 1921.—Early in August before these illegalities were so prevalent as they afterwards became the Commander-in-Chief pressed for a better definition of the terms of the Agreement, and submitted to the Secretary of State for War[h] and the Chief of the Imperial General Staff[i] a memorandum of the conditions on which he considered that these terms should be based.[3]

[h]   Sir (Worthington) Laming Worthington-Evans, 1st Baronet GBE, PC (b.1868–d.1931).

[i]   Field Marshal Sir Henry Wilson.

In this memorandum it was submitted that, if the cessation of activities was to continue, it was essential that the law and lawful authority should be obeyed and acknowledged and that the rebels should at once cease from openly trying to establish and enforce obedience to their own alleged law, and the orders of persons purporting to act under it.[j]

[j]   The simple retort should have been that the Cabinet had already admitted equality by conducting a formal truce. Any attempt to force the republicans to submit to British law would have been appropriately seen as a violation of the Truce, since it was predicated on entering negotiations. Adding conditions to these negotiations *ex post facto* is a demonstration of bad faith at the least.

Commander-in-Chief's recommendations for truce conditions.—Based on experience of the rebels activities since the Agreement of 11th July, the measures suggested for placing matters on a more definite basis were as follows:—

(a)   No interference with Government or with the person or property of individual, or with the personnel of the forces of the Crown.

(b)   No recruiting or collection of funds for organizations which have been declared illegal.

(c) No carrying of arms without a permit, or wearing of unauthorized uniforms.[k]

(d) No importation of arms, ammunition or explosives, or transfer of arms, ammunition or explosives within the country.

(e) No parades, inspections, drilling or military training.

(f) No usurpation of the functions of the courts (civil or military), Government department or local bodies.

(g) No provocative actions likely to cause a breach of the peace.

In case of any infringement of the above, such action as is considered necessary will be taken by the civil forces of the Crown, supported, if necessary, by the military forces.

[k] This was tantamount to calling for surrender.

Except as provided for above, the Government agrees to refrain from—

(a) Military and police activities directed against illegal organizations.

(b) Despatch of reinforcements of troops or police to Ireland, except drafts and reliefs required for maintenance.

(c) Despatch of munitions to Ireland other than those required for maintenance and training.

(d) Interference with the movements of members or with the property of organizations which have been declared illegal, except in cases where they infringe the law of the country.

(e) The imposition of further restrictions under R.O.I.R.[4]

Decisions of Joint Committee.—Subsequently, the "Terms of the Truce" were considered in London by a Joint Committee of British Ministers and Sinn Fein representatives. The recommendations of the Commander-in-Chief were not, however, adopted. Certain decisions were made by this Committee. The commandeering of houses and the raising of forced levies by the I.R.A. were said to be unauthorized by the Sinn Fein representatives. It was agreed that Sinn Fein courts should cease, except those which existed prior to the "truce." Drilling was to be allowed so long as it was not provocative.

These decisions were not satisfactory, so far as the military situation was concerned. The legalizing of the drilling of the I.R.A. went far towards recognizing this rebel body as a regular force; such recognition had always been steadfastly resisted by the military authorities.[1] The permission given for

Sinn Fein courts, as constituted before the "truce," to continue implied that the activities of the rebels prior to 11th July were legitimate. The fact that the Sinn Fein leaders did not authorize commandeering of houses and forced levies did not prevent these illegalities taking place, and no redress was obtained, in the great majority of cases, by reference to the liaison officials. The liaison arrangements in fact were little more than a farce. The men originally selected by Sinn Fein were in many cases leading extremists, whose complicity in outrages and murder was well known to the British officers who were required to deal with them. The replies of these officials to complaints of breaches of the agreement, were usually either a bald statement that the facts of the incidents were not as reported, or that the perpetrators had no connection with the I.R.A.

[l] This is the true crux of the army's angst about this situation. In their eyes, the IRA had not constituted a lawful combatant force because it did not meet the criteria laid out in the Hague Conventions. That they had done so during the Easter Rising, and the leaders were shot regardless, does not appear to have occurred to them; the Irish Volunteers were going to be executed whether they abided by the laws of war or not, and so there was absolutely no legal reason for them to adhere. Even as late as May 1921, that the police and soldiers could surrender safely to the IRA, while the same could not be said for the Irish Volunteers, goes a fair way towards outright dismissal of the British army's complaints. See the end of this chapter, 'Note on Belligerency'.

False impressions that Crown forces failed.—In view of the fact that an impression was allowed to gain publicity, and is likely to be handed down in history as a fact, to the effect that the Crown forces had failed in their task, and had been worsted by the I.R.A., it is well to consider what the task before the Crown forces had been, and what had been the aim of the I.R.A.[m]

[m] In many respects, this seems to have occurred. It is by no means clear that the Irish Volunteers or Sinn Féin 'won' the war. It would be more accurate to say they incurred successes rather than victory.

The aim of the I.R.A. was to drive the Crown forces out of the country and to set up a Republic. Neither of these objects was accomplished, and was never really within reasonable chance of accomplishment until a final settlement was reached. In a speech in the Dail during the discussions of the terms of settlement in December, 1921, Richard Mulcahy, "Chief of Staff" of the I.R.A., stated that the I.R.A. had not been able to drive out the Crown forces, and that the greatest success of which it had been capable was the taking of a moderated-sized police barracks.

The solution of the Irish problem and the pacification of Irishmen was not, and never could be, the task of soldiers. That was a political problem, and no military operations could bring it about. All that the military authorities ever claimed that the troops could do was reduce the armed rebels to a state of sufficient impotence, to create a situation in which a political solution would have a reasonable chance of acceptance.[n] The political solution was accepted, and the part played by the Crown forces in attaining the result may be estimated by a reference to the following facts:—

[n] This appears to be the first statement of an actual military objective. It was, indeed, their mission—as much as can be said to be. The problem is that it is not entirely consistent with the statements of the military leadership during the war. They consistently spoke of retaining Ireland, which was unlikely to happen. Their goals appear to have changed *ex post facto*. They did not 'reduce the armed rebels to a state of sufficient impotence'.

Early in 1921 certain tentative proposals for a settlement were made. In spite of persistent rumours that peace was in the air, there was absolutely no response from the leaders of the Sinn Fein movement. The following statement was made in *An T'Oglac* on 1st February, 1921[5]:—

The Minister responsible for the waging of war against the enemy is interpreting the unanimous wish of the Republican Government in using every weapon at his command against the brutal instruments which the enemy is employing against the Irish people. It is necessary to emphasize this fact in view of statements about "negotiations for a settlement" propaganda which has been helped by the action of erratic individuals representing nobody but themselves.

This was at a time when the troops had only just begun to be used in close co-operation with the police, and when the Sinn Fein leaders, in order to counteract the slight improvement in the situation which had resulted, were making every effort to intensify their campaign of outrage and intimidation. The extremists were then in the ascendant, and the "erratic individuals" lost their seats at the May elections.

Desperate position of the rebels at commencement of truce.—Very different was the situation when, on 24th June, 1921, the Prime Minister issued his invitation to Sir James Craig and Mr. De Valera. The rebel organization throughout the country was in a precarious condition, and the future from the Sinn Fein point of view may be said to have been almost desperate. The flying columns and active service units into which the rebels had been forced, by the search for prominent individuals, to form themselves were being harried and chased from pillar to post, and were constantly being defeated and broken up by the Crown forces; individuals were being hunted down and arrested; the internment camps were filling up; the headquarters of the I.R.A. was functioning under the greatest difficulty, many of its offices having been captured complete; De Valera himself had been captured and released for political reasons; a number of rebels found in possession of arms, or actually engaged in warlike operations against His Majesty's forces had been condemned to death, and execution was only delayed pending an appeal on a particular case; Martial Law was about to be imposed in the 26 southern counties.[6]

On the other hand, the activities of the I.R.A. had been restricted almost entirely to murders of unarmed soldiers, policemen and ex-soldiers, the burning of houses, the kidnapping of individuals, the cutting of their own roads and the boycotting of Belfast and English goods. Added to this was the fact that, although the rebel leaders had for months been explaining o their followers that England, with all her other commitments, could not spare another soldier for service in Ireland, yet during the end of June and beginning of July 18 battalions arrived in the country.[o]

[o] This is quite an overstatement. The IRA certainly was not defeated by the summer of 1921. How the Irish Volunteers would have fared against the planned British military sweeps, which essentially constituted an invasion, remains a matter of conjecture. It is hard to see how they would have been able to put up any significant resistance to such forces. The British would have been able to counter almost every advantage the IRA could employ. It is also unclear whether Macready's plan would have received the full political support that would have been necessary.

These were the conditions in which the Sinn Fein leaders agreed to go to London and discuss the political solution, and they should be remembered when statements are made to the effect that "military tactics had been a disappointing failure."

Rebels encouraged by long truce.—The protracted discussions which took place concerning the very generous offer of the British Government were, in all probability, the result of a growing feeling of power inspired in the minds of the leaders by the long period which had been allowed to them for recuperating and reorganizing without interference from the Crown forces. Had the Prime Minister's offer delayed until the winter, when the large reinforcements received would have had three summer months for further reducing the rebellion, it is not unreasonable to believe that, had he so wished, he might have offered terms less favourable to the rebels, or, at any rate, that the terms he did offer would have been more readily accepted.

As it was, with the chance that negotiations might suddenly break down, and a possibility of the troops being again called upon to assume active operations, the recruiting, reorganizing, re-equipping and training of the I.R.A. was a serious consideration. The Commander-in-Chief pointed out to the War Office the increased difficulties with which the troops would be faced by reason of the lack of authority to enforce the spirit of the terms of the agreement of 11th July.

"Treaty," January, 1922p.—The contingency, however, did not arise, for on 7th January, 1922, Dail Eireann, by a majority of seven votes, agreed to endorse the Sinn Fein representatives' acceptance of the Government's Terms of Settlement. Shortly afterwards these Terms of Settlement were ratified by the members who had been elected to the Southern Parliament.

p The Anglo-Irish Treaty, signed Tuesday 6 December, 1921.[7]

The British soldier is quick to forget. During the 6 months which had elapsed since 11th July, 1921, the sense of humiliation and disappointment at the situation then created had to a great extent disappeared from the mind of all except the more senior officers, and the feeling uppermost in every officer, non-commissioned officer and man in the country was one of intense pleasure at the thought of a speedy and permanent departure from Ireland.q

q This appears to have been the general consensus amongst the military forces as they left.

Factors common to all rebellions.—Apart from the tactical lessons which this particular type of guerrilla warfare brought out, there are certain points in strategy, political and military, which were revealed, chiefly by their omission, but which would appear to be common to all forms of rebellion:—

(1) Rebellions start from small beginnings; a few men of fanatical[r] tendencies, whose views are not at first shared by the majority of their countrymen, can by armed intimidation induce the adherence of a large majority of all classes, and the active support of practically all the young men. In 1919 the armed rebel movement was in a minority; by the end of 1920 it dominated the country.

[r] Research on revolutions since the 1930s has demonstrated that the leaders are rarely extremists. Indeed, Brinton found that moderates generally start these movements, which are later taken over by extremists. The extremists fight the war to the conclusion, at which point the moderates reassert themselves. For Brinton, the last stage of revolution is civil war between the moderates and extremists.[8]

(2) The time to strike, and strike hard, is at the very beginning so that waverers may see which side means to control the situation.[s] This might have been done even as late as the spring of 1920.[t]

[s] Insurgent or revolutionary movements are weakest at the beginning. A move against the Volunteers and Sinn Féin would have required careful political and propaganda preparations that the British were not sufficiently ready to perform at that time. Such action might have strengthened the republicans, and could have damaged relationships with the Americans, since it would have been viewed as nothing but political repression.

[t] Outright victory against dispersed rebel groups in 1920 would have been unlikely. This would have required greater troop strength than had been provided by the Cabinet by the summer of 1921 (55,000), since they would have needed to hold ground and hunt rebel groups simultaneously. Such operations require large numbers of troops.

(3) A policy once started should never be given up. The release of the hunger-strikers from Mountjoy Prison in April, 1920, and the consequent cancellation of policy gave the opportunity for the unmolested organization

and stabilization of the rebel forces, civil and military, and lost the support of many waverers.[u]

> [u]   They appear to be correct in this. These actions emboldened the less militant republicans, and gave hope that the Government would eventually collapse.

(4) Early efforts should be made to enlist loyalists and moderate people on the side of law and order, and to organize them into civil guards. Those who refuse this must be made to understand that they run the risk common to all persons who live or own property in a theatre of war. No steps were taken to make use of loyalists or of the numerous ex-soldiers, who were mostly loyal and who were kept aloof from the rebel movement for a considerable time.[v]

> [v]   This is not entirely true; the RIC created the Ulster Special Constabulary in 1920 and intended them to perform duties that could free up military and regular RIC men for use in other areas of the country. One wonders what sort of response they would have received in the south. The strengths of such groups are much the same as their weaknesses. Recruited from the local population, they knew the members of the IRA and Sinn Féin; of course, this was true in the reverse, potentially placing their families at risk. Many had military training, but how useful this was to a policing function is questionable. Other issues concerned command and control, in a sectarian environment at worst, or a civil war at best.
>
> The other issue with this was that the Irish war veteran was liable to be either a Unionist or a home ruler. Every moderate nationalist killed in the war was one fewer man to oppose Sinn Féin later at its end. The Government had not been kind to home rule and, while technically loyal *and* nationalist, a home rule war veteran was necessarily more loyal to the Crown than to his fellow Irishman. Indeed, the Government had foreseen this problem, hence the deployment of both battalions of all the Irish regiments overseas.

(5) Military areas should be formed by taking possession of whole towns, forming them into defended areas, forcing loyal persons to live in them and take over the civil administration of them. The areas to be gradually extended by the operations of the troops in clearing the surrounding country of rebels.[w]

(6) Preparations in men and material must be made from the start as though it was likely to be a long process. This will have a great effect upon the moral of the rebels.[x]

[w] The points 4 and 5 go together: the problem with enlisting 'loyal' people is that this turns the struggle into a civil war. If the Cabinet were willing to let loyal groups in the south to undertake limited defensive operations, they might have been able to control their actions. Otherwise, they would have turned into the Ulster Special Constabulary. The other problem with this is that it would only have worked if the Government demonstrated that they were not going to abandon Ireland. How they could give such surety, given the Home Rule Act and their eventual actions, it is difficult to determine. It recalls the Listowel Mutiny, when the policemen declared that they had to live in Ireland after the leaders left. The same held true for loyal people in the south.

[x] This depends on the expectation of the people. Later twentieth-century revolutionaries fought protracted wars. Culturally, they were able to do so, but the same may not have been the case in Ireland. Since the war ended as it did, it is impossible to say. The later rebel republican groups really do not provide an answer, as their popular support amongst the people was never as strong.

(7) Martial Law should be declared early, even if there are not sufficient troops to enforce it all over the country, and it must be complete Martial Law without appeal to civil law courts, and without any executive civil authority in the country. If this is done at the beginning, there will be a sufficient number of loyalists to run necessary civil services, such as telegraph, water and gas supplies, &c. The partial application of a limited form of Martial Law caused endless complications and rendered the administration of it ineffective.[y]

[y] Martial law extended over the whole of the country would have been likely to speed up the revolutionary process, as the British were incapable of applying it fairly. The people of the south would have seen how they would not have used it in the north, just as they saw the British stand by and allow the anti-Catholic rioting in 1920 continue without any real intervention. The application of martial law would have played

into republican propaganda, as it stripped away the rights of everyone. Arresting those not involved in the republican movement would provide more volunteers. Executions after dubious trials would make the situation worse. Without mobilizing broad popular support, the British would have failed. While such support may have existed, the British proved incapable of mobilizing it.

(8) Whether Martial Law is made universal or not all the force of the Crown must be under one supreme control, and whoever administers Martial Law must command all these forces.

The dual control of troops and police was a source of serious lack of co-ordinated effort, and might have led to friction.

(9) Improvised force should be grafted on to existing organizations and not made into units of an independent force, otherwise a new system of discipline, or a lack of discipline, will result. The Auxiliary Division, R.I.C., which contained a magnificent set of men, lost half its value through a bad form of discipline.[z]

[z] This was a constant source of frustration for the police and the Army officials in Ireland. The original plans for the ADRIC were for them to be under military discipline. The failure to maintain discipline in the force, however, was only one problem with it; they also needed to strike proper targets. Lack of intelligence hampered their operations greatly.

(10) Newspapers must be severely censored and controlled, or suppressed altogether, both in the country concerned and in England. The hostile Press in Ireland was one of the strongest weapons in the hands of the rebels.[aa]

[aa] British propaganda and counter-propaganda was virtually non-existent during the war. There were, however, some few instances of brilliance. There were occasions when they issued false *Irish Bulletins* and *An t-Óglác*. Otherwise, they operated under not only a cloud of suspicion, but also a lack of credibility. The former stemmed from their issues of discipline and targeting, the latter from their long history in Ireland. Essentially, anything said by the Irish administration was suspect.

(11) The Home Government must state its policy in clear and unequivocal terms as soon as possible, and must explain to the public at home and abroad what this policy is and how and why the forces of the Crown are carrying it out.

There was no clear enunciation of Government policy, and the terms which the Government were prepared to concede were published too late. No attempt was made to explain the situation to the public in England, and the Crown forces had to put up with much unmerited abuse in consequence.

(12) A Military Intelligence Section, with which should be amalgamated whatever civil detective or secret service force which exists in the country, must be formed from the beginning. To this must be attached a publicity department, with two functions—

(1) To disseminate facts officially.
(2) To spread propaganda unofficially.[bb]

[bb] This reflects the immaturity of intelligence as a discipline at the time. Intelligence includes the collection of information, its analysis, its safeguarding and dissemination to the appropriate people for action. Propaganda is the use of information to convince any targeted group to do or not to do something. Modern public affairs is the dissemination of the 'official' message. While these disciplines may work together, they should not be considered as interchangeable. Obviously, these are modern distinctions and the authors were somewhat ahead of their time in identifying these aspects missing from their campaign.

(13) In arresting and interning rebels it is not sufficient to take "officers" of the armed forces only; every man belonging to an illegal body must be liable to be arrested and interned. This will necessitate internment camps outside the country concerned.

(14) The political leaders of the rebel movement should be arrested and tried for high treason or conspiracy, and should not be allowed to go free on the chance of their being willing to treat with the Government.

Arthur Griffith in prison was easier to treat with than De Valera free.

Note On Belligerency

Effect of admitting belligerent status of I.R.A.—During September, 1921, when it appeared possible and even likely that the "truce" might be brought to an abrupt termination, much thought was given to the problem as to whether it would be advisable to admit the belligerent status of the I.R.A. This was not a matter which, even in a state of universal Martial Law throughout Ireland (or Southern Ireland), could be said to affect the military authorities alone, as the recognition on their part of the I.R.A. as belligerents, might *ipso facto*, be said to involve the Imperial Government in the recognition of an Irish Republic.[cc]

[cc] The army still did not want to admit that the Truce, being registered with the League of Nations, was *ipso facto* recognition of the IRA's belligerent status.

Special penalties in force in June, 1921.—The state of affairs in July, 1921, when by agreement military and police activities ceased, was as follows:—

In the Martial Law area proclamations had been issued, by virtue of which the death penalty might be inflicted—(*a*) on any person found in possession of arms, ammunition, &c., without a permit, and (*b*) on any unauthorized person wearing a British uniform. It was further an offence against the R.O.I.R. (9 a.a.) for any person to use, wear or possess uniforms of a naval or military character—but the death penalty could not be inflicted for the last offence.

Outside the Martial Law area the death penalty could only be inflicted (except in cases of murder) on individuals who were actually proved guilty of high treason or who had taken part in an operation involving "levying war on His Majesty."

Impossibility of Civil Government recognizing belligerent status of I.R.A.—Had the military authorities desired to recognized in any way within the Martial Law area, the belligerent status of members of the I.R.A. found to be wearing uniforms and conforming in other respects to the "Regulations respecting the Laws and Customs of War on Land"[dd] as laid down in Annex to the International Convention concerning those Laws and Customs, signed at

Hague on 18th October, 1907, such recognition would have been impossible in the view of the fact that the same organization (I.R.A.) was not and could not be recognized in the rest of Ireland as a belligerent force by the Civil Government of Ireland, without stultifying any justification there might be for their continued presence in the country and their refusal to declare Martial Law throughout Ireland.

> [dd] The Hague Conventions' qualifications for belligerent status were that forces had 'To be commanded by a person responsible for his subordinates; To have a fixed, distinctive emblem recognizable at a distance; To carry arms openly; and To conduct their operations in accordance with the laws and customs of war.'[9] Since the British had outlawed the basic elements of wearing uniforms and carrying arms openly, they nullified the laws of war. Further, since this was an 'internal' war, the Hague Conventions did not apply.

Bad effect of partial Martial Law.—Considerable propaganda use had been made of these conditions, not only in the British Isles but also in Europe and America, and our attitude was unintelligible to the ordinary man in the street, who could not be expected to understand difficulties involved in our having to act simultaneously under two codes—Martial Law and R.O.I.R. As one American writer puts it "...we all quite agree with Lloyd George that Irish soldiers ought to wear uniforms. Then we were shocked to learn that England would not permit the Irish army to wear uniforms and made the wearing of it an offence, and your great opportunity was lost."[ee] In September, 1921, the situation had changed and conditions contemplated in the event of a breakdown of negotiations were those in which Martial Law would be universal throughout Southern Ireland. This meant that the Military Governor-General would be free to act as he desired.[ff]

> [ee] This admission is surprising considering their hostility to the IRA.
>
> [ff] This is questionable at best; without an act of indemnity, the soldiers were still liable to civil law.[10]

Military commanders' opinions.—From the soldiers' point of view it was eminently desirable that the I.R.A. should be recognizable and easy to differentiate from the ordinary civilians. All military commanders were in agreement that men who wore uniform and fought cleanly and in accordance with the laws and customs of war should, if captured, be interned and given the treatment of prisoners of war, irrespective of whether they were in possession of arms or not—provided always that leaders and others might be tried for high treason, or for offences against the laws and customs of war committed prior to their capture.[gg] From the legal point of view it was urged that no proclamation should be issued, or promises made, which would in any way tie the hands of the Military Governors in any action they might be compelled to take for the purposes of suppressing the rebellion.

[gg] In the instance of Seán McEoin, when he conducted the ambush at Clonfin, 2 February 1921, he prevented any abuse of the police prisoners, tended their wounds and allowed them to evacuate their wounded in the remaining undamaged vehicle. He was later captured and tried. While the authors of *The Record of the Rebellion* stated that prevention of 'the massacre of the wounded and prisoners was noticeable and unusual; it counted much in his favour when he was subsequently brought to trial for the murder of a District Inspector, R.I.C.' His reputation was such that two ADRIC cadets who were at Clonfin testified on his behalf. He was sentenced to death regardless.[11]

Precedent of American Civil War.[h]—A precedent for this line of action existed in the case of the 1861–65 campaign, when the North treated the Southern rebels according to the laws and customs of war without definitely recognizing them as belligerents, and dealt with all breaches of international law as war crimes, though they reserved the right to deal with leaders for high treason.

[hh] This was a reference to General Orders No. 100: 'Instructions for the Government of Armies of the United States in the Field' (also called 'The Lieber Code' after Francis Lieber, LLD, its author), signed by American President Abraham Lincoln on 24 April 1863 to govern the conduct of the war. It later served as a guide for the development of the Hague Conventions of 1899 and 1907. See Hague II, 'Laws and Customs of War on Land', 29 July 1899 and Hague IV, 'Laws and Customs of War on Land', 18 October 1907.

Decision to treat I.R.A. in uniform favourably.—It was therefore decided, and confidential orders were issued to the effect that, though no proclamation should be issued on the subject, rebels wearing a uniform (other than British uniform) which can be recognized at a distance, would not be tried by drumhead court on the charges of being in possession of arms, ammunition or explosives, nor by Court Martial (under R.O.I.R.) in respect of wearing uniform. Such men would usually (in default of other charges) be interned.

Rebel views on belligerency.—In view of the above it is interesting to note the views of the rebels as given by Michael Collins in his first article to the Hearst newspapers of America on 6th February, 1922, in which he writes: "… Another thing I believe, and I have not said it except to my personal friends, is that on resumption of hostilities, the British would have been anxious to fight with us on the basis of belligerent rights. In such circumstances I doubt if we would have been able to carry on a conflict with the success which had previously attended our efforts. I scarcely think that our resources would have been equal to bearing belligerent rights and responsibilities."

NOTES

1 See Townshend, *Political Violence*, p. 359.
2 For breaches of the Truce, see 'Investigating Breaches of the Truce', NAUK WO 35/182 pt. 1/3.
3 See commentary in 'Report by the GOCinC on the Situation in Ireland', 2 August, 1921, NAUK CAB 24/126/646–50, pp. 1–5.
4 Appendix V, 'Report by the General Officer-Commanding-in-Chief on the General Situation in Ireland for Week Ending 9 July, 1921', NAUK CAB 24/126/283–4 CP 3134. See Additional Appendices for copies of the GHQ IRA and GHQ Irish Command communiqués.
5 *An t-Óglác: Official Organ of the Irish Volunteers*, vol. II, No. 22, (1 February, 1921), p. 133.
6 See 'Ireland Military Law Committee Report', 1 August, 1921, NAUK CAB 24/126/602–4, pp. 1–3; Memorandum by Col Sir Hugh Elles, 24 June, 1921, CAB 24/125/572, pp. 1–2 CP 3075; and Memorandum by Secretary of State for War, 'Internment of Irish Rebels', 25 June, 1921, CAB 24/125/600, p. 2, CP 3082.
7 F. Gallagher, *The Anglo-Irish Treaty* (1965); Lord Longford, Pakenham, Frank. *Peace By Ordeal: The Negotiation of the Anglo-Irish Treaty 1921* (1967); T. R. Dwyer, *'I Signed My Death Warrant': Michael Collins and the Treaty* (2006); J. Knirck, *Imagining Ireland's Independence: The Debates over the Anglo-Irish Treaty of 1921* (2006); and T. R. Dwyer, *Michael Collins and the Treaty: His Differences with de Valera* (1981).
8 See C. Brinton, *Anatomy of Revolution* (1938).
9 Annex to the Convention, Regulations Respecting the Laws and Customs of War on Land Section I On Belligerents, Chapter I, 'The Qualifications of Belligerents', Laws and Customs of War on Land (Hague IV); October 18, 1907.
10 See Townshend, *Britain's Civil Wars*, pp. 19–27; K. Jeffery, 'Colonial Warfare 1900–39', *Warfare in the Twentieth Century* (London: Unwin Hyman, Ltd. 1988), pp. 35 and 36; Pimlott, 'The British Experience', p. 17; 'Report of Gen Sir Nevil Macready's Committee on the Safe-keeping of Lethal Weapons', 26 February, 1920, NAUK CAB 24/99 C796; and Hare, Maj-Gen Sir Steuart, K.C.M.G., C.B. 'Martial Law from the Soldier's Point of View', *Army Quarterly*, Vol. VII (October, 1923 and January, 1924).
11 *The Record of the Rebellion*, Vol. IV, p. 51, Nat. Archives, WO 141/93.

APPENDIX I

THE MILITARY SITUATION IN IRELAND AT THE END OF SEPTEMBER, 1921[1]

On 11th July, 1921, there came into operation an agreement which was to ensure "a peaceful atmosphere" during the progress of the negotiations between the Prime Minister and Mr. De Valera.

Since that date considerable changes have taken place in the military value of the rebel forces, and the General Officer Commanding-in-Chief wishes commanders of all formations and units to study and think over the following notes, so that they may be prepared to face somewhat new conditions should the conferences now taking place fail "to bear fruit" and active rebellion break out again:—

It is not the intention of this paper to discuss how the terms of the agreement have been kept or disregarded by the rebels, but to endeavour to show in what respect the I.R.A. has become a more formidable organization than it was prior to the date on which the military and police activities ceased.

Three months ago the rebel organization throughout the country was in a precarious condition, and the future, from the Sinn Fein point of view, may be said to have been well nigh desperate. The flying columns and active service units into which the rebels had been forced, by the search for prominent individuals, to form themselves, were being harried and chased from pillar to post, and were constantly being defeated and broken up by the Crown forces.[a] Individuals were being hunted down and arrested; the internment camps were rapidly filling up; the Headquarters of the I.R.A. was functioning under the greatest difficulty, many of its offices having been captured to complete. De Valera himself had been captured and released for political reasons; a number of rebels found in possession of arms, or actually engaging in warlike operations against His Majesty's forces, had been condemned to death, and execution was only delayed pending an appeal on a certain case to the House Lords. The coal strike in Great Britain was over, and reinforcements were pouring into Ireland; Martial Law was about to be proclaimed throughout the 26 counties, and 3 months of suitable weather for operations was still before us. On the other hand, the rebels had scored successes in a few cases where they had surprised small parties of Crown forces, but otherwise their achievements were limited to murders of unarmed soldiers, policemen and ex-soldiers, the burning of houses of loyal persons, the kidnapping of individuals, many of whom were only remotely connected with the civil administration, the destruction of Government property, the cutting of their own roads, and boycotting of English and Belfast goods. The total casualties which had been inflicted on the troops in 18 months were little, if any, more than many a battalion suffered in a single morning during the war in France, and of those approximately 50 per cent. were cold-blooded murders of unarmed individuals.[b] The police had suffered more severely than the troops. Such were the conditions on 11th July, and it is small wonder that the rebel leaders grasped at the straw that was offered, and agreed to negotiation accompanied by cessation of activities on both sides.

[a] Essentially, this is wishful thinking; while the IRA was not winning the war in May and June 1921, neither were they losing outright. On Sunday 8 May 1921, one of the Belfast columns suffered significant loses when ten of their number were captured in the Lappinduff Mountains, Co. Cavan.[2] This might have been alluding to the 80 or more men captured at the burning of the Custom House in Dublin on Wednesday, 25 May.[3] There were many other rebel attacks during those two months that inflicted the highest casualties on British forces of the war.

b Invoking the Great War's casualties as a standard seems to be more a balm to the British army's ego than a comment on IRA efficacy. The IRA was still confounding the Army's best efforts. By denigrating the IRA and its successes, and brushing off casualties, as well as overstating British forces' successes, the army accomplished two goals. They demonstrated that they were not losing the undefined war when it ended. This removed military inadequacy from the list of what went wrong, allowing them to retain pride in what they had accomplished. Regardless of the reasons for failure, soldiers do not like accepting defeat in any of its forms. The second goal, clearly related to the first, was their argument to lay the blame squarely at the feet of the Cabinet. This was a demonstration of how wrong the Government was about Ireland and, therefore, how illegitimate was their decision. This was a direct attack on the Truce.

How the period of immunity from search and arrest has been used by the I.R.A. is well known to all who have been serving in Ireland, and it is proposed to consider in detail what will be the effect of recruiting, organizing, arming and equipping, drilling and training that had been going on without let or hindrance all over the country during the past 2½ months.

Quite early in the days of the "truce" reports were received that a *recruiting* campaign for the I.R.A. was being undertaken in various parts of the country. This has since became universal. Recruiting meetings have been held and speeches made by some of the best known rebel leaders; funds have been openly collected and levies have been made practically by force. Numbers of young men have been enrolled and even ex-soldiers, who in the main had kept aloof from the rebel organization in the past, have now been induced to join. In some parts of the country it is reported that practically every young man has now become a member of the I.R.A. Whether the quality of the new recruit is even up to standard of the Irish Volunteer of the past is more than doubtful[c], and many men have probably joined in the belief that their military activities will be limited to a mild form of training during the week ends in camps or in country houses, commandeered from men who have hitherto been their masters and landlords. Whether the increased numbers will be an advantage to the rebels or not remains to be seen.

c There is little to suggest that these men were conscripted. Their choice of words about the quality of Irish Volunteers is interesting.

In the past it has been difficult to distinguish the active rebel from the harmless civilian; in this respect, at any rate, the work of the Crown forces will be facilitated in those districts where all the young men have joined the I.R.A.

As regards *organization*, we have no information which points to any great changes during the past 2½ months beyond rumours of the formation of a new brigade and of one or two new battalions. One thing, however, is certain, and that is that, owing to various causes—to release of leaders from prison or internment camps—to the return of active rebels from active service units, flying columns and from "the run"—to the impulse imparted by the influx of new recruits and of arms[d]—many of the battalions and companies which were collapsing through inanition have now been reorganized and rejuvenated. The divisional organization, which was being introduced in circumstances of considerable difficulty, has had an opportunity of finding its feet, and is now doubtless integral and effective link in the chain of I.R.A. organization. All rebels units have had time to fill up vacancies caused by casualties to their leaders and in their ranks. The arrival of a number of Thompson sub-machine guns (*see* below) has been followed by the organization of machine-gun squads.

d Large quantities of arms were en route from Hamburg, but had not yet arrived. Thus, there was little upon which to base this statement.

Owing to the withdrawal of all check on importation and smuggling of weapons and ammunition, considerable progress has been made in the *arming and equipping* of the rebel forces.

The most important new adjunct in the Sinn Fein armoury is the Thompson sub-machine gun, a considerable number of which, we know from *An T'Oglac*[4], have arrived in this country. A brief description of this weapon was given in General Headquarters Intelligence Summary of 6th January, 1921, and efforts are being made to obtain a number of handbooks of the gun for general distribution. The possession of this weapon undoubtedly make the I.R.A. a more formidable organization from the military point of view, but, on the other hand, its weight and the conveyance of its ammunition (.45) will tend to make its crews less "volatile" and will possibly assist the troops in close order, or in trains, or lorry convoys, particularly if employed from a height or from buildings overlooking barracks. Such a weapon cannot be ignored, and plans must be made rapidly to deal with situations resembling those suggested above, should they arise. During the present period of training, officers and non-commissioned officers should frequently be confronted with tactical problems necessitating the rapid issue of orders for the attack and capture of machine-gun positions. Cases will probably occur which will admit of the employment of weapons on our side which have not hitherto been used in Ireland, such as field guns, trench mortars, machine guns and bombs from aeroplanes, the 6-pr. guns carried by tanks.

No definite information has been received of the importation of other arms and ammunition, but there have been constant reports of gun-running and there is little doubt that the I.R.A. has been freely used at training camps.[e] There is no doubt that advantage has been taken of the truce to continue the manufacture of bombs and the repair of damaged weapons.

> [e] Charlie McGuinness landed a large shipment of arms in Cork from Germany just after the Truce began.[5]

Beyond the fact that camps, both for the *training* of officers and specialists and for local units and their recruits, are in existence all over the country, few details as to the type of training carried out have been ascertained. Drilling has been going on openly now for nearly two months, and cases of practice ambushes have been reported, from various sources, reports of musketry training, revolver, bombing and machine-gun practice have been received. The lines on which the training has been conducted are certainly based on the instructions contained in our own drill books and manuals—guerilla warfare training has probably been freely carried out. Attendances have varied; at some of the camps in the west large numbers have been reported.

Whatever the *quality* of the personnel of the newly reinforced I.R.A., we must expect to meet better organized, better discipline and better equipped bodies of men than those we met in the past. On the other hand, courage is a quality, which, except in a few instances, has not been conspicuously exhibited by the rebels. Like all irregular or guerilla troops, the I.R.A. are particular sensitive about their flanks and lines of retreat. They invariably collapse in the face of resolute attack. *An T'Oglac* has instilled into them the cult of the initiative, and they are gifted with exceptional cunning and powers of deception. Their aim and object is always to lull their opponents into a sense of security, and then to rely primarily on surprise for success.[f]

> [f] This betrayed their bias: the primary aims of the guerrilla force are to remain functional and to remain alive.

In considering the measures necessary to meet the new situation which would arise, it must be borne in mind that although increase in numbers and weapons may induce the rebels to operate in larger numbers than formerly, it is probable that their methods will continue to be those of guerilla warfare; and that it is almost certain, that the difficulty of insufficient rifles having been overcome, there will be a large increase in single or pairs of snipers firing from vantage points whenever Crown forces move and whenever barracks, &c., can be commanded.

Another point in which the forces of the Crown have been handicapped during the period of military and police inactivity, is *Intelligence*—owing to the very nature of the agreement, but little information has been received in comparison with that obtained prior to 11th July—Sinn Fein has not been limited in this way. Details as to the positions and routine of our guards and sentries are probably well known to them; and it is important that this point should not be overlooked during the *two or three days which will, in all probability, elapse between the breakdown of negotiations and the termination of the "Truce"* so that dispositions may be altered or posts strengthened, as may seem desirable.

It is a fatal error, and possibly one to which Britishers are addicted, to under-estimate an enemy. It is an equally fatal error to over-estimate his value, and the above the somewhat lengthy notes are intended simply as a guide as to what we may expect, and in no way to place the I.R.A. on a pinnacle. To defeat the rebels we must understand them, and bear in mind their weak points and failings as well as their strong points and natural advantages.[g]

g Considering how little they understood of republican motivations, this statement is somewhat ironic.

It is unfortunately not possible to foresee what line of action Sinn Fein is likely to adopt on the breakdown of negotiations, but it may be taken as extremely likely that they will attempt some dramatic coup, which will, in their opinion, give proof of their strength and military ability. It is by no means unlikely that, in order to obtain good propaganda in British and foreign Press, they will stay their hand until we have taken the first step, and that they will reserve their initial efforts until after the first few searches or arrests have been carried out by us.

This initial effort may take the form of universal attacks on small military posts or police barracks, or, as has been rumoured, of attacks on prisons and internment camps, with the object of releasing prisoners, or of incendiary attacks on Government buildings, or it may be directed against the persons or property of loyal individuals. Whatever their plans may be, they can best be frustrated by vigilance and by intense activity on our part. We may expect an interval between the receipt of information that the negotiations have broken down, and the actual termination of the "truce." During this period the greatest vigilance will be necessary, not only to guard against any overt action on the part of the rebels, but in order to obtain clues or indications as to the line of action they intend to employ. Advantage should be taken of this "warning period" to withdraw any isolated military or police posts, and to alter or strengthen the disposition of guards and sentries.

Directly the "truce" terminates we must be prepared to act. Every unit and detachment must endeavour to seize the *initiative*. The difficulty, as in the past, will be the selection of an *objective*. If the existing rebel camps were to remain standing the task would be simple, but at the first sign of the termination of the "truce" these will most probably be struck. The individual rebels will either return to their homes where they must be searched for, and if away without good reason, noted as "on the run" (the unexplained absence of young men from their homes at this period will be fairly convincing proof of their connection with the rebel organization), or the various companies of I.R.A. may be concentrated elsewhere, but most probably still within their battalion area, where they must be sought out and hunted down. Likely places for such concentrations should be noted beforehand. When armed rebels are met, they must be relentlessly pursued, and no opportunity must be neglected for the effective use of every weapon.

In Dublin the primary objectives will be the personnel and various offices of the headquarters of the I.R.A. In the country the headquarters of the various divisions and brigades. These must be sought for and be harried and hunted with ceaseless energy. No organization can adequately function for long if it is constantly on the move, and no peace should be given to these headquarters until all important leaders have been arrested or satisfactorily accounted for.

Plans for the individual or combined employment of all units and detachments must be drawn up in advance; objectives must be selected and revised from time to time. Blows in the air and operations and searches without result are unavoidable, and it is only by good intelligence and careful appreciation of the information obtained that "blank days" can be minimized. It must be impressed on all ranks that operations that fail to bring the rebels to battle, though disappointing, are by no means without result. Being ceaselessly harried and hunted day and night, has more effect on the moral of irregular levies than anything except the infliction of heavy casualties.

The morale of the I.R.A. was at a low ebb 3 months ago—it has revived enormously during the truce—and, should hostilities recommence, no stone must be left unturned to break it completely in the shortest possible time.

In operations such as those which are likely to take place in Ireland, where the rebel forces employ guerilla tactics, remain scattered in small bodies all over the Island, and avoid concentration in large bodies; the opportunities for seizing the initiative and striking the rebels must, in the majority of cases, come to the commanders of units and detachments, and it is to them that the G.O.C.-in-C. looks to let no opportunity pass of inflicting loss and defeat on the rebels. The policy and line of action to be adopted must be laid down from above, and larger scale operations and drives may from time to time be organized, but experience in the past has shown that 90 per cent. of the most successful operations undertaken against the rebels have been due to the enterprise and initiative of commanders of battalions and smaller units.

It must be the ideal of every unit and detachment commander to make existence for the I.R.A. impossible within the area for which he is responsible. This can only be accomplished by watchfulness, by careful planning of operations, by rapidity of action and by boldness in attack.

L'audace, l'audace, toujours l'audace.

J. Brind,
Colonel on the Staff,
General Staff.

G.H.Q., Ireland,
1st October, 1921.

APPENDIX II

Some Examples of Gallant Actions for which Rewards have been Granted

Amongst the many acts of gallantry performed by the troops in Ireland, certain stand out as particularly deserving of notice. In all, 74 decorations were awarded for specific acts of gallantry, a few of which are enumerated below:—

1. On 9th October, 1920, a Major[a] of the Essex Regiment displayed considerable skill in the handling of his party when two lorries were ambushed by rebels and succeeded in driving off the enemy with loss and evacuating his party, several of whom had been wounded. He showed great personal bravery in carrying to safety two wounded officers lying in an exposed position. Unfortunately both of these subsequently died.[b]

> [a] Maj Arthur Ernest Percival (b.1887–d.1966).
>
> [b] Flight Lt Gurth Alwyn Richardson, RAF (d.10 October, 1920) and Lt Robert Douglas Finch Robertson (b.ca.1895–d.12 October 1920). Cmdt Sean Hales was leading the Cork flying column to Newcestown when they were caught on the open road by two lorries of troops. They attacked the vehicles, and in the ensuing gunfight the officers were mortally wounded. The fighting occurred at night, and Deasy said that it was too dark to see well. He reported that Vol. Jim Hodnett shot Robertson as the latter led his men in a flank attack. Rebel prisoner Dan Corcoran escaped the convoy during the fighting. There were no casualties on the rebel side. Deasy said that Percival received a DSO for this, but he received an OBE. Deasy also stated that CSM Harry Benton received an MBE and Pte Wootton received a BEM[6]

2. An officer[c] of the R.A.S.C. accompanied a raiding party in a motor launch on the Shannon on 17th October, 1920. The launch was heavily fired upon from the banks of the river and the engine was stopped, two officers[d] and two men being severely wounded. The officer mentioned above, at great personal risk, climbed along the outside of the launch and worked the rudder with his hand, exposed to full view and fire. He had previously repaired, under heavy fire, the magneto and restarted the engine. His gallantry undoubtedly saved the launch from drifting out of control under the close fire of the hidden enemy. He was assisted in his gallant work by a lance-corporal[e], who also showed utter disregard for himself.[7]

> [c] T/Lieut Albert Nelson Cannon, RASC was awarded an MBE.[8]
>
> [d] Major C. F. Adams, RASC and Lt St.J. Hodson, 1st Leicesters.
>
> [e] L/Cpl Herbert Roger Cantrill, 1st Leicesters was awarded the BEM, and Cannon an MBE.[9]

3. At Bruree, on 29th July, 1920, during the ambush of a small party by about 50 armed rebels, a private soldier[f] of the 1st Bn. Machine-Gun Corps volunteered to replenish the ammunition which was running short. The action lasted about one and a-half hours, and it was extremely dangerous for anyone to leave the building. This man dressed himself in civilian clothes and seized a bicycle

which was beside the building and made off on it. He succeeded in making his escape and brought back help to the beleaguered force. It was entirely owing to his courage and initiative that the party escaped annihilation.

> f   This was likely Pte Charles John Flemming, who received the BEM on 17 January 1921.[10]

4. On 12th/13th December, 1920, when a police barracks was besieged at Camlough, a party of the King's Royal Rifle Corps; under a young officer[g], was sent to its relief. The party was ambushed *en route*, but the officer, displaying great coolness, got his party out of the car in which they were travelling and attacked the rebels, inflicting severe casualties. By skilful handling he managed to avert casualties, and succeeded in relieving the barracks.[11]

> g   This was likely Lt James Herbert Theobald Charles Butler, K.R.R.C., who received an MBE on 7 February 1921.[12]

5. At Clonmult, on 20th February, 1921, an officer[h] of the Dorsetshire Regiment was one of an attacking party on a house strongly occupied by rebels. Troops and police attempted to capture the house but no headway could be made. The officer in question procured some petrol and making his way to the house from which the rebels were firing, poured it on the thatch of the roof and then set light to it. He was throughout under point-blank fire and his action led to the surrender or death of the entire party of rebels, and undoubtedly saved any further casualties being inflicted on the Crown forces. This officer was handicapped by the fact that he had lost an arm in the European War.[13]

> h   Lieut Henry Hammond, Dorsetshire Regiment, who received an OBE.[14]

6. An officer of the South Staffordshire Regiment showed continued initiative, skill and bravery for several months in carrying out specially hazardous duties. He succeeded in arresting single handed, a prominent rebel leader in a hotel where he had registered under a false name. He brought him back, single handed, to barracks, through the town of Cork. On 3rd January, 1921, he arrested another prominent rebel leader, inducing him to enter a car on the plea that he was being taken to make enquiries about the Cork fire; he overpowered him and brought him to barracks. Assisted by another officer he carried out a similar arrest of 17th January, 1921, in plain clothes, bringing the man he was after from a dangerous quarter of the town to barracks. These are among his exploits of a similar nature, all of which would have cost him his life if he had shown the slightest hesitation.

7. On the night of 7th/8th January, 1921, an officer of the Devonshire Regiment[i], with a mixed force of his regiment and R.I.C., was moving to the relief of a police barracks which was being attacked by rebels. The party was ambushed on the way and the officer handled his party with skill and succeeded in driving off the ambushers with the exception of a party posted in a position; he personally accounted for the majority of killed, first, with a bomb, and, secondly, with his revolver.[j] He showed great courage in this hazardous hand-to-hand affair. The rebels were in greatly superior numbers.

> i   According to Dr McCarthy, 'Two officers of the Devonshire Regiment, Lieutenants [Frederick Charles] Yeo and [Archibald William] Valentine, were decorated for their part in this action.' They received MBEs.[15]
>
> j   According to Dr McCarthy, 'Two I.R.A. volunteers, Michael McGrath and Thomas O'Brien, were killed, and one, Nicholas Whittle, was seriously wounded.'[16]

8. In Co. Cork on 31st July, 1921[k], a motor lorry was ambushed by rebels, a bomb being thrown into it which wounded the driver and four out of six of the escort. A serjeant of the Lincolnshire

Regiment was left with two men only, but engaged the rebels—numbering about 30. He put up a gallant fight and though wounded in the wrist, led his two men and cleared the house in which the rebels were. The engagement lasted about 2 hours and the mails and all the arms in the lorry were saved.

k   This was the Tramore (Pickardstown) ambush. It is clear that they meant 1920.

9. At Churchtown, Co. Cork, on 27th August, 1920, a private soldier[l] of the Cameron Highlanders was one of the occupants of a lorry ambushed by rebels. An officer, who had taken the wheel from the driver, who had been killed, was wounded in four places, and the soldier in question climbed from the back of the lorry into the driver's seat, exposing himself quite regardless of danger in doing so. He succeeded in keeping the lorry on the road and driving it to safety.

l   Pte Cecil Harry Smith.

10. On the 28th October, 1920, near Thomastown, Co. Tipperary, an officer of the Royal Engineers[m] was proceeding in a lorry with one non-commissioned officer and 11 men.[n] The lorry was ambushed. The first intimation that there was anything wrong was the appearance of a cart drawn across the road. The officer immediately stopped the lorry, on which heavy fire was directed from both sides of the road. The party returned the fire effectively, but owing to the severe casualties they sustained it was found impossible to bring the lorry through. Accordingly the party left the lorry and occupied a cottage, bringing their seven wounded to safety, and covering the lorry with fire to prevent it from falling into the hands of the rebels. A very gallant defence was put up, which lasted until assistance arrived. The officer's skilful handling of his small force, three-quarters of whom had been put out of action, showed a quick grasp of the situation and a very cool head.[17]

m   This may have been Lieut Joseph Parker, RE, TF who received an MBE.

n   Two soldiers, Ptes T. Crummey and F. A. Short, were killed. [18]

11. An officer and a corporal of the Lincolnshire Regiment, at Killenaule, on 31st October, 1920, put up a most gallant and skilful fight against a number of armed civilians, who they heard had just arrived in the town. They went out together and hunted them out. They were fired upon, and a hand-to-hand struggle ensued in which several of the civilians were killed or wounded, and one was dragged back to barracks, where he died. He turned out to be the most desperate murderer in the district, and it was proved that the civilians had arrived for the purpose of arranging ambushes and murders.[o]

o   Killed in the fighting was Thomas Donovan, former hunger striker and commandant in Tipperary Bde. He was labelled by the British as 'one of the most formidable murderers in the [6th] Divisional Area'.[19]

12. At Cross Barry, on 19th March, 1921, a serjeant[p] of the Essex Regiment displayed great gallantry and initiative in leading his men against the rebels. He succeeded, after repeated attempts, in bringing in an officer of his regiment who was lying wounded in an exposed position under the rebels' fire.

p   The only record of a sergeant from the Essex Regiment receiving a decoration near this time was Sgt Frank Poole, MM, who received the BEM.[20]

13. At Headford Junction[q] a party of the Royal Fusiliers was ambushed on the arrival of their train in the station. The rebels, who occupied positions in trucks near the platform, opened positions in trucks near the platform, opened fire on the party which consisted of an officer and some 28

men, half of whom were killed as they stepped on to the platform, the officer being the first to fall mortally wounded. A young lance-corporal took charge of the survivors and put up a very gallant fight, keeping the enemy at bay for 2½ hours and inflicting casualties on them in spite of the great disadvantage under which he was fighting. A Lewis gunner contributed very largely the skilful defence, working his gun on the platform continuously throughout the action, although three times wounded.[r] The party held out until extricated by the arrival of a train which had been commandeered by an officer[s] of the regiment who heard that firing was taking place at Headford Junction.

[q] Near Killarney, Co Kerry, 21 March, 1921.

[r] They were: Lieut C. E. Adams (b.ca.1891), Sjt G. Brundish (b.ca.1890), L/Cpl Edward Albert Chandler, Ptes A. George, Frederick George West, Frank Edward Woods and G. E. L. Young. Civilians John Breen, Michael Cagney and Patrick O'Donoghue were killed; Timothy McCarthy 'tried to shield his young daughter, but was hit in the leg; the same bullet passed through both legs of his three-year-old daughter, doing horrific damage in the process'.[21]

[s] This may have been Lt Cecil Harry Wreford Clarke, Royal Fusiliers, who received the MBE.

14. At Belfast, on 14th April, 1921, a serjeant[t] of the Norfolk Regiment displayed great presence of mind and courage by throwing two bombs out of the Ulster Club, which had been thrown by civilians at the guard over the building. One of these bombs exploded immediately it left this non-commissioned officer's hand.

[t] This may have been Acting Sgt Thomas Jefferson Whitfield.

15. An officer[u] of The Buffs, near Dungarvan, on 19th March, 1921, displayed the greatest courage in attacking a party of 100 rebels, with one serjeant of the Royal Irish Constabulary and one corporal.[v] The officer went ahead against the rebels and inflicted severe casualties on them until all his ammunition ran out. He was then taken prisoner, one of his two men, who had also been taken prisoner, was murdered before his eyes and he was threatened with death unless he disclosed certain information which the rebels wanted. He was kept in captivity but was rescued by the arrival of a party some hours later.

[u] Capt Donald Victor Thomas received an OBE.[22]

[v] This was the so-called 'Burgery Ambush'. The policemen were Sgt Michael Joseph Hickey (b.1885) and Const. Sydney R. Redman (b.1895). It appears that Sgt Hickey was the one executed; he had a blindfold and a placard reading 'executed'. Also killed in the fighting were Volunteers Patrick Keating and John Fitzgerald.[23]

16. Near Lackelly, on 2nd May, 1921, a party of the Green Howards[w] and R.I.C., numbering 14 in all, was ambushed by about 200 rebels and put up a most gallant fight by counter-attacking the rebels and inflicting severe casualties on them. The engagement lasted for some 5½ hours and resulted in the rebels being driven off. The small party was at a great disadvantage, and it was only their fine military spirit and the skilful leadership that enabled them to bring the action to such a satisfactory conclusion.[24]

[w] Lieut Francis Clifford Ainley, Green Howards, was awarded an MBE, and appears to have been the officer present.

17. At Stranolar, on 2nd June, 1921, an officer[x] and two riflemen of the Rifle Brigade were proceeding in a car and saw the road was blocked in front of them. Instead of retiring from this the officer decided to take action against any would-be ambushers. He proceeded to reconnoitre

and drew the rebels' fire. The rebels, only five or six of whom could be sighted, were at a distance of some 250 yards from the party. The officer determined to attack them, which he did with such success that two of the rebels were killed[y] and one wounded[z] and the remainder made off.

[x] Capt Charles Colquhoun McGrigor was awarded an OBE.[25]

[y] Volunteers James McCarron and Michael Carty.[26]

[z] Volunteer Edward Doherty.

18. At Adavoyle, on 24th June 1921, a troop train was derailed by rebels and thrown down an embankment. The train was conveying a squadron of the 10th Royal Hussars and their horses from Belfast. The squadron attacked the ambushers, and one warrant-officer and a staff-serjeant of the regiment acted with the greatest courage in attempting to save the horses, which were maddened and kicking amongst the debris. Fifty-four horses were saved, of which 40 were actually "dug out" under the immediate supervision of this warrant-officer and non-commissioned officer who risked their lives repeatedly in going among the wreckage and releasing the buried animals.

19. At Srah, on 3rd May, 1921, two officers of the Border Regiment, with one non-commissioned officer and five men, were sent to intercept some rebels who had successfully ambushed a party of R.I.C.[aa] They got into touch with the rebels and attacked them. One of the officers[bb] got several hundred yards ahead of the party and engaged in a hand-to-hand fight with the rebels. He shot their leader[cc] and the remainder of the party put up their hands, whereupon the wounded rebel fired and hit him. The officer was wounded through both arms but his action had so far delayed matters that the party under the other officer were able to get up to the scene of action and account for the remainder of the rebels.

[aa] This was the Tourmakeady Ambush.

[bb] Lieut Geoffrey Ibberson.

[cc] Ibberson shot Cmdt Tom Maguire and killed his Adj. Michael O'Brien. The fighting did not go 'hand-to-hand' as indicated.[27]

20. In view of the constant burning of lorries it was decided to construct a special camouflage lorry to trap the rebels. An officer of the Hampshire Regiment designed this lorry and brought off several remarkable coups with it. On one occasion fire having been opened on the lorry he and a few men concealed themselves under a tarpaulin in it. Several rebels approached the lorry with petrol cans and mounted it with the intention of setting it alight. The concealed party attacked the intruders, driving them back and inflicting casualties on them. There were several other actions of this kind all of which the officer took part in and displayed great courage and disregard for personal safety.[dd]

[dd] Historian N. Charlie Browne stated that the British killed only one rebel, and that the other man killed was an innocent civilian.[28]

APPENDIX III

SPECIAL ORDER OF THE DAY

BY

LIEUT.-GENERAL RIGHT HON. SIR F. C. SHAW, K.C.B.,
COMMANDING-IN-CHIEF, IRELAND.

General Headquarters, Ireland
Parkgate, Dublin,
Wednesday, 14th April, 1920.

Lieut.-General Sir Frederick Shaw relinquishes to-day the Command of the Forces in Ireland.

The period of his Command has been one of exceptional stress and difficulty requiring skill on the part of the commanders and steadiness and devotion to duty on the part of all others.

All ranks have not only been efficient, but have also been most tactful in the way they have carried out their duties, which have called for a high standard of discipline and training.

He wishes all ranks of the Army in Ireland good-bye and good luck, and in doing so can wish nothing better for his successor than the same unfailing support which he has himself received.

F. F. READY, *Major-General i/c Administration.*

SPECIAL GENERAL ROUTINE ORDER

BY

GENERAL RT. HON. SIR C. F. N. MACREADY, G.C.M.G., K.C.B.,
COMMANDING-IN-CHIEF, IRELAND.

General Headquarters, Ireland
Parkgate, Dublin,
Tuesday, 17th August, 1920.

"Statements appear from time to time in the Press and in correspondence to the effect that, especially on occasions when searching of houses and persons has been carried out, articles are found to be missing, the inference being that they have been taken by the troops.

"I know that such statements are to a great extent put abroad purely for purposes of propaganda against the Government, but recognize that instance may occur with young troops not yet fully imbued with the spirit of discipline that is so essential, not only for the credit and good name of the Army in general and their own regiment in particular, but also to enable the Army to succeed in the difficult task which it is called upon to perform in Ireland.

"It has been inferred that soldiers indulge in acts of retaliation on the civilian population as a whole, for acts committed against them, as distinct from defending themselves when threatened or attacked. Such action would reflect the utmost discredit on the Army and would indicate a lapse from discipline, which, if committed on active service, renders the offenders liable to a death sentence.

"To uphold the discipline of the Army and prevent any discredit falling on the good name of the regiment must be the determination of all ranks.

"I therefore look to all officers to ensure that there will not be the least grounds for allegations of looting or retaliation, and though confident that these orders will be rigidly adhered to, must point out that any dereliction would be met by the severest disciplinary measures.

The above remarks of the Commander-in-Chief will be read to all units on parade and kept posted on the unit order board.

WILLIAM RYCROFT, *Major-General,*
i/c Administration, Ireland.

SPECIAL ORDER OF THE DAY

BY

MAJOR-GENERAL SIR H. S. JEUDWINE, K.C.B., COMMANDING-IN-CHIEF, IRELAND.

GENERAL HEADQUARTERS, Ireland
Parkgate, Dublin,
Thursday, 2nd December, 1920.

The circumstance of the recent cold-blooded murders of officers and men have emphasized the difficulties and danger which face His Majesty's Army in Ireland. At the same time they have demonstrated in the face of great provocation the discipline and self-restraint with which all ranks of the Army, largely composed, as it is, of young and partially trained soldiers, are imbued.

This discipline and self-restraint is a source of pride to all connected with the Army, and will, the Commander-in-Chief is confident, be maintained even though greater trials may be in store.

The Army may rest assured that such steadiness does not pass unnoticed, and that the difficult and arduous nature of its duties is appreciated both by those in authority in Great Britain and by the people generally.

The reverence which was paid at the funerals of the victims of the recent murders, both in Dublin and in London, was not only a tribute to the memory of those soldiers themselves but was also a symbol of the respect which the Army in Ireland has won and is winning. Personal assurances to this effect have recently been received from the highest authorities of the Army and of the Government. As an illustration of this the following extracts from the report of what took place in the House of Commons on 24th November 1920, will be of interest.

In the course of a debate on Irish Affairs Sir Hamar Greenwood, Chief Secretary for Ireland, said:—

"In Dublin on Sunday morning 12 of your kinsmen were murdered in cold blood and not a pane of glass was broken in the city (cheers). There were no reprisals. How many of us would have stood the same strain? (Loud cheers.)

"As an example of provocation to the Commanders of British officers, soldiers and police, I may instance the circumstances attending the murder of Lieutenant Hambleton…This is only one instance out of many of the struggle of British officers in keeping discipline in face of inhuman provocation." (Cheers)

At the close of the debate the following amended resolution was proposed by Colonel John Ward, Member for Stoke-on-Trent, and was carried without a division:—

"That this House condemns the outrages committed against the forces of the Crown and civilians in Ireland and expresses its deep abhorrence of the brutal assassination of His Majesty's officers and other British subjects on Sunday last and thanks the military and police forces and other servants of the Crown for the courage and devotion with which they are fulfilling their duty in Ireland in circumstances of unexplained difficulty, and expresses its approval of the steps which are being taken by His Majesty's Government to restore peace in Ireland."

J. E. S. BRIND, *Brig.-General,*
General Staff.

SPECIAL ORDER OF THE DAY

BY
GENERAL RIGHT HON. SIR C. F. N. MACREADY, G.C.M.G.,
K.C.B., COMMANDING-IN-CHIEF, IRELAND.

General Headquarters, Ireland
Parkgate, Dublin.
Friday, 25th February, 1921.

During the last few days two appalling outrages have been committed by the rebels against the troops in Ireland.

On 22nd February, 1921, three unarmed soldiers of the Oxfordshire and Buckinghamshire Light Infantry were captured and shot in cold blood at Woodford, Co. Galway. On 23rd February, 1921, two unarmed soldiers of the Essex Regiment were kidnapped at Bandon and murdered.

Quite apart from the savagery which has always been a marked feature of the tactics employed by the rebels, there is no doubt but that these crimes are a deliberate attempt to exasperate the troops and tempt them to break the bonds of discipline, thereby providing copy for that scurrilous campaign of propaganda on which the rebel leaders so much rely for sympathy in Great Britain and abroad.

The Commander-in-Chief looks to the troops, even in the face of provocation such as would not be indulged in by the wildest savages of Central Africa, to maintain the discipline for which the British Army is, and has always been, so justly renowned. It is only by the maintenance of that discipline that our ultimate object, the restoration of peace in Ireland, will be achieved.

J. E. S. BRIND, *Brig.-General,*
General Staff.

SPECIAL ORDER OF THE DAY

BY

GENERAL RIGHT HON. SIR C. F. N. MACREADY, G.C.M.G.,
K.C.B., COMMANDING-IN-CHIEF, IRELAND,

General Headquarters, Ireland.
Parkgate, Dublin,
Monday, 2nd May, 1921.

His Excellency Field-Marshal Right Hon. Viscount French, K.P., G.C.B., O.M., G.C.V.O., K.C.M.G., having expressed a desire to take a formal farewell of the Army serving in Ireland was received by me at the Royal Hospital, Dublin, on the 29th April, the General Officers Commanding the 5th Division and Dublin District, together with members of their staffs and of general headquarters being present.

His Excellency in his speech expressed his thanks to both officers and men for their splendid conduct and discipline in most trying circumstances. It was a deplorable thing, he said, that they, who by their courage, skill, and perseverance had brought to a successful conclusion the greatest war in history, after 4 years' of hard fighting, should have been compelled by disloyal and traitorous enemies of the Crown to take up arms in its defence once more, but he had absolute confidence that those great qualities which they had already shown would carry their present task, disagreeable though it was, to a successful conclusion. He wished the Army in Ireland a speedy release from their labours and that they would soon attain that rest and quiet to which they were justly entitled.

He asked me to convey to the troops under my command His Excellency's appreciation of the magnificent support they had afforded him during his term of office.

C. F. N. MACREADY,
General.

SPECIAL ORDER OF THE DAY

BY

GENERAL RIGHT HON. SIR C. F. N. MACREADY, G.C.M.G.,
K.C.B., COMMANDING-IN-CHIEF, IRELAND,

General Headquarters, Ireland.
Parkgate, Dublin,
Monday, 15th August, 1921.

On the 26th July, 1921, the Master of the Rolls, Ireland[a], delivered judgement and issued a Writ of *Habeas Corpus* in the case of two men under sentence of death in the Martial Law area.

The Military authorities, in pursuance of the well-known principle that in an area where Martial Law applies Writs of *Habeas Corpus* do not run, refused to comply with the writ. On this the Master of the Rolls directed Writs of Attachment to be issued against the Commander-in-Chief, the Military Governor of the Martial Law area, and other officers.

Subsequently by order of the Government, the two men under sentence of death were released.

On the 10th August the matter was raised in the House of Commons, and the Lord Privy Seal[b], answering for the Government, stated that:—

"This action in releasing the two men was based solely upon the existing situation in Ireland and the importance, at the present time, of avoiding conflict between the civil and military authorities. The releases were not due to any decision given by a civil court in Ireland; civil courts have no power to over-rule the decisions of the military courts in the Martial Law area in Ireland. The decisions of the Military Officer Administering Martial Law in Ireland will be upheld."

In view of the prominence given in the Press to the above cases, and in order that officers, both now and hereafter, who are, or may be, called upon to administer Martial Law may know their powers in regard to interference by civil courts, the Commanding-in-Chief wishes the above facts to be made known throughout the Command.

C. F. N. MACREADY, *General.*

[a]   Charles Andrew O'Connor (b.1854–d.1928).

[b]   Sir Joseph Austen Chamberlain (b.1863–d.1937).

SPECIAL ORDER OF THE DAY

BY

GENERAL RIGHT HON. SIR C. F. N. MACREADY, G.C.M.G.,
K.C.B., COMMANDING-IN-CHIEF, IRELAND,

General Headquarters, Ireland.
Parkgate, Dublin,
17th January, 1922.

The Government have decided that the time has arrived to commence withdrawing troops form Ireland, I wish to express to every officer, warrant officer, non-commissioned officer and man my deep appreciation of the services they have rendered during the time they have formed part of the Irish Command.

While I feel there is no desire on the part of the Army to rake up past animosities or bitterness, you have been called upon to perform a duty in many respects repugnant to our traditions and devoid of all the glamour of war, though in many ways entailing greater strain and greater individual danger.

The call has been answered in a manner worthy of the best traditions of the Service. I honestly believe that no other troops in the world would or could have carried through the work on which you have been engaged without loss of morale or prestige. You, officers and men, have accompanied the most difficult task that any soldier can be called upon to undertake, and you have emerged with your discipline unshaken and your conduct in the eyes of all fair-minded men blameless.

When history is written you will find that by your pluck, vigilance, and discipline, you have contributed no inconsiderable share towards what we hope may prove eventually to be the settled peace and prosperity of Ireland.

I tender to you all my personal and grateful thanks for lightening the burden incidental to the Command of the Forces in Ireland during the last 20 months, and it will ever be an honour and a pride to me to have had the privilege of commanding soldiers who, whether in peace or war, or under the abnormal conditions in which we found ourselves, have proved second to none.

C. F. N. MACREADY,
General.

APPENDIX IV

NOTE ON THE VIEWS EXPRESSED BY MILITARY AUTHORITIES IN IRELAND IN DECEMBER, 1920, WITH REGARD TO THE PARTIAL OR UNIVERSAL DECLARATION OF MARTIAL LAW IN IRELAND

1. Extract of letter from Major-General Sir H. S. Jeudwine (temporarily Commanding-in-Chief) to C.I.G.S., dated 2nd December, 1920:—

"I saw Sir Hamar Greenwood yesterday, who informed me that the Government were prepared to proclaim Martial Law. He asked me:—
"(a) Was I in favour of the application of Martial Law?
"To this I answered 'Yes.'
"(b) If so, should Martial Law be proclaimed over the whole of Ireland?
"I answered 'Yes.'
"(c) What defined areas should be brought within the full scope of Martial Law, and in what order?
"(d) What additional troops, if any, would be necessary?
"To these last two questions, after some discussion, I answered that I was not prepared to give exact answers at short notice, that I would do so after having had an opportunity of conferring with Divisional Commanders."

2. Extract of reply to above from C.I.G.S. to General Jeudwine, dated 3rd December:—

"......I am delighted to find that you agree with me in thinking that Martial Law should be applied to the whole area, and that it should be carried out as regards intensity in varying degrees in different parts of the country. That seems to me to be by far the wisest course, and I hope you have been able to persuade Hamar Greenwood and Anderson to this view."

3. Extract of letter from General Jeudwine to C.I.G.S., dated 3rd December:—

"Since I wrote you last I have conferred with Boyd (Commanding Dublin District), and Bainbridge (Commanding 1st Division, Ulster)......Both were in full agreement as to the advisability of proclaiming Martial Law and its application to the whole of Ireland. They also agreed that its application should vary in degree according to the situation in various localities, and to our resources in making it effective.
"This is in accordance with an application which I think has already been submitted to you by Sir Nevil Macready."

4. Extract from letter dated, 4th December, from C.I.G.S. to General Jeudwine:—

"I am obliged to you for your letter of yesterday, which again makes the position exceedingly clear, and with all of which I am in complete agreement."

5. Extract of letter from General Jeudwine to C.I.G.S., dated 4th December:—

"I have now discussed the situation with General Strickland, and further with Boyd and Tudor. I find we area all in complete agreement."

6. Extract of letter to Chief Secretary, dated 5th December, from General Jeudwine:—

"The following are the conclusions reached, and I believe that these conclusions are in conformity with the views of General Sir Nevill Macready:—
"The Commanders whom I have consulted are unanimously in agreement with me:
(*a*) I am ready to undertake the enforcing the Martial on the lines of the Proclamation, draft of which was sent you yesterday, at any time;
(*b*) I am of opinion that Martial Law should be proclaimed throughout Ireland; it can be intensified in defined areas as and when considered desirable."

7. Exact of letter from General Jeudwine to C.I..G.S., dated 5th December:—

"This afternoon I saw the Chief Secretary, in company with Brind, Wroughton, Anderson and Tudor, and submitted to him a memorandum, of which I enclose a copy...Sir Hamar, however, expressed surprise at the proposal to proclaim Martial Law over the whole of Ireland, for which apparently, in spite of my reply to him when the subject was first mooted, he was not prepared. In the end I think he saw the force of the argument in favour of it. On this point I feel that it is essential that there should be no misunderstanding. He had accepted my memorandum in the spirit in which it was submitted, viz., as an expression, at the request of the Government, of the soldiers' views; it is now for the Government to decided whether to accept or reject it."

8. Extract of letter from General Jeudwine to Sir Nevill Macready, dated 6th December:—

"Yesterday, with Brind, Wroughton, Anderson and Tudor, I saw the Chief Secretary, and in accordance with my undertaking given on the 1st December, submitted to him a memorandum, of which I enclose a copy. I trust by what I have said in it I may have exercised my vicarious responsibility only in the terms which will meet with your agreement and approval. Brind, Wroughton, Strickland, Bainbridge and Boyd are solid behind me on every point...In spite of the fact that I had given the Chief Secretary a positive opinion (when Martial Law was first mooted on 1st December), that Martial Law, if proclaimed, should be proclaimed over the whole of Ireland) so that there should be no geographical inequality in offences and punishments), he expressed surprise at this recommendation, and exerted some pressure towards inducing reconsideration. On this point, however, I felt that no weakening was possible, and eventually I think that our arguments told. He accepted the memorandum as it stands, and in the spirit in which I tendered it, viz., as the advice of the soldier, *in response to the request of the*

Government, for an opinion as to the advantages of proclaiming Martial law, and as to the general procedure which should be adopted in giving effect to it."

9. Extract of letter from C.I.G.S. to General Jeudwine, dated December:—

"I am glad to see that you adhere to your opinion that Martial Law should be proclaimed over the whole of Ireland, and not over part, but that you enforce it in different areas with varying severity."

10. Extract of letter from General Jeudwine to Sir Nevill Macready (in London), dated 10 December:—

"You will appreciate the exceedingly complex situation which ensues from the Government's decision" (*i.e.* to declare Martial Law in four counties only), "so it is no use my harping on this point."

NOTES

1   The original version of this document is in the National Archives at Kew (WO 32/9533) contained in a folder with a memorandum dated 17 October, 1921 from General Macready detailing much of the same information.
2   Hopkinson, *Irish War of Independence*, pp. 147.
3   Hopkinson, *Irish War of Independence*, pp. 103; Traynor, 'Burning of the Custom House in Dublin Crippled', pp. 405–13 and 'The Burning of the Custom House', pp. 313–21; and Townshend, *British Campaign*, p. 180.
4   Vol. III, No. 18, 22 July, 1921, p. 2.
5   See A. Roth, 'Gun running from Germany to Ireland in the early 1920s', *The Irish Sword*, Vol. XXII, No. 88 (Winter 2000); C. McGuinness, *Sailor of Fortune: Adventures of an Irish Sailor, Soldier, Pirate, Pearl-Fisher, Gun-Runner, Rebel, and Antarctic Explorer* (1935), p. 172 and R. Briscoe, *For the Life of Me* (1958), pp. 95–6.
6   See Deasy, *Towards Ireland Free*, pp. 144–6; Townshend, *British Campaign*, p. 123 and *Fourth Supplement* to *The London Gazette*, 15 February, 1921, No. 32231, p. 1361.
7   See account in 'History of the 5th Division', *The Record of the Rebellion* Vol. IV, Appendix XIII, pp. 99–102.
8   *Fourth Supplement* to *The London Gazette*, 15 February, 1921, No. 32231, p. 1361.
9   See *Fourth Supplement* to *The London Gazette*, 15 February, 1921, No. 32231, p. 1361.
10 *Fourth Supplement* to *The London Gazette*, 15 February, 1921, No. 32231, p. 1361.
11 See RIC I-G Monthly Confidential Report for Co. Armagh for December 1920, Nat. Arch., Kew, CO 904/113.
12 *Second Supplement* to *The London Gazette*, 15 March, 1921, No. 32259, p. 2171.
13 For an overall examination, see O'Neill, *The Battle of Clonmult* and *The Irish Rebellion in the 6th Divisional Area*, pp. 84–5.
14 *Third Supplement* to *The London Gazette*, 19 April, 1921, No. 32298, p. 3175.

15 See, *The Irish Rebellion in the* 6th *Divisional Area*, p. 74n and *Second Supplement* to *The London Gazette*, 31 May, 1921, No. 32341, p. 4375 and *Third Supplement* to *The London Gazette*, 19 April, 1921, No. 32298, p. 3175 respectively.

16 See, *The Irish Rebellion in the* 6th *Divisional Area*, p. 74n and *The Last Post*, p. 113.

17 See E. J. Delaney, 'A Tipperary Column Laying for IC had to Fight Military at Thomastown', *With the IRA*, pp. 182–92; Statement of Tadhg Crowe (MA WS/1658), pp. 13–4; Statement of Michael Fitzpatrick (WS/1433); and Statement of Patrick O'Dwyer (WS/1432, pp. 24–5).

18 See, *The Irish Rebellion in the* 6th *Divisional Area*, p. 63.

19 See, *The Irish Rebellion in the* 6th *Divisional Area*, pp. 18n and 64; *The Last Post*, p. 106, and O'Farrell, *Who's Who*, p. 72n.

20 See *Second Supplement* to *The London Gazette*, 31 May, 1921, No. 32341, p. 4376.

21 Dwyer, *Tans, Terror and Troubles*, p. 291 and E. Gallagher, 'Too Early Arrival of Train Robbed IRA of Fruits of Victory at Headford', *With the IRA*, pp. 343–55.

22 *Rebel Heart: George Lennon: Flying Column Commander* (2009), pp. 124–6 and *Second Supplement* to *The London Gazette*, 31 May, 1921, No. 32341, p. 4375.

23 Abbott, *Police Casualties*, pp. 211–12 and *The Last Post*, p. 119.

24 See D. Ryan, 'Daring Rescue of Seán Hogan at Knocklong', *Limerick's Fighting Story*, pp. 111–12 and *The Irish Rebellion in the* 6th *Divisional Area*, p. 105 and note. See also *Fourth Supplement to The London Gazette*, No. 32406, 29 July, 1921, p. 6009.

25 See *Fourth Supplement to The London Gazette*, No. 32406, 29 July, 1921, p. 6009.

26 See *The Last Post*, p. 125; L. Ó Duibhir, *The Donegal Awakening: Donegal & the War of Independence* (Cork: Mercier Press, 2009), pp. 276–8.

27 See Buckley, D., *The Battle of Tourmakeady*; Kautt, *Ambushes & Armour*, pp. 243–8; Statement of Major Geoffrey Ibberson (MA WS 1307); Statement of J. H. Gouldon (MA WS 1340); Abbott, *Police Casualties*, pp. 228–9; and O'Malley, *Raids and Rallies*, pp. 118–21.

28 *The Irish Rebellion in the* 6th *Divisional Area*, pp. 55 & 138 and N. Browne, *The Story of the* 7th: *A Concise History of the* 7th *Battalion, Cork No.1 Brigade, Irish Republican Army from 1915 to 1921* (2007), pp. 36–7.

Additional Appendices

Text of The Defence of the Realm Act and Regulations 9aa and 14b

The Defence of the Realm Consolidation Act, 1914
(5 Geo. 5, c. 8)[1]

An Act to consolidate and amend the Defence of the Realm Acts. 27th November, 1914

BE it enacted by the King's most Excellent Majesty, by and with the advice and consent of the. Lords Spiritual and Temporal, and Commons, in this present Parliament assembled, and by the authority of the same, as follows :

1.—(1) His Majesty in Council has power during the continuance of the present war to issue regulations for securing the make public safety and the defence of the realm, and as to the powers and duties for that purpose of the Admiralty and Army Council and of the members of His Majesty's forces and other persons acting in his behalf; and may by such regulations authorise the trial by courts-martial, or in the case of minor offences by courts of summary jurisdiction, and punishment of persons committing offences against the regulations and in particular against any of the provisions of such regulations designed—

(a) to prevent persons communicating with the enemy or obtaining information for that purpose or any purpose calculated to jeopardise the success of the operations of any of His Majesty's forces or the forces of his allies or to assist the enemy; or

(b) to secure the safety of His Majesty's forces and ships and the safety of any means of communication and of railways, ports, and harbours; or

(c) to prevent the spread of false reports or reports likely to cause disaffection to His Majesty or to interfere with the success of His Majesty's forces by land or sea or to prejudice His Majesty's relations with foreign powers; or

(d) to secure the navigation of vessels in accordance with directions given by or under the authority of the Admiralty; or

(e) otherwise to prevent assistance being given to the enemy or the successful prosecution of the war being endangered,

(2) Any such regulations may provide for the suspension of any restrictions on the acquisition or user of land, or the exercise of the power of making byelaws, or any other power under the

Defence Acts, 1842 to 1875, or the Military Lands Acts, 1891 to 1903, and any such regulations or any orders made thereunder affecting the pilotage of vessels may supersede any enactment, order, charter, byelaw, regulation or provision as to pilotage.

(3) It shall be lawful for the Admiralty or Army Council—

(a)   to require that there shall be placed at their disposal the whole or any part of the output of any factory or workshop in which arms, ammunition, or warlike stores or equipment, or any articles required for the production thereof, are manufactured

(b)   to take possession of and use for the purpose of His Majesty's naval or military service any such factory or workshop or any plant thereof and regulations under this Act may be made accordingly.

(4) For the purpose of the trial of a person for an offence under the regulations by court-martial and the punishment thereof, the person may be proceeded against and dealt with as if he were a person subject to military law and had on active service committed an offence under section five of the Army Act:

Provided that where it is proved that the offence is committed with the intention of assisting the enemy a person convicted of such an offence by a court-martial shall be liable to suffer death.

(5) For the purpose of the trial of a person for an offence under the regulations by a court of summary jurisdiction and the punishment thereof, the offence shall be deemed to have been committed either at the place in which the same actually was committed or in any place in which the offender may be, and the maximum penalty which may be inflicted shall be imprisonment with or without hard labour for a term of six months or a fine of one hundred pounds, or both such imprisonment and fine; section seventeen of the Summary Jurisdiction Act, 1879, shall not apply to charges of offences against the regulations, but any person aggrieved by a conviction of a court of summary jurisdiction may appeal in England to a court of quarter sessions, and in Scotland under and in terms of the Summary Jurisdiction (Scotland) Acts; and in Ireland in manner provided by the Summary Jurisdiction (Ireland) Acts.

(6) The regulations may authorise a court-martial or court of summary jurisdiction, in addition to any other punishment, to order the forfeiture of any goods in respect of which an offence against the regulations has been committed.

2.—(1) This Act may be cited as the Defence of the Realm Consolidation Act, 1914.

(2) The Defence of the Realm Act, 1914 and the Defence of the Realm (No. 2) Act, 1914, are hereby repealed, but nothing in this repeal shall affect any Orders in Council made thereunder, and all such Orders in Council shall, until altered or revoked by an Order in Council under this Act, continue in force and have effect as if made under this Act.

The Defence of the Realm (Amendment) Act, 1915
(5 Geo. 5, c. 34)

An Act to amend the Defence of the Realm Consolidation Act, 1914. 16th March 1915.

BE it enacted by the King's most Excellent Majesty, by and with the advice and consent of the Lords Spiritual and Temporal, and Commons, in this present Parliament assembled, and by the authority of the same, as follows :

1.—(1) Any offence against any regulations made under the Defence of the Realm Consolidation Act, 1914, which is triable by court martial may, instead of being tried by a court martial, be tried by a civil court with a jury, and when so tried the offence shall be deemed to be a felony punishable with the like punishment as might have been inflicted if the offence had been tried by court martial.

(2) Where a person, being a British subject but not being a person subject to the Naval Discipline Act or to military law, is alleged to be guilty of an offence against any regulations made under the Defence of the Realm Consolidation Act, 1914, he shall be entitled, within six clear days from the time when the general nature of the charge is communicated to him, to claim to be tried by a civil court with a jury instead of being tried by court martial, and where such a claim is made in manner provided by regulations under the last-mentioned Act the offence shall not be tried by court martial Provided that this subsection shall not apply where the offence is tried before a court of summary jurisdiction:

> Provided also that before the trial of any person to whom this section applies, and as soon as practicable after arrest, the general nature of the charge shall be communicated to him in writing and notice in writing shall at the same time be given, in a form provided by regulations under the said Act, of his rights under this section.

(3) In addition and without prejudice to any powers which a court may possess to order the exclusion of the public from any proceedings, if, in the course of the trial of a person for a felony under this section, application is made by the prosecution, in the interests of national safety, that all or any portion of the public should be excluded during any part of the hearing, the court may make an order to that effect, but the passing of sentence shall in any case take place in public.

(4) The Vexatious Indictments Act, 1859, as amended by any subsequent enactment shall apply to a felony under this section as if it were included among the offences mentioned in section one of that Act, but a felony under this section shall not be triable by a court of quarter sessions.

(5) For the purpose of the trial of a person for a felony under this section the offence shall be deemed to have been committed either at the place in which the same actually was committed or in any place in the United Kingdom in which the offender may be found or to which he may be brought for the purpose of speedy trial.

(6) An indictment under this section shall not be deemed void or defective by reason that the facts or matters alleged in the indictment for the felony amount in law to treason; and if the facts or matters proved at the trial of any person indicted for any felony under this section amount in law to treason, the person shall not by reason thereof be entitled to be acquitted of such felony; but no person tried for such felony shall be afterwards prosecuted for treason upon the same facts.

(7) In the event of invasion or other special military emergency arising out of the present war. His Majesty may by Proclamation forthwith suspend the operation of this section, either generally or as respects any area specified in the Proclamation, without prejudice, however, to any proceedings under this section which may be then pending in any civil court,

(8) The expression "British subject" in this section include a woman who has married an alien but who before the marriage was a British subject.

(9) In the application of this section to Scotland "a civil court with a jury" means the High Court of Justiciary, and subsection (4) shall not apply.

(10) This section shall apply in the case of offences committed and persons arrested before as well as after the passing of this Act.

2. In Ireland a person charged with an offence against any regulations made under the Defence of the Realm Consolidation Act, 1914, before a court martial shall not, nor shall the wife or husband, as the case may be, of a person so charged, be a competent witness, whether the person so charged is charged severally or jointly with any other person.

3. This Act may be cited as the Defence of the Realm (Amendment) Act, 1915.

The Defence of the Realm (Amendment) No. 2, Act, 1916
(5 Geo. 5. c. 37)

An Act to amend the Defence of the Realm Consolidation Act, 1914. 16th March, 1915.

BE it enacted by the King's most Excellent Majesty, by and with the advice and consent of the Lords Spiritual and Temporal, and Commons, in this present Parliament assembled, and by the authority of the same, as follows:

1.—(1) Subsection (3) of section one of the Defence of the Realm Consolidation Act, 1914, (c) (which gives power to the possession and use for the purpose of His Majesty's naval and military services certain factories or workshops or the plant thereof), shall apply to any factory or workshop of whatever sort, or the plant thereof; and that subsection shall be read as if the following paragraphs were added after paragraph:—

> "(c) to require any work in any factory or workshop to be done in accordance with the directions of the Admiralty or Army Council, given with the object of making the factory or workshop, or the plant or labour therein, as useful as possible for the production of war material; and
> "(d) to regulate or restrict the carrying' on of work in any factory or workshop, or remove the plant therefrom, with a view to increasing the production of war material in other factories or workshops; and
> "(e) to take possession of any unoccupied premises for the purpose of housing workmen employed in the production, storage, or transport of war material."

(2) It is hereby declared that where the fulfilment by any person of any contract is interfered with by the necessity on the part of himself or any other person of complying with any requirement, regulation, or restriction of the Admiralty or the Army Council under the Defence of the Realm Consolidation Act, 1914, or this Act, or any regulations made thereunder, that necessity is a good defence to any action or proceedings taken against that person in respect of the non-fulfilment of the contract so far as it is due to that interference.

(3) In this section the expression "war material" includes arms, ammunition, warlike stores and equipment, and everything required for or in connection with the production thereof.

2. This Act may be cited as the Defence of the Realm. (Amendment), No. 2, Act, 1915.

Reg. (9aa) as to Power to Prohibit Meeting, Procession, Wearing of Uniforms, and Carrying or Having Arms or Explosives, &c

9aa.—(1) In any area in respect of which the operation of section one of the Defence of the Realm (Amendment) Act, 1915, is for the time being suspended, the competent naval or military authority may make orders prohibiting or restricting—

(a) the holding of or taking part in meetings, assemblies, or processions in public places
(b) the use or wearing in public places of uniforms of a naval or military character, or of uniforms indicating membership of any association or body specified in the order;
(c) the carrying in public places of weapons of offence or articles capable of being used as such; and
(d) the carrying, having or keeping of firearms, military arms, ammunition or explosive substances.

(2) Any order under this regulation may be made so as to apply generally to the whole of the area aforesaid or to any special localities in that area, and so as to prohibit all or any of the acts and

matters aforesaid absolutely or subject to such exceptions or save upon such conditions as may be specified therein.

(3) If any person contravenes, or fails to comply with, any provision of any order made under this regulation, or fails to comply with any condition subject to which anything is authorised under any such order, he shall be guilty of an offence against these regulations.

(4) The competent naval or military authority or any person authorised by him, or any police constable (without prejudice to the powers given by any other regulation):—

(a) if he suspects that any firearms, military arms, ammunition or explosive substances are, or are kept, in or upon any house, building, land, vehicle, vessel, or other premises in contravention of an order under this regulation, may enter, if need be by force, the house, building, land, vehicle, vessel, or premises, at any time of the day or night and examine, search and inspect the same or any part thereof, and may seize any firearms, military arms, ammunition or explosive substances found therein or thereon which he suspects to be, or to be kept, therein or thereon in contravention of the order; and

(b) if he suspects that any person is carrying any firearms, military arms, ammunition or explosive substance in contravention of any such order, may stop that person and search him; and

(c) may seize any firearms, military arms, ammunition, explosive substances or other articles carried by any person in contravention of any such order.

Any firearms, military arms, ammunition, explosive substances or other articles seized under this regulation may be destroyed or otherwise disposed of as may be ordered by the competent naval or military authority or chief officer of police.

Regs. (14a, 14b) as to Persons Proceeding to or from Ports in Outlying Islands; Restrictions on, or Internment of, Persons of Hostile Origin or Associations

14b. Where on the recommendation of a competent naval or military authority or of one of the advisory committees hereinafter mentioned it appears to the Secretary of State that for securing the public safety or the defence of the Realm it is expedient in view of the hostile origin or associations of any person that he shall be subjected to such obligations and restrictions as are hereinafter mentioned, the Secretary of State may by order require that person forthwith, or from time to time, either to remain in, or to proceed to and reside in, such place at may be specified in the order, and to comply with such directions as to reporting to the police, restriction of movement, and otherwise as may be specified in the order, or to be interned in such place as may be specified in the order:

Provided that any such order shall, in the case of any person who is not a subject of a state at war with His Majesty, include express provision for the due consideration by one of such advisory committees of any representations he may make against the order.

If any person in respect of whom any order is made under this regulation fails to comply with any of the provisions of the order he shall be guilty of an offence against these regulations, and any person interned under such order shall be subject to the like restrictions and may be dealt with in like manner as a prisoner of war, except so far as the Secretary of State may modify such restrictions, and if any person so interned escapes or attempts to escape from the place of internment or commits any breach of the rules in force therein he shall be guilty of an offence against these regulations.

The advisory committees for the purposes of this regulation shall be such advisory committees as are appointed for the purpose of advising the Secretary of State with respect to the internment and deportation of aliens, each of such committees being presided over by a person who holds or has held high judicial office.

In the application of this regulation to Scotland, references to the Secretary for Scotland shall be substituted for references to the Secretary of State.

Nothing in this regulation shall be construed to restrict or prejudice the application and effect of Regulation 14, or any power of interning aliens who are subjects of any State at war with His Majesty.

APPENDIX B

[CAB 24/110/263 (CP 1750)]

<u>SECRET</u>.

THE CABINET.

S.I.C.55.　　IRISH　　SITUATION　　COMMITTEE.

THE PRESENT MILITARY SITUATION IN IRELAND AND THE PROPOSED MILITARY POLICY DURING THE COMING WINTER.

MEMORANDUM BY THE SECRETARY OF STATE FOR WAR.

I circulate herewith, for reference to the Irish Situation Committee; a memorandum by General Macready, setting forth his views on the present military situation in Ireland, together, with a general forecast of the arrangements which it may be necessary to make during the coming winter.

W. S. C.

THE WAR OFFICE,
6th *August*, 1920.

It cannot be said that the Military situation to-day is more advanced than it was in the middle of April of this year.

The troops are certainly more experienced in the peculiar conditions in this country, but this is discounted to some extent by the increased activity and boldness of their opponents, who are daily becoming better armed, better disciplined and better established. While the troops in Ireland have been very considerably reinforced, they are of necessity more scattered, entailing increased responsibilities and difficulties of supply and transport. The demands for transport are being met rapidly by the Army Council, but this again has during the last month been considerably discounted by the partial paralysis of the railways, a paralysis which will probably result in a very short time in the total shutting down of railway communications throughout the country, except possibly in Ulster.

The increased efficiency of our opponents is without doubt very largely due to the release of leaders who were interned without trial during the early part of this year; a policy Which probably paralysed the organization; but the Continuance of which, for political reasons, it was impossible to maintain. Individuals who came back froth internment are reported as being more active than they were before arrest.

Under present circumstances, the army continues to act "in aid of civil power;" and the initiative lies mainly with our opponents. In my opinion, while both men and officers, are keen upon their work, and are daily improving in powers of initiative and self-reliance!, the police forces of the country ate in a much worse state than they were three months ago, with the result that the task of the army is increasingly difficult.

Additional Appendices

In a few words, the position is this, that while our opponents are making war on us; we are acting in support of civil power, the forces of which are less reliable thin, they were six months ago, and, as a necessary corollary to our support, a great number of troops are engaged in purely passive defence of localities, buildings, &C.

At the same time, great strides in certain brigades have been made with musketry, and a good deal of training has been done, not only according to Regulation, but also what is necessary to meet the peculiar situation here, which is; without doubt, valuable in that it stimulates initiative, responsibility and alertness. From a purely training point of view, I do not think that it will be found that units coming from this country will, when looked at from a broad point of view, be in any way inferior to those who are being trained under more peaceful Conditions.

From time to time, criticism has been levelled at unfortunate incidents which have occurred in connection with the raiding of unguarded buildings, and the overpowering of weak guards mounted for purposes of protection. It is often forgotten by critics that the capacity to afford protection depends upon the limitation of numbers, and the "nights in bed" which it is possible to obtain for troops, more especially for the young and partially trained soldiers of whom the army is at present composed. If the army were composed of veteran troops, the situation would be much easier, and small detachments would give us no anxiety in regard to their capacity for resistance.

Speaking generally, the Divisional Generals, the Brigade Commanders, the Staff, and, with a few exceptions, the Commanding Officers of battalions in this Command, are the very best that can be imagined, but there is a shortage of good company officers, and when it comes to non-commissioned officers, the weakness of the Army is woefully apparent, though they are willing and anxious to learn. The men, though keen and equally willing, are in many cases averse to using their weapons with effect for reasons of youth and inexperience. While, as I have said, all ranks are interested in the work and show increased keenness, the number of desertions and applications for discharge are heavy, which indicates that service in this country is not popular. This, of course, varies in units and depends to a great extent on the personality of Battalion and Company Commanders.

I have already officially put forward a protest against drafts being called for from Ireland during the coming winter, because if the political situation remains as at present the removal of the older and best trained non-commissioned officers and men from units will, in my opinion, constitute a very great danger, not only to the troops themselves but also to the larger question of the maintenance of British supremacy in the Island.

I am well aware of the difficulties with which the Army Council are faced in this respect, but I trust that some way will be found to avoid drafting men from this country, at all events until the spring, as the long winter nights are always the most dangerous.

One of the great difficulties both in regard to the command of troops, and to the troops themselves, is that under present conditions it is necessary for the troops to be on as good terms with the inhabitants as possible, and at the same time to be willing and ready to shoot if occasion requires. It is this that makes it so difficult to bring home to young lads the fact that they are liable to be attacked at any moment by people who pretend to be on good terms with them, or who seem to be carrying out their daily avocations (this was very marked in the attack on troops at Kingsbridge Station on the 19th July, when the majority of the attackers were apparently railwaymen dressed in blue overalls).

Generally speaking, relations with the inhabitants are good, due probably to the fact that the British soldier is always inclined to be careless and friendly individually whether his opponent be an Irishman or a Ghazi. In the same way, eliminating the fanatical faction, the people of the country generally are friendly towards the soldier.

From my own observation, and after consultation with the General Officers throughout the Command, I am satisfied that while the great Irish question will never be solved by force, it is necessary that increased power should be given to those responsible for maintaining the Government of the country, if the Royal Irish Constabulary is to be saved, and a semblance of law and order preserved. The Dublin Metropolitan Police are, in my opinion, quite past redemption, and the policing of Dublin, except so far as the appearance of occasional men in police uniform is concerned, must be, as at present, undertaken by the military.

The Government are, I understand, taking certain measures to replace by military courts the civil courts of the country, which, as shown by the late Assizes, have completely lapsed, and also further measures to bring members of illegal societies within the grip of courts-martial.

There is no doubt but that the arrest and trial (for arrest without ultimate trial will, I am convinced, never be tolerated for long by the proletariat of Great Britain) of the leaders, both male and female, of the illegal societies will- result in a general improvement of the situation, and possibly, although this is by no means certain, produce a resurrection of public spirit by which it may be possible to secure convictions, in civil courts.

A further measure, which to my mind is of the first importance, is the regulation of the Press in this country, which is, I am convinced, responsible for many of the murders and outrages that have been committed.

If these measures become effective in the near future, I believe that much may be done toward the enforced tranquillity of the country, except possibly in certain wild and inaccessible parts of the south and west.

It must be remembered, however, that owing to the railway paralysis, the troops, even with the increased transport which has been lavishly poured into the country, will not be as mobile as if the railway service was effective.

As regards the location of troops during the winter months, it is extremely difficult to foretell with any accuracy what the position may be, but assuming that there is no very marked improvement of the conditions obtaining to-day, I think the following general outline may prove to be more or less correct:—

We are faced with two diametrically opposed principles:—

(a) Dispersion in order to afford immediate and constant support of the police.
(b) Concentration to allow of some comfort, training, leave, and rest to the troops.

During the present summer, we are tending toward an extreme of dispersion in order to help the police to the utmost, and to maintain them in positions from which they would otherwise have had to withdraw. It must be fully realized that as long as the Forces of the Crown maintain a defensive attitude, concentration of troops will be followed by a withdrawal of police, and the consequent abandonment to our opponents of the evacuated area. This must be faced to some extent during the winter, in order to avoid indiscipline, discontent, and incompetency in the ranks of the Army.

I propose therefore that during the winter months, *i.e.*, from the 15th October:—

1. The withdrawal of all detachments of less strength than a company or squadron.
2. To accommodate all detachments in buildings, commandeered when necessary.
3. To transfer' a portion of held and heavy artillery to England in order to make use of the accommodation thus released for infantry and cavalry.
4. If found necessary, when the details are worked out, to send back to England such cavalry as cannot be suitably housed, but I doubt if this step will be necessary as it may be possible to obtain accommodation.
5. Schemes are being worked but in divisions on the above lines, but it will take a little time before the details can be completed.

The survey of buildings which might be suitable for the future accommodation of troops has to be very carefully undertaken, otherwise the buildings are invariably destroyed by our opponents.

Without wishing to be in the least optimistic, I have hopes that if the measures now being considered by the Cabinet bear fruit and are sufficiently drastic, a more vigorous offensive policy against the illegal organizations, and especially their leaders, will enable us, as the winter approaches, to carry out the concentration of troops without necessarily withdrawing police and abandoning districts to Sinn Fein.

As a corrollary to the above policy, I propose during the winter to keep districts under observation by means of small motor flying columns at irregular intervals.

One point I consider most essential, and that is the granting of full leave to all ranks during the winter. The men are deprived under present conditions of their amusements and those recreations which are so necessary for the contentment and health of young men, and many officers have been serving under conditions which are even worse than' actual warfare for nearly a year with practically no leave. This cannot continue without deterioration setting in, and I, therefore, am strongly of opinion that leave must be granted freely to all ranks from Divisional Commanders downwards.

In putting forward this Memorandum, it must be remembered that the situation in Ireland to-day is far worse and more difficult to all ranks of the Army than if they were engaged in actual warfare against an acknowledged enemy. There is no clearly defined "Front," the lines of communication are liable to instant and sudden dislocation by the very people who the moment before appeared to be on friendly terms, and the action of the troops is dependent upon the civil officials of the Crown, including the police. At the same time, the troops are working willingly and cheerfully, and there is no want of cordiality between civil and military authority in any branch of either Service.

C. F. N. MACREADY, *General,*
Commanding-in-Chief the Forces in Ireland.

General Headquarters, Ireland,
Parkgate, Dublin,
26th *July*, 1920.

APPENDIX C

[CAB 24/110/29–30]
DRAFT
OF A
BILL
TO

Make provision for the Restoration and Maintenance of A.D. 1920.
Order in Ireland.:

BE it enacted by the King's most Excellent Majesty, by and with the advice and consent of the Lords Spiritual and Temporal, and Commons, in this present Parliament assembled, and by the authority of the same, as follows:—

1.— (1) Where it appears to His Majesty in Council that, Regulations owing to the existence of a state of disorder in Ireland, the restoration ordinary law is inadequate for the prevention and punishment of crime or the maintenance of order, His Majesty in Council in Council may issue regulations under the Defence of the Realm Consolidation Act, 1914, (hereinafter referred to as the principal Act) for securing the restoration and maintenance of order in Ireland, and as to the powers and duties for that purpose of the Lord Lieutenant, the Chief Secretary, and of members of His Majesty's forces and other persons acting on His Majesty's behalf, and in particular regulations for the special purposes hereinafter mentioned.

(2) Regulations as so issued may extend the provisions of the principal Act with respect to the trial by courts-martial or courts of summary jurisdiction and punishment of persons committing offences against the Defence of the Realm Regulations, to the trial and punishment of persons committing crimes in Ireland, whether before or after the passing of this Act, including persons

committed for trial or against whom bills of indictment have been, found, so, however, as to provide that—

    (a)   any crime when so tried shall be punishable with the punishment assigned to the crime by statute or common law;

    (b)   a court-martial when trying a person charged with a crime punishable by death shall include as a member of the court one person (who need not be an officer) nominated by the Lord Lieutenant, being a person certified by the Lord Chancellor of Ireland or the Lord Chief Justice of England to be a person of legal knowledge and experience.

(3) Regulations so issued may also—

    (a)   provide that a court of summary jurisdiction, when trying a person charged with a crime or with an offence against the regulations, shall, except in the Dublin metropolitan police district, be constituted of two or more resident magistrates, and that a court of quarter sessions, when hearing and determining an appeal against a conviction of a court of summary jurisdiction for any such crime or offence, shall be constituted of the recorder or county court judge sitting alone;

    (b)   confer on a court martial the powers and jurisdiction exerciseable by justices at petty sessions or any other civil court for binding 'persons to keep the peace or be of good behaviour, for estreating and enforcing recognisances, and for compelling persons to attend as witnesses, to give evidence and to produce documents before the court;

    (c)   provide for any of the duties of a coroner and coroner's jury being performed by a court of inquiry constituted under the Army Act instead of by the coroner and jury;

    (d)   provide that where the court house or other building in which any civil court is usually held has been destroyed or rendered unfit for the purpose, the court may be held in such other court house or building as may be directed by the Lord Lieutenant;

    (e)   in the case of a local authority which has in any respect refused or failed to perform its duties, provide for the retention of sums payable to the authority from the Local Taxation (Ireland) Account, or from any Parliamentary grant, or from any fund administered by any Government department or public body, and for the application of funds so retained in or towards the discharge of compensation awarded against the local authority for criminal injuries, or other liabilities of the local authority.

(4) Any such regulations may be issued at any time, whether A.D. 1920. before or after the termination of the present war, and may apply either generally to the whole of Ireland or to any part thereof, and shall have effect as if enacted in this Act, and may include such adaptations of any enactment and such incidental, supple mental, and consequential provisions as may be necessary for carrying out all or any of the purposes of this Act.

(5) In this Act, unless the context otherwise requires—

The expression "crime" means any treason, treason felony, felony, misdemeanour, or other offence punishable, whether on indictment or on summary conviction, by imprisonment or by any greater punishment other than offences against the Defence of the Realm Regulations.

2. This Act may be cited as the Restoration of Order in Ireland Act, 1920.

Appendix D

[CAB 27/108/275, p.1]

S E C R E T.   C A B I N E T.
S.I.C.55. IRISH SITUATIONCOMMITTEE.

Report of the Situation in Ireland by the General Officer Commanding-in-Chief for Week Ending 13th November, 1920

1. GENERAL SITUATION.

The general Military situation continues to improve. The number of cases of rebel attacks on troops has been very small during the week, and it is probable that the disorganisation in Units of the Irish Volunteers, caused by the absence, enforced or voluntary, of many of their leaders, is beginning to affect the situation appreciably. It has been ascertained that men "on the run" are to be organised as flying columns for the perpetration of outrages, but it is doubtful whether the men concerned will not prefer to remain in hiding.

In addition to the decrease in the number of attacks on troops, the raiding of mails on the railways has, at any rate for the time being, ceased.

The number of railway employees dismissed for refusing to operate trains carrying troops, still increases, but, in view of the fact that Union funds are low, it is thought that before long pressure exerted by Republican leaders will be insufficient to compel the railway employees to continue their present policy. An Order has been made restricting the use of Motor vehicles, and it is expected that these restrictions will have a good effect in preventing the use of motor vehicles for the perpetration of outrages.

The cumulative effect of the above circumstances tends greatly to the disorganisation and depression of the rebel forces and their leaders, and there is reason to believe that not only is moderate and loyal opinion becoming more self-assertive, but even those who have previously been ardent supporters of rebellion are beginning to change their attitude for reasons of expediency, if not from conviction. One of the chief obstacles to further and more rapid improvement is the fact that a majority of news-papers in England, and many public men, use their influence and the freedom of speech which they enjoy, on the side of organised opposition to authority in this country. The result is that the disloyal element in Ireland feel that they have a large backing in England, and the destruction of the moral of the forces of disorder becomes consequently a slower and more difficult process than it might otherwise be.

Appendix E

[WO 32/9537][1]

GENERAL HEADQUARTERS, IRELAND
PARKGATE, DUBLIN
1st September, 1920

No:- 2/26908(A).

Sir,

I have the honour to submit the following remarks on the discipline of the Army in Ireland to the Army Council for their consideration and comments thereon.

To sum up the situation as shortly as possible as it affects the Army, the troops are ostensibly working "in aid of Civil Power", and every detachment of troops employed in carrying out arrests or preserving order is accompanied by one or more men of the Royal Irish Constabulary. The attitude of the men of the Royal Irish Constabulary towards the Army, and their methods of preserving order depend entirely on the personality of the Head Constables, District or County Inspectors concerned, and in many cases these Officers are not all that they should be. Lately the Royal Irish Constabulary has been reinforced by recruits from England, usually ex-soldiers - known by the sobriquet of "Black & Tans" - who on account of their Uniform are often mistaken by the populace for soldiers. It is not for me to criticise the methods employed by the Police for keeping order, but in certain parts of the country this is attained by promiscuous firing, with the object, presumably, of keeping the people off the streets, and I am informed that such methods are necessary and effective. Retaliatory measures are often indulged in, especially by the "Black & Tan" contingent, when incensed by the murders of their comrades. I mention these facts merely to illustrate the atmosphere in which the young soldiers who compose the Army to-day are called upon to serve.

As regards the troops themselves, they are the object of daily attacks in towns, and while moving about the country, by persons whom it is impossible to distinguish from ordinary civilians, and often the very nature of a duty necessitates guards and sentries being posted where crowds of civilians are apparently pursuing their ordinary avocations, but who suddenly, turn upon and attack the soldiers. The result of this state of affairs is that the troops are gradually getting - to use a slang expression - "fed up" with the unsatisfactory situation in which their find themselves, and retaliation for the wounding and murders of their officers and comrades is prevalent.

After the kidnapping of Brigadier-General LUCAS the troops broke out at Fermoy, and did considerable damage. A short time ago a case was brought to my notice where an officer who had successfully maintained order in a small town, hearing that there was an intention on the part of the rebels to burn the Police Barracks, intimated that in the event of the Barracks being burnt, the Sinn Féin Hall would be wrecked. The Barracks were burnt, and the officer in a methodical manner carried out the wrecking of the Hall. Last week and officer of the Cameron Highlanders was very seriously wounded, and the men of the Battalion incensed at the outrage, broke out and wrecked a large number of houses and shops in Queenstown.

If a state of recognised war existed in this country these incidents would not occur, or if they did, discipline would be enforced as in any theatre of war, but under present conditions when outrages are committed, often with the sold object of annoying and baiting the troops, any attempt to punish troops concerned in retaliations for attacks on and murders of their comrades will, in my opinion, result in a feeling of resentment which might break the bonds of discipline altogether.

---

1 Note: This is the original letter sent in September; it is not clear whether this was in response to an earlier conference called by the Chief Secretary in September 1920. See NAUK, CAB 23/22/211 and 251 WO 32/9537/1–10.

The situation therefore is this, that owing to the atmosphere in which they are serving, the example set by the Police, the constant outrages and insults to which troops are daily subjected, a spirit of retaliation is rapidly growing, which if checked by the ordinary drastic disciplinary methods that would be employed under normal conditions of peace or war, may result in the break-down of all discipline, and the triumph of the "rebels" at the success of their tactics. The fact is that the human endurance of the troops is rapidly reaching a point where restraint will be impossible.

I think it right to place these facts before the Army Council, not so much in regard to the effect on the present situation in Ireland, as to the effect on the discipline of the Army as a whole in time to come.

Apart from the growing tendency towards retaliation, the discipline of the troops is good, and the unpleasant duties they are called upon to perform are carried out which keenness and increasing efficiency.

I have the honour to be,

Sir,

Your obedient Servant,

GENERAL,

COMMANDING-IN-CHIEF, IRELAND

The Secretary,
WAR OFFICE
LONDON
S.W.I.

APPENDIX F

[CAB 23/23/84]

THE CABINET

THE IRISH SITUATION.

MEMORANDUM BY THE SECRETARY OF STATE FOR WAR

I would ask that a meeting of the Cabinet or a Conference of Ministers should take place next week on the situation in Ireland.

1. Very strong representations are being made to me by the military authorities that reprisals within certain strictly defined limits should be authorized by the Government and regulated by responsible officers of not less than Divisional rank. Complaint is made that the troops are getting out of control, taking the law into their own hands, and that besides clumsy and indiscriminate destruction, actual looting and thieving as well as drunkenness and gross disorder are occurring. In consequence of this, a number of courts-martial are being held upon soldiers, yet the position of the troops, always liable to be murdered by the Sinn Feiners, is such that it will not be possible to restrain their anger when outrages occur in their neighbourhood. I do not consider that the present Government attitude on reprisals can be maintained much longer. It is not fair on the troops, it is not fair on the officers who command them. Although the spirit of the Army is absolutely loyal and very hostile to the Irish rebels, there is no doubt that service in Ireland is intensely unpopular.

I have repeated requests from officers of middle and senior rank to be allowed to retire or to be transferred. When a post is vacant in Ireland, sometimes six or seven officers refuse it in turn. This is not because these men are not resolute and loyal, but because they feel themselves to be in a false position.

It is for consideration whether a policy of reprisals within strict limits and under strict control in certain districts, in which it should be declared that conditions approximating to a state of war exist, would not he right at the present time. It is thought by many that such a policy would be less discreditable and more effective than what is now going on. The recent formidable increase in outrages in particular districts affords an opportunity for a review of the position. I cannot feel it right to punish the troops when, goaded in the most brutal manner and finding no redress, they take action on their own account. If they were to remain absolutely passive, they would become completely demoralized and the effectiveness of the military force would be destroyed. On the other hand, when these responsibilities are thrown upon privates, serjeants and lieutenants, many foolish and wrong things will be done which cannot be passed over by higher authority.

I ask that this matter shall be formally and definitely considered by the Cabinet, in order that the excesses of the troops may be controlled and the discipline of the Army maintained.

2. I am advised that a system of identity cards, which every male in Ireland would have to take out and produce whenever required, would be a most decisive step against the Sinn Fein organization. I am advised that this measure is practicable. It was applied without the slightest difficulty in the districts occupied by our armies on the Rhine. A wanted man who is on the run dare not apply to the police or the military authorities for such a card, and would not get one without having his case and conduct searchingly investigated. On the other hand, a system of sweeps and roundings up in large areas would reveal those who had not taken out their tickets, and consequently lead to the arrest of many men now being sought in vain. This system might be applied in some districts first.

3. I consider that a system of passports should be introduced between Great Britain and Ireland. There is no reason why the Irish desperadoes should be permitted to transfer their operations over here at any moment they think fit, or come over here for rest and peace whenever the hunt gets too hot for them in Ireland.

4. I am advised that the methods by which the importation of arms and explosives into Ireland is now checked are extremely defective, and that there is no guarantee that considerable quantities are not passing in.

I conclude by repeating my request that these matters may be considered at an early date.

W.S.C.

THE WAR OFFICE,
3rd November, 1920.

Additional Appendices

Appendix G

[CO 904/232, pp. 1–4]

5.12.20

THE CHIEF SECRETARY

In accordance with the decision arrived at at the Conference held at the Chief Secretary's Lodge on the 1st December, I have during the past three days discussed the proposal to proclaim Martial Law in Ireland with the General Officers Commanding the 1st Division (Belfast), the 6th Division (Cork), and Dublin District.

The following are the conclusions reached, and I believe that these conclusions are in conformity with the views of General Sir Nevil Macready. The Commanders whom I have consulted are unanimously in agreement with me.

(a) I am ready to undertake the enforcing of Martial Law on the lines of the Proclamation, draft of which was sent to you yesterday, at any time.

(b) I am of opinion that Martial Law should be proclaimed throughout Ireland; it can be intensified in defined areas, as and when considered desirable.

(c) Four extra battalions of Infantry will be required to commence with to enable me to make Martial Law effective. Of these, one is already under orders to sail; one is being held in readiness in England; two more should be ready to sail as soon as it is decided that Martial Law shall be proclaimed. The War Office has been so informed.

(d) In addition to the points enumerated in the proposed proclamation I intend

(i) To inform the Press that Newspapers will not be interfered with as long as nothing is published calculated to cause disaffection among His Majesty's subjects, or to interfere with the enforcement of Martial Law. Any offence will be dealt with by Military Court, suspension or suppression. The formation of a Press Censor's Office will be essential and this I shall ask the Civil Government to undertake.

(ii) Institute at once a system of passports for ingress and egress to and from Ireland. I hope the administration of Passport Offices will be undertaken in England, Scotland and Wales by the Home Office, and in Ireland by the Irish Executive.

(iii) To prepare to institute as soon as the administration to enforce it can be arranged, a scheme by which every householder, hotel (or inn) keeper, etc., etc., shall be compelled to maintain a register or list of all persons accommodated in the building.

(iv) To proclaim as outlaws and publish the photos of a number of leading rebels now in hiding or on the run, making it an offence to harbour or assist the persons named.

(e) Arrangements will be made to tighten up Martial Law in defined areas as required by controlling ingress and egress, by insisting on the use of identification cards, by intensification of the Curfew Order and by controlling movement.

(f) It is proposed to introduce gradually a system of voluntary identification cards, in such a way as to make law-abiding persons realise that the possession of an identification card will relieve the possessor of many of the unpleasantnesses (search, detention, interrogation) which will be unavoidable under the conditions of Martial Law.

(g) Owing to the lack of accommodation on the internment camps in the first instance will be reserved principally for officers of the I.R.A., "gunmen", and known extremists. It may be necessary at a later date to intern the rank and file, and it is essential that preparations for at least 5,000 internees should be made in Great Britain (or the Isle of Man). This has already been represented to the War Office.

(h) With regard to the railway situation, it is intended to inform the Managers of all railways that refusal to accept troops or Military Stores will, after a certain date, be treated as an offence against Martial Law. Ample time will be given for this to be communicated to the men, after which, troops and Military Stores will be offered again in a limited number of cases to commence with.

(i) Very considerable Naval reinforcements will be required to deal with conveyance of troops, police, and prisoners, and to establish a really efficient watch around the coast, to prevent importation of arms and evasion of passport order.

As Sir Nevil Macready will be responsible for the conduct and enforcement of Martial Law, if proclaimed, and the whole brunt of its administration will fall on him, I am strongly of opinion that he should be given an opportunity of submitting his personal views before it is brought into operation.

SIGNED Jeudwine
Major-General
Commanding-in-Chief, The Forces in Ireland.

GENERAL HEADQUARTERS, IRELAND
PARKGATE, DUBLIN
5.12.20.

Appendix H

[CAB 23/23/337]

MEETING held at 10 Downing street, on Wednesday, 29 December 1920.

With reference to Cabinet 77 (20), Conclusion 6, General Macready, General Strickland, General Boyd, General Tudor and Sir John Anderson attended the Conference to express their opinions regarding the present state of affairs in Ireland

General Strickland, Commanding the Cork area where martial law had been proclaimed, stated that he had not yet received any report regarding the number of arms which had been surrendered. The last day on which they could be handed in was December 27th. His opinion was that the loyalists would fall in with the order, but that the majority of the extremists would bury their arms. As time went on the military might be able to ascertain where these arms had been buried. Referring to the raid by the Police at a dance in Limerick, where 138 men had been captured and 5 armed sentries who were standing outside the hall had been shot. General Strickland said that so far he had only received a telegraphic report of what had happened from the Brigadier in charge. As far as he could ascertain there were no women present at the dance, and in all probability it was in reality a conference for/future operations. All those captured, were now in prison.

General Macready said that, generally speaking, the situation, from a military point of view, was improving. The internment camps were going on satisfactorily, although there was rather a shortage of accommodation. He was convinced that everything was satisfactory in the Cork area, and he had now made an application to the Castle for an extension of the martial law area. He would like Kilkenny, Clare, Waterford and Wexford all under martial law. It would not be necessary to apply martial law to its full effect, but it helped the military in their work and was welcomed in many cases by the inhabitants.

General Tudor said that from the Police point of view the position had improved. There were now plenty of men to hold the Police barracks. 13 Auxiliary Companies were now formed, and the transport situation was much improved. Further, he hoped to have 80 armoured cars by the end of January. The moral of the Police during the last six months had made a marked advance. Six months ago the Police were living behind sandbags and wire entanglements, they were boycotted, and life was altogether intolerable; but now things were quite different and they could move about freely, and with the exception of ambushes they were practically out of danger.

Some discussion then took place regarding co-operation between the Military and the Police. It was stated that except as regards discipline and administration, the Police in the martial law area were under General Strickland. As for cases of indiscipline which were tried before a military court-martial, a sentence of dismissal would be carried out by General Tudor, and a capital charge would come under General Strickland, In answer to a question, it was stated that General Strickland had the power to order the Royal Irish Constabulary out of his area should he consider it necessary. Operations General Strickland was responsible for, though he had a District Inspector of the Royal Irish Constabulary on his Staff, The Police, however, acted on their own initiative if they received special information, the area being a very large one.

General Strickland stated that so far there had been no friction between the two Forces, and at the present moment he saw no likelihood of it. If friction did arise, it would only be through lack of discipline. General Strickland added that no military officer under the rank of Brigadier General issued orders to the Police.

Some discussion then followed regarding the arrest by the Military or Police authorities, without reference- to the Chief Secretary, of people of political importance.

The Prime Minister said that if a man like Arthur Griffith, who was well known, was arrested, it at once became & political event, and in the whole history of Ireland an arrest of that kind had not keen made without the sanction of the Chief Secretary. One of the difficulties in connection with Martial law was that it meant the passing of the administration out of the hands of those responsible to Parliament. There should be greater co-ordination between military and political offices.

General Boyd stated that Arthur Griffith was arrested on has order. He did not consult the Chief Secretary because the latter was not there. He had, however, asked the Under-Secretary, in the event of there being murders in Dublin, if he could arrest the leading members of Dail Eireann. He added that if the arrest of Arthur Griffith had not taken place there might have been murders. As there was a good deal of anger amongst the regimental officers at that time he thought it advisable to arrest some of the leading men after what had happened.

Mr Churchill interposed that it was fair to remember that no reprisals had taken place after the Dublin murders ['Bloody Sunday', 21 November 1920].

The Prime Minister said that important arrests of that kind should be taken on the responsibility of the Cabinet. In decisions which had a political complexion the Chief Secretary should be consulted. If, however, a man was guilty of actual crime and there was a prima facie, case on a criminal charge, that was a very different thing.

The Prime Minister then said that all kinds of attempts had been made at obtaining a truce, and when the Cabinet came to consider the policy of such a course they would have to bear in mind the possibility of an Incident happening which might create unpleasantness with the United States, where feeling was dangerous. The Cork incident and the murder of the Canon came near to such a state of affairs. Those were the kind of incidents that drove a country like the United States to do something beyond discretion. If there was a chance of patching up some kind of truce, were General Strickland and General Tudor confident that they could keep their men in hand?

He (the Prime Minister) was afraid that there had been a good deal of drunkenness amongst the "Black and Tans".

General Tudor admitted that drink was the problem with the Auxiliary Divisions, but his Commanding Officers were of the opinion that they were new getting the men under better control. Discipline generally, however, Macroom, after the outrage there, there had been no trouble at all.

The discussion then passed to the Report of the Enquiry into the Cork burnings, and it was stated that the Report would find that these burnings were carried out partly by the Auxiliary Police. As regards the firing of the Town Hall, there was circumstantial evidence against, four men of the Royal Irish Constabulary. The opinion was expressed that the effect of publishing the Report if Parliament was sitting would be disastrous to the Government's whole policy in Ireland.

The Chief Secretary said that he had read the whole Report and not only a telegraphic version, and must say that General Strickland had made a judicial commentary on the facts. Putting the case at its worst, members of the "K" Company of the Auxiliary Corps had set fire to three different shops as a reprisal. Another part of the Report stated that the spread of the conflagration was due to the inadequacy of the Fire Brigade arrangements.

General Tudor said, regarding the finding of the Report, that he thought it went into the discipline of the Auxiliary Company rather unnecessarily, and that the Report reflected on him, inasmuch as after the massacre at Macroom he had sent another platoon of Black and Tans to replace that which had been massacred. This platoon was an experienced one, and reinforcements had to be sent down and no other reserves were available. General Strickland said that, considering the state of the country and that 16 Black and Tans had been massacred, the circumstances were enough to try the discipline of the best troops. Had he been in General Tudor1s place he would have asked for military assistance.

Reference was then made to the discipline of the Army, and General Macready said that he had made it clear that he would break any officer who was mixed up in reprisals; this, not for the sake of Ireland, but for the sake of the Army. He did not think it was possible to have the Police more disciplined they had no code to work under, and the officers were not the standard of men who could enforce discipline. The Divisional Commissioners in the Police were of a rank equal to Brigadier, and he knew from experience how difficult it was to find a Brigadier in the Army suitable for the kind of work required in Ireland.

The Prime Minister asked if a military officer found in the martial law district a number of Policemen behaving in an improper way, would the officer interfere with them?

General Strickland replied that if the officer was in mufti he could not do much, but if in uniform he would take steps and have them put under arrest.

General Tudor said that he thought the discipline of the Police, considering the strain put upon them, was really good. Men who came into the Police Force said that the discipline in it was stricter than in the Army, and anyone who had seen the Black and Tans on parade must admit that their discipline was very fine; they were entirely under the control of their officers. At the present moment, perhaps, there were not as many non-commissioned officers as were necessary, but this was being remedied.

The Prime Minister hoped that General Tudor would realise the importance of preventing such incidents as would add to the difficulties of the Government, and asked that General Tudor would investigate and deal strongly with any case of indiscipline. He put this to General Tudor not because he did not appreciate the fine work which he and the men under him had done, but in order to try and prevent further incidents of the kind.

The Prime Minister then said that there were two questions of a semi-political character which he would like to put to General Macready and the other officers. As was known, conversations in regard to a truce had been going on, and it was suggested that there should be a cessation of strife, without, however, any arrangement as to final terms. What was General Macready's opinion regarding a truce without the surrender of arms by the Sinn Feiners as a condition of such a truce, end was it worth while having a truce of that kind?

General Macready said that, regarding the surrender of arms, he presumed that his opinion was that of a General Officer Commanding who was responsible for the safety of his men. From that point of view, if there was a cessation of outrages on the part of the Sinn Feiners for a month, there would equally be a cessation by the military of raiding. Tie danger with troops was that it was always difficult to keep them on the alert for something that might happen. If it was advisable from a political point of view that such a truce should take place, the risk of effects on the Army might be minimised, and a truce would not, in his opinion, have any very great drawbacks.

The Prime Minister said that he did not know that such a truce would necessarily lead to a settlement, but it might lead to the abandonment of lawlessness. The question was whether General Macready thought he could step lawlessness without a surrender of arms? Michael Collins had said that be could not get his men to surrender their arms even if he tried. If the Sinn Feiners were to stop murdering, what could the military stop in return?

General Macready said they could stop raiding, searching and arresting persons other than those against whom there was a definite charge. By stopping these things, however, the Intelligence machinery would go slower and slower, and if the campaign against the Sinn Feiners was ever resumed the military would find themselves at a disadvantage, as the extremists would have had time to put up a new organisation.

The Prime Minister asked if the Sinn Feiners realised that they had made a miscalculation?

General Boyd said that in his opinion the extreme party was determined to go on, and he would not like to say that they knew they were beaten. Our policy had been very effective, and if there was a truce now the time would be used by the murder party to re-organise themselves, and they would certainly regard a truce as a sign of weakness. The Government would certainly be the losers if the campaign was resumed after a truce.

Sir John Anderson said that when this question was raised, some time ago he was of the opinion that the success of an attack on Sinn Fein depended on the break-up of their central organisation. At Sinn Fein headquarters there was no doubt that they were now badly disorganised, and if there was a truce it would have the effect of enabling them to re-establish their central organisation. This would be a great misfortune He was not at all convinced that it was possible to get a truce observed by the other side, a condition of which was that they did not resume activities which were to be suspended. Another point which the military had not mentioned was the efforts of Sinn Fein to undermine local government, and the Executive were now beating them on this, he thought, however, that everything depended on the line it was possible to get the Church to take. If, during a lull, the Roman Catholic hierarchy came out in strong condemnation of murder and outrage, he thought that a truce would be worth while. As for the attitude of the leaders, it was that they would fight until they dropped. They would not admit that they were beaten. They were men who were kept going by despair, and the forlorn hope that there would be reactions in this country.

Mr Bonar law said that there were two things a truce might result in: first, it might have a discouraging effect on our troops; and, second, the Sinn Feiners might use the lull for intense propaganda in this country regarding the policy of His Majesty's Government in Ireland.

The question arose as to whether, during a truce, it would be possible to arrest people like Michael Collins, and the opinion was expressed that if this -was done the other side would accuse the Government of breaking the truce.

General Tudor, asked for his opinion, said he agreed with General Boyd and Sir John Anderson. The interval would undoubtedly be used by the Sinn Feiners to re-establish their system of communication throughout the country. If murderers were still to be arrested it would not be possible to have a truce.

The Prime Minister then asked if there was no truce, how long they thought it would be before the extremist gang of the Sinn Feiners was entirely broken? The Horne Rule Act might come into operation any time in February, and the North was anxious to get it working at once. It would be very awkward to do this, however, without putting it into operation in the South as well. Sinn Fein was against the Act, and he would like the opinion of the Military Officers as to what would happen If there was an election in the South of Ireland, say, in February and March: would there be any intimidation? General Macready said he thought that if an election was held in February or March there would be a general boycott at the point of the pistol, on the word of Michael Collins.

The Prime Minister observed that if Michael Collins could atop three million people using their vote, it did not say much for the success of the policy His Majesty's Government was not pursuing. General Macready said that he thought thc terror would be broken if martial law was spread all over the country. General Strickland was of opinion that there would be definite and- decisive results in four months' time. Asked if there would be sufficient terrorism to prevent voters from voting and candidates from standing, General Strickland replied in the negative.

General Tudor said that he thought that, in his area, in four months' time the terror would be broken if there was no truce. The great hope of the extremists was a change of policy. General Boyd said he thought that four months was not too optimistic a prophecy, speaking for Dublin, Heath and Wicklow. The Chief of the Imperial General Staff said that in his opinion a truce would be absolutely fatal. There was one party in Ireland which no-one had yet mentioned, and that was the decent peasant, who was nearly on the Government side, but if there was a truce would go over again both the Sinn Feiners. He thought that perhaps in six months' time, if military law was applied to the whole of Ireland, 80 per cent, or 100 per cent, of the people would be on the side of the Government.

There was then a short discussion regarding the extension of martial law to Kilkenny, Clare, Waterford and Wexford, but the Prime Minister said that he would first like to see how it worked in the Cork area.

Appendix I

5th DIVISION AREA.[2]

SITUATION—FEBRUARY, 1921

1. As regards the 5th Division area there is little change. The three Brigade areas present somewhat distinct features. In Galway and Mayo there is on the whole less active unrest, though recently a serious attack on Auxiliaries has taken place. The 13th Brigade area is also less disturbed with the exception of a region in the neighbourhood of Boyle and Longford, in which there has been lately a notable increase in outrages and murders. The 14th Brigade area is practically unchanged, except that within the last six weeks numerous roads and bridges have been trenched and cut with the object of impeding military transport. There is no doubt that the internment of officers of the I.R.A. has favourably affected the situation, in that it has disorganised Sinn Fein command and communication, rendered Sinn Fein courts inoperative, removed those most likely to join in active operations, forced many rebels into hiding and discouraged some who might otherwise have been active.

On the whole the attitude of the bulk of the inhabitants in the Divisional area may be said to be outwardly passive. It will probably ultimately be influenced by the development of the contest in the South. If Sinn Fein is worsted there is probably that it energies will be turned to fomenting trouble in this area. If it obtains the advantage in the South, ill-disposed people in the 5th Division area will be encouraged and would-be loyalists disheartened, so that in either case no improvement is to be looked for in the near future under existing conditions.

2. In considering what measures can be suggested to improve the situation it is impossible to separate military measures from political, since military measures alone can have no lasting effect, and their employment can only be effective when they are directed as the expression of a determined policy towards the foundation of a sound and practical political structure. It follows, therefore, that in the first place there must be a definite conception of the political conditions which it is intended to introduce. Further, it is necessary to consider not only the immediate effect of any military measures, but also the sentiments they may engender, which will last long after the material effect of these measures has passed away. However, putting all details of the political settlement out of the question for the moment, and assuming that the general political

---

2 'History of the 5th Division in Ireland, November, 1919—March, 1922,' Nat. Arch., Kew, WO 141/93, pp. 101–102.

object is eventually to produce a contented self-governing people in close federation with, if not actually subject to, Great Britain, and bound to her by feelings of confidence in the integrity of her government and of respect for its strength and determination, there can be little doubt that the immediate proclamation of Martial Law throughout the whole area would be beneficial. Having regard to the contingencies referred to in para. 1, such a measure would enable steps to be taken in good time to render ineffective attempts on the part of Sinn Fein to foment disturbance and outrage, aid the prevention, detection, and punishment of crime, convince the wavering that the government is determined to repress lawlessness, and encourage them and the loyalists to give their assistance to the cause of order. But what is perhaps the most important argument of all, it would substitute for the present divided control by military and police, which is enforced by different authorities in different ways, according to very diverse standards, and often with more than questionable justice or even advantage, a unified and codified control with definite aims, regulations, and penalties.

3. Having regard, however, to the considerations advanced in para. 2, the administration of Martial Law should be adopted to the needs of the moment in each district, and no more restrictions should be imposed or greater penalties prescribed than are necessary to control the particular district at the particular moment, and to convince its inhabitants of the power and inflexible determination of the governing authority strictly to enforce the regulations with absolute fairness and impartiality. It is, of course, a corollary of the above that whatever regulations may be adopted, there must be sufficient force and resources to make them operative.

4. Although it is possible to make the foregoing general recommendations without consideration of detailed political aims, their reduction to practical measures could not be effective without a comprehension by all concerned of the situation which it is desired to bring about, just as the orders of a superior commander for operations of war require a clear understanding by his subordinates of the "intention" with which he undertakes them.

The people of Ireland may be roughly classified at the present time as follows:—

(a) Extremists, or "gun-men"; i.e., those who, whether actuated by so-called patriotic motives, or impregnated with Bolshevik doctrines, or merely murderers for the sake of what they can make out of it, are resolved to fight to the end and ready to go to any lengths either for complete independence for Ireland, or for the destruction of England, or because they realise that their crimes are beyond forgiveness.

(b) More or less honest patriots, often almost fanatics, whose aims are independence, but who are not prepared to go to the same length as (a), while at the same time they are either afraid to condemn the extremists, or unwilling to forego the advantages which they believe the action of these may bring.

(c) Moderate men whose aims are independent or autonomous government for Ireland, but who support only methods for obtaining their wishes which, if not constitutional, are at all events meant to be bloodless.

(d) The ruck—who desire peace and don't care how they get it, but dare not openly side with Sinn Fein for fear of the consequences if it is unsuccessful, and dare not oppose it for fear of loss of life, property, or business.

(e) Loyalists in name, who perhaps excusably, take no part in aid of law and order for fear of Sinn Fein reprisals.

(f) Active loyalists. An inconsiderable class.

There is, of course, no clear line of demarcation between these classes in every case. They are overlapped by labour and its professional agitators, who sometimes attempt to use Sinn Fein to further their own ends, but are more often made its cat's-paw.

5. It seems to be obvious, from a review of the above classes, that the guiding political aim should be to separate class (a) from the remainder, to hunt them down relentlessly and deal with them when taken with the utmost severity, while at the same time conciliating classes (b) and (c), and endeavouring with all the resources of finesse and diplomacy to create a cleavage between them and (a). if these tactics are successful all the remaining classes will come to heel. It is submitted,

therefore, that it is with this end in view that all Martial Law regulations should be framed and carried out so as to provide concrete expression of the determination to persecute the really wicked while conciliating those who are only mistaken, or misled, or over enthusiastic. For instance, the extreme penalty should be relentlessly enforced for levying war, or carrying or using arms, and heavy penalties awarded for harbouring or assisting murderers on the run, while the mere membership of the I.R.A., or possession of seditious documents not involving active rebellion should be quite leniently treated. It is certainly advisable to continue the internment of all officers of the I.R.A., but it is certain that, if marked success is obtainable against the real extremists many of these will be willing to recant, and might be sent under definite recognisances, to their homes, where they would automatically act as propagandists.

CONDITION OF INHABITANTS

I have consulted persons who have had the best opportunities of judging of the present prosperity or want among the average inhabitants of Ireland. Their unanimous opinion agrees with the results of my own observation during journeys in my district. At no time within the memory of man were the peasants and small farmers of Ireland so prosperous as at present. The farmers have accumulated riches during the war, their labourers have had their wages very largely increased, and in all trades and occupations not directly affected (as, for instance, the motor trade and horse dealing are) by the present situation, the result of this prosperity is felt. Probably almost the only cases in which there has been want during this winter have been among unemployed ex-soldiers and their families.

(*Signed*) H.S. JEUDWINE, *Major-General*,
Curragh Camp, Commanding 5th Division.

14th February, 1921.

APPENDIX J

[CAB 24/123/366 (CP 2948)]

S E C R E T.

CABINET.

C.P. 2948.

REPORT BY THE GENERAL OFFICER COMMANDING -IN-CHIEF ON THE SITUATION IN IRELAND FOR WEEK ENDING 14th MAY, 1921

(Circulated by the Secretary of State for War.)

1. GENERAL MILITARY SITUATION

During the week the Military Situation has not materially changed, hut the week-end has produced a large number of outrages of the most cowardly and cold-blooded nature, in which women and unarmed men have been done to death by large bodies of armed rebels. In order that a clear appreciation of the Whitsun weekend may be formed, these murders have been shown separately in Appendix I (A). It has become apparent that, in spite of my many representations, little or nothing is being done to rouse public opinion in England from the complacency with which it views the attacks on Military and police patrols when in the execution of their duty; but I am strongly of opinion that the events of this week-end, involving as they do the murder of civilians, troops, and police engaged in private business or recreation, should not be allowed to pass without wide publicity being given to them by influential members of the Government

During the period May 5th to May 12th, operations were carried out in the Mullingar-Tullamore district. The operations which took the form of "drives" by Cavalry, were carried, out under the orders of the G.O.C. 5th Division, Four Cavalry regiments were employed, assisted by local Infantry units, and provided with Mobile Wireless Stations. A different Area was driven each day by the Cavalry, the exits to the Areas being blocked by Infantry piquets, The Colonel Commandant 3rd Cav. Bde, was in command of the operation and his column was self contained as regards supplies etc. A considerable number of individuals were arrested and arrangements had been made for local police to be available to identify these men on the spot. Although the number of arrested persons retained was not large, about 35.wanted men were captured. The operation was particularly useful as an experiment to discover the value of cavalry in this kind of work. The general conduct of the "drives", the administrative and supply arrangements worked very well and have been a good guide for any future operations of the same kind which it may be desirable to carry out in other areas, There was practically no opposition to the troops, and the only casualty was one trooper slightly wounded.

The nomination of candidates for the new Irish Parliaments on Friday 13th, has been the most important event of the week. I all constituents in Southern Ireland, except Dublin University, Sinn Fein has had a complete "walk-over", not one single Unionist, nationalist or Labour Candidate being even nominated for any of the remaining 124 seats.

There are only two conclusions to be drawn from these results. Either the people of Southern Ireland are solidly republican and support and approve of the Dail Eireann's policy of murder, outrage and boycott, or the gunmen have so terrorized their fellow country men that no one dare nominate or support an individual whose views are other than republican. Sinn Fein would have the world believe that the former is the correct conclusion, and that Southern Ireland is unanimously republican. This is not the case, though it is probable that Sinn Fein would have obtained a substantial majority had the Elections been contested, and it seems a pity that arrangements were not made to nominate candidates in order to farce a contest and ascertain that proportion of the electors were prepared to vote for the republican party.

The ascendency of the gunmen is amply proved by examination of the lists of individuals nominated for the Southern Parliament approximately 50% of whom are important members of the H.Q. Staff of the I.R.A. or of Brigades in the provinces. Among the newly nominated members, there is if anything a greater proportion of leaders of flying columns and active service units who are on the run as fugitives from justice, than among the old re-elected members of Dail Eireann. The moderate element as represented by persons like Father O'Flanagan and John Sweetman, has disappeared.

The results of the election in the South have demonstrated that there is only one question to be dealt with - "Is Ireland to have a Republic or not"? The people of Southern Ireland have acquiesced either from choice or through fear in the election of individuals who maintain that Ireland is at War with England, who have taken an oath to do all in their power to establish a Republic who maintain that every form of outrage is justifiable against Crown Forces, loyal civilians and Government property. Until these men understand that they are beaten and that the Republic is possible, there can be no hope of moderate people coming forward to discuss a reasonable settlement.

The Election has been a "revolver election". No one but extreme republicans have been nominated. Practically all the nominated representatives of the people in Southern Ireland are men who have taken the oath of the Irish Republican Brotherhood or of the Irish Republican Army. The greatest publicity should be given to these facts in Great Britain, and quickly otherwise the public will be led by the very effective system of Sinn Fein propaganda to believe that the results of the election express the wishes of the Irish people.

The task before the troops and police, though difficult (chiefly owing to the impossibility of' differentiating at sight between armed rebels and peaceful civilians) is by no means stupendous. At the outside the drilled and trained men of the I.R.A. amount to 25,000 men. A "parade state" of the I.R.A. recently captured, but undated, shows only 4,076 of which 3,386 are in Munster. This figure is considerably below the estimate formed from other captured documents, but might well represent the number of men with Flying Columns and Active Service Units, sometimes referred to in rebel documents as their "Standing Army". Whatever the exact interpretation of this return, there is no doubt that the main obstacles to peace, in Ireland are the individuals who have recently been nominated for election to the Southern Parliament, and those who form, the Flying Columns and Active Service Units. The total number of these individuals, is probably not in excess of the figures given in the return, viz:-

Munster	3,386
Leinster	320
Connaught	450
Ulster	320
Dublin	600

Once those men are dealt with and once their arms are captured there will be some chance of peace in Ireland.

On May 14th, an Armoured Car which had escorted a lorry and party of R.A.S.C. to the Abattoir in Dublin to fetch meat, was captured by rebels whilst stationary at the Abattoir. The rebels numbered about 30. One of the drivers of the car was shot as he was getting out of the Car, and the remainder of the crew were surrounded and compelled to get out of the Car. The whole party were lined up against the wall and some of their uniforms taken, The rebels, of whom two were dressed as officers, then got into the car and drove to Mountjoy Prison where their uniforms gained them admission. The rebels dressed as officers were taken to the Governor of the Prison and informed him they had been sent to take a prisoner from Mountjoy to Kilmainham. The Governor became suspicious and the rebels then produced revolvers and locked the Governor in his room. In the meantime five or six more rebels had gained admission at the gate, holding up the warders with revolvers. A sentry fired and wounded one rebel, and the whole rebel party, including those dressed as officers then made good their escape in the Car. The car was subsequently found abandoned outside Dublin, The two Hotchkiss guns and the ammunition had been removed; the Car was s lightly damaged. A Court of Enquiry is being held on the affair, The whole incident has caused me to consider seriously the adequacy of the personnel at present available for manning the armoured cars, and I am strongly of opinion that the number of trained men of the Tank Corps in Ireland must be increased if the armoured cars are to reach their full efficiency. This question has previously been raised by me, and I propose how to send £mother letter to the War Office asking for the increase which, after consultation with the Officer Commanding the 3rd. Battalion Tank Corps, I consider necessary. I should be glad if the matter could be treated as urgent.

C. F. N. MACREADY, *General*,
Commanding-in-Chief the Forces in Ireland.

General Headquarters, Ireland,
Parkgate, Dublin,
17th *May*, 1921.

Additional Appendices

SECRET.   CABINET.

C.P. 2872.

REPORT BY THE GENERAL OFFICER COMMANDING-IN-CHIEF ON THE SITUATION IN IRELAND FOR WEEK ENDING 23RD APRIL, 1921

(Circulated by the Secretary of State for War).

1. GENERAL MILITARY SITUATION

The number of minor outrages shows no diminution, "but there is still an absence of rebel activities on a large scale, and the general situation remains unchanged.

In Dublin the principal feature of the week has been the capture of arms. These captures, following those of last week, are the result of information au to the existence of hidden arms.

In the country, the only operations of any magnitude were the rounding-up of armed rebels drilling at Ballymurphy, Co. Carlow, in which five rebels were killed and eight captured; and an attack on ration wagons at Clogheen, Co. Tipperary, in which a Hotchkiss Gun on a farm cart was captured from the rebels.

Several police barracks have been attacked, both in the vicinity of Dublin and in the country, but none of these attacks has been pressed home.

The rebels appear to be concentrating their efforts on out rages on a smaller scale, such as the shooting of horses, the cutting of roads, and the sniping of individual members of the Crown Forces and murder of loyalists.

This policy of avoiding risk vas the usual rebel method until the formation of the Flying Columns and Active Service Units. The inauguration of these units led to more active operations, involving large numbers of rebels and considerable risk to their lives. In the Martial Law Area, at any rate, this semblance of Military operations has for the time disappeared, and it may be assumed that the policy has not met with the success which had been hoped for by the I.R.A. leaders, or that the rank and file do not consider their achievements justify the risk involved.

The An T'Oglac is now published weekly instead of fortnightly as has previously been the case. This is significant in view of the known reliance which I.K.A. Headquarters place upon the influence of this paper on the moral of the Volunteers, Recent numbers have shown an increased incitement to murder, and to small outrages as compared with larger activities. The article which dictates this policy is hardly consistent with the heading of the leading article in the previous number which was entitled "All or Nothing."

The G.O.C. 6th Division has recently submitted to me a review of the Situation in the Martial Law Area and of the progress made by the methods adopted. In considering this question it must be borne in mind that the Area in which Martial Law was imposed contained the counties in which the rebels had made most headway and that the situation there was rapidly becoming worse. The degree of success attained must, therefore, be viewed in the light of the probable state of affairs which would have existed in Munster to-day had Martial Law not been imposed.

The principal points brought out in the report of the G.O.C. Martial Law Area are as follows:-

    (a)   The intense rebel activities on a scale previously not attempted, which marvel the beginning of the Martial Law period, have died down, and for a month there has been comparative immunity from such operations. This is probably due to re action after ill-success, the desire of some men to get back and attend to their farms, and, possibly, instruction to keep quiet till after the elections,

(b) Rumours, apparently well-founded, as to intended attacks on isolated garrisions in Kerry and elsewhere, have come to nothing, although it is believed that the preliminary concentrations of rebels took place.

(c) Individual murders of Protestant Land Owners and Farmers and other moderate people are numerous, and are probably due to an attempt to frighten inhabitants from Giving information. The murders increase as the larger outrages decrease, and it is thought that they are the work of members of Flying Columns in their spare time. These murders of individuals are particularly, difficult to prevent.

(d) Information has not been coming in so well recently. This is due partly to the increased wariness of the rebels in their movements - previously they moved about freely in confidence that their movements would not be reported by inhabitants. In Cork City, however, information has increased since the murder of unarmed soldiers.

(e) Interning has undoubtedly done good.

(f) The attitude of the Press in the Martial Law Area has much improved, thanks to firm control, and also probably to the recognition of the fact that intimidation does not now have such a free hand as before.

(g) Inconvenience is no doubt caused to the population by Martial Law restrictions, and certain sections of the inhabitants are apt to attribute the cause for these restrictions entirely to the Troops and Police.

(h) Generally speaking, Martial Law has justified itself and the rebels have been driven back to their old position of small outrages involving little risk. Two courses appear to be open to the rebels for future action. To organise strong surprise attacks; but the rebels will probably be in no better position to do this in the future than they are now. Or, to play a "Waiting game" in the hope that we may be worn down by the cumulative effect of minor outrages and that political propaganda will supplant military operations.

I am in agreement with these views of the G.O.C. Martial Law Area, and I have no hesitation in saying that our policy, not only in the Martial Law Area, but all over Ireland, must be to be ready to strike when intelligence is received and to enforce restriction rigorously in order to bring home to moderate men and neutrals alike, that the forces of the Crown are gaining control of the Military situation.

(Sgd.) C.F.N. MACREADY,
GENERAL, Commanding-in-Chief, Ireland,

H.Q., Ireland
26th April, 1921.

Additional Appendices

Appendix L

[CAB 24/123 (CP 2965)]

MEMORANDUM "A" BY THE COMMANDER-IN-CHIEF, THE FORCES IN IRELAND

C.I.G.S.,

I understand that under certain conditions it may be possible for you to reinforce the troops under my command in Ireland with, say, 20 Battalions of Infantry, 8 Regiments of Cavalry, and a certain proportion of armoured cars, wireless personnel, and aeroplanes, in the event of the Government deciding to throw the whole of the forces at their disposal into Ireland in order to take the greatest 1 possible advantage of the weather during the summer and early autumn. Should this decision be reached, it will, of course, be necessary that the Navy should equally throw the whole of their available weight into the scale. The activity of the troops at present serving in Ireland is directed towards countering the pressure of the Irish Republican Army whenever that becomes prominent in various areas and localities, and little more than this can be done on account of insufficiency of numbers, and the consequent strain on young troops by having few nights in bed. At the present moment in certain parts of Ireland the troops are getting only two nights. Apart from little expeditions of a couple of subaltern officers and from 12 to 20 men, extending over from 24 to 48 hours, and directed against a spot where information has been received of a collection of rebels, a course of action which is taking place almost daily in different parts of the country, the only possibility of taking the offensive is with the Cavalry, and now that the weather has become suitable for mounted work, one "drive" has already taken place, another is about to take place, and a third on a very much larger scale is planned for the middle of June. If, however, the Government decide to take thorough and drastic action in the direction of imposing Martial Law throughout the country (omitting the six counties of Ulster) and of instituting such blockade as may be considered necessary by the authorities in Ireland, accompanied by passport regulations and residential permits, I propose to utilize the extra forces which may be placed at my disposal, broadly, in the following manner :—

At least 7 Battalions, together with 3 Cavalry Regiments, would be apportioned to Munster, 9 Battalions to the 5th Division and 4 to the present Dublin District, which, as soon as the Ulster Government is formed, will extend up to Monaghan and Cavan.

As regards general policy, I attach the greatest importance to "showing the flag" in districts where there are a considerable number of loyalists and people who "sit on the fence." The arrival of fresh troops and the obvious determination of the British Government to "see the thing through" will encourage waverers and will make all except the irreconcilable extremists realize that the success of the rebels is out of the question. Until the populated districts have been quieted, I do not propose to waste force on the mountainous districts into which the extremists will fly, and who will be comparatively easily rounded up as soon as the civilized areas have settled down. Another important factor is to re-establish all police posts which have been abandoned, except those which the military authorities decide need not be re-occupied.

On arrival, the new battalions will be at first located as complete units at certain centres, where they will have the opportunity of learning something about the conditions which prevail in the country and of becoming acquainted with many points, both tactical and administrative which are unknown outside Ireland. Battalions will then be moved out each into a certain area and distributed according to circumstances, but on no account will any detachment be smaller than a company. A Battalion thus distributed will cover a considerable area, and mobile columns from the companies will perpetually move about the district, thereby assuring that every village and farm sees the Army. All movements will be by route march or bicycles, transport only being required for baggage and supplies, but even if new battalions are not equipped with first line transport, they must, at any rate, have one cooker and one water-cart per company, water being a great difficulty in certain parts. I hope by this means to keep down extra transport to the lowest possible limit, but, of course, there are certain localities where extra transport will be required for extra troops.

The rôle of the infantry therefore will be:—

    (a)   To move through the country, get in touch with the inhabitants, obtain information, hearten the loyalists and depress the extremists.

    (b)   Assist in the re-occupation of stations vacated by the Royal Irish Constabulary,

    (c)   Despatch mobile columns to act against rebels who have been located.

As regards Cavalry, I propose to use the three regiments in Munster as -one force to carry out concerted movements through certain districts, and according to the information available to tackle each locality. In the 5th Divisional Area, the Cavalry would be employed in two brigades acting in the same way, either separately or together, and action may arise, according to information received, where the whole of the Cavalry might be turned on to one large "drive." It is difficult to give a more detailed appreciation at the moment, because everything depends upon the situation at the time and the information received. The more armoured cars that can be provided, the better, as they are of great value.

If the Government decide to place at my disposal all possible troops and material, every effort will be made to stamp out the extremists while the fine weather lasts, that is up to the end of September, but I am not prepared to guarantee that this object will be attained, as it is impossible to forecast with any certainty happenings which may take place in Ireland in the future.

One last point I would urge, and that is that should the Government decide to take drastic steps to stamp out the rebellion now existing, efforts should at the same time be directed towards countering the rebel propaganda which is at present pursuing its course unchecked in the Press, at meetings presided over by prominent persons, and by certain members in both Houses of Parliament.

C. F. N. MACREADY, *General,*
Commanding-in-Chief the Forces in Ireland.

23rd May, 1921.

APPENDIX M

MEMORANDUM "B" BY THE COMMANDER-IN-CHIEF, THE FORCES IN IRELAND

C.I.G.S.,

Following the discussion we had this morning in regard to my Weekly Report, dated 14th May, I understand that you wish to be informed as to my candid opinion in regard to the *morale* and feelings of the troops at present stationed in Ireland.

It is extremely difficult for anyone not living in Ireland at the present time to realize the "atmosphere" under which officers and men are at present serving. The rank and file are in excellent health, keen on their work, and thoroughly under discipline. During the last few months, instance after instance has occurred where officers and men have been murdered by the rebels, and yet in not one single instance has there been the least attempt at outbreak or retaliation of any kind. This, I think, speaks volumes for the state of discipline in which the troops are held by their officers. I mention that the health of the troops is good, but my Deputy-Director of Medical Services is continually impressing on me that, while this is the case at present, anything in the shape of an epidemic might suddenly have a very disastrous effect among the men who are for the most part very young and "fine drawn." I have on several occasions drawn attention to the number of nights in bed which in certain areas is now down to two, and this cannot be remedied except by reinforcement. While from a purely military standpoint of the well-being of the troops, the above might be considered satisfactory, I- feel impelled to point out that the situation from this point of view gives me the very greatest anxiety, because there seems to be at the present moment no definite end to the state of affairs now existing. I make it my constant endeavour to keep in as close touch as may be possible with the troops, and to discover their ideas and feelings by conversations with officers of all ranks, and I believe that the following remarks are a picture of the true facts of the case:—

While the rank and file are in no way discontented, there is a feeling among them that their efforts and the danger which hourly besets them are not appreciated by people in Great Britain. The idea is strengthened by the want of anti-rebel propaganda, and by what is read in the papers about Parliamentary debates and meetings held under the auspices of various influential people. The result is that the men cannot be expected to go on indefinitely without the conditions under which they are serving having effect upon their *morale,* discipline and future from the point of view of military usefulness. Married men have been separated from their wives and families for a considerable time and see no prospect of either returning to them or having them out to live with them, and the unmarried men, except in the larger cities (and there only with increased danger) are denied the usual amusements which normally exist when serving in the British Isles.

As regards the officers, the strain upon them from the junior to the highest ranks is incomparably greater than it would be in time of actual war. The Lieutenant or Captain in charge of a village or post not only has the hourly danger of assassination hanging over him, but has to be at any moment prepared to come to a decision in regard to the defence of his charge, or to act on a sudden call from the Police, or to exercise his discretion in regard to setting right complaints which are often libellous, brought to his notice by sympathizers with rebels. In addition to this, he may be continually worried to render reports in order that questions by rebel sympathizers may be answered in the House of Commons. The strain of this situation increases in proportion to the rank of the officer concerned and in the case of General Officers Commanding Divisions, more especially in the 6th Division whose headquarters are at Cork, it is often astonishing to me how the officers manage to bear up under the strain as they do.

Events lately have shown that the rebels stick at nothing in order to carry out their policy of endeavouring to secure their ends by outrage and murder, under the impression that the further they go, the more chance there is that the British Government and public will be cowed into submission. At the same time, it is only right to form a clear opinion of what the effect of continued service under these conditions will be upon the troops.

It is my considered opinion that the troops as at present situated will continue to do their duty during the present summer, although I am not prepared to say that, if pressed too far by the campaign of outrage directed against them, there may not be cases where they will take the law into their own hands and break out. It is difficult for the rank and file and junior officers to understand why it is that the members of Dail Eirann are left untouched by the Government, and even though Arthur Griffiths has now been under arrest for 6 months, no action is taken against him, seeing that the campaign of murder now in progress is, if not directed by the members of Dail Eirann, at all events concurred in by them. While, as I have said, I am of opinion that the troops at present in Ireland may be depended on to continue to do their best under present circumstances through this summer, I am convinced that by October, unless a peaceful solution has been reached, it will, not be safe to ask the troops to continue there another winter under the conditions which obtained during the last. Not only the men for the sake of their *morale* and training should be removed out of the Irish "atmosphere," but by that time there will be many officers who, although they may not confess it, will, in my opinion, be quite unfit to continue to serve in Ireland without a release for a very considerable period.

To sum up, it amounts to this. Unless I am entirely mistaken, the present state of affairs in Ireland, so far as regards the troops serving there, must be brought to a conclusion by October, or steps must be taken to relieve practically the whole of the troops together with the great majority of the commanders and their staffs. I am quite aware that troops do not exist to do this, but this does not alter in any way the opinion that I have formed in regard to the officers and men for whom I am responsible.

C. F. N. MACREADY, General,
Commanding-in-Chief the Forces in Ireland.

23rd May, 1921.

APPENDIX N

SPEECH OF KING GEORGE V OPENING THE NORTHERN IRELAND PARLIAMENT

Members of the Senate and of the House of Commons—

For all who love Ireland, as I do with all my heart, this is a profoundly moving occasion in Irish istory. My memories of the Irish people date back to the time when I spent many happy days in Ireland as a midshipman. My affection for the Irish people has been deepened by the successive visits since that time, and I have watched with constant sympathy the course of their affairs.

I could not have allowed myself to give Ireland by deputy alone. My earnest prayers and good wishes in the new era which opens with this ceremony, and I have therefore come in person, as the Head of the Empire, to inaugurate this Parliament on Irish soil.

I inaugurate it with deep-felt hope, and I feel assured that you will do your utmost to make it an instrument of happiness and good government for all parts of the community which you represent.

This is a great and critical occasion in the history of the Six Counties, but not for the Six Counties alone, for everything which interests them touches Ireland, and everything which touches Ireland finds an echo in the remotest parts of the Empire.

Few things are more earnestly desired throughout the English speaking world than a satisfactory solution of the age-long Irish problems, which for generations embarrassed our forefathers, as they now weigh heavily upon us.

Most certainly there is no which nearer My own heart than that every man of Irish birth, whatever be his creed and wherever be his home, should work in loyal co-operation with the free communities on which the British Empire is based.

I am confident that the important matters entrusted to the control and guidance of the Northern Parliament will be managed with wisdom and with moderation, with fairness and due regard to every faith and interest, and with no abatement of that patriotic devotion to the Empire which you proved so gallantly in the Great War.

Full partnership in the United Kingdom and religious freedom Ireland has long enjoyed. She now has conferred upon her the duty of dealing with all the essential tasks of domestic legislation and government; and I feel no misgiving as to the spirit in which you who stand here to-day will carry out the all-important functions entrusted to your care.

My hope is broader still. The eyes of the whole Empire are on Ireland to-day—that Empire in which so many nations and races have come together in spite of ancient feuds, and in which new nations have come to birth within the lifetime of the youngest in this Hall.

I am emboldened by that thought to look beyond the sorrow and the anxiety which have clouded of late My vision of Irish affairs. I speak from a full heart when I pray that My coming to Ireland to-day may prove to be the first step towards an end of strife amongst her people, whatever their race or creed. In that hope, I appeal to all Irishmen to pause, to stretch out the hand of forbearance and conciliation, to forgive and to forget, and to join in making for the land which they love a new era of peace contentment, and goodwill.

It is My earnest desire that in Southern Ireland, too, there may ere long take place a parallel to what is now passing in this Hall; that there a similar occasion may present itself and a similar ceremony be performed.

For this the Parliament of the United Kingdom has in the fullest measure provided the powers; for this the Parliament of Ulster is pointing the way. The future lies in the hands of My Irish people themselves.

22 June 1921

Appendix O

[Appendix V, CAB 24/126/283–4 CP 3134]

APPENDIX V

(a). Copy of G.H.Q. Communiqué issued to the Press on morning July 9th

Mr. de Valera having decided to accept the Prime Minister's invitation to confer with him in London, is issuing instructions to his supporters.

(a) To cease all attacks on Crown Forces and civilians.
(b) To prohibit the use of arms.
(c) To cease Military manoeuvres of all kinds.
(d) To abstain from interference with public or private property.
(e) To discountenance and prevent any action likely to cause disturbance of the peace which might necessitate military interference.

In order to co-operate in providing an atmosphere in which peaceful discussion may be possible, the Government has directed that

(a) All raids and searches by military or police shall cease.
(b) Military activity shall be restricted to the support of the police in their normal civil duties.
(c) Curfew restrictions shall be removed.
(d) The despatch of reinforcements from England shall be suspended
(e). The police functions in Dublin to be carried out by the D.M.P.

In order to give the necessary time for these instructions to reach all concerned, the date from which they shall come into force has been fixed at, 12 noon, Monday July 11th. 1921.

(b). Extract from "Irish Bulletin" published in the Press on evening of July 9th.

On behalf of the British Army it is agreed as follows:-

1. No incoming troops R.I.C. & Auxiliary Police and munitions and no movements for military purposes of troops and munitions except maintenance drafts.
2. No provocative display of forces, armed or unarmed.

3. It is understood that all provisions of the truce apply to Martial Law Area equally with the rest of Ireland.'
4. No pursuit of Irish Officers or men or war material or Military stores.
5. No secret agents, noting descriptions or movements, and no interference with the movements of Irish persons, military or civil, and no attempt to discover the haunts or habits of Irish officers and men. (Note - This supposes the abandonment of Curfew restriction)
6. No pursuit or observance of lines of communication or connection.
7. No pursuit of messengers. (Note - There are other details connected with Courts martial, motor permits, and R.O.I.R. to be agreed to later.)

"On behalf of the Irish Army it is agreed:-
(a) Attacks on Crown Forces & civilians to cease
(b) No provocative display of forces, armed or unarmed.
(c) No interference with Government or private property
(d) To discountenance and prevent any action likely to cause disturbance of the peace which might necessitate, Military interference".

(C) COPY OF CIRCULAR MEMORANDUM ISSUED TO ALL FORMATIONS. 11TH JULY

In order to avoid any possible misconstruction of the terms referred to in G.H.Q. official statements and those issued as a supplement to the Irish Bulletin, it is notified for information that the wording of the G.E official statement is taken from the letter written by G.O.C-in-C. to Lord Midleton (and agreed to in principle by Mr. de Valera) and is in no sense a draft. The wording as issued in the Irish Bulletin is their interpretation of the same terms issued after discussion at G.H.Q- in a form more acceptable to Mr. de Valera's adherents. The spirit of the two documents is identical.

NOTES

1   HMSO, *Defence of the Realm Manual, Revised to February 28th, 1918*, 5th edition (HMSO, 1918)

Bibliography

Published Sources

1916: Easter Rebellion Handbook (Mourne River Press, 1998) aan de Wiel, Jerome. *The Irish Factor 1899–1919: Ireland's Strategic and Diplomatic Importance for Foreign Powers* (Dublin: Irish Academic Press, 2011).

Abbott, R. *Police Casualties in Ireland, 1919–1922* (Cork: Mercier Press, 2000).

Allen, Cmdt Mary, OBE, *The Pioneer Policewoman* (London: Chatto & Windus, 1925).

The American Commission on Conditions in Ireland, *Interim Report* (1921)

Andrew, C. *Her Majesty's Secret Service: The Making of the British Intelligence Community* (New York: Viking Press, 1986).

Ash, Bernard. *The Lost Dictator: A Biography of Sir Henry Wilson, Bart, GCB, DSO, MP* (London: Cassell, 1968).

Augusteijn, Joost (ed.), *The Irish Revolution, 1913–1923* (Basingstoke: Palgrave, 2002).

Augusteijn, Joost. *From Public Defiance to Guerrilla Warfare: The Experience of Ordinary Volunteers in the Irish War of Independence, 1916–1921* (Portland, OR: Irish Academic Press, 1998).

Augusteijn, Joost. *The Memoirs of John M. Regan: A Catholic Officer in the RIC and RUC, 1909–48* (Dublin: Four Courts Press, 2007).

Barry, Tom. *Guerrilla Days in Ireland: A Personal Account of the Anglo-Irish War* (Boulder, CO: Roberts Reinhart Publishers, 1995).

Barton, B. *From Behind a Closed Door: Secret Court Martial Records of the 1916 Easter Rising* (Belfast: Blackstaff Press, 2002).

Beckett, Ian F. W., Ed. *The Roots of Counter-Insurgency: Armies and Guerrilla Warfare, 1900–1945* (London, Blandford Press, 1988).

Begley, Diarmuid. *The Road to Crossbarry: The Decisive Battle of the War of Independence* (Bandon, Cork: 1999).

Bennett, Richard. *The Black and Tans: The British Special Police in Ireland* (New York City: MetroBooks, 2002).

Bew, Paul. *Ideology and the Irish Question: Ulster Unionism and Irish Nationalism* (University of Chicago Press, 1998).

Borgonovo, J. 'Revolutionary violence and Irish historiography', *Irish Historical Studies*, vol. XXXVIII, N°. 150, pp. 325–31.

Borgonovo, John. *Spies, Informers and the 'Anti-Sinn Féin Society'* (Dublin: Irish Academic Press, 2007).

Bowman, T. *Carson's Army: The Ulster Volunteer Force: 1910–22* (Manchester University Press, 2007).

Boyce, D. George. *Englishmen and Irish Troubles: British Public Opinion and the Making of Irish Policy, 1918–1922* (Cambridge, MA: MIT Press, 1972).

Boyce, D. George. *Nationalism in Ireland* (Abingdon, Oxford: Routledge 1995).

Breen, Daniel. *My Fight for Irish Freedom* (New York: Anvil, 1964).

Brinton, Crane. *The Anatomy of Revolution* (Prentice Hall, 1938).

Briscoe, Robert. *For the Life of Me* (Boston: Little, Brown & Company, 1958).

Browne, Charlie. *The Story of the 7th: A Concise History of the 7th Battalion, Cork No.1 Brigade, Irish Republican Army from 1915 to 1921* (Ballydehob, Co. Cork: Schull Books, 2007).

Browning, Edward. *Slaughtered Like Animals: A detailed examination of the killing of 17 members of the Royal Irish Constabulary Auxiliary Division by the IRA at Macroom, County Cork on 28th November 1920, and similar notorious incidents in that period* (London: Grosvenor House Publishing Limited, 2011).

Buckley, D. *The Battle of Tourmakeady, Fact or Fiction: A Study of the IRA Ambush and Its Aftermath* (Dublin: Nonsuch, 2008).

Butler, Ewan. *Barry's Flying Column* (London: Leo Cooper, 1971).

Campbell, Colm. *Emergency Law in Ireland 1918–1925* (Oxford University Press, 1994).

Campbell, F. *Land and Revolution: Nationalist Politics in the West of Ireland 1891–1921* (Oxford University Press, 2008).

Carroll, A. *Seán Moylan: Rebel Leader* (Cork: Mercier Press, 2010).

Carroll, Francis M. *American Opinion and the Irish Question, 1910–23* (Dublin: Gill and MacMillan, 1978).

Chappell, B. *The Regimental Warpath 1914–1918* (General Data LLC, 2008).

Christenson, Timothy, Ed. *Can't We All Just Get Along? Improving the Law Enforcement-Intelligence Community Relationship* (Washington, D.C.: Defense Intelligence College, 2007).

Clausewitz, Carl von. *On War*. Ed. and trans. Sir Michael Howard and Peter Paret (Princeton, NJ: Princeton University Press, 1984).

Coates, T. *The Irish Uprising: Papers from the British Parliamentary Archive* (London: The Stationary Office, 2000).

Coleman, Marie. *County Longford and the Irish Revolution, 1910–1923* (Dublin: Irish Academic Press, 2003).

Colum, Padraic. *Arthur Griffith* (Dublin: Browne and Nolan, 1959).

Coogan, Tim Pat. *De Valera–Long Fellow, Long Shadow* (London: Arrow, 1993).

Coogan, Tim Pat. *The Man Who Made Ireland: The Life and Death of Michael Collins*. First American edition (Niwot, Colorado: Roberts Rinehart Publishers, 1992).

Costello, F. J. *Enduring the Most: The Life and Death of Terence MacSwiney* (Tottenham: Turnaround Publishing Services, 1995).

Costello, Francis. 'The Republican Courts and the Decline of British Rule in Ireland, 1920–1921', *Éire-Ireland* (Samradh/Summer 1990), pp. 36–55.

Costello, Francis. *The Irish Revolution and its Aftermath, 1916–1923: Years of Revolt* (Dublin: Irish Academic Press, 2003).

Crane, Charles P. *Memories of a Resident Magistrate 1880–1920* (London: T. A. Constable, 1938).

Crozier, Brig.-Gen. Frank P. *Impressions and Recollections* (London: T. Werner Laurie, 1930).

Davis, Richard. *Arthur Griffith* (Dundalk: Dundalgan Press, 1976).

Deasy, Liam. *Towards Ireland Free: The West Cork Brigade in the War of Independence, 1917–1923* (Cork: Mercier Press, 1973).

Denning, B. C. 'Modern Problems of Guerilla Warfare', *Army Quarterly* (January 1927), pp. 347–54.

Doherty G. and D. Keogh, eds, *1916: The Long Revolution* (Dublin: Mercier Press, 2007).

Dolan, Anne. 'Killing and Bloody Sunday, November 1920', *The Historical Journal*, Vol. 49, No. 3 (2006), pp. 789–810.

Dublin Brigade Review (Dublin: Cahill, 1939).

Duffy, Stephen M. *The Integrity of Ireland: Home Rule, Nationalism, and Partition, 1912–1922* (Madison, New Jersey: Fairleigh Dickinson University Press, 2009).

Dwyer, T. Ryle. *'I Signed My Death Warrant': Michael Collins and the Treaty* (Blackrock, Co. Cork: Mercier Press, 2006).

Dwyer, T. Ryle. *Michael Collins and the Treaty: His Differences with de Valera* (Blackrock, Co. Cork: Mercier Press, 1981).

Dwyer, T. Ryle. *Tans, Terror and Troubles: Kerry's Real Fighting Story, 1913–23* (Dublin, Mercier Press, 2001).

Dwyer, T. Ryle. *The Squad: and the Intelligence Operations of Michael Collins* (Cork: Mercier Press, 2005).

Ebenezer, L. *Fron-Goch and the birth of the IRA* (Pwllheli: Gwasg Carreg Gwalch, 2005).

English, Richard. *Irish Freedom: The History of Nationalism in Ireland* (Dublin: Gill & MacMillan, 2006).

Enright, Seán. *The Trial of Civilians by Military Courts* (Dublin: Irish Academic Press, 2012).

Fanning, Ronan. *Fatal Path: British Government and Irish Revolution, 1910–1922* (London: Faber and Faber, 2013).

Farrell, B. *The Founding of Dáil Éireann: Parliament and Nation Building* (Dublin: Gill and Macmillan, 1971).

Farrell, Michael. *Arming the Protestants – the formation of the USC and the RUC 1920–5* (London: Pluto Press, 1983).

Farry, M. *The Irish Revolution: 1912–23: Sligo* (Dublin: Four Courts Press, 2012).

Ferguson, K. ed. *The Irish Rebellion in the 6th Divisional Area* (Dublin: The Military History Society of Ireland 2009).

Ferriter, Diarmuid. *Judging Dev: A Reassessment of the Life and Legacy of Eamon de Valera* (Dublin: Royal Irish Academy, 2007).

Fitzpatrick, David, ed. *Terror in Ireland, 1916–1923* (Dublin: The Lilliput Press, 2012).

Fitzpatrick, David. *The Two Irelands 1912–1939* (Oxford: University Press, 1998).

Fitzpatrick, David. *Politics and Irish Life, 1913–1921* (Dublin: Gill and MacMillan, 1977).

Flynn, B. *Irish Hunger Strikes 1912–1981: Pawns in the Game* (Cork: Collins Press, 2011).

Follis, B. A. *A State under Siege: The Establishment of Northern Ireland* (Oxford University Press, 1995).

Foy, Michael. *Michael Collins's Intelligence War: The Struggle between the British and the IRA, 1919–1921* (Charleston, SC: The History Press, 2006).

French, Gerald. *The Life of Field-Marshal Sir John French, First Earl of Ypres* (London: Cassell, 1931).

Gallagher, Frank. *The Indivisible Island: The Story of the Partition of Ireland* (London: Victor Gollancz, Ltd., 1957).

Gallagher, Ronan. *Violence and Nationalist Politics in Derry City, 1920–1923* (Dublin: Four Courts Press, 2003).

Gardiner, Eamonn T. *Dublin Castle and the Anglo-Irish War: Counter Insurgency and Conflict* (Cambridge Scholars Publishing, 2009).

Garvin, Tom. *Nationalist Revolutions in Ireland, 1858–1928* (Oxford: Clarendon Press, 1987).

Garvin, Tom. *The Evolution of Irish Nationalist Politics* (Dublin: Gill & Macmillan, 2005).

Gaughan, J. A. *The Memoirs of Constable Jeremiah Mee, RIC* (Cork: Mercier Press, 2012).

Gleeson, James. *Bloody Sunday: How Michael Collins's Agents Assassinated Britain's Secret Service in Dublin on November 21, 1920* (London: The Lyons Press, 2004).

Greaves, C. Desmond. *Liam Mellows and the Irish Revolution* (London: Lawrence & Wishart, 1971).

Greaves, C. Desmond. *The Irish Crisis* (New York: International Publishers, 1974).

Gregory A, and S. Pašeta. *Ireland and the Great War: 'A War to Unite Us All'?* (Manchester University Press, 2002).

Grob-Fitzgibbon, B. *Turning Points of the Irish Revolution: The British Government, Intelligence, and the Cost of Indifference, 1912–1921* (Palgrave, 2007).

Hannan, Kevin. 'Winifred Barrington', *The Old Limerick Journal*, vol. 24, (Winter 1988–Barrington's Edition), pp. 107–113.

Hannigan, D. *Terence MacSwiney: The Hunger Strike that Rocked an Empire* (Dublin: O'Brien Press, 2010).

Hare, S. 'Martial Law from the Soldier's Point of View', *Army Quarterly*, vol. VII (October, 1923 and January, 1924), pp. 289–300.

Harnett, M. *Victory and Woe* (UCD Press, 2002).

Harnett, Mossie. *Victory and Woe – The West Limerick Brigade in the War of Independence* (Dublin: UCD Press, 2002).

Harris, Mary. *The Catholic Church and the Foundation of the Northern Ireland State* (Cork University Press, 1994).

Hart, Peter, ed. *British Intelligence in Ireland, 1920–21:The Final Reports.* 'Irish Narratives', (Cork: University Press, 2002).

Hart, Peter. *Mick: The Real Michael Collins* (New York: Penguin, 2005).

Hart, Peter. *The I.R.A. & Its Enemies: Violence and Community in Cork, 1916–1923* (New York: Oxford University Press, 1998).

Hart, Peter. *The IRA at War, 1916–1923* (Oxford University Press, 2003).

Harvey, A. D. 'Who Were the Auxiliaries?', *The Historical Journal*, vol. 35, No. 3 (1992), pp. 665–69.

Hay, Marnie. *Bulmer Hobson and the Nationalist Movement in Twentieth-Century Ireland* (Manchester University Press, 2009).

Hayes, Karl. *A History of the Royal Air Force and United States Naval Air Service in Ireland 1913–1923* (Dublin: Irish Air Letter, 1988).

Hennessey, Thomas. *Dividing Ireland: World War One and Partition* (Milton Park, Abingdon: Routledge, 1998).

His Majesty's Stationery Office (HMSO), *Statistics of the Military Effort of the British Empire During the Great War, 1914–1920* (first published by HMSO 1922, reprinted 1999 by Naval And Military Press).

Herlihy, Jim. *The Dublin Metropolitan Police: A Short History and Genealogical Guide* (Dublin: Four Courts Press, 2001).

Herlihy, Jim. *The Royal Irish Constabulary Officers: A Biographical Dictionary and Genealogical Guide, 1816–1922* (Dublin: Four Courts Press, 2005).

Herlihy, Jim. *The Royal Irish Constabulary: A Short History and Genealogical Guide* (Dublin: Four Courts Press, 1997).

Hittle, J. B. E. *Michael Collins and the Anglo-Irish War: Britain's Counterinsurgency Failure* (Washington, D.C.: Potomac Books, 2011).

Hobson, Bulmer. *Ireland Yesterday and Tomorrow* (London: Anvil Books, 1968).

Holmes, R. *The Little Field Marshall: Sir John French* (London: Jonathan Cape, Ltd., 1981).

Hopkinson, Michael. ed., *The Last Days of Dublin Castle: The Mark Sturgis Diaries*, (Dublin: Irish Academic Press, 1999).

Hopkinson, M. *The Irish War of Independence* (Ithaca, New York: McGill-Queen's Press, 2004).

Jackson, Alvin. *The Ulster Party: Irish Unionists in the House of Commons, 1884–1911* (1989).

Jeffery, Keith and P. Hennessy. *States of Emergency: British Governments and Strikebreaking since 1919* (Boston: Routledge and Kegan Paul, 1983).

Jeffery, K. ed, *The Sinn Féin Rebellion as They Saw It* (Dublin: Irish Academic Press, 1999).

Jeffery, K. *The GPO and the Easter Rising* (Dublin: Irish Academic Press, 2006).

Jeffery, Keith. 'The road to Asia, and the Grafton Hotel, Dublin: Ireland in the "British world"', *Irish Historical Studies*, xxxvi, no. 142 (Nov. 2008), pp 243–56.

Jeffery, Keith. *Field Marshal Sir Henry Wilson: A Political Soldier* (Oxford University Press, 2006).

Jeffery, Keith. *Ireland and the Great War* (Cambridge University Press, 2000).

Jeffery, Keith. *The British Army and the Crisis of Empire, 1918–22* (Manchester University Press, 1984).

Jeffery, Keith. *The Military Correspondence of Field Marshal Sir Henry Wilson, 1918–1922* (London: The Bodley Head, 1985).

Jones, Thomas. *Whitehall Diary*. Vol. III, *Ireland*, 1918–1925. Keith Middlemas ed. (1971).

Joy, Sinead. *The I.R.A. in Kerry, 1916–1921* (Cork: The Collins Press, 2005).

Kautt, W. H. *Ambushes & Armour, 1919–1921: The Irish Rebellion* (Dublin: Irish Academic Press, 2010).

Keegan, M. ed. *Rebel Cork's Fighting Story, from 1916 to the Truce with Britain* (Tralee, Co. Kerry, *The Kerryman*, 1947).

Kenna, G. B., (Fr John Hassan). *Facts and Figures of the Belfast Pogrom, 1920–1922* (1922).

Kenneally, Ian. *The Paper Wall: Newspapers and Propaganda in Ireland, 1919–1921* (Cork: Collins Press, 2008).

The Kerryman. *Kerry's Fighting Story, 1916–21: Told by the Men Who Made It* (Tralee: *The Kerryman*, 1942).

The Kerryman. *With the I.R.A. in the Fight for Freedom: 1919 to the Truce* (Tralee: *The Kerryman*, 1955).

The Kerryman. *Dublin's Fighting Story, 1916–1921: Told By the Men Who Made It* (Cork: Mercier Press, 2009).

The Kerryman. *Rebel Cork's Fighting Story, from 1916 to the Truce with Britain.* (Cork: Mercier Press, 2009).

The Kerryman. *With the I.R.A. in the Fight for Freedom: 1919 to the Truce* (Tralee: *The Kerryman*, 1955).

The Kerryman. *With the IRA in the Fight for Freedom: 1919 to the Truce* (Cork: Mercier Press, 2010).

Knirck, Jason. *Imagining Ireland's Independence: The Debates over the Anglo-Irish Treaty of 1921* (Plymouth. Rowman & Littlefield, 2006).

Kostick, C. *Revolution in Ireland: Popular Militancy, 1917 to 1923* (London: Pluto Press, 1996).

Kotsonouris, 'The Dáil Courts in Limerick', *The Old Limerick Journal* (Winter, 1992), pp. 37–40.

Kotsonouris, Mary. 'The Dáil Courts in Limerick', *The Old Limerick Journal* (Winter, 1992), pp. 37–40.

Kotsonouris, Mary. *Retreat from Revolution: The Dáil Courts, 1920–1924* (Dublin: Irish Academic Press, 1994).

Kotsonouris, M. *The Winding Up of the Dáil Courts 1922–1925* (Dublin: Four Courts Press, 2004).

Labour Party of Great Britain. *Report of the Labour Commission to Ireland* (London: Caledonian Press, 1921).

Laffan, Michael. *The Resurrection of Ireland: The Sinn Fein Party, 1916–1923* (Cambridge University Press, 1999).

Laffan, Michael. *The Partition of Ireland 1911–1925* (Dundalk: Dundalgan Press, 1983).

Lankford, Siobhan. *The hope and the sadness: Personal recollections of troubled times in Ireland* (Tower Books of Cork, 1980).

Lawlor, Pearse. *The Outrages 1920–1922: The IRA and the Ulster Special Constabulary in the Border Campaign* (Cork: Mercier Press, 2011).

Leeson, David M. *The Black and Tans: British Police and Auxiliaries in the Irish War of Independence, 1920–1921* (Oxford University Press, 2012).

Limerick's Fighting Story: From 1916 to the Truce with Britain (Cork: Mercier Press, 2009).

Lord Longford (Frank Pakenham) & T. P. O'Neill, *Eamon de Valera* (London: Arrow Books, 1974).

Lord Longford (Frank Pakenham). *Peace By Ordeal: The Negotiation of the Anglo-Irish Treaty 1921* (London: Nel Mentor, 1967).

Lynch, Robert. *The Northern IRA and the Early Years of Partition, 1920–1922* (Dublin: Irish Academic Press, 2006).

Macardle, Dorothy. *The Irish Republic 1911–1925* (London: Gollancz, 1937).

MacCurtain, Fionnuala. *Remember It's for Ireland: A Family Memoir of Tomas MacCurtain* (Cork: Mercier Press, 2008).

MacEoin, Uinseann. *Survivors: The story of Ireland's struggle as told through some of her outstanding people* (London: Argenta Press, 1987).

MacLysaght, E. 'Larkin, Connolly, and the Labour Movement', *Leaders and Men of the Easter Rising: Dublin 1916*, F. X. Martin, ed. (Cornell University Press, 1967).

Macready, General Sir Nevil. *Annals of an Active Life*, vol. II (London: Hutchison & Co., 1925).

Magill, C. ed., *From Dublin Castle to Stormont: The Memoirs of Andrew Philip Magill, 1913–1925* (Cork University Press 2003).

Maher, Jim. *The Flying Column: West Kilkenny, 1916–21* (Dublin: Geography Publications, 1988).

Malcolm, Elizabeth. *The Irish Policeman, 1822–1922: A Life* (Dublin: Four Courts, 2006).

Mansergh, N. Nicholas. *The Irish Free State: Its Government and Politics* (G. Allen & Unwin, 1934).

Mansergh, *The Unresolved Question: The Anglo-Irish Settlement and Its Undoing* (Yale University Press, 1991).

Martin, F. X. ed. *Leaders and Men of the Easter Rising: Dublin 1916*, (Ithaca, NY: Cornell University Press, 1967).

Matthews, Anne. *Renegades: Irish Republican Women 1900–1922* (Cork: Mercier Press, 2011).

Matthews, K. *Fatal Influences: The Impact of Ireland on British Politics 1920–1925* (Dublin: University College Dublin Press, 2004).

Maye, Brian. *Arthur Griffith* (Dublin: Griffith College Publications, 1997).

McBride, Lawrence W. *The Greening of Dublin Castle: The Transformation of Bureaucratic and Judicial Personnel in Ireland, 1892–1922* (Washington, D.C.: Catholic University of America Press, 1991).

McCall, E. *The Auxiliaries: Tudor's Toughs, A study of the Auxiliary Division Royal Irish Constabulary 1920–1922* (Red Coat Publishing, 2010).

McCarthy, C. *Cumann Na mBan and the Irish Revolution* (Cork: Collins Press, 2006).

McCarthy, Col. J. M. ed. *Limerick's Fighting Story: From 1916 to the Truce with Britain* (London: Anvil Books, N.D.).

Mcconville, S. *Irish Political Prisoners 1848–1922: Theatres of War* (London: Routledge, 2003).

Mcconville, S. *Irish Political Prisoners 1848–1922: Theatres of War* (2003).

McCoole, S. *Guns and Chiffon* (London: Stationery Office Books, 1997).

McCoole, S. *No Ordinary Women: Irish Female Activists in the Revolutionary Years 1900–1923* (University of Wisconsin Press, 2003).

McDermott, Jim. '*Northern Divisions. The Old IRA and the Belfast Pogroms 1920–22*' (Belfast: Beyond the Pale Publications, 2001).

McDowell, R. B. *Crisis and Decline: The Fate of the Southern Unionists* (Lilliput Press, 1998).

McGarry, Feargal. *Rebels: Voices from the Easter Rising* (Dublin: Penguin Books, 2011).

McGarry, Feargal. *The Rising: Ireland: Easter 1916* (Oxford University Press, 2010).

McGee, Owen. *The IRB: The Irish Republican Brotherhood, from the Land League to Sinn Fein* (Dublin: Four Courts Press, 2007).

McGuinness, Charles John. *Sailor of Fortune: Adventures of an Irish Sailor, Soldier, Pirate, Pearl-Fisher, Gun-Runner, Rebel, and Antarctic Explorer* (London: Macrae-Smith Company, 1935).

McInnes, Colin and G. D. Sheffield. *Warfare in the Twentieth Century: Theory and Practice* (London: Unwin Hyman, 1988).

McKenna, J. *Guerrilla Warfare in the Irish War of Independence, 1919–1921* (Jefferson, NC: McFarland & Co., 2011).

McLaughlin, Robert. *Irish Canadian Conflict and the Struggle for Irish Independence, 1912–1925* (University of Toronto Press, 2013).

McMahon, P. *British Spies and Irish Rebels: British Intelligence and Ireland, 1916–1945* (Boydell Press, 2008).

Mitchell, A. *Revolutionary Government in Ireland: Dáil Éireann, 1919–22* (Gill & Macmillan Ltd, 1995).

Mitchinson, K. W. *Defending Albion: Britain's Home Army, 1908–1919* (Palgrave, 2005).

Moylan, S. *Seán Moylan in his own words: His memoir of the Irish War of Independence* (Cork: Aubane Historical Society, 2004).

Murland, J. *Departed Warriors: The Story of a Family in War* (Kibworth Beauchamp, Leicester: Troubador Publishing Ltd, 2008).

Murphy, Brian P. OSB, *The Origins and Organisation of British Propaganda in Ireland, 1920* (Cork: Aubane Historical Society, 2006).

National Association of Old IRA, *Dublin Brigade Review* (Dublin: Cahill & Co., 1939).

National Graves Association. *The Last Post*, American Edition (New York: National Grave Association, 1986).

Neeson, E. *The Battle of Crossbarry* (Cork: Aubane Historical Society, 2008).

Nelligan, David. *The Spy in the Castle* (London: Prendeville, 1999).

Ó Duibhir, Liam. *Prisoners of War: Ballykinlar Internment Camp 1920–1921* (Cork: Mercier Press, 2013).

Ó Duibhir, Liam. *The Donegal Awakening: Donegal & the War of Independence* (Cork: Mercier Press, 2009).

Ó Ruairc, Pádraig Óg. *Blood on the Banner: The Republican Struggle in Clare* (Cork: Mercier Press, 2009).

Ó Broin, Leon. *The Chief Secretary: Augustine Birrell in Ireland* (Archon Books, 1969).

O'Broin, Leon. *Revolutionary Underground: The Story of the Irish Republican Brotherhood* (Dublin: Gill and MacMillan, Ltd., 1976).

O'Broin, Leon. *W. E. Wylie and the Irish Revolution 1916–1921* (Dublin: Gill & Macmillan Ltd, 1989).

O'Callaghan, J. *Revolutionary Limerick: The Republican Campaign for Independence in Limerick, 1913–1921* (Dublin: Irish Academic Press, 2010).

O'Callaghan, Micheál. *For Ireland and Freedom: Roscommon's Contribution in the Fight for Independence* (Blackrock, Co. Cork: Mercier Press, 2012).

O'Callaghan, Seán. *Execution* (London: Muller, 1974).

O'Connor, Emmet. *A Labour History of Ireland, 1824–1960* (Dublin: Gill and Macmillan, Ltd., 1992).

O'Day, A. *Irish Home Rule, 1867–1921* (New York: Oxford University Press, 1998).

O'Donoghue, Florence. *No Other Law: The Story of Liam Lynch and the Irish Republican Army, 1916–1923* (Dublin: Irish Press, 1954).

O'Donoghue, Florence. *Tomas MacCurtain Soldier and Patriot: A Biography of the first Republican Lord Mayor of Cork* (Tralee, Co. Kerry: Anvil Books, 1971).

O'Farrell, Padraic. *Who's Who in the Irish War of Independence and Civil War, 1916–1923* (Dublin: Liliput, 1997).

O'Halpin, Eunan. *Decline of the Union: British Government in Ireland, 1892–1920* (Gill and Macmillan Ltd, 1987).

O'Mahoney, Sean. *Frongoch: University of Revolution* (Killiney, Co. Dublin: FDR Teoranta, 1987).

O'Mahony, S. *The First Hunger Striker: Thomas Ashe* (Dublin: 1916–1921 Club, 2001).

O'Malley, Ernie. *Raids and Rallies* (Dublin: Anvil Books Limited, 1982).

O'Neill, Frank and Thomas P. Gallagher. *The Anglo-Irish Treaty* (London: Hutchinson & Co., 1965).

O'Neill, Tom. *The Battle of Clonmult and the I.R.A.'s Worst Defeat* (Dublin: Nonsuch Publishing, 2006).

O'Reilly, Terrence. *Rebel Heart: George Lennon: Flying Column Commander* (Blackrock, Co. Cork: Mercier Press, 2010).

Officer, Lawrence H. 'Five Ways to Compute the Relative Value of a UK Pound Amount, 1830 to Present,' (MeasuringWorth, 2008, measuringworth.com).

Petter, Martin. ' "Temporary Gentlemen" in the Aftermath of the Great War: Rank, Status and the Ex-Officer Problem', *The Historical Journal*, Vol. 37, No. 1 (March 1994), pp. 127–52.

Pinkman, John A. *In the Legion of the Vanguard* (Irish American Press, 1999).

Price, Dominic. *The Flame and the Candle: War in Mayo 1919–1924* (Cork: The Collins Press, 2012).

Robertson, Sir William. *From Private to Field-Marshal* (London: Houghton, Mifflin and Company, 1921).

Roth, Adreas. 'Gun running from Germany to Ireland in the early 1920s', *The Irish Sword*, Vol. XXII, No. 88 (Winter 2000).

Ryan, Annie. *Comrades: Inside the War of Independence* (Dublin: Liberties Press, 2007).

Ryan, Louise. and M. Ward, eds. *Irish Women and Nationalism: Soldiers, New Women and Hags* (Dublin: Irish Academic Press, 2004).

Ryan, Louise, '"Drunken Tans": Representations of Sex and Violence in the Anglo-Irish War (1919–21)', *Feminist Review* Nº. 66 (Autumn 2000), pp. 73–94.

Ryan, Meda. *Tom Barry: IRA Freedom Fighter* (Cork: Mercier Press, 2005).

Scanlon, Mary. *The Dublin Metropolitan Police* (London: Minerva Press, 1998).

Seedorf, Martin F. 'Defending Reprisals: Sir Hamar Greenwood and the "Troubles", 1920–21', *Éire-Ireland: A Journal of Irish Studies*, (Geimhreadh/Winter 1990): 77–92.

Sheehan, Tim. *Lady Hostage* (Mrs. Lindsay) (Dripsey, Co. Cork: 1990).

Sheehan, William, ed. *Hearts & Mines: The British 5th Division, Ireland 1920–1922* (Cork: The Collins Press, 2009).

Sheehan, William. *A Hard Local War* (The History Press, 2011).

Sheehan, William. *Fighting for Dublin: The British Battle for Dublin 1919–1921* (Cork: The Collins Press, 2007).

Smith, Jeremy. *Britain and Ireland: From Home Rule to Independence* (Harlow, Essex: Longman, 2000).

Staunton, Enda. *The Nationalists of Northern Ireland 1918–1973* (Dublin: Columba Press, 2001).

Steele, K. *Women, Press, and Politics During the Irish Revival* (Syracuse University Press, 2007).

Stewart, A. T. Q. *The Ulster Crisis: Resistance to Home Rule* (London: Faber and Faber, 1967).

Street, Maj. Cecil John Charles. *Ireland in 1921* (London: Philip Allen & Co, 1922).

Street, Maj. Cecil John Charles. *The Administration of Ireland, 1920* (London: Philip Allen & Co, 1921).

Taillon, Ruth. *When History Was Made: the Women of 1916*, (Belfast: Beyond Pale Publications, 1999).

Tansill, C. C. *America and the Fight for Irish Freedom* (New York: Devin-Adair Publishers, 1957).

Thompson, W. I. *The Imagination of an Insurrection: Dublin, Easter 1916: A Study of an Ideological Movement* (New York: Harper Colophon Books, 1972).

Townshend, Charles. *Easter 1916: The Irish Rebellion* (Chicago: Ivan R. Dee, 2006).

Townshend, Charles. 'The Irish Railway Strike of 1920,' *Irish Historical Studies*, Vol. XXI, No. 81 (March 1978), pp. 265–82.

Townshend, Charles. *Britain's Civil Wars: Counterinsurgency in the Twentieth Century* (London: Faber and Faber, 1986).

Townshend, Charles. *Political Violence: Government and Resistance since 1848* (Oxford: Clarendon Press, 1983).

Townshend, Charles. *The British Campaign in Ireland, 1919–1921: The Development of Political and Military Policies* (Oxford: Oxford University Press, 1975).

U.S. Army Field Manual 100-6, *Information Operations* (Washington, D.C., U.S. Army, 27 August 1996).

U.S. Army, FM 3-13 *Information Operations: Doctrine, Tactics, Techniques, and Procedures* (Washington, D.C., U.S. Army: 28 September 2003).

Walsh, Louis J. *'On my keeping' and in theirs: A Record of Experiences 'on the run,' in Derry Gaol, and in Ballykinlar Internment Camp* (Dublin: The Talbot Press, 1921).

Walsh, Maurice. *G2: In Defence of Ireland: Irish Military Intelligence 1918–45* (Cork: Collins Press, 2010).

Walsh, Maurice. *The News from Ireland: Foreign Correspondents and the Irish Revolution* (London: I.B. Tauris, 2008).

Ward, Alan J. *Ireland and Anglo-American Relations 1899–1921* (London: Wiedenfeld and Nicolson, 1969).

Ward, Mary. *In Their Own Voice: Women and Irish Nationalism* (Cork: Attic Press, 2001).

Ward, Mary. *Unmanageable Revolutionaries: Women and Irish Nationalism* (London: Pluto Press, 1995).

Wheatley, Michael. *Nationalism and the Irish Party: Provincial Ireland 1910–1916* (Oxford University Press, 2005).

White, Joseph, ed. *Dublin's Fighting Story, 1913–21: Told by the Men Who Made It* (Tralee: The Kerryman, LTD., 1947).

Williams, Desmond, Ed. *The Irish Struggle 1916–1926* (London: Routledge & Kegan Paul, 1966).

Winter, Brig-Gen Sir Ormonde de L'Épée. *Winter's Tale: An Autobiography* (London: The Richards Press, 1955).

Woodcock, Caroline. *Experiences of an Officer's Wife in Ireland* (Galago Books, 1994). Originally published in *Blackwood's Magazine*, No. MCCLXVII Vol. CCIX, May 1921, pp. 553–98.

Yeates, P. 'Irish craft workers in a time of revolution 1919–1922', pp. 37–56 *Saothar* 33, 2008, pp. 37–54.

Periodicals

An t-Óglác: The Official Organ of the Irish Volunteers.
The Army List, 1920.
The Army Quarterly
Freeman's Journal
Irish Bulletin: a full reprint of the official newspaper of Dáil Éireann giving news and war reports, Vol. i, 12 July, 1919–1 May, 1920 (2012) Aubane Historical Society.
The London Gazette

Unpublished Sources

Theses:

Barndollar, G. 'British Military Use of Armoured Cars, 1919–1939', D.Phil Thesis, Oxford University, 2011.

Kautt, W. H. 'Logistics & Counter-Insurgency: Procurement, Supply & Communications in the Irish War of Independence, 1919–1921', D.Phil. Thesis, University of Ulster at Jordanstown, 2005.

Leonard, Paul B. 'The necessity for de-anglicizing the Irish nation: boycotting and the Irish war of independence', PhD Thesis, University of Melbourne, 2000.

Archival Sources:

Republic of Ireland
Archives Department, University College Dublin
   IRA 2nd Southern Division Papers
   Mulcahy Papers
   O'Malley Papers

Cork Archives Institute, Cork City
   Liam de Róiste Diaries
   Séamus Fitzgerald Papers
   Siobhán Lankford Papers

Military Archives, Cathal Brugha Barracks, Dublin
   Bureau of Military History Chronology
   Bureau of Military History Witness Statements
   Collins Papers

United Kingdom
Imperial War Museum, London
   Field Marshal Sir Henry Wilson Papers
   General Sir Hugh Jeudwine Papers
   General Sir Peter Strickland Papers

Liddell Hart Centre for Military Archives, King's College, London
   Papers of Brigadier Frederick Arthur Stanley Clarke, DSO
   Papers of Lieutenant Colonel Evelyn Lindsay-Young
   Papers of Major General Charles Howard Foulkes

Public Records Office, Kew, Surrey
   Admiralty Papers
   Colonial Office Papers, Dublin Castle Records
   Home Office Papers
   Labour Ministry Papers
   Metropolitan Police Papers
   Ministry of Munitions of War Papers
   Railway Company Papers

Railways Staff Conference Papers
Records of the Boards of Customs, Excise, and Customs and Excise
Records of the Cabinet Office
Sturgis Diaries
Treasury Board Papers
Treasury Solicitor and HM Procurator General's Department Papers
War Office Papers

Index

Note: Page references in bold refer to tables.

active service units, 96
adoption of conciliatory policy by
    government, 45–6, 47–8; effect of,
    56–7
ADRIC (Auxiliary Division, RIC), 92,
    101, 124, 131, 138; C Company, 4;
    carrying out of reprisals, 90, 95, 228;
    disciplinary problems, 134, 191, 233;
    K Company, 105, 135, 234
Ainley, Lt. Francis Clifford, 205
albumin, as used in water, 74
Allgood, Lt-Col. W.H.L., 161
ambush, the, as guerrilla tactic, 4–5,
    58, 81, 82, 146–7, 158 (*see also*
    ambushes; rebel tactics)
American Civil War, the, and belligerent
    status, 94, 195
Anderson, Sir John, 45, 235
Anglo-Irish Treaty, the, 187 (*see also*
    truce, the)
aristocracy, the, and Army officers, 131
armoured cars, 119–21, 135, 240
    (*see also* lorry patrols)
armoured tactical lorries, 121, 135
arms seizures, 34
arrests, policy on, 31–6, 37, 41, 46,
    104–5, 141

Ballykinlar internment camp, 106, 107,
    119
Barry, Cmdt. Tom, 105, 107, 108

Barton, Robert Childers, 34, 169, 171
Battle of Clonmult, the, 136–7
behaviour in combat, 1–2, 181
belief of intended rising in Kerry, 139,
    159
belligerent status of rebels, 5–6, 25, 94–5,
    183–4, 194–6
Biggs, District Inspector Henry 'Harry,'
    153
Birrell, Augustine, 21, 35
Black and Tans, the, 92, 95, 124, 228,
    234 (*see also* ADRIC (Auxiliary
    Division, RIC))
Bonar Law, Andrew, 235
boycott of RIC, 22, 23, 25, 40
Boyd, Maj-Gen. Sir Gerald Farrell, 28,
    101, 131, 233, 235, 236
Braine, Lt. Col. H.E.R.R., 9, 10
Breeze, Second Lt. Alfred Donald Hugh,
    154–5
Brind, Lt-Col. J.E.S., 9, 109
British army, the: affect of truce on, 180,
    181, 187, 199–200; and counter-
    insurgency, 7, 92, 118, 141, 167;
    leadership after World War 1, 131; as
    military police force, 97–8; military
    thought, 2, 7, 8, 236–8; mission, 8,
    97, 126, 141, 167, 185; morale of,
    42, 46, 164–5, 187, 229, 244–6; new
    infantry formations, 70; post-World
    War I, 2–3; proposed increase in

troops, 164, 165–6; re-organization of Ulster area, 161; Training Reserve Battalions, 29–30; troop reinforcements, 43, 67, 68–72, 119, 167–9, 175–6, 186, 243–4; troop strength, 42–3, 119, 125 (*see also* Orders of Battle)

British troop distribution, **26–30, 68–72**

Butler, Lt. James Herbert Theobald Charles, 203

Cabinet and government, criticism of, 7, 8, 10–11

Cabinet meeting, December 1920, 232–6

casualties, 61, 63, 87–8, 91, 138, 141, 165, 177, 197–8

cattle driving, 66

Churchill, Winston, 229–30, 233

claims for damages to property by British troops, 36–7

Clancy, George, 137–8

Clancy, Peadar, 99, 104

class system and obstacles to social advancement, the, 131–2

Clausewitz, Carl von, 4

Clune, Conor, 99

C.M.A. (Competent Military Authorities), 31, 32, 33, 46, 73, 75, 114, 115; powers, 31, 32, 46, 73, 75

coal strike in Britain, 75, 146

coercion in revolutions, 56

Collins, Michael, 10, 105, 196, 235

common law and state of insurrection, 92

Cope, Sir Alfred (Andy), 45, 170, 173

Cork, disturbances in, 62–3, 234

counter-insurgency tactics and progress, 7, 92, 118, 125–9, 141, 167 (*see also* guerrilla warfare)

counter-propaganda, 191 (*see also* press, the, and propaganda)

Craig, Sir James, 169

Creedy, H., 9

Croke Park killings, 100–1

Crossbarry, Battle of, 138–9

Crossley 'Tenders,' 135

crowd handling by British troops, 43–4

Crozier, Brig-Gen. Frank, 99, 134

Culhane, Lt. Seán, 42

Cumann na mBan, 57

Cumming, Col. Hanway Robert, 137, 138

curfew restrictions, 39–40, 64, 115–16, 172

Custom House, burning of the, 155–6

Dáil, 20, 21, 56, 57, 187

Danford, Lt-Col. B.W.Y., 61, 62

De Valera, Eamon, 98, 169, 170, 171, 175, 176, 180, 186, 192, 247

death penalty, the, 47, 193; by Sinn Féin courts, 66, 73

decorations, 177 (*see also* gallantry, examples of)

Defence of the Realm Act, 217–22

Detective Division of DMP (*see* DMP)

detention of men without trial, 36

discussions for a political solution after the truce, 186–7

divided control of military and police, 133–4, 135

DMP (Dublin Metropolitan Police, 22, 23, 25, 39; Detective 'G' Division, 23–4, 35

dockers strike (*see* Munition Strike)

Donovan, Thomas, 204

Drew, Maj. J.S., 9

drives, use of, 158–60, 166–7

Dromkeen ambush, the, 147

D.R.R. (Defence of the Realm Regulations), the, 30, 31, 32, 73

Dublin Castle, 23, 58

Dublin District of British Army, **28–9**, 39, 44, 119

Dublin murders of November 1920, 98–9

Duggan, E.J., 169, 170, 171–2

Dwyer, Tadgh, OC, 78

Easter Rising, the, 3–4

economic blockade, idea of an, 128

Edgeworth-Johnstone, Lt-Col. Sir Walter, 25

Index

extension of Martial Law area, 113–14

fairs and markets, restriction of, 115
Fitzgerald, Michael, 47, 74
Flemming, Pte. Charles John, 202–3
flying columns, 96, 105, 136, 138, 143, 158
force, authorisation for use of, 25, 26
Forde, Liam, 157
Freeman's Journal, the, 130
French, Field Marshal John Denton, 26

Gaelic League, the, 57
gallantry, examples of, 202–6
Garvey, Sgt. Denis, 73
Gaunt, RAdm Sir Ernest Frederick
    Augustus, 160, 161, 175
general election, May 1921, 151–3, 239
general strike in Dublin, 44
George V, King, 169, 246–7
G.Os.C. Divisions, 31, 32–3
government policy on controlling the
    rebellion, 30–8, 90–1; abandonment
    of, 45–6, 47–8, 56–7; additional
    powers granted by R.O.I.R., 87, 89,
    97; internment of I.R.A. leaders, 104,
    106; memoranda by Commander-in-
    Chief, 90–2, 93, 164, 165–7
Greenwood, Sir Hamar, 5, 45, 208
Griffith, Arthur, 20, 98, 101, 169, 192,
    233
guerrilla warfare, 3–4, 58, 64, 126, 128,
    129, 139, 199 (*see also* counter-
    insurgency, problems with)
gun-running and arms importation,
    160–1, 198–9

Hague Conventions, the, 94, 193–4, 195
Hammond, Lt. Henry, 203
Haugh, Cmdt. Liam, 66
Hely-Hutchinson, Col. Richard, 107
Henry, Sir Denis Stanislaus, 30, 31
Hill-Dillon, Bvt. Maj. S.S., 57
Hobson, Bulmer, 20
Holmes, Maj. Philip Armstrong, 35
home rule, support for, 26

hostages, carrying of in lorry convoys,
    116
hunger strike for political status, 43, 44,
    73, 74
Hynes, Sgt. Michael J., 89

Ibberson, Lt. Geoffrey, 206
identity card and passport system, 230
IGS (Imperial General Staff), the, 67
incendiarism and arson, 155–6, 234
individual murders, rebel tactic of, 21,
    37, 60, 126, 144, 153
informants, 37–8, 127, 137
inland waterways and arms concealment,
    145
intelligence, 9, 35, 36–7, 141, 192,
    199–200, 235; DMP intelligence
    gathering, 23, 25; intelligence
    officers, 59; Military Intelligence
    Section, 34, 56–7, 133, 192 (*see also*
    Dublin murders of November 1920)
internment of rebels, 40, 104, 106–7,
    110, 119, 141, 160, 192
intimidation of local population, 37, 40,
    46–7, 57, 73, 76–8
intimidation of policemen, 21, 22–3, 25,
    38–9, 58–60 (*see also* police barracks;
    R.I.C.)
I.R.A., the, 5, 37, 47, 67, 92, 98, 152,
    179, 186, 239–40; 4th Bn. East Cork,
    78; affect of arrests on, 37, 104–5,
    107; aims, 184–5; exploits change
    in Crown policy, 56–7; Limerick
    battalions, 137–8; morale, 46, 87–8,
    97, 201; targets for intimidation, 60,
    166; during the truce, 198–9 (*see also*
    intimidation of policemen and local
    population; Irish Volunteers, the;
    rebel tactics; Sinn Féin)
I.R.B., the, 20
Irish Bulletin, the, 172, 247–8
Irish Free State, the, 8–9
Irish Independent, the, 130
Irish problem, nature of the, 185
Irish Republican Police, 67

Irish Self-Determination League, the, 74
Irish Transport and General Workers' Union, 44, 64
Irish Transport Union, 65
Irish version of Truce terms, 172
Irish Volunteers, the, 4, 20, 21, 22, 25, 33, 57, 96

Jeffrey Quad armoured cars, 120
Jeudwine, Maj-Gen. Sir H.S., 6, 109, 208, 213, 231–2; papers, 13

Keating, Patrick, 158
Kilmichael Ambush, the, 4–5, 107–8, 127–8

Labour Party Commission report, 133, 134
Lambert, Col. T.S., 155
Lambert, G.W., 13
land mines, 155
Lane-O'Kelley, Kathleen, 57
Larkin, James, 44
Leahy, Cmdt. Michael, 78
legal obstacles for Army and R.I.C., 92, 94–5, 111–12
Lieber Code, the, 195
Londonderry riots, 69
lorry patrols, 72, 80, 142–3, 153, 206
Lucas, Brig-Gen. C.H.T., 61, 82, 90, 228

MacCurtain, Thomas, 41–2
MacEoin, Seán, 97, 195
Macksey, Lt-Col. P.J., 9
MacMahon, James, 45
Macpherson, Ian, 45
Macready, General Sir C.F. Nevil, 9–10, 45, 66, 68, 97, 130, 131, 134, 234–5; assessment of situation to CIGS, 144–5; and Martial Law, 110, 176, 232, 242; memoranda, 90–2, 93, 164, 165–7, 173, 176, 222–5, 227–9, 238–46; special orders, 207–8, 209–12; and the truce, 180–1, 182–3

Macroom ambush (see Kilmichael Ambush, the)
maps, cost of, 11–12
Martial Law, 30–1, 91, 109–11, 112–16, 133, 193, 231–2, 237, 242; affect of, 134–6, 140–1, 194; drawbacks of, 111–12; leads to increase in battalions, 119, 119, 175, 176; and "Official Punishments" system, 116–18; partial Martial Law, 111, 194; proposed extension of, 165, 174–5, 190–1, 213–15; question of in Dublin, 143, 144
Maxwell-Scott, Col. W.J., 9
McKee, Richard (Dick), 99, 104
McSwiney, Mary, 74
McSwiney, Terence, 47, 66, 73–4
Midleton, Lord, 170, 171
military, use of as labour, 64, 65, 75
Military Governor, role of, 135, 136, 140
Military Intelligence Section, 34, 56–7, 133, 192
military officers, kidnapping of, 61
military situation: April 1921, 140, 141, 145, 241–2; August 1920, 72–3, 222–5; end of 1919, 20; February-March 1921, 136–9, 143–5, 236–8; May 1921, 153–6, 238–40; November 1920, 97, 227; September 1920, 228–9; September 1921, 197–201; at time of the truce, 186, 197–201
military tactics, 4, 200
M.O.3 (Administration and Special Duties Section), 9
Moran, Patrick, 100
motor launches, use of, 145
Motor Restrictions Order, 114–15
Mountjoy Prison, 43–4
Moylan, Seán, 146, 147
Mulcahy, Richard, 89, 104, 143, 185
Munition Strike, the, 64, 65–6, 92
murders of policemen and detectives (see R.I.C. (Royal Irish Constabulary))
Murphy, Joseph, 47, 74

officer class in the British Army, 131, 132
"Official Punishments" system, 116–18
  (*see also* Martial Law)
O'Flanagan, Father Michael, 152, 239
O'Neill, Cmdt. Ignatius, 89
Orders of Battle, **26–30, 68–72**; 1st Bn.
  Duke of Wellington's Regiment, 176;
  1st Bn. Gloucester Regiment, 119;
  1st Bn. King's Royal Rifle Corps,
  119; 1st Bn. Lancashire Fusiliers, 43;
  1st Bn. Loyal Regiment, 176; 1st Bn.
  Somerset Light Infantry, 146; 1st Bn.
  Wiltshire Regiment, 43; 1st Infantry
  Division, 12, **70**; 2nd Bn. Duke of
  Wellington's Regiment, 146; 2nd Bn.
  King's Own Yorkshire Light Infantry,
  146; 2nd Bn. King's Shropshire
  Light Infantry, 146; 2nd Bn. North
  Staffordshire Regiment, 176; 3rd
  Bn. Rifle Brigade, 119; 3rd Cavalry
  Brigade, 159; 3rd Regiment, Royal
  Artillery Mounted Rifles, 176; 5th
  Armoured-Car Company, 120; 5th
  Infantry Division, 7, 11, 12, 38, 57,
  70–1, 166; 6th Infantry Division, 6,
  9, 11, 13, 38, 57, **71**; 13th Infantry
  Brigade, 155, 161; Border Regiment,
  206; Cameron Highlanders, 204,
  228; Devonshire Regiment, 158, 203;
  Dorsetshire Regiment, 203; Essex
  Regiment, 138, 139, 202, 204; Green
  Howards, 205; Hampshire Regiment,
  136, 138, 155, 206; Lancashire
  Regiment, 136; Lincolnshire
  Regiment, 20; Manchester Regiment,
  136; Norfolk Regiment, 205; Royal
  Engineers, 204; Royal Fusiliers,
  204–5; South Staffordshire Regiment,
  203 (*see also* British Army, the)
outrages committed or attempted in
  Martial Law area, 146–8

Peck, Capt. C.H., 9
Peerless armoured cars, 120
pensioners and veterans, attacks on, 60, 76

perception and war, 4–5
Percival, Maj. Arthur Ernest, 202
personation and intimidation at elections,
  152–3
police barracks, attacks on, 24, 37, 38,
  40, 41, 48–50, 60, 78–9, 88, 127,
  228; success of, 61, 72–3 (*see also*
  R.I.C. (Royal Irish Constabulary))
political and ordinary crime, 108–9
Poole, Sgt. Frank, 204
popular support for the I.R.A.,
  measuring, 115
press, the, and propaganda, 21, 23,
  24, 63, 65, 137, 152, 191; Army
  complaints about bias, 129–33, 227;
  promotion of the war as legitimate,
  40, 58, 62, 179
Price, Lt-Col. Ivon Henry, 35
print volumes and distribution, 13
propaganda, 36, 191
proposed enlistment of ex-soldiers, 175

Raids Bureaus, the, 35
railway strike, 64–5, 141, 227
R.A.S.C. (Royal Army Service Corps),
  156, 166, 202, 240
Rathmore Ambush, the, 165
re-organization of Ulster area of British
  Army, 161
rebel concentration in Kerry, 139
rebel tactics, 38–9, 40, 58–62, 76–82,
  126–7, 135, 141–2, 153–8; ambushes,
  4–5, 58, 81, 82, 88–9, 107–8, 137,
  146–7, 158; flying columns and active
  service units, 96–7, 105, 136, 138,
  143, 158; and guerrilla warfare, 58,
  64; and hunger-strikes, 43, 44, 73,
  74; ignore terms of truce, 181; of
  individual murders, 21, 37, 60, 126,
  144, 153
rebellions and revolution, origin and
  nature of, 56, 64, 188–92
*Record of the Rebellion in Ireland in
  1920-21, The*, 2, 3, 6–12; purpose
  of, 15, 16

Redmond, William Charles Forbes, 24, 26
release of hunger strikers, 44, 45, 46
release of prisoners, 169–70
reprisals and retaliation by Crown forces, 89–91, 93–4, 228–30 (*see also* "Official Punishments" system)
Restoration of Order in Ireland Act, 75, 225–6
revolutions and control of the local population, 64
R.I.C. (Royal Irish Constabulary), 24, 189, 228; killing of policemen and detectives, 21, 22–3, 25, 38–9, 41–2, 58–60, 66, 98–9; recruitment to, 87, 88; relations with Army, 46, 135–6 (*see also* police barracks, attacks on)
Rineen Ambush, the, 89
roads and bridges, destruction of, 58, 141–2
Robertson, Lt. Robert Douglas Finch, 202
R.O.I.R. (Restoration of Order in Ireland Regulations), 87, 89, 97, 127, 194
Rolls-Royce armoured cars, 120, 135
Royal Engineers, 166
Royal Navy, role of the, 106, 110, 160–1, 175

sea transport of I.R.A. internees, 106, 110
searching of individuals and buildings, policy on, 32, 33, 34, 36, 46, 143–4, 169
Secret Service, the, 35
sectarian violence, 69
Shaw, Lt-Gen. Sir Frederick, 33, 42, 45, 207
Sinn Féin, 20–1, 22, 40, 46–7, 57–8, 151–2, 235, 239; claim for mandate, 151
Sinn Féin Arbitration Courts, 20, 21, 56, 57, 66–7, 73, 183, 184
Smith, Pte. Cecil Harry, 204
Smyth, Lt-Col. Gerald Brice-Ferguson, 62, 63, 129, 130
Southern Unionists, 170
'Squad,' the, 23, 24, 105

staff officers, 2
Staines, Michael, 169, 170
Stephens, James, 20
Strickland, Maj-Gen. Sir Peter, 9, **27**, 89, 90, 109, 110, 233, 234, 235; papers, 13
Swanzy, DI Oswald Ross, 42
Sweetman, John, 20, 152

t-Óglác, An, 46, 58, 181, 185, 199, 241
Taylor, Sir John, 45
Teeling, Frank, 99
telegraph and mail facilities, destruction of, 58, 126, 153, 157
telegraph facilities, restrictions on, 157
Thomas, Capt. Donald Victor, 205
Toureengarriv Ambush, the, 147
trains, attacks on, 156
Tramore ambush, the, 203–4
Traynor, Oscar, 156
Treacy, Seán, 82
Trengrouse, Lt. William Trevenen, 153, 154
truce, the, 5–6, 11, 179, 180–4, 235–6, 247–8; affect on British Army, 180, 181, 187, 199–200; differences in interpretation of, 172–3, 179; negotiations for, 169, 170–1, 173–7
Tudor, Lt-Gen. Sir Henry Hugh, 63, 98, 136, 233, 234, 235, 236
Tupper, Adm. Sir Reginald, 106
Tyrrell, Lt-Col. W.G., 61, 62

Ulster Special Constabulary, 12, 189

Whelan, Thomas, 100
Whitfield, Sgt. Thomas Jefferson, 205
Wilson, Field Marshal Sir Henry, 11, 93
Winter, Brig-Gen. Sir O., 35
witnesses, unreliability of, 56
women, attacks on, 60, 77
women, use of by rebels, 126

Young Soldier Battalions for young recruits, 29–30